Thanks to Kathy, Carol, Howard and Sue.

AUTHOR'S NOTE

Please appreciate that my relationship with people I work with is one of strict confidentiality. This book is filled with stories of people I know and have helped in my role as a volunteer financial counselor. But I've disguised the circumstances, so hopefully these people won't even recognize themselves. Furthermore, I am associated with some of the finest organizations to be found. Through these associations, I have learned many of the principles in this book. But this book is my own, and these organizations are in no way responsible for my opinions.

Richard P. Halverson

For information contact Harbor Publishing, 1668 Lombard Street, San Francisco, California 94123.

Printed in the United States of America.

ISBN: 0-936602-21-X

Contents

◇ Preface ◇

There are probably hundreds of reasons why authors write books. I would like to tell you why I wrote *Financial Freedom* and why I believe you should read it. In doing this, I am aware that much has been written on the general subject of personal finance and investment already (much of which doesn't ring true).

In a word, I believe this book can help you achieve financial freedom. And if it does, that will please me.

Today I find a great majority of Americans wanting a little help and looking for some sensible answers. Here's why:

First, personal financial matters have been a common concern of most people for decades. Making ends meet has never been easy.

Second, the world surrounding our personal finances has changed dramatically and abruptly: inflation and financial upheaval, on one hand, to new financial products, on the other. Many laypeople want to understand these startling events and prosper with them.

Third, most people are fully capable of handling their personal financial affairs. But most people also find tools that are oriented to explanation, self-evaluation, and how-to-do-it procedures are very useful. Such tools are particularly popular in today's environment.

But what of the many other books written on this subject? Won't they fulfill these needs?

I believe *Financial Freedom* is distinctive. There are on the market today personal finance and investment books scanning the spectrum from financial encyclopedias, to single-purpose investment programs, to get-rich-quick schemes, to crisis and calamity books. The encyclopedias (as I define them) tend to be good reference works. Several are well written and easy to understand. (For some reason, they tend to be written by literary, rather than financial people, however.) I have several of these encyclopedias in my personal library and recommend them in many situations.

But as a real program to financial freedom, the encyclopedias fail because they are *too complete*. They delve into things such as wise buying of cosmetics and the cost of birth control and hundreds of other subjects. They are so complete, in fact, that no one sits down and reads them to develop an overall strategy for financial freedom. The reader needs to know what his or her problem is in order to find the reference and solve it. Most people who want financial freedom want a resource to help them diagnose their needs and create a program to meet them.

There is a second problem with the financial encyclopedias—timeliness. The financial world has changed so dramatically in just a few years that even the most recent fail to deal with new forms of home financing, new insurance products, new cash management products. If you are to achieve financial freedom in the 1980s, you must understand the financial products that have been created for this decade.

Many books on the market deal with a single type of investment, such as real estate, stocks, money market funds, or gold. Many of these books are responsibly done. The truly responsible ones have two characteristics. First, no matter how well written, they are complicated. *All* forms of investing can require substantial sophistication if one intends to achieve truly superior results. (This does not mean a person cannot invest until he or she acquires great sophistication. This book will help you invest in a diversity of investments. But to specialize in any one area, much needs to be learned.)

Second, the responsible single-purpose book will not imply that a single form of investment will solve all financial problems—no single investment type will.

Unfortunately, many single-investment concept books on the market are not responsible. In fact, these books can be very harmful to unsuspecting readers. They preach complete dedication to a single investment concept. Furthermore, they usually teach a highly unorthodox approach to the investment. Often the approach is characterized by excessive leverage or questionable legal and ethical practices. Without exception, *all* investments go through cycles. Excessive concentration, especially through unsound practices, can lead an investor to ruin in the down cycles.

Many single-purpose investment books are also get-rich-quick books. Get-rich-quick books are the pornography of financial books. Ask yourself, "How many people do I know that have read some form of get-rich-quick book?" How many do you know that ever got rich quick? It is my privilege to know a large number of wealthy people. Not one of them made their money on get-rich-quick schemes.

Simple logic explains why. First, we all know there aren't enough of the world's resources for everyone to be a millionaire—only a few will attain that status. But there is enough paper and ink to supply us all with many copies of get-rich-quick books. The law of limited resources tells us most readers will be disappointed.

Most readers are disappointed, because the get-rich-quick schemes really don't work. But let's assume some foolproof scheme has been found. And assume that the author has made so much money he or she is now happy to share the scheme with you.

As you apply the system, the market for the scheme tightens. The system works less well for you than for the previous user. Then imagine hundreds of thousands of readers applying the scheme. Because investment markets depend on balance, soon the market will be so inefficient no one makes money. In fact, all schemers lose. And by the law of the market, those who sold to the schemers will be the winners. You might come out OK if you are early. But by the time the get-rich-quick scheme is in book form, it's too late.

A fourth category of books on the market are the crisis and calamity books. It is hard to know if these are financial or political books. Their theme is that capitalist countries (especially the United States) have been so destroyed by government conspiracy that disaster is unavoidable. These books can also be harmful to readers who adhere to the advice without balance and wisdom. In fact, it is already possible to say the doomsayers have been wrong and many of their disciples have been badly hurt.

We do face problems as a country. In fact, there is a possibility of complete collapse. But that chance is not more than 2 or 3 percent. People who feel collapse is inevitable do not understand the checks and balances in the system. Furthermore, they completely underestimate America's socioeconomic ability to adjust.

If you adopt financial crisis strategy, there are two probable ways of being wrong. First, the system will not collapse. Second, in the unlikely event the U.S. capitalist system does collapse, the odds are great that your financial strategy will not protect you. Chances are a financial crisis and calamity system will lead you to a personal financial crisis.

I recognize there are problems in the United States today—severe problems. Much of this book is devoted to analyzing them. Gaining financial freedom in the 1980s will not be easy, but it is possible.

The author of the book capable of doing what I've just described would need a unique background. May I explain why I feel my background qualifies me to write the book? I think you will also see why I wanted (in many ways feel obligated) to write the book.

First, I've been fortunate to receive an excellent education. My college and graduate work were financed through scholarships and part-time work. I pursued a keen interest in finance. I graduated *magna cum laude* in banking and finance from the University of Utah. I was then accepted by Harvard University, where I received a Master of Business Administration Degree, graduating with distinction and being named a Baker Scholar.

My education set the foundation for this book—but it opened the door for my career—a career that has been exciting and stimulating to me. I broke into the world of professional investing with Waddell & Reed, Inc., manager of the United Mutual Funds, one of the largest (and best-managed) mutual fund complexes in the world. I began as a security analyst. My responsibility was to study industries and companies in detail in order to judge which stocks represented money-making values.

Studying companies included spending considerable time in the corporate suites of some of America's finest corporations analyzing their methods and interviewing their managements. (This opportunity is open to analysts of large investment institutions.) Through my experience as an analyst, I've become acquainted with hundreds of the world's most successful business executives.

I believe American corporations are financially the most efficiently run organizations in the world. I've also discovered that most of the key principles of inflation and energy management, budgeting, and cost control they use can be adapted for personal use. This book is full of those principles.

I've enjoyed progress in my profession and increasing responsibility. In 1977 I was offered the opportunity to join the First Trust Company of Saint Paul, one of the country's finest financial institutions. Today I am executive vice president of the company. I have as one of my responsibilities the investment department of the company. There is a staff of twenty investment professionals engaged in everything from stocks and bonds to real estate, to money market investing, to economic forecasting. First Trust Saint Paul has fiduciary assets of more than $4.5 billion. On a day-to-day basis, I am deeply a part of the world of billion-dollar investing and financial management.

But significant as my education and career have been, there is yet another aspect of my life which is even more significant. For the past eleven years I have voluntarily donated from twenty to thirty hours of my time each week to charitable, religious, and civic activities. Much of this activity has involved financial counseling to individuals and families looking for answers to managing their financial affairs. These people range from hard-core welfare recipients trying to become independent, to wealthy people trying to make more. Most of them are ordinary middle-class Americans trying to gain a measure of financial independence.

My counseling work has given me a genuine understanding of the day-to-day problems of ordinary personal finance. It has helped me discover several things. First, nearly everybody feels financial pressure to some extent. Second, most people feel the pressure of today's inflation. Third, a lot of what you read in books today just will not work with most people, for a variety of reasons.

What is written in this book will work for most people.

In this book, I bring together my experience in the world of billion-dollar finance and my experience in personal financial counseling. It leads to a book that is filled with explanations about what's right, what's wrong, and how you can prosper in today's financial environment. The book is filled with self-diagnosis opportunities. It's a how-to-do-it financial manual oriented to helping you work through financial needs to a conclusion. Finally, there is a great deal of what I call pro and con explanation about various financial products. In using any product, you must understand both the good and bad parts to avoid getting financially trapped.

This book will explain step by step how to achieve personal financial freedom in the 1980s without taking advantage of the misfortunes of others.

This book does not promise to help you get rich quick. It does promise that you can get rich gradually. This book will help you gain your financial freedom.

Sincerely,
Richard P. Halverson

◇ Introduction ◇

There's been an upheaval resulting in a great massacre. Millions of people are casualties. It has affected every family in America.

You didn't hear about it?

Don't feel bad. Most people didn't, at least not in so many words. But it did occur. This modern American financial upheaval has been going on for more than half a decade, and is still continuing today. It's affecting every American, from youngest to oldest.

Of course, no one is actually dying in this upheaval. Yet the fact that you are reading this book indicates that you may be a casualty yourself.

The upheaval I'm speaking of has taken place at the savings and loan institutions, where depositors found their life savings were worth less than they had thought; at the banks that charged historically high interest rates. It took place in the office of the real estate agent who turned buyers away because they couldn't have qualified for the new, expensive mortgages even if the mortgages had been available; at the broker's office, where securities losses mounted; in the money markets, where mutual funds exploded a hundredfold in just a few years. It took place at the grocery store, where the price of meat and potatoes moved out of reach of many Americans; at the gas pump, where prices eliminated the "optional" drive; at the auto assembly plant, where the unavailability of competitively priced cars eliminated tens of thousands of jobs. And it took place in the typical American family, which found itself saddled with a huge load of expensive debt.

This litany describes a scene of modern American financial devastation. But *this is not a book about financial doom.* In fact, this probably is the most optimistic book you can read at this time. It is optimistic for two reasons. First, it recognizes that the worst of the upheaval may already be over. The book fully recognizes that, despite the upheaval, the American system has survived, and that is encouraging. But the book also somberly recognizes the upheaval that has occurred. Like people on the day after a volcanic eruption, this book recognizes that the world has changed.

Evidence of the change is everywhere. For example, inflation has driven prices out of reach. If inflation were to stop tomorrow (it won't), the average price of gasoline would still be four times what it was a few years ago. The average price of a home would still be beyond the reach of the average family. The price of normal health care would still be crippling. The cost of living would still be astronomical.

And personal debt is higher than at any time in history. If borrowing were to stop tomorrow (it won't), the average American household would still owe $38,982 for their personal debts as well as their share of public debt ($13,627 for every man, woman, and child in the country).

Personal savings are lower than at any time in fifty years. If people could afford to start saving again tomorrow (they can't), they would still be saving at a rate 50 percent below normal.

Two-income families are the rule where there are two people who can work. In many cases, women want to work. But in many more cases, women *must* work. If women were no longer being pressured into the labor force tomorrow (they will be), there still would be a majority of school-age children whose mothers work.

Resources are scarce. If conservation were perfected tomorrow (it won't be), we would still be uncomfortably short of energy and other key resources.

Unemployment is stubbornly high. If the economy ceased stagnating tomorrow (it probably won't), the nation would still have more than 8 percent unemployed.

So, even if the upheaval is subsiding, even if the worst is already behind us, we must recognize the world has changed. Today people must manage their finances better than ever before. There is less margin for financial error. People must be more aware of new financial tools and how to use them.

This leads to the second reason for optimism in this book. There is hope! There are things you can do to adjust to the change, and even prosper from it. There are new tools available, such as higher-yielding investments, money market funds, and new mortgages. This book explains them.

More important, perhaps, the book explains in detail new techniques for using old tools and making them work for the new circumstances. It is very encouraging to know that something can be done.

But what about you, personally?

Do you feel you need to adjust to the recent upheaval? A person does not have to be visibly poor to be financially trapped. Take this little test:

1. Have you reached the financial objectives you had planned to achieve by this time?

2. Do you see achieving your financial goals for the future as being easier or more difficult than in the past?

3. Do you feel more financially secure now than in the past in light of such financial obligations as debts and such financial resources as savings?

4. Do you feel you are having less difficulty, or more, in maintaining your standard of living (despite increases in your income)?

5. Can you realistically see yourself achieving financial freedom at some point in the near future?

If your answers, like most people's, are no! then you are indeed a victim of the economic upheaval that has taken place. Like most others, you feel financially trapped. You've lost mobility and freedom. You may feel frustrated, even confused. You may take the situation personally. You may not realize that big changes in the world may be largely responsible for making your own personal financial pressures much worse.

What is a person to do?

Well, don't panic. The worst is probably over (as I'll show later). Panic can make your situation worse. It can lead you to look for a quick fix. At best, quick-fix solutions amount to financial Band Aids. Band Aids tend to cover up the problems, not cure them.

Today, the country is awash in these quick-fix solutions. Financial crisis books are everywhere. Each is filled with financial Band Aids. Seminars are given on them. Each suggests a quick-fix answer: "Buy gold and enjoy inflation!" "Buy real estate and make millions without working!" "Borrow your way to wealth and riches!"

The trouble with all these quick-fix solutions is that they don't work. Usually they are too extreme to be practical. And to the extent they do work, they don't deal with the problem itself. Like Band Aids, they only cover up the symptoms. They don't cure the problems. They don't go into your own personal financial needs and show how to meet them. They don't realistically analyze the economic upheaval that's racking our country and show how to deal with it. Quick fix solutions can lead to long term problems.

Once you understand you do not have to act impulsively, you can learn the five steps to financial freedom outlined in this book.

1. Understand what has happened and why the world is now dramatically different.

2. Understand yourself and your ability to handle financial challenges, especially in the decade of the 1980s.

3. Learn the skills of managing your resources for greater financial freedom.

4. Learn how to deal successfully with the three largest areas of potential financial entrapment: credit, risk and insurance, and retirement.

5. Learn how to make your money work for you through investing for financial freedom.

The book is divided into five sections that correspond to these five areas. Please understand that *all* five are important in achieving the financial freedom I know you want.

Part I.
Understanding
the World
of the 1980s

The world of the 1980s will be very different from the world of the 1970s. The 1970s witnessed protracted, relentless inflation; high and unstable interest rates; the disappearance of abundant, inexpensive energy; deep economic recession; and persistent stagflation. The 1970s were a time of unequaled political mistrust, massive encroachment of federal regulation, and major disaffection of the ordinary citizen toward the governmental, corporate, and institutional establishments influencing his or her life. The worst of this is probably over. But the devastation has already affected the shape of the 1980s.

This section will explore the upheaval, especially inflation. It will discuss where it came from and how it is even now being corrected. When we understand what has happened, we can understand what adjustments must be made.

Adjustments must be made to survive, prosper, and be financially free in the 1980s. Unfortunately, too many will try to adjust by doing what appeared to work in the 1970s. But history is clear: Adjusting today to yesterday's problems leads to wrong solutions for tomorrow. This part of the book will introduce you to some of the right solutions for tomorrow—the all-new 1980s.

Finally, Part I points out that despite the upheaval of the 1970s, there is more opportunity for financial success now than at any other time in history.

◇ 1 ◇

The Changing Face
of Inflation

Perhaps the nation's upheaval is most visible in the nation's high inflation rates. Public opinion polls indicate that inflation is the number one concern of most Americans. It's become a national issue—big enough to bring down presidents, embarrass economists, and frighten nearly all of us.

Runaway inflation can burn up an economy like a forest fire can burn up trees. If there is enough fire, the forest will be gone. Just as a small campfire cannot be ignored in parched timberland, today's inflation can't be ignored in our parched economy. In succeeding chapters, we'll deal with specific methods of handling our personal money management so that we don't succumb to the fires of inflation. But for now, let's consider what inflation truly is and what our strategies for handling it should be.

First off, we should realize that inflation is only temporary!

I realize that this is a startling statement to make given the economic climate of today. But we have to realize that inflation such as it is today has not always been with us and it may not continue to be with us in the distant future. The past ten to fifteen years have been characterized by an unusually large number of inflationary forces, all hitting the economy at the same time. Many of these are now subsiding and will continue to do so in the later 1980s. This observation is important in our planning today.

But regardless of what inflation does in the future, it is here today, and we must understand and deal with it. To begin, let's understand that inflation is only a measure of change, it is not a price level itself. For example, gasoline may double in price from $1 to $2 a gallon. That's a lot of change and a lot of inflation—100 percent. Most people would agree that $2 a gallon is a very high price (most people thought even $1 was a very high price). If the doubling reduces demand for gas, the upward pressure on prices may subside. With reduced upward pressure, the price may stabilize at its new high of $2 a gallon. Because the price is not going up any more, inflation drops to 0 percent, but gas is still uncomfortably expensive.

Things may stay uncomfortably expensive in the next ten years, but inflation should slow considerably. In fact, inflation could disappear. How? By the natural subsiding of inflationary pressures on many of the unusually strong pricing forces of the 1970s and early 1980s. What is the case for this complex point of view?

Demographics

Population mix was an important inflationary force in the 1970s. After World War II, the soldiers returned home and got married; they and their wives had children. This great postwar "baby boom" has flowed through the economy like a pig through a snake. In the 1950s and 1960s, no city could build schools fast enough. But now schools are being shut down. In the late 1960s and early 1970s, college dorms were overcrowded. Now colleges are beginning to wonder what to do with the space. During the late 1970s, those postwar babies moved into the 25- to 35-year-old age group and formed households of their own. Traditionally, this age is the time in life when demand for goods and services is highest. These new families are buying homes, furniture, color television sets, expensive recreation equipment, and cars, and are having children of their own. Demand for many goods and services ran unusually high in the late 1970s and early 1980s. This increased demand is a major cause of inflation.

Things will change as the 1980s progress, however. The postwar babies will become 40 and 45 years old. Their households will be established; their heaviest spending for heavy durables will be behind them. Certainly they will keep spending, but their spending patterns will shift substantially. In fact, much of their spending will go toward repaying debts, such as the mortgages they assumed in the 1970s. These spending shifts will greatly reduce inflationary pressure. Some people argue that this will never happen. They may, however, be the same people who predicted a permanent shortage of kindergarten teachers.

Productivity

Productivity is an economic measure of output (products) per
worker input (labor). Productivity has generally increased since the
onset of the Industrial Revolution centuries ago. There have been
some periods, of course, when productivity increased less than at
other periods. Unfortunately, the 1970s was a bad period for the
United States. The rate of improvement declined steadily. Sometimes productivity was actually negative: Worker output was less
per hour worked than the month before.

Low or negative productivity is a major source of inflation. In
the early 1960s, productivity was running around 5 percent. In 1963
an employer could raise wages 5 percent and still not need to raise
prices to maintain profits. Today, a mere 5 percent wage increase
would anger the employee, and the company might still be forced
to increase prices by 4 to 6 percent just to stay even.

Low productivity effectively means higher costs and "cost push"
inflation. The productivity problem is as complex and frustrating as
inflation itself. This book cannot attempt to deal with productivity
completely except to say that there is hope for improvement in the
1980s. A key reason for hope stems from technology, which is always improving. The age of the microprocessor is here, for example. The microprocessor can be to the 1980s what the computer
was to the 1960s. A second important hope comes from an expected
increase in the level of plant and equipment expenditures during the
1980s. New plants have led to greater productivity than in the past.
The third hope for productivity improvement results from demographics. Our labor force was getting younger during the 1970s.
During the 1980s, it will gradually grow older. Workers in the 35 to
55 age group have historically been more productive than those 25
to 35, probably because of more experience and better attitudes
toward work. This phenomenon should continue to be true and
should result in higher productivity in the 1980s.

Scarce Natural Resources

Economists have discovered an interesting pattern of pricing during
the life cycle of many scarce natural resources, such as oil. What
might be expected is frequently not what actually happens. Because
there is only a fixed amount of the natural resource in the world and

a steadily growing number of people wanting it every year, what might be expected is gradual price increases as demand increases. Frequently, however, the price remains fairly flat or declines for years. Then suddenly the price explodes upward, increasing maybe 1000 percent or more in a short time. Ultimately, the explosion is followed by a sharp drop, bringing the price back nearly to its starting point.

What causes this "hump-theory" roller-coaster pricing to occur, instead of the nice, steady increase that might be expected? Well, initially there is more of the resource readily available to the market than the economy demands. This is true despite the fact that there is only a given total amount of the resource in the world. With more of the resource available in the short run than is needed, prices hold steady. Over time, the easily developed resources are exhausted; demand continues to climb, and pressures on prices build; but still the price does not rise. Countervailing forces (often political) hold them artificially low. Suddenly there is a breaking point. The breaking point may be triggered by a natural disaster, a strike, or a political event. Prices explode upward, rising dramatically in a short period of time. The economy cannot quickly reduce its dependence on the resource; new technologies cannot be developed fast enough; and inflation runs wild.

Over time, the situation produces change. High prices induce conservation and substitution. The passage of time allows new technologies to develop. The new technologies often result in major breakthroughs that permanently reduce society's dependence on the resource. The conservation, declining demand, substitution, and new technology finally produce actual price declines that are often as sharp as the price increases that preceded them.

During the 1970s, an unusual number of scarce resources seemed to reach the point of price explosion. Some examples include molybdenum, potash, land, certain food commodities, and, of course, oil.

Economists are divided in their opinions regarding the outlook. But the economic theories suggest that sometime in the 1980s many of these commodity prices should decline.

It is not only conceivable that energy costs could decline, it is *likely*. Oil costs should decline, perhaps substantially, sometime in the late 1980s. Oil seems to be a classic example of hump-theory roller-coaster pricing. So far, all we have experienced is the ride up. For years, we were buying and consuming energy at prices well below what it actually cost to replace energy. Then along came the Organization of Petroleum-Exporting Countries (OPEC) and the 1973 Arab-Israeli war. OPEC existed long before 1973, and it had always wanted to raise oil prices. What finally gave OPEC the chance was not the Arab-Israeli war—it was the fact that the United States couldn't produce enough of its own oil to say no any more.

U.S. energy production had fallen because prices were below replacement costs in the United States. But OPEC's ability to raise oil prices may even now be waning. Political problems have erupted within OPEC (the OPEC countries never have gotten along very well with each other). Pricing discipline has collapsed.

Far more important than OPEC solidarity, however, is the fact that prices are now high enough to encourage broad conservation, intense exploration, substitution, and new energy technologies. It is almost certain that oil prices will not rise in the first half of the 1980s as fast as they did in the last half of the 1970s. Oil prices will hit $500 a barrel by 1986, from around $34 today, if they don't slow down. But there are a lot of energy alternatives to consider before oil reaches $500 a barrel. Furthermore, there is real hope that energy costs may be declining—perhaps sharply—by the late 1980s. We may find it hard to fathom such a decline today, but history and logic suggest it will occur. Imagine what such a decline would do to inflation!

Income Redistribution Policies

There is a feeling in society that the richest people can, and should, carry a bigger share of society's financial load than the poor. This feeling is manifest in such things as graduated income taxes, which take from the rich, and social programs, which give to the poor. These policies may be excellent social policies, but they aren't necessarily excellent antiinflation policies. There is an economic rule that society gets less of what it taxes and more of what it subsidizes. People with high incomes tend to be the most productive people in society; those with low incomes tend to be the least productive. Redistribution, if carried too far, tends to drive productive people out of the economy and increase the number of those who are nonproductive. Such a trend is economically expensive and adds to "cost push" inflation.

Income redistribution is not a new philosophy. Nor were the 1970s the decade of greatest redistribution change—that honor probably goes to the 1930s. But the 1970s may stand as the decade with the most expensive social programs. Examples include food stamps, Aid to the Families of Dependent Children (AFDC), Medicare, Medicaid, the national school lunch program, the Job Corps, and so on. Substantial differences of opinion regarding the value of each program are possible. But most economists agree that after all the bureaucracy, red tape, and mismanagement is considered, these social redistribution efforts were highly inflationary.

As the 1970s ended, there were small but clear signs of social change. Grass-roots pressure was building to slow the pace of income redistribution in our society. The first signs were at the local municipal level. Voters began regularly defeating bond issues. Then came the California Proposition 13 phenomenon. Voters told politicians what the tax rates should be. This reversal is being followed by greater voter interest in how tax dollars are being spent.

As the 1980s begin, there are even more signals that taxpayers want relief. A major effort to convene a constitutional convention to consider an amendment requiring a balanced federal budget is being mounted. And many interpret the 1980 national election as a clear signal that voters want a reduction in government spending. Don't count on any miracles, but a simple slowing of the redistribution trend of the 1970s will take some pressure off inflation in the 1980s.

Social Protection

Society must do many things to be certain the quality of life remains high. But inflationary costs may be involved. For instance, in the late 1960s the nation realized that pollution was becoming a serious problem. During the 1970s, corporations were required to spend billions installing antipollution devices in their plants. Few of these devices increased output or efficiency. Your own automobile is an example. Think of the antipollution items such as catalytic mufflers you must pay for. They increase the cost, lower the gas mileage of your car, and don't increase the performance. It is the same for corporations. The result—higher costs without additional revenues. This is "cost push" inflation. Corporations have had to make enormous antipollution investments. Of course, this means the corporations have had to raise their prices to stay even.

Pollution is just one example of social protection expense. There are many others. There have been huge costs for crime prevention, safety control, consumer safety, worker protection, and so on. These costly programs result in higher prices and inflation, at least in the short run. (Incidentally, I am not expressing any value judgments about the worth of these programs; my sole purpose here is to examine their role in creating inflation.)

As we move into the 1980s, we can see that much pollution retrofitting has been accomplished. Many U.S. cities have cleaner air and water now than twenty years ago. The pressure seems to have relaxed in other areas, as well. But this doesn't mean we've seen the end of government intervention. The government will be deeply involved in areas such as energy during the 1980s. But hopefully programs such as a synthetic fuels program should eventually reduce inflationary pressures.

Government Regulation

Federal, state, and local governments all impose regulations. In order to supervise compliance with all these regulations, those being regulated are frequently required to file reports stating they are complying. In the late 1960s and throughout the 1970s, the growth of government regulation became absolutely cancerous. Many new laws were passed, and their complexity increased. All this resulted in enormous increases in nonproductive costs to corporations. Some companies report that 10 to 15 percent and more of their costs are for government reporting.

You can see examples of regulation in your own life. Income tax reporting keeps getting more complicated. Millions of ordinary Americans feel compelled to pay experts to prepare their tax returns. The fees paid to tax preparers are lost costs. When a corporation incurs such costs, they must pass them on in higher prices.

Is there hope for fewer regulations in the 1980s? Probably not fewer regulations in total—bureaucracies don't work that way. But there is a lot of grass-roots pressure on government to slow it down. For example, we see what may be a changed regulation attitude in trucking, broadcasting, airlines, railroads, the Federal Trade Commission, and others. There is hope that new regulations won't expand as fast in the 1980s as in the 1970s, and that should help win the inflation battle.

A key in controlling regulation is controlling the amount of money the government is willing to spend on the bureaucracy. For the first time in fifty years, the government seems willing to tackle this problem.

Monetary Policy

The Federal Reserve System, affectionately known as the FED, is responsible for the supply of money in the United States. During the 1970s, the FED frequently let money supply grow rapidly for extended periods of time. They hoped to stimulate business, produce a strong economy, and provide lots of jobs. Along the way, they also stimulated, produced, and provided lots of inflation. As inflationary problems grew, the FED eventually panicked, over-reacted by slamming on the monetary brakes, and then created a deep recession. The recession naturally led to high unemployment, which prompted even greater stimulation to create jobs—and away we went again back into inflation.

Many economists are highly critical of the way things went. They feel the FED's stop-and-go policies produced both inflation and unemployment. They feel the FED should have picked a constant rate of money growth and then stuck with it through boom *and* bust.

The steady-as-you-grow policy is a theory that should work. And as we enter the 1980s the FED seems determined to try it. If the theory does work, it should help cool inflation. But its inflation-fighting benefits may not be fully evident for several years. It's just theory, and there are lots of politics and reality ahead, but it leaves room for hope.

Government Fiscal Policy

After World War II, the federal government decided it had a responsibility to see that jobs were available for everyone. The idea was for the government to spend enough money during the bad times to keep people working. The government was to spend the money even at the risk of running deficits. The plan was to repay the deficits during the good times.

Unfortunately, during the 1960s and 1970s the government was not disciplined. In its enthusiasm to keep everyone working, happy, and voting the right way, the government ran huge deficits all the time—even during the good times. All this deficit spending created lots of demand and tremendous inflationary pressures.

Will the deficit pressures ease in the 1980s? Again, there is hope. There is much grass-roots pressure on the government to do something about its budget. The election of 1980 installed a president and a Congress who seem willing to tackle the federal budget. It won't be easy, but the chance to make real progress is here.

Wage and Price Controls

During the early 1970s, the government tried to interfere with the nation's important pricing mechanism by imposing wage and price controls. This program backfired completely. Today the persistent rhetoric of more controls is continuing to push inflation. The rhetoric is unfortunate. Some people forget, or do not realize, the controls didn't work—except cosmetically and for a short time. When controls were imposed in August 1971, many businesses were caught off guard. In many cases, they found themselves with several products whose prices needed to be raised to be profitable. Often the only alternative was to withdraw these products from the market. Soon shortages of many items began to develop. Consumers and businesspeople panicked. They began hoarding products, which led to more shortages, and the shortages led to pressure for higher prices. When controls were finally lifted, prices exploded everywhere. This explosion was followed by a massive recession as people worked off their hoarded inventories. The result? Prices were as high, or higher, than they would have been anyway, and the nation was dragged through its worst recession since the 1930s.

Although controls were officially phased out in 1974, people continue talking about new controls even today. The talk is making inflation worse. Business and labor both feel they must raise their prices high and fast to avoid being caught by surprise with another controls program. Consumers, in turn, act rationally to avoid new shortages by purchasing in advance of their needs. Just when the "controls psychology" will subside is anyone's guess. But probably it will subside in the next few years.

So far, I have briefly touched on nine important causes of inflation. I have tried to outline a case for a reduction of inflationary pressures from these sources in the 1980s. If all or some of these forecasts prove true, inflationary pressures will be eased.

There were, however, at least six other important causes of inflation in the 1970s as well. Unfortunately, improvement isn't likely to occur soon in these six.

Pricing Power

When truly free markets exist, prices adjust quickly to supply-demand conditions. Prices go up and prices go down. The problem is that we don't have many truly free markets. If markets aren't truly free, then someone, such as a handful of corporations, can control prices. When prices can be controlled, they are then set to maximize profits, not to satisfy demand. Frequently, the profit-maximizing process means artificially high prices, and prices that rise quickly but decline slowly if at all. A few important examples of industries that are not completely free include all utilities (legal but regulated monopolies); automobiles (dominated by a few huge companies); airlines (regulated); banking (local areas usually dominated by a major bank or two); packaged foods (usually dominated by big companies)—the list goes on and on.

Pricing in these markets is not free. Demand is frequently a secondary concern. Therefore, some prices can be increased almost irrespective of the natural forces trying to hold them down. During the 1970s, the situation probably became worse. A number of basic industries that had always shown characteristics of heavy price competition began to change: industries such as paper, cement, gypsum, insurance, gasoline, and chemicals. Executives of these formerly price-competitive businesses came to the conclusion they would be better off worrying only about profits. They decided to maintain prices and forget about market share. The official rationale for this change in operation was the volatile profits they had experienced in the 1950s and 1960s. Their shareholders became angry over the sudden drops in earnings every few years. Practically speaking, it became possible for many formerly price-competitive industries to achieve some level of price control in the 1970s, because fewer new plants were built than in the 1960s. Today new plants are badly needed again. But it is impossible to be sure they will be built in the 1980s. And if they are built, it's hard to know just what influence that will have on prices.

Strong Labor

Labor is a key national resource. Labor unions are an important force in today's economy. In the 1960s and 1970s, the unions' efforts have been inflationary in several ways. First, they have pushed for wage increases that exceed inflation rates. Second, they have opposed work rule changes that would lead to higher productivity. Third, in the last fifteen years they have concentrated on improved benefits such as insurance, pensions, and paid holidays. These benefits are hidden costs that can be especially inflationary. For example, pension increases are usually retroactive. Sometimes the new benefits even apply to employees already retired. The increase per employee may not look big, but the total cost to the company, including catching up, can be enormous. Furthermore, many benefits are in areas of the greatest inflation, such as health insurance. So the cost of the benefit increases much faster than the company or union originally imagined. And, to complicate matters, benefits often restrict the firm's ability to manage its expenses. When business is bad, the company can't "lay off" its benefits in order to reduce costs. Fourth, unions have in recent years concentrated on organizing workers in the service sectors of the economy, such as police, teachers, bank employees, office personnel, and retail employees. These workers are least subject to new productivity gains. Also, they are workers in areas where labor expense is a high percentage of the total cost. Higher wages thus very directly result in higher prices.

Union membership has actually declined as a percentage of the work force. But unions haven't declined in influence. Employers everywhere watch what the unions do. Then they tend to match, or exceed, what the unions get. Today most employees, union and nonunion, expect frequent pay raises, more time off, greater job security, and even improving benefits. These are good, but they cost money, and the increased expenses mean high prices.

The Declining Dollar

During much of the 1970s, the good old dollar took a beating. It declined in value against the currencies of many other countries. This decline was partly (or largely) due to the United States' insatiable appetite for foreign oil. As we paid for our oil, we flooded the world with dollars. And when there is too much of something sloshing around, its value goes down—including the dollar.

A declining dollar *is not* inflationary in itself as many people believe. It does, however, contribute to inflation. Consider Toyotas. Most Toyota owners know their cars are built in Japan. Suppose that in January each U.S. dollar is worth 250 Japanese yen. Suppose at that level Toyotas cost $5000 or 1,250,000 yen (5000 × 250 yen). Then imagine that the dollar's value declines or, conversely, that the yen's value rises. Say the new relationship is one dollar equals 200 yen. Now $5000 is only equal to 1,000,000 yen. That's OK as far as the U.S. buyer is concerned. But it is not OK as far as the Japanese manufacturer is concerned. He or she must pay salaries in yen, buy materials in yen, and pay taxes in yen. The manufacturer needs 1,250,000 yen on each Toyota in order to make a profit. So he or she must raise the dollar price of the Toyotas to $6250 (6250 × 200 yen = 1,250,000 yen).

A price increase from $5000 to $6250 is a lot of inflation to the U.S. Toyota buyer. It is an increase of 25 percent even before the Toyota buyer considers getting any fancy options. But the inflation doesn't stop at the Toyota dealership. Let's say General Motors had priced its competing cars at $5000. Naturally, GM would love to charge more but it has been afraid of losing sales to Toyota. But if Toyota is forced to increase its prices to $6250, GM can increase its prices. GM might now price its cars at $6000. This is a smart move. GM gets a 20 percent increase in price without any increase in costs, and it is left with a $250 price advantage over Toyota. All this is terrific for GM, but it is inflationary for car buyers. The trend of the dollar has been better recently. But we can not assume all the weakness is behind us.

Third World Development

Less-developed countries of the world are often referred to as Third World countries. In the 1970s, many of these nations began pushing to raise their standard of living: countries in Africa, South America, and the Far East. Many of these countries have thrown off oppressive dictators and are now being led by governments that want to improve the living standards of all their people. These improvements create more demand for the world's scarce resources, putting upward pressure on costs everywhere, including in the United States.

Value Added

Consumers like convenience. Convenience frequently comes in the form of value added. For instance, Americans have long had a love affair with chocolate cake. Years ago, Mom made chocolate cakes from scratch. Today the cake probably comes in a box and the icing in a can, or the whole thing comes frozen, ready to be heated in the microwave oven. Consumers pay for much more than just flour, eggs, and milk when they buy a cake. Today they also pay for special boxes, testing, advertising, and transportation. They also pay for profits and overhead all along the way. So cakes cost more.

Cakes aren't the only item to which expensive value has been added. Just about everything is fancier today: Cars have seat belts and carpets; houses have two bathrooms and extra insulation; vacations have air fare and swimming pools. Things are fancier, which adds to inflation.

Inflation

Inflation itself is one of the biggest causes of inflation. Costs for basic materials rise, so prices of finished goods must rise. Costs of finished goods rise, so labor rates must rise. Labor rates rise, so the cost of basic materials must rise, and around we go again. Soon everyone begins anticipating inflation. Consumers buy two cans of soup, not one. They buy one to eat and one to save so they can beat the next price increase. But the hoarding increases demand, and results in "demand pull" inflation. Inflation anticipation affects labor contracts. The workers demand wage increases higher than inflation. Then they also demand a cost of living adjustment built right into the contract, in case inflation rises yet higher. Naturally, cost-push inflation results. Furthermore, inflation anticipation affects the way businesspeople price products, write contracts, figure bids, and on, and on. Once inflation gets started, it feeds on itself. It can be very difficult to shut off. Inflation is as close to a perpetual motion machine as you'll find.

Inflation is the most difficult economic problem in our time, but it's not completely hopeless. The 1970s witnessed an unusual confluence of inflationary forces. There is good reason to believe that the 1980s will not see as many inflationary pressures. In fact, before the

1980s are gone we may see the reversal of some of the 1970s' most important inflationary forces. By 1990, inflation may well no longer be considered a problem.

Such a change in concerns is typical. Every decade dawns with concerns and problems that are not around ten years later. Depression was the concern in 1930, war in 1940, rebuilding in 1950, Sputnik in 1960, social priorities in 1970, inflation, economics, and energy in 1980—and who knows in 1990? Our 1990 problems may be worse than our 1980 problems, but they will be different.

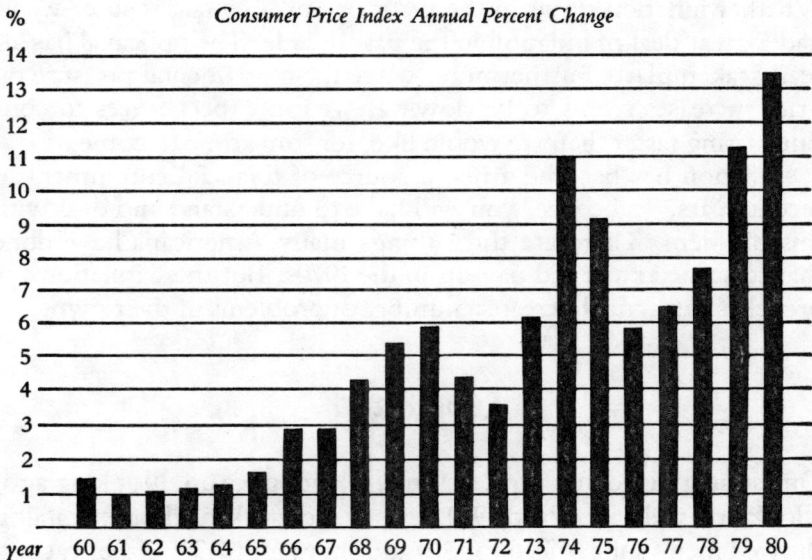

Consumer Price Index Annual Percent Change

◇ 2 ◇
Prospering
in Spite of Inflation

Whether inflation slows in the 1980s or not, one fact is sure: We've had a great deal of inflation in the past decade. The upheaval has already taken place. Furthermore, while the fundamental pressure on price increases seems to be slowing, we can expect prices to continue rising faster than we would like, for some time to come.

Inflation has become a major source of financial entrapment in recent years. To be free, you will have to understand and deal with this problem. There are three things many Americans have done that to some extent did pay off in the 1970s. But these inflation approaches can actually create a number of problems of their own.

Approach 1

One strategy is to buy now, before the price goes up. Not long ago, a look at a well-preserved 1910 Sears & Roebuck mail order catalog showed men's suits priced for $10 and shoes for $1.25. Other catalog items were comparably priced. Of course, the catalog is usually a little cheaper than the store, but you couldn't help wishing you'd done all your 1985 Christmas shopping in 1910. But buying a whole lifetime's worth of Christmas presents to protect against inflation is impractical, probably impossible, and not even smart. One reason it's not smart is because styles have changed. Another reason is that the same $10 invested in common stocks in 1910 would be worth more than $4000 today—that would buy a pretty stylish suit even at today's prices.

Smart or not, "buying now" is a strategy being used by many Americans today. Numerous buying decisions are being settled on the rationale that "I'd better buy it now before the price goes up." Using this rationale, people buy cars and appliances sooner than necessary. They buy a case of soup when they only need a few cans. They buy a house before they can really afford it. This accelerated buying can become a serious national economic problem. First, all the accelerated buying creates artificially high demand. The artificially high demand causes inflation. The inflation causes more accelerated buying, and a vicious cycle gets started. Then, when everybody is all bought out, people stop buying completely. The artificial demand evaporates, and business plunges into a serious recession. Many people get hurt by the hyperinflation-recession cycle. And, in addition, many hurt themselves with their inflationary buying habits. Buying now before the price goes up forces people to spend all their savings and go heavily into debt. Then, if for any reason their incomes are interrupted, debt-burdened individuals are severely hurt. Becoming completely engrossed in a "buy now" strategy will almost certainly lead to financial ruin in the changing 1980s.

There are several reasons why "buy now" is not a good idea. First, you can tie up a lot of capital with accelerated buying. As we will see later, this seriously reduces your options to make your money work for you. And making your money work is the key to future financial flexibility.

Second, accelerated buying tends to become an irrational rationale for overconsumption. Too many people buy an item they don't really need just because it will cost more later. Salespeople really feed on this phenomenon. How many times have you been pressured by a salesperson to buy something now before the price increases?

Third, the accelerated buying phenomenon is symptomatic of short-range planning. Any real attempt to gain control of your finances will require long-range planning and discipline.

Please do not misunderstand. Buying items you need at good prices is wise. Furthermore, storing certain basics such as food, emergency supplies, and medicine as insurance against unforeseen emergencies is a very good idea. These things are usually done as part of a conscious long-range strategy.

Approach 2

Another strategy is to invest in assets that go up or appreciate in value. Certainly, that's a good idea. But there are risks. Assets that can appreciate can also depreciate in value. Such assets include, among others, land, gold, diamonds, art, antiques, coins, and common stocks. As a particular investment becomes recognized as a good hedge against inflation, more and more investors flock to it. Prices may be driven up beyond any reasonable level. When the bubble finally bursts, great numbers of investors may find their inflation hedges dropping in value a lot faster than their dollars ever dropped. Paying too much for assets just because they have been good inflation hedges in the past is risky and unwise.

During the 1970s, a lot of attention was given to buying so-called hard assets like gold, diamonds, and land. These assets have their place. This book devotes considerable attention to them. But using them solely as inflation hedges presents some serious problems. To be blunt, they are probably overpriced at this time. Making money in them from this point on will require real skill. Furthermore, if inflation does subside in the 1980s you could find yourself really trapped in hard assets.

Approach 3

Yet another strategy is to borrow to buy everything you can, and repay with cheaper dollars. If land for example is inflating at 15 percent, it seems to make sense to borrow at 10 or 12 percent to buy the land.

I will have much more to say on interest rates and credit later on. But here let me say that this strategy, carried to extremes, is very foolish for several reasons. First, you really tie up today's and tomorrow's cash flow, strangling you financially. Second, what if inflation slows? You may find yourself repaying an expensive loan with dollars that were far more costly than you imagined.

Approach 4

A fourth strategy is to increase your income. Everyone likes raises. Sometimes the raise does not seem high enough to offset the inflation. By the time Uncle Sam takes his share of the raise, it often feels like you're farther behind. To keep ahead, Dad may feel like he has to take another part-time job, or, as has become common in the United States, Mom goes back to work.

Many women really want to work, but many working women are working just to make ends meet. When people are taking extra jobs and both spouses are working just to stay ahead of inflation, they have suffered a reduction in their standard of living. A large number of women who really don't want to work have returned to the labor force. How will families keep their incomes growing ahead of inflation in the future? Maybe the child labor laws will be repealed!

Approach 5

Try to prevent inflation. As with many global problems, very few people feel there is anything they can do individually to solve the problem. In fact, as with many global problems, most people fail to appreciate that they are part of the problem. Usually they blame big government, or big business, or big labor, and so forth. But hundreds of millions of individuals *do* collectively add to the problem. And it is possible for those individuals to do a great deal to solve it.

Individuals can do a lot to solve inflation. Basically, what they have to do is stop participating in strategies that involve excess spending and buying. If people curtailed their accelerated spending and inflation hedge investing, many of today's inflation problems would vanish. The extra buying demand forces prices up.

People can also pressure their elected officials to slow the pace of government spending and to curtail the formation of expensive government regulation. They can pressure their companies and even their labor organizations to moderate price and wage increases. Individuals can join buyer strikes against goods and services if prices have been raised unreasonably. Individuals can do more than anyone else to solve inflation. But they can't do anything until they are pulled together into a large group and lose their individuality.

Unfortunately, this strategy is too far-sighted and patriotic for most people. I suppose people can't be blamed for looking out for themselves even if their collective looking out makes it hard on everyone.

It's like a fire in a crowded room. Everyone's impulse for self-preservation creates a stampede for the exit. The result? Few get out, and many burn. If instead the crowd would move out in an orderly fashion, the result would be many saved and almost no one burned.

There are some very sound things you can do to manage with inflation.

First, manage your expenditures better than ever. Much of this book will be devoted to principles to help you do just that.

Second, make your current dollars work as hard as possible. This book will help you learn about many new financial products, such as new money market funds, higher yielding investments, and certificates. You cannot afford to let cash sit idle.

Third, improve your earning capabilities as much as possible. Inflation is forcing changes. Many jobs will stagnate or be eliminated altogether. Don't stagnate with them. Take advantage of the numerous opportunities to learn new skills, cross-train, and upgrade your job. Training adds flexibility—and flexibility will be a key theme for the 1980s.

Fourth, plan for bigger risks. Inflation means everything costs more—including unpleasant experiences such as accidents. The chapters of this book devoted to insurance are important. You must learn how to manage for the inflated loss. It is possible to do so and frequently to lower your cost at the same time.

Fifth, engage in more careful long-range planning for such things as inflated college and retirement expenses. Anticipating them now improves your chances of dealing with them later.

Sixth, diversify your investments. This is always a good principle. But it is more important with the uncertainty of inflation. This means you will need to know about more investments. This book will acquaint you with them.

There is hope. You really can prosper in spite of inflation and avoid being trapped by some of the unwise strategies people used in the 1970s. Prospering with inflation means dealing with it if it continues, but not being trapped if it doesn't.

◇ 3 ◇
Dealing with
High Interest Rates

Inflation is almost always accompanied by high interest rates. The level of interest rates has changed dramatically. It is important to understand them for the 1980s.

Understanding high interest rates is *simple* when we take a moment to consider where money we borrow comes from. It comes from someone who lends money. The lender may be a good friend, or a financial giant such as a multibillion-dollar bank. But regardless of who lends the money, that person or institution wants to be sure that, at the end of the period of the loan, at least as much is returned as was originally loaned out.

For example, if the loan amount is $10,000, then the lender wants to be sure that the full value is ultimately returned. If there were no inflation, the amount to be paid back would be $10,000. But with inflation, that amount may be considerably more. With inflation, we must consider buying power, not just nominal dollars.

Let's say that you are the lender, and you loan out $10,000 for one year. Yet during that one-year period inflation is 10 percent. That means that your dollar loses roughly 10 percent in buying power over the course of time. Because inflation is eroding buying power, that $10,000 you loaned out is only worth about $9,000 at the end of the year. As a lender, would you settle for lending out $10,000 worth of buying power and one year later receiving $9,000 back?

I certainly wouldn't, and I don't think you would either. In order to get back just the amount you loaned out, you would need to get back about $11,000 at the end of one year. That's about $1,000 more to compensate for inflation. That's 10 percent interest.

As the lender in this example, you would charge roughly 10 percent interest just to be sure that you got back the same amount of money in terms of buying power that you loaned out. Please keep in mind that we're not talking about profit here. The lender (you) isn't receiving any profit yet. The 10 percent interest is just to recoup the initial money loaned.

Now we can add on profit. What's a fair profit? Two percent? Three? Four? Let's say it's 4 percent. The lender wants 4 percent profit on the loan of money over one year. The interest rate on the loan now becomes 14 percent. That's 10 percent to compensate for inflation and 4 percent for profit.

This is one reason why interest rates are so high during high inflationary periods. In order to get a real rate of return, the lender has to charge more than the rate of inflation. During 1980 and 1981, when inflation ran at about 13 percent at times, prime bank interest rates rose to more than 20 percent. Personal secured loans (mortgages and auto loans) reached 16 and 17 percent. On the surface, 17 percent may seem an outrageous rate of interest. But it's not all profit. A 17 percent interest rate translates to only a 4 percent profit once a 13 percent inflation is taken into account.

Other reasons why interest rates rise and fall concern the government borrowing money in the marketplace (refinancing the national debt), commercial borrowing from major banks and even the borrowing of private individuals. Competition for a limited supply of funds influences interest rates. (I'll examine these functions in more detail later.)

During the 1970s, interest rates rose substantially, in many years hitting new high levels. But even with these increases, the rates seem low compared with the inflation of the time. How could this happen?

The answer is that, for much of the 1970s, most people kept their money in savings accounts in banks and in savings and loan associations. These accounts usually paid only about 5 percent interest. These institutions could easily afford to lend money out at, say, 8 or 9 percent, when it was being deposited with them at 5 percent. As long as the public kept depositing money in these lending institutions at the low interest rate, it really didn't make all that much difference what inflation was doing. The banks and savings and loans could keep loaning out money cheaply because their cost of acquiring it was cheap.

Eventually, however, high inflation caused savers to look elsewhere for higher interest rates. They began looking for new money products that would give them competitive rates of return. From this demand grew money market mutual funds, high-interest savings certificates, and other products, which I'll also discuss later. When the general public started taking its money out of low-interest deposits in savings institutions, these institutions were no longer able to make low-interest rate loans. Instead, because they now had to begin borrowing money themselves at high interest rates, they charged more for their loans. That's what happened during 1980. That's what a large part of the financial revolution of this decade was all about.

Today, high interest rates (coupled with fluctuations up and down) are commonplace. They are as accepted as, and as ordinary as, high-priced gasoline and $100,000-plus homes. It's the way things are.

But knowing the way things *are* doesn't necessarily mean we like high interest rates or understand how to deal with them. What can we *do* about them?

During the 1970s, conventional wisdom was "get in as much debt as you can." People borrowed to buy homes, and second and third homes. They borrowed to buy automobiles, furniture, and just about everything that one can think of. Most of us, in fact, got into the habit of thinking "Borrow." It made good sense.

The reason it made good sense was that we could borrow at a relatively low fixed interest rate and pay back tomorrow with cheaper dollars. We would not only make money on what we bought (because it would cost more tomorrow than it cost today), but we also made money just on our borrowing (we paid back less in dollar value than we borrowed). Borrowing made great sense.

With high interest rates, however, this old wisdom no longer makes much sense. Today, interest rates tend to be significantly higher than either current or anticipated inflation. Therefore, we no longer can pay back with cheaper dollars. The money we formerly were saving in borrowing through inflation is now going directly to the lenders in the form of interest. Borrow today and pay back with dollars of equal value *plus real interest* tomorrow. Borrowing is no longer as keen an idea as it was only a year or two ago.

But what is one to do?

Strategy 1

Don't borrow unless you have to. Don't borrow to buy unless you know that either you must have the item (it's a necessity) or you can sell it in the future for a profit that will more than compensate for the cost of borrowing. In the old days, the cost of interest was a minor part of calculating profit on investments. Today, it's one of the most important parts. When people buy real estate, for example, high interest rates lead to negative cash flows (the investor has to take money out of his or her pocket just to keep the property).

These negative cash flows can be so significant that they can turn what otherwise used to be a profitable deal into a loss. What's the good of making $25,000 profit on the sale of a house, for example, if it costs you $26,000 negative cash flow (after taxes) during the time of ownership?

The same holds true for buying a car or making a credit card purchase. Although generally these types of purchases are not investments and although we're not looking for a profit, we still have to take into account the high interest rates. We all only have so much income. If we have to give a larger share of it to pay interest charges, then we have less to use for making actual purchases. The more interest we pay, the less actual goods we may be able to buy. Paying cash suddenly makes sense.

Strategy 2

If you have to borrow, shop around. In the old days, borrowing was simply a matter of accepting the financing that the car dealer offered, or going down to the savings and loan institution and taking whatever mortgage was offered, or just charging it on any credit card.

Today, shopping around pays off. Interest rates charged differ from one institution to another. Rates also differ on the type of loan being made, what the collateral is, and how long it's being made for. Many institutions don't like long-term loans. They were burned once when they had long-term low-interest loans and interest rates skyrocketed. They don't want to be burned again.

You don't want to be burned either. A complete section on credit follows later. At this point, I'll just summarize by saying properly used credit is a marvel. It allows you to time and manage your wealth. It extends your ability to attract goods and services. Properly used, it adds financial flexibility, and flexibility is key to the 1980s. But improperly used credit is the biggest financial trap of all.

It is crucial to understanding the world we currently live in to first understand how high and volatile interest rates make using credit more difficult than ever before. Much of what you thought about borrowing in the 1970s will not be true in the 1980s.

Average Annual Mortgage Rate

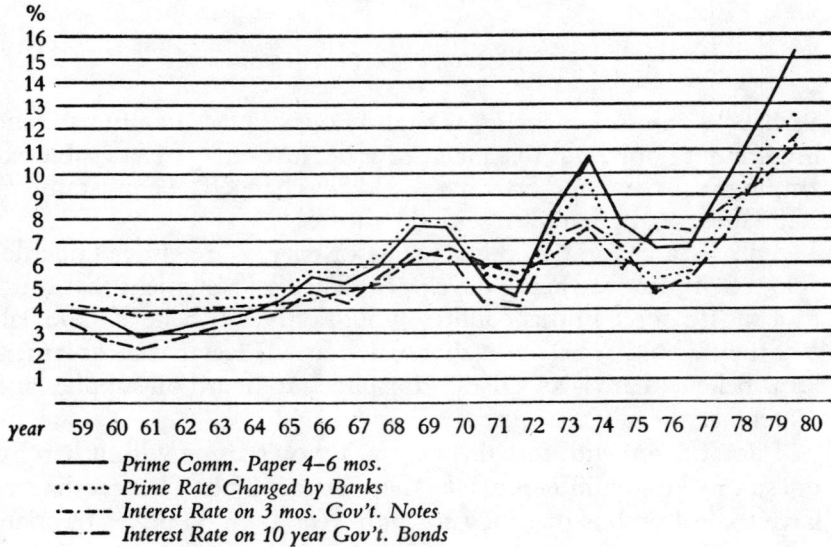

year 59 60 61 62 63 64 65 66 67 68 69 70 71 72 73 74 75 76 77 78 79 80

——— Prime Comm. Paper 4–6 mos.
······· Prime Rate Changed by Banks
—·—·— Interest Rate on 3 mos. Gov't. Notes
—·—·— Interest Rate on 10 year Gov't. Bonds

Average Annual Mortgage Rate

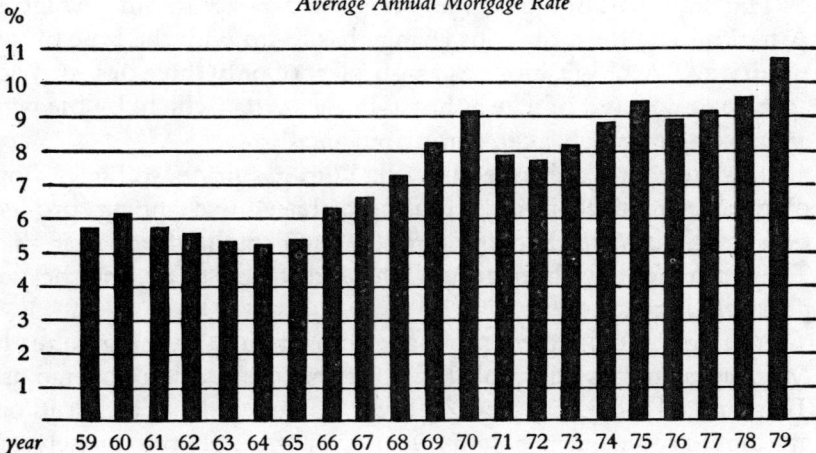

year 59 60 61 62 63 64 65 66 67 68 69 70 71 72 73 74 75 76 77 78 79

◇ 4 ◇
Coping with Scarce Energy

Perhaps a chapter on energy is slightly out of place in a finance and investment book. But I've included it because energy is a visible example of upheaval and how the world has changed. We must understand these changes to deal with the future.

Oil is scarce, and all other forms of energy are either underdeveloped or just now being developed. That is a statement that I suspect most people in this country would only half believe. The half that they wouldn't believe is that oil is scarce. I feel that most Americans believe there is an OPEC conspiracy to hoard oil supplies and thereby artificially raise prices.

I don't agree with that theory, but I won't argue with it here. It doesn't make any difference *why* oil prices are high. The fact that we have to deal with is that they *are* high. And high oil prices translate into high prices for a whole variety of products, from gasoline to fertilizer. Ultimately, we pay more for transportation, food, shelter, and even clothing.

Higher prices for gasoline have made a significant change in America. The most obvious change has to do with the type of cars we drive. The old-fashioned gas-guzzlers of only three or four years ago are now as out of date as horse-drawn carts (which, by the way, are making a comeback in some rural areas!).

There are other changes as well. With gas prices so high, shopping patterns are changing. Housing patterns are changing, production techniques are changing, and building standards are changing. These changes have been abrupt, they are visible to all, and they are probably here to stay.

You have almost certainly made adjustments for energy already. More adjustments will probably be necessary. But don't overadjust. This, and all the recent changes must be well understood, or in our attempt to solve our problems we may unwittingly trap ourselves.

For instance, it is obvious we should become as close to energy self-sufficient as possible. This means driving a low-consumption car, living in a well-insulated house, driving frugally, and so forth.

However, remember that energy is in transition. Don't go into bankruptcy trying to save a few pennies on energy costs.

Take the example of an automobile. Let's say Joe has a gas-guzzler that only gets 15 miles to the gallon, but that he owns free and clear and that runs very well.

Every time Joe goes to the gas station, his gas-guzzler gives him a pain in his wallet. He keeps thinking about all those tiny cars that get between 25 and 30 miles to the gallon. If he only had one of those, he could save up to half of his gas costs.

Eventually, the thought of 15 miles to a gallon drives Joe to dump his gas-hog (for which he gets next to nothing, because nobody else wants a gas-guzzler either) and to pay between $6000 and $10,000 for a gas-stingy car.

Did Joe make a good move?

Maybe. It depends on a lot of factors. For example, how much does Joe drive a year? How long would he have kept his old car if gas consumption hadn't been a problem? How much is it going to cost to obtain a new car? And so on.

If Joe only drives about 10,000 miles a year, for example, and had planned on keeping his old car for three more years, buying a new gas-stingy car may make poor sense. Consider the following:

10,000 miles at 15 miles per gallon = 666 gallons

$$\times \ \underline{\$1.35 \text{ per gallon}}$$

$$\$899$$

10,000 miles at 25 miles per gallon = 400 gallons

$$\times \ \underline{\$1.35 \text{ per gallon}}$$

$$\$540$$

$$\$899$$

$$- \ \underline{540}$$

$$\$359 \text{ savings per year}$$

$$\times \ \underline{3 \text{ years}}$$

$$\$1077 \text{ savings in three years}$$

Joe would have saved $1077 just by switching from his gas-guzzler to a more fuel-efficient car. But consider the cost: A $7000 car financed over three years at 20 percent interest yields total interest charges of roughly $3000.

That means that Joe ends up paying about $3000 in interest. Joe has saved $1077 on gas and spent $3000 on interest. All other things being equal (if Joe was satisfied with the original car, would have kept it for three more years, it ran well, and so on), Joe hardly made a good bargain.

If Joe makes many more bargains like this, such as moving to a more expensive house close to work, paying a lot of money for insulating, and installing solar heating and cooling, Joe may save so much money that he could end up in bankruptcy!

The point is that making transitions to energy efficiency must make economic sense. Making the move without looking at the true arithmetic makes no sense. People can lose more, in the long run, than they save. It might make sense, given Joe's economic condition, to stick with an energy-*in*efficient car, if it runs well, is paid off and if he doesn't plan to trade it in for a few years. Of course, when it comes time to trade in the car, then Joe would opt for the energy-efficient model.

Becoming energy-efficient should be a major goal. But it should not be the only goal. We should try to make such transitions smoothly.

Conclusion

We have been examining some of the more visible and awesome examples of the financial upheaval our nation has been experiencing, such as inflation, interest rates, and energy. Of course, there are many others, which are less visible.

Many feel the financial dislocation of these forces is too great to handle. They feel financial freedom is out of reach.

I disagree. Not only can you deal with the world as it now is, but I believe that on balance the opportunities are greater in the 1980s than at any time in the past. Let me close this part of the book by outlining why I express such optimism.

1. America is still strong. There are a lot of problems—but there always have been. Our social, political, and economic fabric has tremendous resiliency and is capable of adjustment. As one example, I point to the 1980 election. The people of the country

wanted a change in leadership. Not only was it made, it was made without riots, bloodshed, or turmoil. In fact, it was made with pledges of support and cooperation. The American people are in charge. As long as a majority of Americans are in favor of correct principles, the country will be strong.

2. There are new products available in all fields to cope with new problems. This book discusses many of the new financial products.

3. There is more information available in terms of education at all levels. Greater understanding leads to greater opportunities.

4. There are fewer barriers. Minorities and women, for example, can pursue alternatives previously unavailable to them. It is not necessary to be wellborn to succeed.

5. Greater opportunities for advancement are open to well-trained workers in nearly all fields than ever before.

6. There is more mobility. People are free to pursue opportunities wherever they exist.

7. Technology is moving at an extraordinary pace, opening new horizons. Minicomputers and microprocessors are revolutionizing our lives and opening new doors.

8. There are actually greater opportunities for entrepreneurs than at any time in history. Venture capital financing is available for sound ideas. Traditionally stuffy financial institutions are more flexible in their lending practices.

This list can go on. Anyone who fails to comprehend the opportunities of the 1980s will miss the future. Anyone who fails to understand the world and its very real problems will be buried by them.

With the right kind of management, there are more opportunities for financial freedom now than a decade ago.

Part II.
Understanding Yourself
Financially

We have been looking at the new world of the 1980s trying to comprehend the financial upheaval that has occurred and how it changes our lives.

But barriers to financial freedom are not just in the world around us. Many people remain financially trapped because of their own attitudes and actions.

Frequently it is difficult for us to see ourselves as others see us. We have mannerisms we really don't realize we have—unless we purposefully try to identify them. Some of our mannerisms lead to self-defeating behavior. The same is true of financial mannerisms. Some lead us to financially self-defeating behavior. In these circumstances, we cannot be free until we really understand ourselves and change.

Of course, many people find themselves struggling simply because of their circumstances. These people don't need pity—they need good advice.

This part of the book is devoted to helping each reader understand the most important variable in his or her personal financial picture—him- or herself. It will also try to offer some good advice, up to and including telling you where to find a financial counselor and what the counselor will do for you. Fortunately, nearly everybody can achieve financial freedom on his or her own. Hopefully this book can help.

◇ 5 ◇
Personal Financial Crises
of the 1980s

I have spent years helping people work through some of their personal financial struggles. Often, outsiders can quickly see self-defeating behavior on the part of financially trapped people. In this chapter, I will share with you briefly ten cases of self-defeating financial behavior. My experience is most people can see some of themselves in these stories. And when they do, they can make some adjustments.

These cases are true, but disguised. Only the financial principles are apparent.

Case 1
"Money Is for Spending"

Sam and Marge were the kind of people you might find as your neighbors. They had two children and lived in a pleasant suburb. Sam had a good job, and on the surface they seemed financially well off. But both Marge and Sam knew they were sitting on a financial volcano.

Sam and Marge were horribly in debt and getting more in debt every day. They both agreed that something had to be done. But they violently disagreed on what.

Sam said it was all Marge's fault—she continued to spend money even when they had none. Marge said that it couldn't be her fault—it was just that they needed things and with inflation the cost of everything was so high. It simply cost more and more to buy the same things. One thing was clear: Within a few months, they would be nearing the end of their ability to make ends meet, and then bankruptcy was a real possibility. So they went to see a financial counselor.

In their interview with the counselor, several things became obvious. First, Sam put all the burden of shopping on Marge. He rarely went out and bought anything himself. He left her to shop for food, clothing, and just about all her needs. In addition, he made demands on the type and quality of products she was to buy.

Marge, to get Sam what he wanted, acceded to his every request. In fact, acceding to Sam's request was easy because Marge had a problem of her own. Like many women who have not been allowed full financial responsibility, she had no concept of money. She did not understand the relationship between income and expenses. She only knew that Sam made money and that she spent it. She knew cash was money, and when that ran out, she could still buy with credit cards and checks. Sam paid all the bills and balanced the checkbook, so she never had to think about any limitations.

Also, because she was the spender and had a feeling of unlimited income, she didn't bother to take advantage of sales or price reductions. Because it was difficult figuring out which of two products was the best value on a per-ounce basis, for example, she usually bought the one in the brightest package. To her, $100 in cash seemed like a lot of money. She didn't understand that the $100 only bought a week's worth of groceries, the way she spent. She really needed to make the money stretch farther.

In addition to meeting Sam's demands for purchases, Marge had demands of her own. She wanted new furniture and drapes. Sam would explode in fury, shouting, "No! We can't possibly afford it."

Marge couldn't figure out why they couldn't afford the things she wanted when she always bought what Sam wanted. Marge retaliated by accusing Sam of not being a good provider. She occasionally accused him of not loving her. And he would call her stupid, irresponsible, and a spendthrift. With the higher cost of everything, what had been a difficult problem was quickly becoming an impossible, marriage-threatening concern.

The financial counselor told them that they had to come to terms with their financial problems at once or face a complete collapse of their personal relationship. Both Sam and Marge nodded. They foresaw disaster, and they wanted to avoid it.

The counselor pointed out that inflation was making life tough for all families, not just theirs. Income in many cases was not going up as fast as inflation, and the result was that the same dollars bought slightly less each month. Until Sam could make more money (or Marge went out and got a job), they would have to live on what they had. The only way to do so was to stick to a budget.

Marge agreed to spend only a set amount of money for household operations. The money would be in cash. This amount would have to last through the month. She also agreed to use no credit cards and checkbooks. The counselor also gave her a pocket calculator and showed her how to determine the best prices for what she was buying.

Sam agreed not to make any demands for food, clothing, and other items, unless there was a pressing need. The counselor pointed out that a "pressing need" probably wouldn't occur more than once in every two or three months. Both Sam and Marge agreed to try out the budget.

Sam didn't ask for his favorite food, oysters, nor for a new green sweater he was dying to have. He wanted the plan to succeed.

Marge also wanted the plan to succeed, but still didn't really know what money was. A budget was just an abstract theory. She seemed to have an internal resistance to learning math. And shopping for value was too confusing, so she gave up. She ran out of money after two weeks.

In the midst of a fight in which Marge was demanding more money and Sam was pointing out all the things he was giving up, they called the counselor. The counselor said that the solution was simple. Sam couldn't have what he wanted, and Marge couldn't have a cent more until next month.

The rest of the month was a disaster. For the last week, the family subsisted on dry cereal and canned goods stored in the pantry. There was no more food money.

The second month wasn't much better, and the arguments between Sam and Marge were still bad. But the counselor suggested trying the budget for a bit longer.

By the third month, Marge had become an expert with the calculator. She started watching for sales, checking prices, buying only those items the family needed. By the last day of the month, she had enough money left over to splurge by taking the family out for dinner at a fast-food restaurant. And Sam had realized that he didn't really need expensive foods and clothes.

Marge and Sam learned two important lessons. First, rising prices don't mean you can spend more money. Rising prices mean you must understand money even more. You can only spend according to income. To make ends meet, you must control the middle more than ever.

Case 2
"Spend Your Way Out of Depression"

Cindy worked as a "Girl Friday" for an insurance agency. She made about $1100 a month. She lived alone, she was a little overweight, she felt she was not pretty, she had a terrible self-image, and she was depressed. And picking up the morning paper and reading about high interest rates, rising gas prices, and escalating everything sure added to her depression.

Cindy recently wanted to buy a car, but was turned down. The price of the car and the cost of financing were more than she could afford. That really depressed her. Besides her own personal problems, she felt that society as a whole was out of control. She was frustrated about it, but because there was nothing she could do, she just felt more depressed.

Of course, Cindy didn't like feeling bad, and there was one thing she could do that always seemed to perk her up—spend money. It was fun to have new things; at least, it was fun for a while. Besides, Cindy somehow felt a little more in control when she spent money. She felt she was getting things before there would be nothing left to have.

Overall, Cindy's income and expenses should have balanced. She was paying about $300 a month for an apartment, and about $265 for food, utilities, and personal items. She owned an old gas-guzzler free and clear. But, for some reason ends weren't meeting.

Lots of long-distance phone calls to her old friends and family members helped cheer her up. And then there were clothes, lots and lots of clothes, and jewelry and perfumes. Nothing she purchased was that expensive by itself. But, altogether they added up to hundreds of dollars a month. Cindy always found that her paycheck was never enough. She was continually broke and going further into debt, and that only depressed her even more.

When Cindy went to a financial counselor, they quickly agreed that both her personal and her financial self-image were poor. Helping her conquer her financial problems was a good step in improving both. To help her solve her financial problems, she agreed to give her counselor an itemized list once each week of every penny she spent.

Knowing that the counselor would review her expenses each week gave Cindy the incentive to stick to her budget. She didn't want to be embarrassed, so she watched her spending.

Sticking to the budget did wonders for Cindy. Her self-image improved. She felt more in control. She no longer felt broke; she decided she was as well off financially as most other people. She no longer had to spend to relieve her depression. She even started dating again.

Depression is not new; neither is spending to relieve it. But Cindy illustrates the added frustration that many people feel in our society today because of the financial (and personal) constraints imposed by inflation, high interest rates, and other factors. Realizing that we're not alone and that it is possible to live well within these constraints often relieves the depression they cause.

Case 3
"Browsing to Relieve Boredom"

The Johnstons appeared to be a model upper middle class family. They have a good family life. He was a sales manager for a small surgical instrument company and a Scout Master; she was a school-teacher, church worker, and musician. Between them they made more than $50,000 a year. But although they should have been secure, they weren't. They were badly in debt. They got in debt by browsing and they browsed just for fun.

Browsing through what they really couldn't afford had become a kind of hobby for the Johnstons. They looked around their house and found that it was not nearly as nice as they would have liked it to be. "Let's go look at some furniture," Mrs. Johnston might say. "We'll just look, we won't buy anything."

So they would get in their car and go to the shopping center. "It's the perfect antidote to boredom," Mr. Johnston would remark.

Of course, just looking at fine furniture, paintings, clothing, dishes, silverware, and so forth was terribly frustrating. "Oh, couldn't we just have that cute little end table," Mrs. Johnston might say. Or Mr. Johnston might decide that he had to have that pin-stripe suit. And so they would do more than window shop— they also purchased.

These purchases led to bickering and arguments over where their money went. They knew that at their income level they should have money, but they didn't. They didn't have any savings, and in fact they had debts, and barely enough to make ends meet month after month.

The Johnstons never did see their problem. When they went to a financial counselor, they couldn't understand where their money went. Only after the counselor made them go back and list each check and credit card charge for an entire year did the true pattern begin to emerge.

Shopping for recreation has always been a bad idea. It's even worse at today's prices. Once the problem was identified, a solution became possible. The Johnstons wanted to live "better," and they found they could. Simply by not shopping on a whim, but instead saving their money for specific purchases on which they both agreed, they found they actually could get much of what they wanted.

Then, and most important, they learned that other activities could relieve their boredom besides window shopping. They found that going to the public library, attending free concerts in the park, and joining various clubs took up much of their time and provided them with opportunities to meet people who thought the Johnstons were well off. It gave them a new perspective both on what was really happening in society around them and about themselves.

The Johnstons learned to like what they had and to plan on how to get what they wanted, even in today's economy.

Case 4
"I Want What They've Got"

Bert and Becky came from definitely middle-class families. Both of them had always liked nice things, especially the nice things their friends always had but that they themselves somehow couldn't afford. The hope of breaking out of middle-class mediocrity was a prime motivation for their decision to go into dentistry. They knew some dentists, and in their opinion dentists were well above the ordinary middle class. Dental school wasn't easy. It was a struggle for both of them. First Becky trained to be a dental assistant, and then got a job. Bert struggled with the books, and Becky struggled with her job. When graduation finally came, they were really ready to begin enjoying the rewards of their struggle.

Perhaps if times had not changed, Bert and Becky might have succeeded in achieving their desires. But, given the tight economy of today, quickly getting what they wanted was totally unrealistic. The high cost of borrowing, high inflation, and all the problems of the 1980s were against them. That didn't mean, of course, that they couldn't try.

They soon discovered the local banks were more than eager to loan a promising young couple all the money they wanted. Bert and Becky decided to take advantage of the bank's generosity and "do it 'right' the first time." For example, there were lots of choices for dental equipment and office furniture. Bert and Becky wanted the best. They had been in several very nice offices run by established dentists. They thought they too should have a nice office.

They also decided to buy a home. One of the dentists they knew before they went to school lived in one of the best suburbs in town. Bert and Becky also wanted to live there.

A new car was yet another matter. One óf their dental student friends owned a particularly nice car, and Bert and Becky felt they ought to have one like it.

And so it went with furniture, clothes, social organizations, and so on. Bert and Becky always found someone, usually a dentist, they wanted to be like.

Soon problems began to set in. A practice was harder to get established than they had counted on. And collecting from the patients that did come in was harder still. Soon they discovered the banks' generosity was conditional on keeping up with payments. Frankly, Bert and Becky couldn't keep up with the payments. Before they knew it, the banks repossessed their living room furniture, and threatened to take one of their cars.

The repossession came at a particularly bad time as far as Bert and Becky were concerned. They had joined a prestigious social group composed mainly of dentists. This organization met monthly for dinner at someone's home. This month it was Bert and Becky's turn. All the other homes seemed to have expensive living room furniture. But at the time, Bert and Becky had no living room furniture at all. They weren't about to be embarrassed. So they took money that they absolutely couldn't afford to spend and rented some expensive-looking living room furniture. At the party, they both felt a little sick, except for a moment when they overheard one envious woman say to her husband, "They've redone their living room already. How do they do it? I wish we could afford some new furniture."

Initially, when Bert and Becky went looking for financial help, what they wanted was advice on collecting from patients. Indeed, a review of their office management procedures indicated they did have some problems. But more study quickly revealed that their biggest financial problems were at home. Helping Bert and Becky see the real problem was difficult. Eventually they were asked to write down precise reasons why they bought the things they did, instead of less-expensive alternatives. With their written answers in front of them, they were finally persuaded that they were afflicted with a serious case of the "keeping up with their peers." But simply understanding intellectually didn't help much. They had to change the way they thought and felt inside.

A good dose of humility was clearly in order. Bert and Becky were persuaded to sell their fancy car and buy a small compact. Their financial thinking improved dramatically when they finally learned that they could still get back and forth to work in a compact and all their friends seemed to accept them anyway.

Bert and Becky are good at their work, and they are going to enjoy prosperous careers. Fortunately, they no longer feel like they are in a race to prove it. Toning down or at least decreasing yesterday's goals may be a necessity in today's world.

Case 5
"Do It for the Kids"

At forty-five years old, Barbara was ambitious and independent. She had worked her way nearly to the top of a medium-sized accounting firm. Yet although she made over $46,000 a year, she was in serious financial trouble.

The cause of her trouble was the personal side of her life. On the road to success, Barbara did not have much time for traditional wife and mother responsibilities. She had been married and divorced twice. She had three teenage children and she worried about them. Neither of the fathers paid child support or alimony.

Barbara's children were having problems, and she felt the problems were her fault. She wanted to spend more time getting close to them, but business matters always interfered. They always seemed to want something, and their friends always seemed to have these things. But prices were so high these days that she just knew they couldn't afford much by themselves.

She felt as if she were already depriving them of her time. She didn't want to deprive them of the things they wanted. So she bought them presents. She gave them clothes, stereos, and even plane fare to go see friends. Barbara paid tuition to college for one of the boys twice. He only went for a few months each time before deciding it was too hard and dropping out.

Whether it was misplaced guilt over not being able to spend time with them, or concern for them in today's society, or a combination of both that caused Barbara to act as she did, she really didn't know. All she knew was that she was getting deeper and deeper into debt. She had purchased cars for the kids, expensive skis and equipment for her daughter, and many other items. Last year alone, Barbara spent over $13,000 on things she couldn't really afford for the children. She felt guilty about the kids, but she also felt guilty because she was getting close to bankruptcy.

Helping Barbara figure out why she was spending wasn't difficult. Deep down inside, she knew it all the time. But getting her to do something about it was another matter. At the start, even the threat of bankruptcy didn't give her enough incentive to stop covering up her misplaced guilt with toys. Finally she realized that bankruptcy might hinder her career and make everything worse. She held many conversations with friends on the subjects of guilt, spending, the current state of the economy, relationships with children, and so on. Eventually she realized she was really hurting the kids. She realized it was tougher to make a go of it now than ever, and she wasn't doing her kids a favor by not helping them realize that. She also became convinced that it doesn't take great amounts of time or money to express love to someone. She came to believe that sincere interest in another person shows right through without buying a lot of expensive gifts to prove it. Nor was it impossible for someone with incentive to build a life and career even in today's tougher society.

Barbara's change of mind was only half the problem. The kids were the other half. None of them had ever worked a day in their lives. They were hooked on material handouts like drug addicts are hooked on heroin. Mom had been trying to show her love with money for so long that simply telling the kids "Things are going to be different around here!" really would have been viewed by them as some sort of rejection. Nevertheless, they had to be told. Honesty seemed to be the best policy.

A family meeting was scheduled and held. Barbara explained the details of her financial mess and proposed a plan of financial recuperation. She asked for full cooperation. Two of the children did cooperate. They sold some things and got jobs to help pay for the others. Unfortunately, one son, for whom she had bought a race car, did not. He decided he loved his car more than he loved his mom. He would rather see her go bankrupt than sell the car. And, as for a job, that would interfere with working on the car. When the car was sold anyway, he moved out. The improved relationship with her first two children is something Barbara counts as a blessing. Now she's hoping time will heal her financial wounds and that time will also mend her relationship with the son who moved out.

Case 6
"You've Got to Be Smart if You're Going into Business"

John always figured that the way to get rich was to find a little business that would make a bundle and require very little work. He kept this fantasy in his mind for most of his life. But when the tough economic climate of the 1980s hit, he decided to turn it into reality.

He thought he had just the thing in buying a coin-operated, wand-type car wash. He borrowed from his folks and mortgaged his house to open the business. According to the figures the company gave him, he could repay everyone within eighteen months after opening. John envisioned owning dozens of car washes all over town. Six weeks after he opened for business, a competitor opened just up the street with an automatic system. One year later, two service stations within a mile installed automatic systems and gave washes free with gasoline purchases. At this point, John is afraid he's the one that got cleaned.

John didn't need much outside help to solve his problems. He realizes now that he hadn't investigated the car wash business thoroughly. He realizes he should have talked to more people first. He realizes he should have at least considered the questions all those Doubting Thomases were raising. He realizes if he had used a little common sense, he could have seen those same competitive trends occurring all over town. He realizes that "get rich quick" schemes aren't the solution. Now he is struggling to repay the debts and dispose of his business. He figures it will take him five years. He also figures in the future his "excessive enthusiasm" will be tempered with "cautious consideration."

Case 7
"End of the World"

Mac was a solid citizen. He owned a home, a car, and a boat, and he had a good job. The only debt he had was a modest mortgage. Three years ago, his wife sued for divorce. Mac didn't fight it. He took his old pickup truck and left her everything else. He also left his job, his friends, and his common sense.

He began to drink. He borrowed money to live on and to gamble with. He bought expensive presents, such as television sets and freezers, for casual friends. He frequently contemplated suicide and lived as though he might do it at any time.

Six months ago, a concerned relative finally helped him settle down. Mac met another woman and fell in love again. They decided to get married. But after the euphoria of the courtship, Mac began to realize that he still owed more than $8000 to Master Card, VISA, oil companies, and small loan organizations. His only asset was his pickup truck, worth about $1250. He couldn't get a decent job because of his recent work history.

Mac never did physically commit suicide, as he had contemplated. But Mac had committed financial suicide along the way.

Thoughts of some sort of suicide began creeping into Mac's mind again. His despair began to rise. His past bills and current state of helplessness quickly began to affect the relationship with his new wife, and within weeks of their marriage a second divorce was being threatened.

Because Mac's despair had lifted once when a few people had shown they cared, maybe the same thing could happen again. Only the people who had to care were Mac's creditors. An interested third party persuaded Mac to visit his creditors in person. The theory was that the employees of the firms he owed money to were people like anyone else. The theory was that these people would be easier to deal with if they met Mac in person.

The theory was correct. The people at these firms did sympathize with Mac's problems and wanted to help. One of them even helped him find a job in a warehouse, a job that Mac took promptly. Knowing that people—even creditors—cared again gave Mac hope. He kept the job, held on to his second marriage, and began making headway on his bills.

Mac learned that as tough as the world is, particularly today, for someone with the desire a way out can almost always be found.

Case 8
"Not Communicating About Money"

Roland and Suzie had been married seven years. Roland handled the finances. When they were first married, they shared the finances. But they found they had great difficulty in discussing money. Roland always felt guilty whenever the subject came up because he couldn't immediately give Suzie everything he imagined she wanted. Like many husbands, Roland thought that he wouldn't be a good husband if he couldn't buy everything his family wanted. And he thought women shouldn't have to deal with financial responsibility. Suzie, on the other hand, only wanted to know exactly how much they had so that she wouldn't overspend.

Eventually, Roland found it easier just not to tell Suzie how much he made. He gave her money to buy food, clothes, and other items.

For a time, it worked. But with inflation, Suzie found she had to spend more money on food. Her other expenses for clothing, laundry, cleaning, gifts, babysitting, and many other items were also accelerating. She worried about the extra costs. But whenever she tried to bring up the subject of money, Roland changed the topic.

Suzie deeply resented the idea of having to beg Roland for more money. So she just didn't. She wrote checks or charged whatever she needed. The bills always got paid anyway, so she decided to trust Roland.

Roland, meanwhile, was having trouble. During the 1970s, it had been hard. But in the 1980s and with high costs plus even higher costs to borrow, he was in a bind. Roland tried to manage the family finances by making mental budgets in his head. He knew how much he gave Suzie for household items. He used the figure for his mental budget.

But somehow he was surprised month after month by how much more she spent than he budgeted. He thought she was wasting money and started yelling at her. Suzie was surprised and tried to discuss money matters with Roland. But he shied away from specific discussions. Instead, he only wanted her to spend less. He called her a spendthrift. She was confused and didn't know what to do. So she continued spending as before.

Eventually the bills got too high. The only way to bail out seemed to be a bill consolidation loan. Roland secured one at high interest rates. Even when Suzie co-signed the second bill consolidation loan, she still didn't realize what serious financial trouble the family was in.

Money wasn't the only thing Roland and Suzie couldn't communicate about, but money was a good place to start in rebuilding their communication. It was good because all the figures were there in black and white. No one could argue they didn't have financial problems. To begin with, the family received help in making a list of all the debts and monthly expenses. Roland was asked to explain each item. Suzie was "flabbergusted"—a combination of being completely flabbergasted and totally disgusted.

Next the family was helped to prepare a simple budget on which both worked. At this session, Suzie gave no indication that the same old household amount was totally inadequate. However, the family also agreed to keep track of everything they spent.

These expenditures were discussed in detail one month later and again three months later. By that time everyone could see that Suzie wasn't a spendthrift. Everyone could see the amount she had been getting was too low. And everyone could see the only way to solve the family money problems was through good financial communication.

Case 9
"Hidden Costs"

Fred was making good money. But he saw that whatever he made was being eroded by inflation. "What I need," he told himself, "is an inflation hedge." The best inflation hedge, he had heard, was a new home. So he decided to buy one.

The broker told him his old home was worth $64,500, leaving him with $28,000 in equity. That would serve as a down payment. But the mortgage on his old home was only at 8 percent interest! The payments now would be nearly twice as high.

To make it, Fred would have to stretch his finances. But he reasoned he'd be saving money with inflation, if he committed every dime of his equity plus took money from savings.

Unfortunately, in his enthusiasm he forgot a lot of things. He forgot that no one ever sells a home for the asking price. Fred finally settled for a price $2000 lower than he thought he would get for his old home.

He also forgot about closing costs, which came to over $1000. He forgot about $890 for a new refrigerator, $1100 for moving, and on and on. In all, he forgot $9895, and he hadn't even started on new drapes, new furniture, landscaping, or air conditioning for the new home.

"But," he reasoned, "appreciation will take care of things. I'll eventually sell for far more than I paid."

Fred borrowed $10,000 for five years at 20 percent interest, payable at $400 a month, just to complete the deal, without the furnishings. When the new payments were added to the mortgage payment, he found that he was up against the wall. He could make things work, but only by taking money out of savings each month. He judged he could just hold on by his fingernails until his income increased.

But Fred had forgotten a few other things.

He forgot that other expenses would be increased in a new house. He had to pay higher utility bills, higher gas costs for the greater driving distance to work, and the generally higher cost of everything as inflation took its toll.

A few months after Fred moved into his new house, he realized he was in trouble. Big trouble. Hidden costs were killing him.

Fred analyzed his problem as an inability to make a sound purchase. He only looked at the initial price, never the hidden costs. He discovered that this was always the case whenever he bought. He never bothered about the sales tax or the carrying charges. In small purchases, it rarely mattered. But in a big purchase it was critical.

A few years ago, Fred might have been OK in spite of his shortcomings. Today, however, high interest and inflation coupled with a big purchase did him in.

Two suggestions could have helped Fred. First, buy a book on the subject. There are "How to Buy" books for just about every big purchase a person can imagine: houses, cars, boats, planes, stereos—you name it. A good "How to Buy" book will deal extensively with costs.

Second, show a written budget to an expert. By making out a budget of all anticipated costs and allowing an expert to review the figures, hidden errors are often found. The best place to find an expert is to call the establishments that sell or finance the item. They will talk with you, and they won't charge you anything. Of course, don't just ask the salesperson working with you. His or her objectivity may be clouded. For example, if Fred had made such a budget on his new house and had shown it to a mortgage loan officer at a savings institution or to a friendly real estate agent, they would have noticed just about all the hidden costs that Fred forgot. This would have allowed a more rational buying decision to begin with. And it would have avoided disappointment later on.

Case 10
"I Can't Resist It!"

Jerry had a good job, made $20,000 a year, and was always broke. Not long ago, he saw an ad for a fancy sports car. Just for the fun of it, he took a test drive. ("What could that hurt?" he asked himself.) Jerry knew he couldn't possibly afford the car, but at least he could pretend.

Jerry loved the car. He just couldn't stop thinking about it after the test drive. He thought about how much fun it would be to own, to drive, even to wash. He regularly went eight blocks out of his way just to drive by the dealership. At work his performance was actually starting to slip because he spent so much time thinking about the car.

Jerry thought of every rationale in the world why a new sports car was a practical decision for him. Of course, there was that stack of bills to pay from other items he had recently bought—a new camera, a new suit, even a boat. In each case, Jerry had just gone to see the item for the fun of it. Eventually he had purchased and now he was stuck with the payments. But the old itch was back. Finally he gave in. He bought the car.

Jerry's wife Lisa didn't know what to do. She would have been glad to go back to the job she had had before their marriage—as an advertising artist. But they had just had their first child, and she felt she couldn't work right now. She sympathized with Jerry's problem, because she knew how appealing advertisements could be. But she also felt desperate.

Eventually Jerry realized he had a problem. After a while, he even knew what his problem was, but he couldn't find the will power to overcome it.

Jerry's problem would be serious in any economy, but in ours it was catastrophic. In order to buy, Jerry had to borrow, and the high interest rates he was paying on his loans were driving him even further into debt. Borrowing to solve his problems was an old stand-by from another era, but in today's tight money economy it was the sure road to bigger problems.

What Jerry needed was another person to talk with him about his periodic "spending fevers" and tell him no if necessary.

His wife Lisa was not the person to do it. She had to live with him. But her father was a good choice. The relationship between Jerry and his father-in-law was excellent. The plan was that every time Jerry became infatuated with a new toy of some sort he would discuss it with his father-in-law. Jerry would routinely submit a list of pros and cons regarding the purchase and a written summary of what the purchase would do to his finances. Jerry's father-in-law was very persuasive. By the time Jerry went through this exercise a few times, anyone could talk Jerry out of buying. Before long, he could even do it himself—and he did.

◇ 6 ◇
Life
and Financial Crises

We've looked at ten different—but common—ways people get themselves into financial trouble. These faults become all the more apparent in today's financial environment.

It wouldn't be fair, however, to assume all financial problems are due to poor financial attitudes. They are not. Some serious problems are thrust on us through no particular fault of our own.

The best hope of gaining financial freedom is to first understand the nature of the problem we are experiencing. There are *layoffs*. There have always been layoffs but inflation, energy, and economic stagnation have compounded the problem. At present, hundreds of thousands of workers are laid off in the automobile field, indirectly because gasoline prices are so high and fewer people are willing to buy Detroit's gas-guzzlers.

There's *sickness*. Remember when you could call a doctor and he or she would come to the house? Well, today doctors won't come to the house and a simple visit to the doctor's office can cost $25 or more. One day in a hospital can cost between $125 and $500. Inflation of costs has probably been higher nowhere else than in medicine.

Like sickness, *disability* is more costly today than ever. The breadwinner suddenly finds he or she can't produce income, yet the expenses don't go away.

Most of us just don't like to talk about *death*. But the untimely passing of a loved one can leave an unsuspecting family financially in chaos.

Then there is what I call *congenital poverty*. Millions of people in this rich country are born to poverty. Inflation hits poor people harder than well-to-do people. The movement out of poverty can be difficult and heartbreaking, as well as inspiring. But inflation actually reduces the chances of escaping from poverty.

And there's *divorce*. Divorce rates continue to increase. Anyone close to these problems knows the high frustration level of living in the financial bind that many people find themselves in frequently leads to divorce; and divorce can be financially devastating.

Case 1
"Laid Off"

Hank and Randi had been married for twenty years. They had four teenage children. They'd had their fair share of life's little problems, but all in all they had counted themselves pretty fortunate. In fact, they had been so fortunate that Hank had enjoyed flaunting it a little. For eighteen years, Hank had worked with a major automobile company. He had some seniority and a skill, so he felt pretty secure. The last thing he ever expected was to get permanently laid off—but he did. The U.S. auto industry was in desperate trouble because of imports. Furthermore, his plant was especially inefficient. And, to make matters worse, even the technology of Hank's skill had been changing—but Hank hadn't upgraded his skill. So suddenly he was out.

Finances were not the first thing Hank worried about. He had both SUB pay (supplementary unemployment benefits) and unemployment benefits. In fact, he took the family to Florida for a week to prove he could handle it. And perhaps he might have, if he had handled matters properly to start with. He had only a few payments to meet, for things such as cars and campers. If he had moved quickly, he might have been able to reorganize these. The family had some savings and a few stocks.

Concern began to set in when Hank and Randi started to realize how hard it was going to be to find Hank a new job. He had always worked for the auto company, but his skills were relatively narrow. Furthermore, as an auto worker his income had been fairly high. At forty-five years of age, he found himself competing with men far younger, frequently fresh out of trade schools, with broader training and more than happy to work for nearly half what Hank figured he was worth. Eventually Randi decided to go to work, no matter how much Hank resented it. Even then, her job and his unemployment compensation weren't even close to what Hank had been making.

Concern turned to panic at six months when the sub payments finally ran out. The family started to sell a few things they owned. It was depressing to see how little some items would really bring.

A year went by, and Hank and Randi's panic turned into total despair. Their aged parents helped a little. The church they attended brought them some food. Hank picked up odd jobs such as painting houses and cutting grass. Hank's self-confidence and pride disappeared. His self-image dwindled to that of a born loser. The family was so deeply in debt that he figured it would take five years to dig out of the hole after he got back to work. His oldest daughter had graduated from high school. It really hurt to think he couldn't send her to college. Hank began to seriously debate leaving the family or committing suicide. He reasoned the family would be better off without him. After all, then they could qualify for more welfare.

Fortunately, Hank went looking for help instead. By the time he did look for help, a lot more than his finances needed straightening out. Hank had begun to see so clearly the mistakes he had made that he couldn't see any solutions. He now realized he should have been keeping up with the trends. He should have seen what his company was getting into. He should have been getting extra training all along. He could see that if he had objectively looked at the situation when he first lost his job, he would have realized he had been overpaid and overspecialized and had almost no serious hope of finding work at his previous level. He would have realized that some downward adjustment in his standard of living was necessary. Unfortunately, he couldn't go back and redo anything.

The first hurdle for the counselor was to convince Hank he could live on half of what he had previously made—and still live with dignity. Then Hank was directed to a retraining program. After the schooling, he landed a job with another manufacturing firm.

With steady jobs, Hank and Randi finally made some tough decisions about their standard of living. Because their standard of living had been "temporarily" reduced during his unemployment, the decision to "permanently" reduce it was almost easy to make. The decision was finalized by selling their home and buying a much smaller one.

With a smaller home, a smaller car, a smaller income, and a large pile of "stretched-out" debts, it would be natural to expect Hank and Randi to be bitter. But they aren't. Two years after the layoff, their family seems closer, somehow. Their first daughter finally did get to college by saving her own money and working after school.

Their second daughter's grades actually improved during this period, and she eventually graduated from high school at the top of her class and won a scholarship to college. The other two kids are also doing well.

Beside realizing their children support them all the way, Hank and Randi were grateful to realize their friends didn't desert them, either. In fact, Hank will tell you the whole experience was worth it to learn that the people who matter most in his life didn't really care how much money he made.

Case 2
"Sickness"

The Bartons were a middle-aged, middle-income couple. They had five children, ages sixteen to six. The Bartons made an average income. The family had normal expenses, a few thousand dollars in savings, average insurance, and the usual financial problems. They had never really suffered anything serious until they discovered that their eight-year-old had a rare heart disease.

Money was never a question: Mike had to have treatment—the best. The doctors, the Bartons, and eight-year-old Mike fought with everything they could against the disease. But after eighteen months of pain, hospitals, and major operations, Mike—on his tenth birthday—told his family not to worry, and he bravely faced death. Mike's faith and courage had sustained the whole family throughout the ordeal, even through the funeral. In fact, not until after the funeral did the Bartons begin to realize fully the cost of Mike's illness. The total was more than $78,000.

Insurance ran out at $10,000. A special government program paid $12,000 more, but the remaining $56,000 still left the Bartons hopelessly in debt. Some relatives advised the Bartons to file bankruptcy. But the Bartons, still inspired by Mike's acceptance of his problems, refused to turn their back on their debts.

There was no magic in what the family did to work out of their situation. They cut all expenses to the bone. Everyone who could work, did work. They made many sacrifices. It took the Bartons ten years to work free of debt. Their children were grown and gone before it was over. But the Bartons will tell you they would spend every dime again without question, trying to save Mike's life. And they would endure every sacrifice a second time to honor his death.

Case 3
"Injury"

Don built homes for a living. Cheryl kept the books and worked part time at a day-care center. Homebuilding is a volatile business at best, so Don and Cheryl were either as flush as a kid with tooth fairy money or as broke as a starving artist without a commission. Through all the ups and downs, Don and Cheryl managed not only to keep going but also to accumulate many very nice things along the way—such as a $200,000 house with a big loan on it, two nice cars financed to the fenders, and a pickup truck that was the company's biggest asset. Neither Don nor Cheryl really worried much about money—they always got by somehow, and they had a lot of fun in the process.

Then one day disaster struck. The roof of a house Don was building collapsed. One of the carpenters was killed, and Don was paralyzed from the waist down. Don and Cheryl were sued by the carpenter's family, the owners of the house, and the owners of two other houses that had been partially completed but now could not be finished. Of course, Don's own medical bills ran to the tens of thousands of dollars. In all, they had debts and liabilities in excess of $300,000 and assets of less than $90,000, including equity in the home.

Ironically, Don and Cheryl had talked about business insurance just one week before the accident—but they hadn't as yet decided to buy it. Now they only had one possible decision left—bankruptcy.

Going into bankruptcy was the hardest decision Don and Cheryl ever made. They knew well most of the people they owed money to, and considered them friends. Don and his wife vowed they would settle their debts regardless of the bankruptcy.

Settling debts, however, soon became only a hope and a dream. Don could no longer do the work he had always done. And Cheryl had a hard time finding a worthwhile job. Soon their daily living expenses completely outstripped the money Cheryl could bring home. Financial disaster was at the door again. But this time even the option of bankruptcy wasn't available for seven more years.

In complete desperation, they came looking for help. Help in such circumstances is not easy to find. But they did find a minister that refused to feel sorry for them, and refused to let them sit around feeling sorry for themselves. His blunt discussions with them filled their heads with resolve, determination, and ideas. Their new resolve helped them face a major cut in their standard of living. They moved to a modest apartment. The location was conveniently close to everything, so that Cheryl could walk most places and rarely use a car. That meant they could get by with one very inexpensive car. Their eating habits changed completely. Meat was almost eliminated from their diet, for example. A host of other changes were made that cut living expenses substantially.

Another idea was that Don could work at home, on the phone. But who would pay for his services? The minister suggested he put a small ad in the paper. It worked.

Don found many potential clients. His first assignments weren't very profitable—prospecting clients for an insurance company and selling magazines. He kept at it, however, improving his ability on the phone. He also ran ads periodically, hoping to upgrade his clientele, which he did. Soon he was working for an auto dealer, encouraging customers to come in for maintenance; for a consulting firm, doing market research; and for a small parts manufacturer, checking on customer inventory levels. He was working twelve hours a day and could have worked around the clock if he had wanted to. In his second full year, he made $20,000 and was still upgrading clients.

Life will never be the same for Don and Cheryl again, no matter how much money they make. Fortunately, they have adjusted to their problems and have learned to live with them. They've learned to live with them so well they haven't started to upgrade their standard of living, although they're making good money again. They want to keep their personal promise to help some of the people to whom they owed money. They especially want to help their carpenter's widow and five children. They know full well her situation was actually more desperate than their own.

Case 4
"Death"

No one ever did figure out exactly what happened to that roof, but Gary was underneath when it collapsed. His long-time friend and boss, Don, suffered a broken back. Gary died of head injuries before the rescue squad ever arrived. Under the circumstances, money isn't the first thing a young widow would normally think of. But for Sherry Robins the issue came to mind within hours. The day had been payday, and she literally had no food in the house. Friends brought in casseroles, but nobody thought of baby food or milk for her little ones.

Gary and Sherry never had accumulated a whole lot of anything, except maybe kids: They had five children under the age of eight. Over the years, they had pretty much lived from one paycheck to the next. And because Gary's work was occasionally slow, even the paychecks weren't all that regular. Now there would be no paycheck at all. Sherry knew that right away. And while no one could describe her grief in losing her best friend and husband, no one could describe the panic that gripped her either.

Sherry had every right to feel panic. There was a mortgage, a car payment, a loan for the last baby's delivery, a couple of doctors' bills, and a $300 bill at Sears. There were no savings, no assets, no checking account, no pension, and no life insurance. Furthermore, Sherry had no employable skills. Sherry felt hopeless.

Her minister helped her find some hope. Initially the church assisted her financially by purchasing groceries and paying the mortgage installments. The minister also helped her with the details of filing for Social Security benefits and Aid to Dependent Children. Sherry had never accepted welfare, and it was hard for her to do.

Even harder were two legal actions she was advised she must file: personal bankruptcy and a lawsuit against Gary's employer. She hated to sue Don and Cheryl. They were friends. But it seemed possible they had some money or insurance; after all, they had a big house. Unfortunately, Don and Cheryl didn't have anything either, and within weeks of Sherry's lawsuit they filed bankruptcy.

Sherry knew she would eventually have to work this out by herself. By cutting literally everything out that could possibly be cut, and by doing her own baking, sewing, and by taking in extra kids to babysit, she almost balanced her cash flow. Then she went to school at night. She really had to finagle to work out babysitting and tuition, but she worked it out. It took more than finagling to handle everything emotionally and physically, but she did that too. She studied to be a dental assistant, and had no trouble getting a job after graduation. The money, after expenses, was only a little better than the welfare she had been receiving, but she felt a lot better about getting it.

Today Sherry feels better about a lot of things, including the fact that Don and Cheryl have started to send her money. But she never really will feel good about the way things are. She feels her children need her at home, she is always tired, and, of course, she's lonely. In fact, now that the panic has subsided there is time for grief. But Sherry is determined. Her determination and backbone will help her survive.

Case 5
"Congenital Poverty"

Ralph had been raised in what might respectfully be called the ghetto. His dad moved Ralph and his eight brothers and sisters north to a big city when Ralph was only three. Ralph's father could barely read or write, but he had been told by relatives there were well-paying jobs in the North. There were—but Ralph's dad could never find one. Then one night, when Ralph was eight, his dad was hit and killed by a drunk driver.

Ralph was young, but he quickly learned the meaning of "abject poverty." He learned that the word *poor* described people a lot better off than his family. The family got some welfare money, but it was never enough. Ralph wore shoes scrounged from garbage cans and old sweaters with holes in them, and he frequently went to bed hungry.

Even as a kid, he missed school a lot. Often he missed because he simply didn't have enough to wear to keep him warm while walking to school. By the time he was fifteen, he had dropped out altogether. He was learning all the time, though. He was learning how to handle himself in the street. He was learning that his hunger was the system's fault. He was learning that it was the government's responsibility to send money every month.

He married when he was seventeen. He and his wife moved in with his mother. A baby came along quickly. Ralph tried to get work, but there wasn't much work available. He worked a little as a janitor, but the pay was low and the work wasn't steady. Ralph's baby was hungry, and Ralph didn't want his baby to be hungry. So he found something steady to do—steal.

Ralph was barely eighteen years old when he was caught robbing a store. His thoughts in the county jail while awaiting trial were confused. He had feelings of bitter resentment, guilt, and hatred. He knew he didn't want to go to the state prison. And he knew he wanted to get out and make something of himself. He was overjoyed when the judge said he could spend his sentence at a technical training school where he could learn a skill. Ralph did well at the electrical technician school he was sent to. The social worker

following Ralph's case knew electrical technicians were in demand
and thought Ralph would land a job easily after he got out. The social worker was wrong. Of course, the social worker never knew he
was wrong: The social worker never checked back with Ralph after
he was released.

Ralph thought he would land a job easily, too. Ralph was also
wrong. After Ralph was released he went home, which, of course,
was still the ghetto. Ralph didn't know anything about finding a
job. He quickly learned there weren't any electrical technician jobs
in the ghetto. So Ralph took the initiative. He looked in the "Help
Wanted" section of the paper. He called several likely prospects, all
of whom wanted him to come in for an interview. Most of the
places were in the new industrial parks located in the suburbs. To
Ralph, the suburbs were like a foreign country. He had never been
to the suburbs. He didn't know how to get there, and even if he did,
he would be scared to go to the suburbs. Consequently, he didn't
keep a single appointment. He did go to one interview near the ball
park. He had been to the ball park and knew how to get there on a
bus. But when the interviewers learned he was a high school drop-
out with a prison record, they abruptly terminated the interview.

The interview was a blow to Ralph. It destroyed what little confidence he had mustered. But the interview was not the only setback Ralph and his family got that day. His wife received notice that
she wouldn't be receiving any more welfare checks, because her
husband was back home. So Ralph moved out again. At least, they
told the welfare people he moved out. The welfare check wasn't
enough, though. Ralph had to have money, too. He started stealing
again. And got caught again. This time the judge gave him an
eighteen-month sentence in the state penitentiary and a lecture. The
judge lectured him on motivation, being a self-starter, gratitude to
society, self-reliance, and the basic American principles the judge
himself had used to get through law school. Ralph listened, but he
didn't understand. It wasn't that Ralph didn't want to understand,
but the concepts the judge was speaking about were so foreign to
Ralph's thinking the judge might have been speaking Chinese.

In nine months, Ralph was out on parole. Ralph's parole officer
was a unique guy. He'd been raised in the ghetto, too, but he had a
lot of the same concepts the judge had. Most importantly, he took
an interest in Ralph. This time, when Ralph heard about jobs in the
suburbs the parole officer showed him how to get there and proved
to Ralph there was nothing to fear. When Ralph was turned down

because of his lack of education, his parole officer showed him how to present himself differently. Finally, Ralph landed a job with decent pay. The parole officer helped him through the first few critical months while Ralph was still frightened of working a long way from home.

Ralph made good. So good that one morning he woke up with a desire to get his high school degree. It took three years of night school, but he made it. Now he's thinking about college. A year ago he moved away from the ghetto and bought a house. He's determined his kids will have things better than he did—but not necessarily the better things you buy with money. Ralph knows he'll never be rich. But he wants his kids to have better values, better concepts, and better attitudes. Ralph feels he has escaped. He feels he was lucky to get a parole officer that cared enough to walk him through the steps to freedom from the ghetto. Ralph is glad for himself, but sad for his family. He's the only one of nine brothers and sisters that did escape.

Case 6
"Divorce"

Dave and Judy had a big fight on their honeymoon, and they never stopped fighting after that. Judy thought Dave was an irresponsible, inconsiderate, inattentive lush. Dave thought Judy was a demanding, hypercritical, nagging shrew. Perhaps the biggest surprise about their marriage was that it lasted seven years before Judy and Dave finally agreed on something—a divorce.

Money was not something they thought about when they filed the papers. But both soon learned that most divorces are financial disasters for everyone involved—except the lawyers. In the end, Judy got the house with a mortgage, half the furniture, and the washer and dryer. She also received custody of their two small children. Dave got "reasonable visitation" rights, the car, the stereo, his tools, and an assortment of household items. Dave was ordered to pay $250 per month in child support and to pay off the credit cards, the banks, and the finance companies they had borrowed from. Neither felt the settlements were enough.

DIVORCED—JUDY'S STORY

As Dave and Judy's marriage ended, their lives and their stories went separate ways. Judy had been working part-time before the divorce. After the divorce, she had to go to work full time. She took a bank job that she quickly learned to hate. Her take-home pay was $1025 a month. Her house payment was $405. Utilities ran more than $105—in a good month.

She also had to buy a car to get around. She couldn't afford much, so the payments were only $80. It cost her $54 a month just to run the car, not counting insurance, which she didn't have. The tires were bad, and breakdowns, which she couldn't afford, were frequent.

She was forced to leave the kids with a sitter who was willing to watch them, along with seven other children, for $7 a day. Food ran $180 a month. Clothes, doctor bills, household expenses, and a host of miscellaneous items were taking up all the rest of her money, and more.

Judy wasn't making ends meet. Judy was broke. She couldn't even afford a babysitter if she wanted to go out for the evening. She thought about selling the house, but she couldn't bring herself to let it go. Then real disaster struck.

Dave disappeared and quit paying child support. Judy was frantic. She didn't know where he was, and she needed her money. She soon found that their creditors were in the same boat. They didn't know where Dave was either. But they did know where Judy was, and no matter how many times she told them the judge had assigned all the bills to Dave, the creditors kept hounding her. They hounded her because she had co-signed all those loans. Life with Dave had been miserable, but life with her finances was more miserable. Judy wished she could divorce her finances.

She couldn't divorce her finances, so she came looking for help. Judy knew a lot of things had changed in her life, but financially she hadn't made the adjustment. The house, unfortunately, was the prime example. Her feelings were understandable. She had worked very hard to get into that home, but the burden was beyond her.

Tearfully, she put it and some of the furnishings on the market and moved into a modest apartment. Her share of the equity gave her some breathing room. She took some of the money and fixed her car up, and was still able to put $13,000 in savings. She reduced her living expenses by more than $170 a month, when utilities and maintenance were considered. Furthermore, she picked up some money in interest on the savings.

She was directed to the local district attorney's office, where she found that new interstate laws now afforded her more protection against runaway ex-husbands. All the authorities had to do was find him.

The financial counselor worked out a consolidated payment program of $50 a month, which kept most of the bill collectors quiet—at least until they could find Dave.

Then Judy was advised to look for several other divorced women with similar problems. She ran an ad in the paper and found lots of them. She got together with five and formed a cooperative. The women traded evening babysitting. They set up their schedules so they could car-pool to places such as the grocery store. They started doing each other's hair. They found they could save money buying some things together, such as cases of food on sale or quarters of beef. They kept careful records of who had received what from whom, so there wouldn't be disagreements. Perhaps the most important things they shared were ideas, common problems, and friendship.

Things are still tight for Judy, and they probably will stay tight, even though the authorities have found Dave. They have threatened to put him in jail if he doesn't keep up with his child support payments. The payments help, but the most important thing is Judy has now adjusted her thinking to fit her circumstances. She is finding she *can* be compatible with her finances.

DIVORCED—DAVE'S STORY

At the time of the divorce, Dave's take-home pay was $1200 a month. His boss didn't see fit to give him a raise just because he got divorced. He was ordered to send Judy $250 a month, leaving $950 for him to live on. He moved into an old apartment for $280 plus utilities. His food was running $75 each month, just for himself. The car was $175 a month plus gas and maintenance. Clothes, haircuts, laundry, and miscellaneous items were eating up all the rest. The court ordered him to pay all court costs plus both lawyers in the divorce. Dave felt that he'd been given a raw deal. He received some expensive items, such as the car, the stereo, and tools, but all of them were financed. He still had some equity in the house, but he couldn't spend it as long as Judy was living there.

Then he discovered creditors really put the heat on as soon as they find out you are divorced. He quickly found out that he and Judy had been spending the $400 per month that she earned from her part-time job to pay bills. His creditors began to hound him so much he took a part-time job pumping gas.

He was so busy working two jobs it is hard to know where he found time to meet other women, but he did. Eight months after his divorce, he remarried. His new wife, Mary, had three children of her own. Mary worked in a dress shop. With the new marriage came an increase in living expenses—Dave didn't want to deprive Mary. So they rented a much bigger apartment, bought Mary a newer car and so on. But they still felt as if they were scrimping.

Mary was tired of scrimping. She had never had much help from her ex-husband. Perhaps she should have been the first to understand when Judy called in tears because she didn't have money to buy clothes or medicine for Dave's children. But Mary did not understand. She would throw a temper tantrum every time it happened. In fact, Mary even got mad when Dave paid the child support, let alone gave Judy anything extra. Dave was caught in the middle. Eventually he couldn't stand it any more. He packed up his new wife and her kids, rented a truck, and disappeared. Dave thought he could disappear for good, but he couldn't.

At Judy's request, the authorities came looking for Dave and found him. He had had no idea how tough the laws were concerning failure to pay child support. Before Dave knew it, he was faced with raising some money fast or going to jail. To make matters worse, the move had been expensive, and his new job paid less than his old one. Dave was in a jam. He thought seriously of running away again. This time he thought he would change his identity, leave no traces, and really disappear.

Fortunately, Dave only thought about running for a short time. Soon he concluded he did not want to live like an outlaw forever, so he went looking for help.

But help was not going to come easily. Dave worried that his financial problems might result in a second divorce—and he was almost right. The plan of rehabilitation included a further reduction in standard of living for Dave and Mary. Dave didn't like it, and Mary figured her standard of living was already at rock bottom. Mary was tired of skimping. In the end, however, she preferred skimping to running or visiting Dave in jail.

Mary, who had worked all along, now worked longer hours. She felt as if she were working to support Dave's ex-wife. That thought kept her constantly steamed up inside. Dave once again took a second job. Dave consolidated his bills and reduced his monthly payments. Finally, he got his cash income in line with his cash outgo.

Dave doesn't like his new circumstances. But, like Judy, he has come to accept them. He compares himself to a man with a physical handicap. He knows it won't go away soon. He also knows he can live with it and can live a nearly normal life if he just accepts the situation. Both Dave and Mary have to accept it, whether they like it or not.

◇ 7 ◇
Divorce and Finance

This is not a book on marriage. But today no book on personal finance can ignore the subject of divorce. For one thing, finances are at the root of many marriage problems that lead to divorce.

Most divorces create extreme emotional pressures for everyone concerned. Less immediately apparent, however, is that most divorces create extreme financial pressures for everyone concerned. The case mentioned at the end of the last chapter is *typical,* not unusual. Divorce is something to be avoided if possible.

But sometimes avoiding divorce isn't possible. When divorce becomes inevitable, financial difficulties nearly always become inevitable as well. A little understanding of the possible financial problems cannot eliminate them, but it can help reduce them. The problems come from two areas. First, two households are usually trying to exist on the same income, which often didn't support one household well. Second, two people are trying to divide up the financial assets and liabilities in some reasonable manner. And there is a third financial problem, the legal cost of the divorce itself.

There's an old saying that two can live as cheaply as one. Most newlyweds probably doubt this statement, but one thing is sure; two can't live apart as cheaply as two can live together. People living together can share a lot of costs: housing, transportation, heat, light, phone, paper, appliances, TV, furnishings, household items, and so on. Even the total cost of food and taxes can be lower for married couples than for two single people. When people separate, many ordinary everyday living expenses increase in total.

The problem with increasing total expenses is that the total income doesn't usually increase by nearly as much. Circumstances vary tremendously, of course. Sometimes a spouse that has not been working can now get an excellent job. But more often both spouses are already working and earning as much as possible. Or the unemployed spouse is not able to get an "excellent" job for some reason. So the total per capita expense of living rises sharply but the total per capita income increases only moderately or not at all. The net result is financial frustrations and a lower standard of living for everyone.

The financial frustrations of the divorce are frequently complicated by the financial frustrations of the marriage. Financial problems are a major contributor to many divorces. And people who couldn't make ends meet during marriage can expect even more difficulty during divorce.

No matter how tough it has been to make ends meet during marriage, most couples manage to accumulate a few things along the way. Some furniture, some appliances, some household items, maybe a house, possibly some investments, and probably a whole bunch of debts. Dividing up the assets can become a knock-down, drag-out fight for two people who've grown so distant they can't agree how to divide up leftover meatloaf. But dividing up the debts can really be awful. At least dividing up assets leaves you with something. Dividing up debts leaves you with less than nothing.

Usually the judge must do the final dividing up. He or she will probably decide who gets what assets and pays which debts. Sometimes, however, the trouble starts with the judge's decision. For example, the judge may decree that the husband will pay off a loan the couple has. But the divorce decree does not legally dissolve the wife's responsibility to the finance company. The company probably has a legally executed contract with both signatures on it. The divorce court has no legal authority to abrogate that contract. The court can order the husband to pay the loan back, but if he does not do so the finance company can demand payment from the wife. In fact, the company can sue her to get payment. Her only hope is to go back through the divorce court and try to collect from her ex-husband. But if creditors *could* collect from him, they probably would already have done so.

This situation, unfortunately, develops quite often. Making matters worse, when the judge made final income distribution decisions (alimony, child support, and so on), he or she did so on the basis of the husband paying off the loan. If the finance company comes after the wife, she'll also find herself without the money to pay.

It seems as if there should be some easy advice to follow, to avoid all these problems. And in fact there is, loads of theoretical advice that can be given to couples contemplating divorce. Unfortunately, following such advice requires a high degree of cooperation, understanding, and general agreement between the couple.

Most couples going through a divorce have stopped cooperating, understanding, and generally agreeing long before the divorce, so the advice is worthless.

There is one suggestion, however, that is not worthless. It has worked very well for many couples. The advice is that couples should use the same lawyer in a divorce.

Normally, each party in a divorce retains his or her own lawyer. But I'm convinced that the lawyers, in proper fulfillment of their jobs, do substantial harm to the already poor relationship between the husband and wife. The lawyer's proper job is to represent his (or her) clients' interests fully. He is supposed to get as much as possible for the party he represents.* He is not supposed to be making a lot of judgments about what's fair to the other party. In fact, if he unilaterally decides his party should make concessions he runs the risk of leaving his client wide open for exploitation. He can't be sure the lawyer on the other side will be as impartial as himself.

The lawyer's normal instinct and training of getting all he (or she) can for his clients is amplified by the fact that he only hears one side of the story—his client's. And in an emotionally charged situation such as a divorce, he doesn't hear a very objective story.

So the stage is set for a bitter struggle between the estranged couple and their lawyers. When the judge gets through untangling it, everyone winds up hating the judge, the lawyers, and each other.

There's already enough hate in most divorce situations. Some can be minimized if the warring couple can agree to use the same lawyer. If one lawyer represents both parties, then his (or her) whole mission changes. Then he is working for fairness, negotiation, and agreement. Furthermore, he's in touch with more of the facts, which means that he can make better judgments. And, as a bonus, total legal fees will be much lower.

If you use the same lawyer, go see him (or her) together the first time. If one party contacts and retains a lawyer, you place the lawyer in a difficult ethical position if you later ask him to represent both parties. If one party has already contacted a lawyer, it is wise to pay him for the services he's performed and jointly retain another lawyer.

Regardless of how many lawyers are used, both husband and wife should adjust their thinking to accept a lower standard of living. Generally, a lower standard of living is inevitable. The income

---

*No sexism is intended by the occasional use of the masculine pronoun where to double pronouns ("his or her") might be clumsy.

simply cannot support two households at the previous standard of living. But frequently the divorced people do not want to reduce their standard of living. And that usually results in intense financial pressures to add to all the other pressures the newly divorced people are facing. A good financial adjustment can help ease all the other adjustments.

Divorce is such a difficult emotional adjustment that financial adjustments aren't always the first thing people worry about—and that's understandable. A few timely financial adjustments can help, but a divorce is still difficult. It seems like everyone gets hurt in a divorce—except the lawyers.

◇ 8 ◇
Financial Counseling

Occasionally people come to realize their financial situation is beyond self-diagnosis. In fact, some people may feel they are so much like the cases we've just reviewed that they need professional financial counseling.

I have listed below several places people can turn to for professional counseling if they do need it. You probably don't. In fact, this book will likely provide you with all the tools you need. If so, skip over the list but read the remainder of the chapter. I think you'll find it interesting. You probably will never go to a financial counselor, but I believe you can learn a lot by knowing what the professionals do. Understanding these steps will help you understand yourself.

What Can Be Done for a Hopeless Financial Situation?

Plenty can be done. The majority of readers will never feel their financial circumstances are completely hopeless. The majority of readers will be able to help themselves—and that's what this book is all about—helping people help themselves. But some people find themselves in a financial jam that seems almost hopeless. Some may need help even beyond this book. For those people, it is useful to know there are sources of potential help. And it is useful to discuss those sources now, before moving on with the most important sources of help—self-help.

Today, there is more hope for a person who is financially ill than there used to be, just as there is more hope for a person who is physically ill than there used to be. But knowing where to go to get help in getting well again is important. Everyone knows how to reach a doctor if one is needed. However, not everyone knows how to reach a financial counselor if one is needed. Here are some possible sources of financial counseling.

Sources of Financial Counseling

◊ *Consumer Credit Counseling Services.* There are more than 150 of these nonprofit organizations throughout the country. They are an excellent resource. They counsel people who are heavily in debt. Their services are free. They are supported financially by hundreds of businesses large and small. These businesses know this organization will help them with their collections. It helps by helping people with their finances. You can find the nearest Consumer Credit Counseling Service in the white pages of your telephone book, or in the yellow pages under "Credit consultants" or "Financial consultants." Or you can write to

    National Foundation for Consumer Credit
    1810 H Street, North West
    Washington, DC 20006

They will give you the address of the consumer credit office nearest you.

◊ *Family Service Agencies.* There are hundreds of family service agencies across the country. They assist families in a wide variety of family problems, including financial problems. You can get more information on these services by writing to

    Family Service Association of America
    44 East 23rd Street
    New York, NY 10010

◊ *Public welfare services.* Frequently state, county, or city welfare services provide financial counseling. If they can not help you, they will refer you to reputable people that can.

◊ *Private financial counseling firms.* Many professional financial planners offer counseling services. They will charge a fee up to 20 percent of your debts and liabilities for their work. The fee is well worth it if they can help you return to sound financial health. Such firms can be found by consulting the yellow pages under "Financial Consultants."

◊ *Lending institutions.* The various banks, finance companies, and credit unions you might owe money to may offer financial counseling. Because they make personal loans, they understand personal finance. Reputable firms will provide counseling free of charge. If you do use this resource, make sure they are providing *objective counseling* rather than presenting a plan designed just to repay them.

◊ Other sources of possible help include (1) churches, (2) labor unions, (3) personnel departments of large companies, and (4) commanding officers if you are in the military.

There are many places to go and get financial help, and most do not charge for their services. None of them can work miracles, but they can help. They can be a source of hope in a seemingly hopeless situation. One of the most important helps they can offer is to help a person stop thinking his or her financial situation is hopeless.

What Can a Financial Counselor Do?

Whether or not you are ever going to need a financial counselor, you should know what he or she will do. If you do know what he or she will do, you won't be surprised or offended by the treatment. You can aid in the diagnosis. You won't be fooled by a quack. And you may learn enough to treat your own financial illness.

Treating yourself for financial illnesses is like treating yourself for physical illnesses. You need to be wise enough to know when you can and when you can't. Like physical illness, many financial illnesses require the skill of a trained professional. And if a trained doctor or a trained financial counselor is necessary, you should not be fooling around with home remedies.

What remedy a trained professional will use to help you get well again depends on what is wrong—each case is different. A doctor treats a dislocation of the thumb differently from the way he or she treats congenital heart disease, for instance. First the doctor must diagnose the problem, and then treat it. Likewise, the financial counselor treats a dislocation of the pocket book differently from the way he or she treats congenital poverty. First diagnose the problem, and then treat it. Solving all problems begins with a proper diagnosis.

DIAGNOSING A FINANCIAL ILLNESS

A physician routinely listens to your heart, checks your blood pressure, and takes your temperature while trying to diagnose your physical ailment. He or she will also ask you where you hurt, if it's not obvious. The doctor may need to ask you a lot of personal questions—questions about your habits, lifestyle, and activities. He has to figure out what is causing your ailment. He has to figure out if you are making yourself sick.

A financial counselor will routinely need certain types of information while trying to diagnose your financial ailment. You can help by being prepared with lists of the following (be sure to list *everything*):

◇ Sources of income
◇ Expenses (list amounts you actually spend rather than amounts you wish or think you should spend)
◇ Assets, and what they are worth
◇ Debts, liabilities, and financial obligations

The counselor will also ask you where you hurt, if it's not obvious. He (or she) will probably need to ask you many personal questions—about your habits, lifestyle, and activities. Many of the questions he'll ask may seem tough. He'll want to know why you made certain financial decisions. Be truthful. Some people have a tendency to gloss over the real truth to make their spending decisions look clever. But if the decision was a bad one, you cannot make it into a good one by altering your reasoning after the fact. Don't withhold information. A financial counselor, like a doctor, can make a better diagnosis when he has all the facts.

When all the facts are known, more often than not the financial counselor finds his (or her) patient is causing the financial illness. This understanding is absolutely vital for proper treatment. Even though some treatments will be common to all financial illnesses, many treatments depend entirely on who or what is causing the trouble.

TREATING A FINANCIAL ILLNESS

When a person is financially ill, the first thing a financial counselor must do is treat the symptoms. Symptoms such as excessive debt, delinquent bills, and too little income are common to most serious financial illnesses, and serious financial illnesses are about all a financial counselor ever sees. Generally he or she doesn't even get the case until after a major financial crisis has already set in. At the time of a financial crisis, things may look pretty hopeless. Debts often exceed assets by many times. Monthly payments may actually exceed monthly income even before necessities. Occasionally, no income is coming in at all. And to complicate things further, when the symptoms are bad they tend to get worse. Normal everyday upsets become major new disasters. In a weakened condition, you are more likely to catch additional diseases. It's like having your resistance lowered by a long bout with the flu, making you vulnerable to viral pneumonia, or like being unable to afford car maintenance, making you vulnerable to an engine breakdown. Conditions such as these can definitely appear hopeless.

With proper treatment, however, many hopeless situations can be salvaged. A financial counselor may use some of the following treatments in treating the symptoms:

A NEW BUDGET. The counselor may help the financially ill person work out a new budget. The budget will be dedicated to slashing expenses. A counselor can be far more objective regarding a person's needs than the person him- or herself. The amount of surgery on the budget is entirely a function of the circumstances. Some items will look like luxuries to the counselor, such as extension phones, magazine subscriptions, or movies. And expensive items such as second homes or second cars may need to be sold. Rarely, however, is anyone required to leave a warm home and take up residence in a tent.

A BILL CONSOLIDATION LOAN. In many cases, bill consolidation loans can be the answer. Consolidation loans are useful in circumstances where the big problem is too many monthly payments on short-term loans. The bill consolidation loan pays off all the short-term debts and spreads the payments out over many years.

For example, consider the following real-life case. The Youngs were in their late 20s. Gary Young's average take-home pay was $1200 a month. Cindy Young had no outside income. She had a full-time job at home with three small children, including a set of twins. They had the following bills:

Creditor	Original loan	Out-standing debt	Months left to repay	Monthly payment	Interest charge
Hospitals	$ 1,200	$ 1,000	10	$ 100.00	0%
Doctors	500	400	10	50.00	0
Bank card 1	Floating	593	12	56.10	24

Bank card 2	Floating	382	12	36.10	24
Retail charge account	Floating	684	12	62.75	18
Finance company	1,670	1,388	24	69.30	18
First National Bank	1,075	636	9	66.55	14
Car loan	5,170	4,254	36	141.30	14
Home loan	50,000	43,600	276	514.30	12
				$1,096.40	

This family was obligated to pay $1096.40 each month in time payments, leaving the Youngs $103.48 to feed and clothe a family of five, pay utilities, gasoline and so on. They were running hundreds of dollars behind each month. They arranged a five-year bill consolidation loan and paid off everything but the car and the house. This was the result:

Item	Debt	Months to pay	Monthly payment	Interest rate
Bill consolidation loan	$ 5,083	60	$129.07	18%
Car loan	4,254	36	141.30	14
Home	43,600	276	514.30	12
			$784.67	

Their monthly payments dropped from $1096.40 to $784.67, a decline of $311.73 a month. In this case, the family's situation improved from absolutely impossible all the way to extremely difficult. But even though the situation was difficult, and was going to be difficult for five years, at least the situation was manageable.

Not all financial counselors use bill consolidation loans. Bill consolidation loans are like strong medicine used by a doctor; there can be negative side effects. For example, a bill consolidation loan keeps the family in debt for a much longer period of time. In this case the family will be working to repay the debt for five years, not just one. Next, a bill consolidation loan increases the amount of interest the family will pay. If the actual rate doesn't go up, the total amount paid to interest will, simply because interest is being paid for many more years. In the preceding example, both the rate and the amount went up. The interest rate on the bills that were consolidated rose from an average of 13.7 to 18 percent. And the total amount of interest the family will pay on these bills over the years rose from $512.47 to $2,661.20. The big difference of course is the fact that the bill consolidation loan runs for five years, with interest being paid the whole time.

Another negative side effect that frequently occurs is that the borrower is forced to use what assets are left as collateral against the consolidation loan. This is called "pledging the assets." The Youngs pledged the equity in their home and their furniture against the loan. If they default, the finance company can repossess their furniture and take their home.

Finally, bill consolidation loans, like some medicines, may become addictive. The problem of addiction is severe in cases where the borrower is a "credit junkie." If the Youngs, having received $311.73 of monthly breathing room, rush out and run up a whole bunch of new charges, they will quickly be in a worse mess than they started with. Hence, bill consolidations are to be used sparingly, in proper dosages, by prescription only, and under the watchful care of a professional.

CREDITOR ASSISTANCE. When you are financially overextended, it is frequently necessary to ask creditors to accept lower payments. First, write down in black and white your income, expenses, assets, and liabilities. Second, hammer out a hard-nosed budget. This budget should show a reduction in monthly payments to creditors as well as severe restrictions on your own spending. Third, arrange visits with all your creditors. Give them your figures. Explain the problem. Discuss the solutions. Ask them to cooperate in spreading out your payments. If they are reputable people, they will cooperate. But they will only cooperate if they think you are sincere, your plan is workable, and you have made sufficient personal sacrifices. Do not disappoint them on any of these counts, or they will never cooperate with you again.

Creditor cooperation has some drawbacks. First, it is very hard for people in debt to force themselves to go see their creditors in person. A letter is an alternative, but it is far less convincing than a personal visit. Second, the personal sacrifices required may be greater than the debt-ridden borrower can really live with. Third, the system may not work at all if the debts are secured by tangible assets. For instance, if there are loans on cars, boats, television sets, and lakeside property, creditors often prefer to repossess the item rather than lower the monthly payments. Creditor cooperation, therefore, is difficult medicine for some people to take. But these negatives are really disciplines, and in the end they should prove to be positive.

TURNING FINANCES OVER TO THE COUNSELOR. Many reputable counselors will only help you if you agree to turn part or all of your finances over to them. They will contact your creditors for you and seek their cooperation. The creditors are generally willing to go along with a counselor, because they know the counselor will do what he or she says. Under this arrangement, your paycheck will be turned over to the counselor, who will pay your bills for you. You will be given a predetermined amount of money with which to buy food, clothes, and so forth. This type of treatment is like being put in the hospital so the doctor can be sure you are taking your medicine. Many people do not like hospital confinement, and many people do not like turning their finance over to a counselor. But, like it or not, this treatment really works.

AVOIDING DEBT. A counselor may require that you surrender all your credit cards, and he (or she) may ceremoniously cut them into pieces. Furthermore, the counselor will insist that you not enter into any additional debts without approval. This is like a doctor trying to help an alcoholic by insisting he (or she) not carry a flask of whiskey around with him or not meet friends in bars.

FRIENDS AND ASSOCIATES. Sometimes there are sources of financial help the debt-ridden person hasn't thought of or hasn't been willing to consider, such as family, friends, churches, and social organizations. Sometimes these resources can help with direct monetary assistance. Often they can offer greater assistance in nonmonetary ways. One church group arranged free babysitting so a young mother could go back to work. A Veterans of Foreign Wars group took up a collection of needed clothing and other personal items. And one man went to considerable inconvenience to drive his brother to work because his brother couldn't afford to operate a car.

Pride may be a real problem for the financially ill person to contend with when friends or organizations are helping out. Hopefully, the luckless individual will realize how much most people really want to help, especially if he or she is really trying to help him- or herself. In most such cases, too, the person who is receiving help agrees that he or she would want an opportunity to help a friend if the tables were turned.

PUBLIC ASSISTANCE. Public programs may offer a source of financial assistance. Pride is still an issue for most people who receive public welfare assistance, but generally it is easier for people to take money from the government than from family or friends. This is probably because the government is an impersonal entity to most people. Similarly, the impersonality of public assistance may be one reason why there are abuses of the system. But impersonal or not, public assistance programs are among the services we buy and pay for as a wealthy nation. These programs can be viewed as services such as schools, roads, and libraries. Most people don't attach any stigma to using schools, roads, or libraries. Public assistance services should also be used—but only if necessary.

Public assistance programs vary widely by state and county all across the country. They vary so much they defy specific description here. However, as a generalization, the following programs are available.

1. *Unemployment compensation.* Unemployment compensation programs are actually a form of insurance. In most cases, the premiums are paid by employers. The purpose of unemployment compensation programs is to assist people who are willing and able to work but who are temporarily without employment through no fault of their own. Generally, to qualify you must be out of work due to the action of your employer; that is, you can't quit. In some cases, you can't receive benefits if you were fired for a good reason such as stealing or drunkenness on the job. However, you probably would qualify if you were let go due to general layoff or plant closing, or even if you lost your job because your employer was not happy with your performance. Many states pay unemployment benefits to union workers out on strike. Benefits are usually a percentage of your previous wage. Normally, you must file frequent reports indicating you are looking for work to keep the benefit coming. And in most cases, the benefits will automatically cease after a given period of time, such as nine months.

2. *Food stamps.* The federal food stamp program is intended to help low-income families buy food. Food stamps work just about like cash in a food store. If you run up a $40 grocery bill, the grocer will accept either $40 in cash or $40 in food stamps. The stamps are not to be used to purchase pet food, liquor, beer, cigarettes, or other nonfood items.

What the program does is allow qualifying people to buy food stamps at a cost below their face value. How much below their value depends on the number of individuals in a family and their total income. The schedules of what price a specific family will pay for a book of stamps changes every six months. If you think you may qualify for food stamps, contact your local welfare office for more information.

3. *Health programs.* Most states have programs to help qualified people with medical bills. Most of the programs are designed to assist people with low incomes. People who qualify under these programs usually receive many basic health services free, or at low cost. These may include visits to doctors, dentists, and hospitals, as well as medication prescribed by a doctor. These services are usually dispensed through public clinics; hence, recipients do not choose their own physicians.

   In many localities, there are health programs that assist individuals regardless of their income. Usually, chronic illness of some kind is involved, such as kidney disease and many diseases that afflict children.

   Finally, there is Medicare and Medicaid, which are principally designed to assist senior citizens by paying a portion of their medical bills. More information can be obtained from your local Social Security office or from your doctor.

4. *Aid to families with dependent children.* The purpose of this program is to assist single parents with low incomes and young dependent children. Requirements vary between locations, but generally the single parent (usually the mother) must be single and receiving little or no assistance from the spouse. Furthermore, there must be little children in the home who cannot be left while the parent returns to work. These programs have received much criticism for encouraging divorces and frauds. However, they are a great resource for many single parents faced with the unbelievable task of raising a family of small children without much money or much help.

5. *Education.* There are many federal, state, and local programs dedicated to helping people receive a basic education and obtain employable skills.

Many overlapping government bodies offer some or all of the programs just mentioned. If you believe your financial ailment can use treatment through public assistance, you should try to get more specific information on what is available and who qualifies. If it can possibly help you, it's worth the effort to phone and find out.

BANKRUPTCY.   Going through bankruptcy proceedings is the ultimate, most severe, and most thorough treatment for financial problems. It's like radical surgery to remove a diseased organ from the body. The surgery may save a life, but it may also leave unwanted scars and side effects. Bankruptcy, too, is likely to leave unwanted scars and side effects. Therefore, like radical surgery, bankruptcy should be avoided if at all possible.

There are two forms of bankruptcy an individual might be concerned with: wage earner's bankruptcy and straight bankruptcy.

In wage earner's bankruptcy, 50 percent of your creditors must approve your filing for wage earner protection. Under the plan you, your creditors, and a court-appointed referee will all get together to figure out a way for you to repay your bills. All this is done under the watchful eye of a federal judge. Your creditors will be legally compelled to accept extended payments. Sometimes the actual amount you owe will be reduced. You will be legally compelled to pay the court-appointed trustee a given sum every month, and the trustee in turn will pay the creditors. Your wages will be protected from garnishment. Your home and personal property will be protected from foreclosure. Your creditors will not be allowed to hound you. And if you miss payments, you will be held in contempt of court.

One of the disadvantages of wage earners' bankruptcy is cost. Yes, it costs something to go bankrupt: lawyer's fees, filing fees, and trustee's fees of up to 5 percent of the debts plus expenses.

Expenses, however, are not the most serious side effects. The most serious side effect is loss of reputation and credit standing. Your wage earner status will be reflected on the records of credit-rating services. You will find yourself answering yes to the "Have you ever been bankrupt?" question on applications for everything from employment to major purchases. Although the experience may haunt you for years, if you successfully complete the wage earner program many people will view your effort positively.

In straight bankruptcy, provisions in the law allow your creditors to put you in bankruptcy involuntarily, or allow you to file bankruptcy voluntarily. Straight bankruptcy is generally simple. You make a complete list of all assets and liabilities. A selected list of your possessions, such as clothing, household items, tools, and so on will be exempted. The rest of your belongings will be sold by the court and the proceeds will be distributed to your creditors. Then your financial slate will be clean.

Recovering from bankruptcy, like recovering from surgery, is painful. Many of your assets will be gone. And whether it should be this way or not, the bankruptcy record will mark you in the eyes of the financial world for years to come.

You or a financial counselor may use these tools to treat the symptoms of financial illness. Knowing which, when and how to use these tools is important. Making a proper diagnosis is important. If you've already tried home remedies without success, then you should find out what a financial counselor can do for you.

Conclusion

All of us want greater financial freedom. The first step in achieving that is understanding the barriers that prevent us from being financially free.

Many of these barriers are new ones in the environment, and we must understand them. Many of these barriers are personal. They would exist no matter what decade we lived in. Often these barriers are the most difficult to identify and thoroughly understand.

It has not been my purpose to imply that everyone suffers from terrible flaws of financial character. But it has been my experience that people often find a little of themselves in the cases in this section. And once a person sees that part of themselves, they are in a better position to really do something about it.

Part III.
Managing Your Money

"I just don't make enough money to keep up with the cost of every-thing!" I can't think of how many times I've heard those words. What's most interesting is that they have been uttered by people from all walks of life and in *every income level!* How can it be possible that the person who makes $100,000 can't afford to survive any more than the person who makes $20,000 a year? How can it be that they both say they need more money to meet the high cost of every-thing?

I've seen families operate at below what the government consid-ers the poverty level and live relatively well. On the other hand, I've seen families with $100,000 a year incomes who couldn't afford to buy food for the dinner table at the end of the month. It's all in how well people manage their money.

You can't do much to change the world and its problems, but you can understand them and learn to respond appropriately. You can do some things to change your own financial attitudes once you understand what they are. One thing all people can do—if they want—is manage efficiently. Efficient money management is at the heart of any financial plan. This section is devoted to these tech-niques. During years of personal financial counseling, I've seen people struggle with basic things such as budgets and checkbooks. I've seen many failures and have come to realize that much advice in this area must be given by people who have never worked with real financial problems.

A fair portion of this section will be devoted to exploring things such as why budgets don't work. But most of the section is devoted to techniques that do work. I know they work because I have been personally involved and seen them work. I think you will find that some are unique.

Of course, nothing will work if you will not put forth a little ef-fort. There are no something-for-nothing gimmicks. I consider this an important part of the book for anyone struggling to make ends meet. I hope you will spend some time here trying these techniques for handling money yourself.

Before exploring how to handle money, it seems worthwhile to make sure we know what money is in our society. This is the subject of Chapter 9.

◇ 9 ◇
What Is Money?

Money—to economists it's a medium of exchange; to accountants it's a unit of value; to children it's a penny; to millionaires it's a measure of success; to paupers it's only a theory; to politicians it's a campaign promise; to government planners it's a tool of management; to bankers it's the commodity they sell; to workers it's what they sweat their life's blood for; to a husband and wife it's something to argue about; to ministers it's the "root of all evil."

To the average person, money is what he or she never has enough of.

Everybody knows what money is, or at least they should. But in reality very few people know everything about money. For example, very few people realize that the invention of money is one of those inventions that rank with the invention of the wheel or the discovery of fire in its importance. As with wheels and fires, our world simply could not run without money. Imagine the chaos if money were suddenly eliminated and society reverted to the old barter system. Consider the plight of the brain surgeon trying to trade services for ten gallons of unleaded gasoline. How many service station attendants need brain surgery anyway? Or the computer programmer trying to work an arrangement to get a toupee styled. Or a steelworker attempting to buy a can of hair spray at a discount store. Without money, these transactions would not take place. In fact, money has become the common denominator of nearly all our dealings. Everybody understands how much various items are worth when they are valued in money. This is because everyone knows what a dollar is worth—even if it does seem to be worth less all the time.

The reason money is worth anything at all, however, is because of faith. The reason people have faith is because they know the money they accept for what they sell will in turn be accepted by the people they need to buy from. The value of money is not in what the money is made of, but in the fact that everyone accepts it. The paper in a $10 bill is worth less than a penny. But you can buy a lot more penny candy with a $10 bill than with a copper penny. Sometimes even valuable materials such as gold can't make the money worth much if people can't exchange it for what they need.

I recall hearing about a man who dreamed he was in a war-ravaged area. All government, law, and society had broken down. He dreamed he was holding a cat, for which he was offered a bag of gold. Without hesitation, he refused the offer. It was a logical decision under those conditions. He had no faith that he could use the gold to buy things he needed, such as food. But he could eat the cat if he needed to, and thus he could stay alive. After all, what good was a bag full of gold pieces if he died of starvation while counting them?

This little dream illustrates another point about money: Money is valuable because it is scarce. In the dream, cats and other good things to eat were apparently more scarce than gold. The average American will quickly agree that money is scarce in our society. But it must be scarce, or it will have no value. If the supply of money in the United States were suddenly doubled and passed out to everyone, inflation would occur. Inflation in prices is the same thing as a decline in the value of money. In this example, the value would probably decline about 50 percent. That would leave everyone right where they started.

Inflation would occur because the large increase in money would not create an equally large increase in things to buy. For example, a doubling of the amount of gold will not result in a doubling in the number of cats available. Similarly, turning out an extra batch of dollars on the nation's monetary printing press will not solve family money problems.

Increasing the nation's money supply by "turning on the printing presses" not only would fail to solve family money problems, but the phrase itself is misleading. It implies that the federal government increases the money supply by printing more money. That's not true. This mistaken idea starts with the popular misconception that money is cash. Of course, cash is money, but most of the money in the country is not cash. Actually, all the cash in everyone's wallets, vaults, and sugar bowls only adds up to about 10 percent of the nation's total money. Most money is nothing more than bookkeeping entries at a bank and notations in your checkbook. For example, very few people pay bills with cash. Most people write checks. Most people do not keep their money around the house;

they keep it in banks. And what is true for ordinary people is even more true for the nation's business enterprises. Nearly all of their money is on deposit at the bank. Bank deposits represent most of the money.

What is actually on deposit at the banks is bookkeeping entries, not cash. Of course, banks do keep some cash in their vaults for cashing checks and supplying retailers with cash register money, but the great bulk of their deposits are not held in cash. Most of the deposits are invested in loans, government securities, and other investments. Customer deposits themselves are just numbers on the bank's ledgers.

Numbers on pages of books representing nearly all the money might strike some people as funny. It doesn't seem to fit with the idea that money must be scarce to be valuable. Obviously, there is an endless supply of numbers in the world. Numbers certainly aren't like gold or silver, which eventually will all be discovered and mined. What keeps these special numbers scarce are the laws that govern them. Take the numbers in your checkbook. It takes no effort at all for you to write down $1,000,000 in your checkbook. But if you try to write a check for $1,000,000 and the bank doesn't have corresponding numbers on your records, you will go to jail. That's pretty good incentive to keep you from writing numbers you don't have.

The banks have laws and rules that control the numbers they write down as well. Ultimately, the only people who really have authority to fiddle with the numbers are the Federal Reserve banks, and their authority is tightly regulated. The Federal Reserve, reverently known as the FED, has the power to create money. The way money is created is rather interesting. The FED has authority to do a number of things that have the effect of creating new deposits in the banking system. The new deposits multiply and become more money.

Here's how it works: Assume there is just one bank in the country. Assume the FED creates $10,000 in new deposits in that bank. Now, having $10,000 of nice new numbers on the books is great, but the bank is in business to make loans. Loaning money is how banks make a profit. So they will loan the new money out. But not all of the new money. The law says the banks have to keep a portion of their deposits in reserve.

Assume, for example, that the reserve is 20 percent. That means a bank can loan out 80 percent, or $8000. Let's assume that the first guy through the bank's door is the owner of the corner drugstore. Let's say he needs $8000 to buy an inventory of bubble gum for the coming gum-chewing season. The bank makes the loan, but the druggist doesn't cart the money out in cash. Instead, the bank deposits $8000 worth of numbers in the druggist's account. Notice, at this point, that the bank has a new deposit for $10,000 from the FED and a new deposit of $8000 from the druggist. Already the new money created is $18,000. But it won't stop there. Now the bank can loan out 80 percent of the new deposit from the druggist, or $6400. The next person through the door may be a homeowner needing a loan of $6400 to remodel her front closet. The loan is made. A new deposit of $6400 is created for the homeowner. The bank can now loan 80 percent of the $6400, and so on. This process goes on and on until the original $10,000 deposited by the FED has expanded into $50,000 worth of new deposits. The total amount of the new deposits depends on the reserve requirement. In this example, the reserve requirement was 20 percent, so the original deposit increased five times (100% ÷ 20). If the reserve requirement were 10 percent, the expansion would be ten times (100% ÷ 10) and so on.

What happens to the money supply when all the people that took out new loans write checks against them? For instance, when the druggist gets around to paying for his bubble gum? Not much will happen at all. The druggist will write some numbers on a slip of paper, called a *check*. He will give the paper to the bubble gum manufacturer. The bubble gum manufacturer will take it to the bank. The bank will then take the numbers it has on the books for the druggist and deposit them in the manufacturer's account. The total deposits at the bank remain the same, and so does the nation's money supply. Only the FED can put in new deposits.

Naturally, this example is very simplistic. In reality, the problem of money creation is very complex. But this is the mechanism by which it occurs. Note that no new greenbacks were printed in this money creation process. All that was created was a lot more numbers on the bank's books.

Does all this matter to the average person? Yes, indeed. But we take the money creation process, like most things that work pretty well, for granted. What really matters to us is the numbers in our own checkbooks, and the cash in our own wallets, and the loans at our own banks. Money matters to us all right, but not the same way it matters to FED. The FED is worried about the nation's money supply, while the average person is only worried about his or her own money supply. The average person is concerned with day-to-day money matters, such as budgets, bills, and bank books; college, retirement, and financial security; and stocks, real estate, and savings accounts. That's what money means to the average person, and that's why *money matters!*

◇ 10 ◇
How Can You Know
What You Are Worth?

As you will soon see, one of the first steps in controlling your money is knowing what you are worth. There are a number of ways to determine what you are worth.

You can ask your boss what you're worth, or you can ask your spouse what you're worth, or you can keep a personal "statement of financial condition." They may all give you answers you don't want to hear, but at least you can be sure the financial statement will tell you the truth—about finances anyway.

The purpose of this chapter is to see whether you *own* more than you *owe*. If you owe more than you own, then technically you're bankrupt. Just fill in the following figures:

Personal Financial Condition

Assets:
1. Cash, checking account   _____
2. Savings account   _____
3. Market value of stocks, bonds, savings certificates, etc.   _____
4. Cash value of life insurance policy   _____
5. Money owed to you   _____
6. Value of furniture, appliances   _____
7. Value of cars, boats, and so on   _____
8. Value of home and real estate   _____
9. Vested pension benefits   _____
10. Value of a private business   _____
11. Value of all other assets   _____
12. Total assets   _____

Liabilities:

13. Balance due, such as utilities or
    other services   _____
14. Balance due on charge accounts   _____
15. Payoff on car loans   _____
16. Payoff on personal loans from finance
    companies, banks, and so on   _____
17. Payoff on home loan   _____
18. Money owed to friends and relatives,
    and so on   _____
19. All other debts and obligations   _____
20. Total liabilities   _____

Personal worth (Total assets, Line 12,
minus total liabilities, Line 20)   _____

The terms "value" and "payoff" as used here deserve explanation. "Value" is the amount you can *really* get for an item today if you absolutely have to sell it. Be candid with yourself. For the purpose of this report, "value" would only be what someone else would pay you for it. Your ideas and theirs might be quite different. Remember to subtract commissions and other selling expenses when valuing homes, stocks, and so forth. One of the most important realizations arising from this "real value" exercise is the recognition of how fast some things lose their value and how much it really costs to own them.

"Payoff" is the amount of money necessary to close out the loan today. Often the only way to get an accurate payoff figure is to call the finance company from which you got your loan. Every type of loan has its own unique payoff schedule. Normally you pay much more toward interest than principal while the loan is new. Among other things, this probably means you won't get the right "payoff" figure by simply subtracting the amount of the payments you've already made from the original value of the loan. One of the most important realizations arising from this "payoff" exercise is how expensive it really is to borrow money to buy the things that lose their value so fast.

Once you've filled in all the figures, you can use the report to analyze your own personal financial worth. Conditions vary so much from one person to another that it is hard to generalize about what your personal statement should look like. However, with that hedge aside, some generalizations are as follows.

Personal Worth

Personal worth is assets minus liabilities. The figure should fall within the broad ranges of the following table.

Age	Personal Worth
20–30	$ 2,000– 7,000
30–40	$ 7,000–25,000
40–50	$25,000–75,000
50–65	$75,000 +

If your figure is well below these guidelines, you probably are spending too much relative to your current income. Spending more than you should may be enjoyable, and even necessary, right now, but you'll regret it later on—when you retire for example. If your worth is negative, and you have been out of school for more than three years, you probably have a serious financial problem.

Personal Liquidity

Your personal liquidity is the funds you could get your hands on quickly if you had to: cash, savings, securities (Lines 1, 2, and 3). These assets should be two to three times greater than the amount you have to pay in the next month or two for monthly bills, credit cards, and so on (Lines 13, 14). Ready cash in hand (Line 1) should be one or two times *this* month's bills (Line 13). If it is lower, you'll find occasions when you are past due or overdrawn. If it is three times greater or more, you are losing interest you could be earning from investments.

Personal Asset Analysis

Where is the bulk of your assets concentrated? If your money is in furniture, cars, and so on, then your personal worth is slipping away through depreciation. If your asset values are mostly tied up in your home, then you are "real estate rich" but "dollar poor." A proper mix of liquid spendable assets, growing assets, and current standard of living assets is the goal.

Personal Liability Analysis

Where are your debts concentrated? Monthly bills should be current. If items such as rent and utilities are consistently two to three months past due, your life is made miserable by the dunning notices you receive and the degrading phone calls you get. Credit card payments should not extend more than two to three months into the future.

It is important to match your borrowing to what you are buying. For instance, borrowing for thirty years on a home that will last thirty years makes sense. But it wouldn't make sense to finance a car for thirty years. After it wears out in ten years, you'll still have twenty years of payments. You should also avoid using your credit card to buy things with big price tags or long usefulness such as television sets. Credit cards involve short-term debt. If you have too much short-term debt, your life will be like a pressure cooker trying to keep it current.

The personal financial statement is intended to be a snapshot of your current circumstances. As a rule, it becomes even more useful if a new statement is made at least yearly. This will help you track your financial progress and lay plans for the future. After all, your boss and spouse probably tell you what they think of you everyday; once a year isn't too often to hear from your financial statement.

◇ 11 ◇
Anyone Can Stick
to a Budget

Sticking to a budget is like sticking to a diet. You use self-control. Overspending is like overeating—both are bad for people. And, like proper weight maintenance, proper financial maintenance requires a lot of self-control—there is no substitute. Lack of self-control is the Number One reason why people suffer physical obesity. It is difficult for most Americans to discipline themselves not to overeat. America is a land of plenty. We tend to let our "eyes get bigger than our stomachs" and to eat more than we should. There is plenty of food to eat, and it tastes so good. But overeating is bad for us, in the long run.

Likewise, lack of self-control is the Number One reason why people suffer financial obesity. Most Americans find it difficult to discipline themselves not to overspend. America is a land of plenty. We tend to let our "eyes get bigger than our pocketbooks" and to buy more than we should. There are plenty of things to buy and spending feels so good. But overspending is bad for us, in the long run.

People are different, of course. Some people can eat or spend more than other people. We all know people who can eat just about anything they want, yet stay skinny as rails. Others seem to gain ten pounds just making out the grocery list. Also, some people can buy just about anything they want, while others can barely afford to make out the grocery list. Most people are somewhere in between. The trick is to figure out the limits of your personal diet and budget and then stick to them. Diets and budgets are different for different people, but they all have one thing in common: They all require self-control. And self-control is difficult for just about everyone. There are no easy ways to achieve greater self-control. Self-control is a matter of personal discipline. But certain principles of self-control, if applied faithfully, will help people control their actions.

These principles are:

- ◇ Decide in advance.
- ◇ Don't reconsider a good decision.
- ◇ Control your thoughts.
- ◇ Start small.
- ◇ Don't be discouraged by failures.
- ◇ Don't excuse yourself.
- ◇ Avoid bad influences.
- ◇ Get others to help.

These principles apply no matter what kind of improvement a person is trying to make in his or her life. These principles can help control everything from overspending to oversleeping, from overeating to overdrinking. These principles are so important they are worth further discussion.

Decide in Advance

When you are trying to limit your spending, your eating, your *anything,* you stand a far better chance of success if you decide what you are going to do in advance. Deciding in advance means deciding when you can be most objective about the problem. It means that you are deciding when you are most free from enticements.

There was a man who was frequently invited out to dinner by suppliers. Weight soon became a major problem. When he sat down in a restaurant, he would be faced with all kinds of decisions. Should he order the Lo-Calorie plate, which didn't appeal to him much, or should he order something fattening—which did appeal to him? Should he eat the hot rolls or pass them by? And what about dessert? Generally he found himself fighting a mental battle over the issue, and generally he lost. Then one day he realized he was trying to make a good decision at a very bad time. He realized he should decide *before* he got in the restaurant. He should decide *before* he got hungry. He should decide away from the influences of tantalizing smells and mouth-watering menu descriptions. He found that decisions made in advance were good decisions—at least as far as his waistline was concerned.

Don't Reconsider a Good Decision

Having made good decisions at good times, people risk changing their good decisions if they allow themselves to reconsider the decision at a bad time. One college student, because of his work schedule, frequently needed to get up early and study. When work prevented him from studying, he would make a good decision to get up early the next morning. But in the morning when the alarm went off, he would start to reconsider his decision of the night before. With one eye half open and the other half shut, and feeling half dead, he would reason, "I don't really have that much to do; I can sleep another thirty minutes." Or he would think, "The work isn't due until tomorrow; maybe I can find time this afternoon." Or he would rationalize, "What good is it to get up and do my homework and then fall asleep in class?" The result of rethinking a good decision at a bad time was that he didn't get up, he didn't get his work done. And he fell asleep in class anyway.

Control Your Thoughts

Perhaps the single most important reason people fail to control what they do is because they fail to control what they think. Thinking is like rehearsing for a school play. After people have rehearsed a thought a long time in their minds, their actions become automatic when time for the performance comes. Naturally, if their thoughts are contrary to what the people should do, their actions will also be contrary.

Jim was a family man who had financial problems and really needed to stick to a budget. But he loved to fish, hunt, camp, and so on. He could not afford to buy a camper, but he could not stop thinking about one either. He told himself there was no harm in daydreaming. But he daydreamed so much that he eventually wore down his own buying resistance. Then one day he found himself signing the papers on a brand new camper. Buying a camper was the wrong thing for Jim to do. It not only complicated his already strained finances, but it also nearly finished his marriage.

Jim really wanted a new pickup truck to go with the new camper. But he finally realized his wife would divorce him if he bought one, and then the only company he would have on camping trips would be a bunch of bill collectors. He also realized he would have to learn to control his thinking in order to control his spending. He decided to try thought replacement. On a small card he could carry with him he wrote, "I save money for my family." Several times each day, he would read the card. As he read the card, he formed a mental image of his children and his wife. He thought about the things they needed. Or he would picture himself feeling secure, with thousands of dollars in the bank. Or he would imagine himself walking by a truck dealership and not stopping.

He followed up these planned thought replacement sessions with spontaneous thought replacement sessions. Whenever he found himself dreaming of new toys he wanted to buy, he would shake his head and force himself to replace that thought with one about his family or his savings, and so on. Jim never was able to prevent unwanted thoughts from involuntarily popping into his mind, but he became very successful in replacing them or pushing them out when they got in there. And much to his delight he found his thought replacement program gave him the self-control to stick to his budget.

Start Small

Frequently, people get a notion to make some major changes in themselves, and they impatiently want to change all at once. But big changes can be like eating whales. No one can eat a whale in a single sitting. However, one *can* eat a whale in a number of meals.

A housewife named Sandra went through periodic stages of wishing she were better educated. She frequently signed up for correspondence courses from a local college. But she had always had a tough time making herself study. She thrust herself into the course with determination, but before long her self-control would lag. She wouldn't force herself to study, and the course went uncompleted.

After a series of uncompleted attempts, Sandra decided to start more gradually. She picked a good book to read. She decided to read one page a day. Some days she really had to force herself to read the page, but the assignment was so small she couldn't rationalize not doing it. Eventually she finished the book. It was a major victory for her. She took on another book, and then another. Her self-control improved, and she eventually graduated from college.

Don't Be Discouraged by Failures

Often people set goals for themselves, even small goals, which they do not achieve. Failure to achieve their objectives damages their self-confidence. Before long, their self-confidence is so low they give up trying altogether. They may conclude they are simply too weak to achieve anything. And they may abandon any attempt at self-control at all.

Dick is an example of someone who gave up. Dick wanted to quit smoking. Three times Dick really got determined, but after four or five days he was a nervous wreck. The pressure at work and his own grouchiness around the house eventually overwhelmed him, and so he would light up a cigarette. After three determined attempts, Dick concluded he was too weak ever to quit smoking. Making such an admission was a real blow to his personal self-respect. In fact, his self-respect slipped so much that his self-control in other areas also declined. His performance slipped at work, and his patience around the house declined. He even had a hard time keeping up with the yard work. To make matters worse, he wound up smoking more than ever. His wife hopes he won't ever try to quit smoking again.

If Dick is ever going to quit smoking, he must realize that quitting is tough for everyone. He must not get discouraged if he has a minor setback. Instead, he must realize that his struggle is normal, and then he must redouble his determination to do better. Avoiding discouragement is the only way he'll ever gain strength to make it.

Don't Excuse Yourself

The human mind can be very creative. If allowed to, it can create all kinds of rationalizations to excuse oneself for not exercising proper self-control. The rationalizer reasons that exercising self-control is either not a good idea, impossible, or not necessary, at that specific moment. Some times the rationalizer simply convinces himself (or herself) that he is exercising complete self-control, when in reality he is using no control at all. Such rationalizations prevent a person from getting the necessary job done.

An example of rationalization is a woman who had a terrible problem of yelling at her children. Jane knew that temper outbursts were a poor way to control her family's behavior. She could also see that her kids were drawing away from her. She often embarrassed herself, her family, and everyone around with her vicious verbal assaults on her kids. She told herself, and her spouse, that she really wanted to control her temper, but somehow she couldn't.

Deeper questioning, however, showed that while she said she wanted to control her temper she could not think of a single incident in which she felt she had acted wrongly. She could rationalize that each flare-up had been an acceptable exception. In fact, she often believed the outbursts were necessary. Sometimes the kids were at fault. She rationalized that they were so disobedient that she had to scream to make them behave. Sometimes it was her husband's fault, because he didn't discipline the kids before she lost her temper. Sometimes it was her health's fault, because she wasn't her normal self when she had a splitting headache. And so on. She could excuse herself for each and every incident of angry temper and loss of self-control.

The only hope for Jane, or for her kids, is to stop rationalizing and excusing herself for each breach of behavior. Once she stops rationalizing, she can start realizing that she is responsible for her temper and her self-control regardless of the situation.

Avoid Bad Influences

Bad influences can be either places or people. The classic example is the alcoholic trying to control his (or her) drinking. He will never stay "on the wagon" if he continues to meet his old drinking buddies in bars. The environment of a bar obviously is conducive to drinking—that's how the establishment makes its money. And the buddies may actually try to talk the drinker into joining them. They don't mean any harm and are usually just trying to be sociable. But in that environment a drinker will want to be one of the group, so he'll relax his self-control and have "just one drink."

To conquer his problem, the alcoholic must give his (or her) self-control all the help he can by finding new influences, such as meeting his new friends at Alcoholics Anonymous gatherings.

Get Others to Help

A person trying to overcome a problem can sometimes get help from other people. If the person says to friends, "I'm trying to stick to a diet, don't let me buy a donut on my work break," his or her friend will act as a reminder. Or the person might say, "I'm trying to stick to a budget, don't let me go shopping at lunch." Again, the friend will act as a reminder. Help from friends can provide the little bit of extra strength needed in critical situations.

All these principles apply in any circumstance where self-control is necessary. All these principles can help a person gain self-control. They will help people stick to a good financial diet and enjoy good financial health.

◇ 12 ◇
The "Anyone Can Budget" Budget

Making out any old budget is relatively easy. Making out a really good budget requires a little more work. Budgets are divided into "income" and "expense" sections. Each section is further divided into numerous categories for major sources of income or expense. The following example includes many common categories. Most families won't need all these; some families may need more.

Budget Worksheet

Income:
Salary, commissions, earnings, etc.   ———————
Dividends   ———————
Interest and investments income   ———————
Alimony   ———————
Government payments   ———————
Pension or Social Security   ———————
Other sources of income
    Gross income   ———————

Less:
Income Taxes withheld   ———————
Social Security   ———————
Other deductions   ———————
    Total deductions   ———————
    Take-home pay   ———————

Expected expenses:
Food   ———————
Mortgage or rent   ———————

House insurance, taxes   _____
Electricity   _____
Heat   _____
Water   _____
Other utilities   _____
Transportation expense   _____
Automobile, gas, oil   _____
Automobile payments   _____
Automobile insurance, taxes   _____
Automobile parking   _____
Medical insurance   _____
Life insurance   _____
Other insurance   _____
Clothing   _____
Personal expenses   _____
Entertainment   _____
Loan payments   _____
Union dues   _____
Charitable donations   _____
Savings   _____
Other regular expenses   _____
                                                 _____
                                                 _____

    Total regular expenses   _____
    Cash before irregular expenses   _____

Unexpected expenses:
Home repairs   _____
Automobile repairs   _____
Medical expenses   _____
Other   _____
    Cash available for major purchases   _____

This budget worksheet separates expenses into "expected expenses" and "unexpected expenses." This treatment is not customary. However, it can be very important, because unexpected expenses are an important part of nearly everyone's budget. Chapter 16 provides more information on budgeting for unexpected expenses.

    Fill the worksheet out, using the very best estimates you can make. If the bottom line shows a deficit, or too small an excess, then you must either (1) figure out a way to increase your income, or (2) figure out a way to lower your expenses.

Most people learn a great deal just by making a budget. They learn how little they know about where their money comes from and goes to. They frequently learn how close they are living to the line. They learn how tough it is to increase income and lower expenses.

And all this learning is good. It is worth the exercise all by itself. But if the effort is to be meaningful, the budget must really influence how you spend and save your money. Otherwise the most important financial tool you have—your budget—will become a source of harassment, depression, and self-inflicted guilt.

◇ 13 ◇
How to Keep
Simple Financial Records
That Work

Families need financial records in order to plan their expenses for the future and to know where they can cut if the need arises.

In handling finances, families can learn a great deal from major corporations. Each year, corporations begin their budget-making process with a complete examination of the previous year's records. How much was spent for office supplies? What was the cost of advertising? Once last year's figures are in hand, good estimates can be made about next year's spending.

Can you imagine the reaction of a corporation president who received financial records that were based on guesses and estimates? Records where large expenditures for items such as entertainment were forgotten all together? And where there was one item simply labeled "Miscellaneous" that accounted for 15 to 20 percent of all the expenses? One thing the bookkeeper could expect to be eliminated from next year's budget is his or her salary!

Families may not be *big* businesses, but they are *important* businesses to their "presidents" and "bookkeepers," namely, Mom and Dad. But most family financial records are a mess. If the family's chief financial officer were asked for a breakdown of the family's expenses, he or she could probably give fairly exact figures for rent, car payments, and insurance. He (or she) would have to guess how much was spent for food, clothing, and gasoline. And the guess probably wouldn't be very close. To make matters worse, he wouldn't have any idea how much was spent on "Miscellaneous" items such as entertainment, presents, haircuts, lunches, and school expenses. Not knowing how much is spent on "Miscellaneous" might not be too serious if these items in total were small, but for most families these unrecorded, unplanned, and miscellaneous expenses add up to 15 to 20 percent or more of their total expenditures.

With this big, and largely forgotten, "Miscellaneous" category, the family members will not even realize they are in no position to afford some luxuries they want. "After all," they may say to themselves, "we make $1500 per month. Surely we can squeeze a mere $19 out of each paycheck for that new computerized air hockey game we've been wanting." Well, enough of that kind of thinking and the family members will get so tied up with payments that they'll wind up playing air hockey with bill collectors.

Here are some ideas that can help. Because cash purchases are the hardest to keep track of, carry a slip of paper in your wallet. Divide it into columns for "Date," "Item," and "Amount." Whenever you pay cash for anything, jot the amount down, even if it's for a minor item such as lunch. Whenever you write a check, be sure to record the purpose of the payment, not just to whom it is written. Some checks may cover several items, such as groceries, notions, and cash. Try to indicate how much of the check is for each. When you use a credit card, record the item next to your signature. Too often the clerk's description says only "Merchandise," which won't help you recall, months later, what the purchase was. For ease in recording, use a code system. Corporations use numbers for their accounts, but most people do not like to memorize account numbers. Because your records aren't as complex as IBM's, you can probably use "initials," which are easier to remember.

Most families' financial records would include the categories shown on the chart found on p. 102. This is intended as an example only. Each family's categories will differ, depending on its spending habits.

Code each purchase faithfully. Once a month, add up the figures by category and record the totals in a permanent book or general ledger. This general ledger can be as simple as a spiral binder, or you might prefer to buy regular six-column ledger paper. Use a separate sheet for each major heading, such as "Food" and "Automobile." Have separate vertical columns for each subcategory, such as "Food—Meat" or "Food—Other." Don't try to record each individual purchase in the general ledger; the totals from your paper slips, checks, and credit cards are enough. You can save all the individual slips for future reference if necessary and thus avoid the work of recopying every transaction. When you've finished for the month, your book will look something like this:

Code	Category	Code	Category
A	Automobile	M	Medical
AG	Gas and oil	MD	Dentist
AM	Maintenance	MP	Physician
AP	Payments	MH	Hospital
AT	Taxes	MD	Drugs
AI	Insurance	MI	Insurance
C	Clothing	P	Personal
CP	Parents	PC	Cosmetics
CC	Children	U	Utilities
D	Charitable	UE	Electricity
	Donations	UG	Gas
		UW	Water
E	Entertainment	UT	Telephone
EV	Vacations	UN	Newspaper
EH	Hobbies	W	Work
F	Food	WL	Lunches
FM	Meat	WE	Equipment
FO	Other	WC	Clothes
H	Household	WT	Transportation
HC	Cleaning supplies	X	Christmas
HR	Repair and Maintenance	XC	Children
HM	Mortgage	XP	Parents
HT	Taxes	XR	Relatives
HI	Insurance	XF	Friends

At the end of each month, you will see a quick picture of your spending.

As you set up your books, you may be tempted to make one of two common mistakes: too much detail or too little detail. You would go crazy trying to keep track of your expenditures on individual quarts of oil, for example. But a single category covering "Automobile" is too broad to be helpful, especially when you want to identify some costs you can cut. As a guide, set up separate subcategories for items that will be at least 2 percent of your total expenses a year. That might be about $300 for the average family. If you think you spend $300 a year on oil, then you should have a separate subcategory for oil.

Reactions to such suggestions may be "I hate book work" or "I'd never keep it up." Maybe so, but I strongly recommend you do it

Automobile

	Gas and oil	Mainte- nance	Payments	Taxes	Insurance	Total
Jan	$82		$197		$112	$391
Feb	74		197			271
Mar	86		197			283
Apr	62		197			259
May	73	$69	197			339
Jun	112		197		112	421
Jly	97		197			294
Aug	87		197			284
Sep	90					90
Oct	85					85
Nov	72	158		$86		316
Dec	75					75
Total	$995	$227	$1576	$86	$224	$3108

anyway. The time involved for a typical family is less than sixty minutes a month. Most families spend more than that worrying over why they can't make ends meet. Without records, you'll never find a solution to that age-old problem of running out of money before you run out of month. All you will find is financial frustration.

◇ 14 ◇
Why It's Important
to Communicate
About Family Finances

A sponge is an aquatic animal with no central nervous system. Without a central nervous system, the sponge can't communicate danger from one part of its body to another. Thus, one side of the sponge can be as happy as a clam while the other side is being *eaten* by a clam.

Financially, many families are like sponges. The members depend on one another and are held together by family ties, but their relationship is full of holes. Sometimes there seems to be no central nervous system for communication from one side of the family to the other. Part of the family is working hard bringing home the clams, while another part is busy spending them, and neither part seems to know what the other part is doing with the clams.

More frequently, however, families do have at least a primitive form of central nervous system—a system that is capable of feeling pain when the family is being eaten alive. And in most families, when one family member is in pain, that person communicates distress all over the household. Unfortunately, this type of communication simply spreads the pain around and seldom leads to corrective action.

Families can improve their financial communications by developing the following rules and procedures:

1. *Expense records.* Expense records kept, even for small cash expenditures. This helps family members remember where their money was spent.

2. *Accessibility.* Expense records made accessible to all family members. Family members find they understand expenditures by others when they review the expenditures frequently.

3. *Budgets and priority lists.* Money stops slipping away when spending decisions are made together—in advance of the purchase.

4. *Spending limits.* Members do not exceed these limits without telling the rest of the family beforehand.

5. *Record-keeping environment.* Each family member is given an assignment for keeping part of the records. In this way, each understands what the records mean and how they work.

6. *Meetings.* The family members establish a practice of meeting together regularly to discuss finances and review the records. In most cases, they meet at least once a month. Regular reviews at predetermined times allow family members to become aware of any problems as they develop. The meetings also promote rational and timely discussions. It is almost impossible to have any type of rational discussion regarding finances when all the "discussions" are started right after a "past-due" notice arrives or a big check bounces.

7. *Keeping up to date.* Family members develop a discipline of keeping their records up to date. They realize that even a single person can fail to communicate with himself (or herself) if he doesn't keep his checkbook balanced.

These simple little rules can be used in most households. They promote good spending habits, good communication, and help to eliminate financial suspicion among family members. When suspicion is removed in a big area such as finances, a more harmonious family environment can exist in all areas. Frequently, when families really begin to communicate, they discover that what's been troubling them has been themselves.

◇ 15 ◇
Why Some Budgets Don't Work

Sometimes budgets fail because they are not reviewed on a regular basis.

For example, Harold just got the news that a $100 check he had written to his church bounced—it came back marked "Insufficient funds." The poor clerk at the bank who had to call and break the news to Harold got the distinct impression he was furious. She couldn't quite be sure who he was mad at, but she knew she got the brunt of his wrath. Harold wasn't really angry, especially with her. Actually, he was embarrassed and frustrated. He's always embarrassed and frustrated when a check bounces. And it happens a couple of times each year. What makes the situation particularly embarrassing is Harold's job—he is the treasurer of a large corporation. As treasurer, he is responsible for the company's budgets and cash management. He is well qualified for his work. He holds a master's degree in accounting, and he is a CPA (certified public accountant). Not only is he qualified for his work, but he handles his job well. For one thing, his firm's checks never bounce.

Harold just can't figure out why he can't manage his own budget and cash. He earns an executive's salary, and he and his wife Martha are anything but reckless spenders. Harold has tried to apply his formal training to the family finances, but somehow it hasn't worked. Each year he and Martha make out an elaborate budget for the family. They estimate expenditures for everything from shoelaces to pet food. The budget always includes a sizable amount for savings and investments, but somehow the savings are never there. He's not sure where the family is overspending. But the overdrawn checking account is evidence that it is. Harold's inability to handle simple family finances when he knows he is capable of handling complex corporate finances is especially frustrating.

106

Adding to his current frustration is his workload this week. It is monthly budget review time, and there won't be much extra time to think about his personal budgeting problems. Each month his office prepares a report showing what has been spent by corporate managers in various accounts. After the totals come in, Harold meets with each manager and reviews the report. They particularly discuss any areas where expenses are running ahead of budget. The reasons for the overruns must be fully explained, and plans must be established to bring expenses back into line. Sometimes it is necessary to adjust the budget due to previously unforeseen circumstances. These reviews help Harold and the managers track their progress and stick to their budget.

Another item Harold reviews often is the cash balance. A daily cash report is prepared, which he reviews carefully. He also keeps track of the bills the corporation must pay in the next few weeks. As he reviews these figures, he makes decisions regarding the timing of various expenditures. In this way he avoids any cash shortage position for the company.

Harold is proud of the company's elaborate review procedures. He knows these procedures help the entire management team efficiently run the company. He also knows that careful financial controls have helped the company earn the reputation of being the best-managed firm in their industry.

Harold *should* be proud. He personally designed and implemented the company's successful budget and review procedures. But Harold should be embarrassed, too. He and Martha never review their personal budget after it is prepared. Neither Harold nor Martha can tell you whether their expenditures for shoelaces or pet food are in line with their budget. For all they know, their pets are eating the family's lunches and wearing its shoelaces. When the cash gets low or a check bounces, Harold usually sits down and makes up a whole new budget. Usually he does this without figuring out why the old one failed. So ultimately the new one fails too. If Harold stopped and reviewed the whole situation, he would realize that lack of financial review is his source of frustration.

Harold's story is dramatized of course, but not much. Basically, budgeting and review are something like driving from Peculiar, Missouri, to Liberal, Kansas. The driver first consults a road map and decides which route he (or she) will follow to Liberal. As he drives, he watches for road signs and mileage markers to reassure himself that he is on the right road. If he sees a sign indicating that he is on the wrong road, he immediately tries to figure out what's wrong and what to do about it. If the driver only looks at a map before leaving and then fails to review his progress along the way, he may wind up in Last Gasp, Wyoming, and not Liberal, Kansas.

Even families who make careful budgets need to watch the financial road signs along the way. At least once a month, all interested family members should review what has been spent. The actual expenses should be compared with the estimated expenses. If there are overruns, the family can figure out what's wrong and what to do about it. Usually, the family will map out a plan for reducing expenses. But sometimes family members will agree that circumstances have changed and a new route is now best to follow. If the family implements good financial review procedures, it can identify wrong turns and take corrective action before it travels many financial miles out of the way.

Making a "Want" List

Organize your spending by making a "want" list. A want list is simply a list of major purchases you want to make, ranked according to priority, with estimated cost and estimated time of purchase. It has proven to be a highly successful tool in my work with people.

There are three steps in developing a want list—listing wants, estimating costs, and establishing priorities.

1. *Listing wants.* Call the family together for a brainstorming session (even if you are the only member of your family). Let everyone make suggestions about the family's wants. Because it is a brainstorming session, any want can be suggested without criticism. When all the wants are listed, go back and eliminate the clearly impractical ones.

2. *Estimating costs.* Next to each surviving want, record an estimated cost. Be realistic about your estimates. For example, if you characteristically wind up getting the deluxe model of everything you buy, use the deluxe price. If you want a trash compactor, and if deluxe models that "burp" and say "Thank you" cost $325, then estimate $325. Don't record the price of some stripped-down model that only grunts and groans, when you're almost certain to pay more.

3. *Estimating priorities.* Most people want all items on their lists, and they want them right now. So deciding which want comes first is really tough. Furthermore, family members won't always agree on priorities. Mom's first want may be a helicopter motor home. Sis may strongly want a thoroughbred racehorse. But Dad's Number One want might be a bathroom—inside the house.

Resolving such differences of opinion isn't easy. Families are well advised to establish criteria for analyzing their wants. Each family's criteria will differ, just as their wants do, but the following questions may be helpful:

◊ Will the item improve the health, safety, or well-being of the family?
◊ Will the item protect existing investment?
◊ Will the item contribute to income?
◊ Will the item reduce work?
◊ Will the item be used often?
◊ Is the item simply for esthetics?
◊ Is the item expensive to maintain or operate?
◊ Is the item a fad?

To see how this works, let's say the members of your family contribute the following list of things they want, at the following estimated costs.

Items	Estimated costs
Racehorse	$ 15,000
Motorized Pogo stick	175
Living room drapery	450
Drinking fountain in the kids' room	750
Grandfather clock	490
Vacation to Dogpatch, U.S.A.	750
TV video recorder	975
Mercedes-Benz delivery truck	22,000
Bed frames	25
Fruit trees for yard	50
New driveway	1,300
Helicopter motor home	187,000
Indoor bathroom	2,500
Trash compactor	325
	$231,790

After this list is completed, considerable "adult" discussion will be necessary. However, you will eventually be able to scratch a few items, change a few, and place priorities on the remainder. For example:

Priority	Items	Estimated costs
11	Regular pogo stick	$ 15
4	Living room drapery	250
9	Grandfather clock	490
7	Vacation to Dogpatch, U.S.A.	650
10	TV video recorder	975
8	Datsun delivery truck	8,000
1	Bed frames	25
3	Fruit trees for yard	50
5	New driveway	1,300
2	Indoor bathroom	2,500
6	Trash compactor	325
	~~Racehorse~~	~~15,000~~
	~~Drinking fountain in the kids' room~~	~~750~~
	~~Helicopter motor home~~	~~187,000~~
		$14,580

Once the items are finally listed, priced and ranked, you are ready to decide when they can be purchased. Your monthly cash flow projection is necessary at this point.

Assume you expect to have the following excess cash to spend on this list:

Jan	$ 175	Jul	$1,500
Feb	175	Aug	700
Mar	2,000	Sept	150
Apr	800	Oct	1,700
May	0	Nov	0
June	0	Dec	0

Total annual cash flow $7,200

You can see immediately that, with $7200 expected cash flow and $14,580 worth of wants, you won't get everything purchased right away. In fact, it may take two years or more.

With all this information in front of you, you can complete your money calendar. Run a cumulative cash flow, subtract the cost of wants as you can afford them, and you will be able to see exactly when you can afford to buy things.

Month	Estimated cash flow	Want	Cost	Accumulated Cash
Jan (this year)	$ 175	Bed frame	$ 25	$ 150
Feb	175			325
Mar	2,000			2,325
Apr	800	Indoor bathroom ($2,500), Fruit trees ($50), Living room drapery ($250)	2,800	325
May	0			325
June	0			325
July	1,500	New driveway ($1,300), Trash compactor ($325)	1,625	200
Aug	700	Vacation to Dogpatch, U.S.A. ($650)	650	250
Sept	150			400
Oct	1,700			2,100
Nov	0			2,100
Dec	0			2,100
Jan (next year)	175			2,275
Feb	175			2,450
Mar	2,000			4,450
Apr	800			5,250
May	0			5,250
June	0			5,250
July	1,500			6,750
Aug	700			7,450
Sept	150			7,600
Oct	1,700	Datsun pickup truck ($8,000), Grandfather clock ($490)	8,490	810
Nov	0			810
Dec	0			810

According to this calendar, you can get your bed frame right now, and your bathroom, trees, and drapes in April. But your new truck doesn't come until October next year, and your video tape recorder is two years away. Sometimes the family members rearrange their want list priorities when they realize how long they must wait to buy some things while saving for others.

A well-constructed, properly used want list can help you spend your money on things you really want, rather than blowing money on momentary whims. It can actually help you do a better job of buying and getting good value for your money, too. When purchases are scheduled and written down, adequate examination of the purchase is more likely to occur than when a purchase is made hurriedly. Timing also improves. For example, purchases can be scheduled during periods when the items are most likely to be on sale. The benefits of a want list can be substantial.

But beware! The want list can create more problems than it solves. Some people don't have much buying discipline. The mere process of writing all their wants down on paper gets them excited. Then they can't resist running out to look, and they wind up buying all the items on their entire want list immediately. Such lack of discipline may be called the "accelerated buying" phenomenon. This phenomenon frequently has a few little extras thrown in that the buyer doesn't count on, such as big debts, heavy finance charges, and frustration.

A subtle form of the "accelerated buying" phenomenon can develop when a big sale comes along for an item scheduled for purchase months away. Without the want list, the item may not have been on the buyer's mind, and the sale may have gone unnoticed. Here the want list can be good or bad. With the want list in hand, the buyer can quickly reexamine all his (or her) wants without forgetting any of them. Then he can intelligently decide whether he should postpone purchase of another want to take advantage of the sale. If the buyer completes this reordering properly, the want list is good. But if the buyer can't stand the idea of missing the sale or postponing other wants, the "accelerated buying" phenomenon occurs, complete with all the "extras" just mentioned, and that's bad!

The want list can become one of your most valuable financial planning tools. Not only can it help you spend your money with greater care, but you also have fun deciding what you are saving for and anticipating the time of its purchase. However, the want list must be a respected tool—one that is consulted and used. Otherwise, the new trash compactor may be "burping" and saying "thank you" as it consumes baskets full of threatening past-due notices and dozens of old want lists.

Being Surprised by Your Bills?

You can stop being surprised by your bills by not forgetting about them. In this age of "Buy now, Pay later," people tend to forget about the "later." Then when that "later" actually comes, they are surprised. Financially speaking, some people surprise themselves right into the poorhouse. This forgetful phenomenon is probably helped along by the human tendency to mentally suppress things we don't like. And most people don't like bills. There are many kinds of surprises:

⋄ *Once-a-year surprises.* Property taxes, insurance, car registration, and so forth.
⋄ *Annual event surprises.* Christmas, vacation, back-to-school, and so forth.
⋄ *"Your credit is as good as cash" surprises.* Credit cards, charge accounts, and "Nothing down, ninety days until first payment" contracts.

You can forget about these surprises if you set up a system for recognizing expenditures when they occur and taking care of them right then—instead of when they are due and payable. Such a system can be called "personal accrual accounting." Accrual accounting *is* recognizing your expenses when they occur. It *isn't* kidding yourself about how much you spent this month. It *is* breaking your expenses into manageable portions. With accrual accounting, you deduct from your current cash balance (1) what you spent and paid for in cash, (2) what you spent and paid for with credit, and (3) one month's portion of items you use up all the time but only have to pay for once a year. Because the checkbook is the key financial management tool for most families, a personal accrual accounting system operates in the checkbook. Here is how it works.

ONCE-A-YEAR SURPRISES

Let's assume your car taxes and registration are due once a year, in November. Because they aren't due on a monthly basis, you tend to forget about them in December, and January, and so on. In fact, you may forget about them until the tax notice comes in November. A big amount such as for taxes can be difficult to handle out of one month's paycheck. Because you forgot about them for eleven months, you may view them as a surprise in November—a bad surprise. Under accrual accounting, you divide your estimated taxes for the year by 12. Each month, you write a check for 1/12 of your taxes. Then the check is sent to your own savings account. When November rolls around, your taxes won't be a surprise. In fact, you may have earned enough interest to avoid being surprised by the fact that they are higher than expected.

The principle of recognizing your expenses monthly applies to all annual and semiannual expenditures: automobile insurance, life insurance, pledges to charitable organizations, as well as taxes. You enjoy these items all year—not just when you pay for them. For instance, you drive your car all year around, not just in November. Consequently, 1/12 of your taxes belong in each month of the year. If you account for it that way in your checkbook, then taxes won't be a surprise in November. And you won't be kidding yourself about the real cost of driving in March.

ANNUAL EVENT SURPRISES

Theoretically, it is difficult to show that the benefit of Christmas or a family vacation is enjoyed equally all twelve months of the year, as is driving your car. But whether the theory fits or not, it is still smart to break these once-a-year events up into twelve equal payments. Banks realized this years ago when they started "Christmas Clubs" for their customers. With a "Christmas Club," the depositor sends money to his (or her) bank once each month. Then at Christmas the bank sends it all back—with interest. Banks aren't the only ones who have learned this trick. Mortgage companies have also learned the trick—people make monthly payments on their homes. Finance companies have learned the trick—people make monthly payments on their cars. And the federal government has learned the trick best of all—many people pay their income taxes with every paycheck through payroll deductions. But the average consumer is still trying to pay for great big expenses such as for Christmas and vacations in one lump sum. They would be better off to write themselves a check every month for 1/12 of the estimated cost of the event and send it to their own savings account.

Then the big events wouldn't be such a financial surprise.

Many people say they *would* be surprised if they kept up the payment to themselves. They say that when things got tight in April the the first thing they would skip is the "big event" payment. And things always seem to get tight in April, and in May, and in every other month of the year. If you think this way, look at it like this: If you spent $600 for Christmas last year, you will spend at least $600 for Christmas next year. And you will do it no matter how tight things are in April. You'll do it because you'll want to do it. You'll find good reasons for doing it. And the money must come from somewhere. You can eliminate a lot of frustration trying to figure out where the money is coming from in December by making that payment to yourself in April, no matter how tight things are. Naturally, the follow-through is up to you and your personal financial discipline.

Personal discipline is also important in spending only what has been set aside for the big event. People tend to spend what has been set aside and more. There was a man who was tired of his lack of discipline when it came to such things as Christmas. He finally gained the discipline he needed by drawing his special event savings for Christmas out in cash. Then he converted the cash to travelers checks for safety. He used the travelers checks to pay for Christmas, and not a penny more. When the travelers checks were gone, his Christmas spending was over. The system kept him within his budget. Staying within his budget really did help him have a Merry Christmas and a Happy New Year.

Some people prefer not to fool around with travelers checks or to pay the 1 percent charge for them. If you are such a person, you can achieve the same result by setting up a special events checkbook. Not a new checking account, just a special events checkbook using your regular checking account. Assume you save $600 for Christmas by sending your savings account $50 a month. When your Christmas shopping starts, transfer the $600 to your regular checking account. But instead of showing the deposit in your regular checkbook, show it as a deposit in your new special events checkbook. As you shop, write checks for gifts and deduct them from this special events checkbook. The running balance in that checkbook lets you know how much you have left for Christmas. When the balance falls to $0, your Christmas shopping should be done. This will help you stay within your budget—just like the man who carried travelers checks.

"YOUR CREDIT IS AS GOOD AS CASH" SURPRISES

The credit card is a great modern innovation. It is probably the most convenient method of payment ever devised—perhaps too convenient. The credit card can be a great source of financial surprise. It shouldn't be a surprise, though, because the consumer receives a receipt at the time of purchase and receives most statements within six weeks. Receipts and statements should eliminate surprises—but they don't. Many people are surprised to see how much they have actually charged when the statement finally comes. They forgot how much they really spent, because they didn't add up the amounts as they went along.

Adding up the amounts and keeping a running total is one way to avoid being surprised when the statement comes. But adding up the amounts still doesn't ensure that you'll have enough in your checking account to pay the amount. I knew a family that devised a better system. Like many families, the members of this family found credit cards easy to use. Like many families, they couldn't believe how big their bill was at the end of the month. Frequently, they found themselves without enough money in the bank to pay the bills. So they sent part payments and let the interest charges pile up on the overdue amount.

Finally they came up with a better idea. When a family member reached for a credit card in the store, he (or she) reached for the checkbook, too. In the checkbook, he made a notation just as if he were writing a check. In this way, he deducted the amount of the charge from the checking account balance immediately. The entries looked like this (note that √ed means "checked in," which is discussed later when we deal with balancing the checkbook):

Check no.	Date	Check issued to	Amount of check	√ed	Amount of deposit	Balance
1431	6/2	Grocery store	45.50			300.00
cc100	6/2	Bank card	25.00			275.00
cc101	6/3	Store charge card	100.00			175.00
cc102	6/3	Bank card	25.00			150.00

In this example, the family has written one check to the grocery store and has used credit cards three times. The members of the family won't actually have to pay for the credit cards until next month. But deducting the amounts of their charges as they are made has several advantages. First, they can't forget about them so they are not surprised when the statement comes. Second, when the statement does come, the money will already be set aside in the bank to pay it. Third, the family members can't kid themselves about how much money they have left to spend. In this example, if the credit cards had not been deducted, the checking account would show a balance of $300. The members of the family might be tempted to spend the money somewhere. But in reality they are not that rich. They only have $150 left when purchases they've already made with their charge cards are considered.

It can be a good thing that the family has considered the credit charges. Assume, for example, that only a few weeks later our family's checkbook balance has dropped to only $20. If that $20 was all they really had left in the checking account, the family would be surprised and financially embarrassed when the credit card statement for $150 arrived. Fortunately, however, the family had already deducted the money for the credit cards and set it aside. Consequently, members were able to pay their bills promptly. Prompt payment avoids embarrassment, and costly interest and late charges.

The system is very easy. It takes very little time. It assures that those credit card statements will not come as a big surprise. This system also goes a long way toward helping the family members keep charge purchases under control, by continuously reminding them what they really have left to pay it all with. And a continuous reminder is good for discipline and avoiding financial surprises.

Many financial surprises should not be surprises at all, because everyone knows they are coming and must be paid for. Everyone knows about taxes, Christmas, and credit card purchases, for example. But these items become surprises when they are forgotten. Families can forget about being surprised if they'll remember to allow for expenses as they occur, rather than just remembering them when they have to be paid.

◇ 16 ◇
A Money Calendar
Can Help

A lot of people ask, "How can I make my money last as long as my month?" Keeping a "money calendar" to know how long the money is supposed to last will help.

A monthly (or quarterly) cash flow projection can be considered a "money calendar." The coming and going of your money isn't quite as precise as the number of days in December or the occurrence of the next full moon. But if you keep this very important personal report, it can help bring some order to your money month.

Some people like to make a money calendar for every month. After all, many bills come every month, such as rent, utilities, and credit card charges. People who want a money calendar that fits the normal cycle of their bills should start with paper that can be divided into fourteen columns. The first column is for the name of the item, the next is for the annual estimate, and the next twelve are for the months of the year.

Many people figure that it would take them a month just to put monthly figures down. These people can probably get by with a quarterly money calendar. They need to start with paper that can be divided into six columns—one for items, one for annual estimates, and one for each quarter of the year. Here we will illustrate a money calendar using quarters. The calendar on p. 119 shows examples of income and expense items many people would use. Each person may also have other items. The figures are just examples, not exact guidelines.

The blank report, whether monthly or quarterly, should be made out *twice*. The first is for estimating (use pencil), the second is for comparing your real experiences with your estimates. Estimate your inflows and outflows for every quarter during the year. Reflect expected raises, bonuses, tax refunds, layoffs, and so on in the quar-

Money Calendar
(Quarters)

	Annual estimate	(1st) Jan Feb Mar	(2nd) Apr May June	(3rd) July Aug Sept	(4th) Oct Nov Dec
Income					
Gross income	$22,000	$5,000	$5,000	$6,000	$6,000
Interest and dividends	600	150	150	150	150
Other income	2,000	1,200		800	
Total income	$24,600	$6,350	$5,150	$6,950	$6,150
Deductions					
Taxes and Social Security	$ 3,000	$ 680	$ 680	$ 820	$ 820
Other payroll deductions	150	37	38	37	38
Total deductions	$ 3,150	$ 717	$ 718	$ 857	$ 858
Take-home pay	$21,450	$5,633	$4,432	$6,093	$5,292
Expected expenses					
Food	$ 1,500	$ 375	$ 375	$ 375	$ 375
Mortgage/rent	5,500	1,375.	1,375	1,375	1,375
Utilities	1,800	550	350	475	425
Transportation	2,800	700	700	700	700
Insurance	600	0	200	0	400
Clothing	480	60	60	300	60
Entertainment	360	90	90	90	90
Loan payments	0	0	0	0	0
Charitable contributions	2,460	635	515	695	615
Property taxes	700	0	0	0	700
Savings	2,000	500	500	500	500
Miscellaneous	300	60	60	60	120
Total expected expenses	$18,500	$4,345	$4,225	$4,570	$5,360
Cash before unexpected expenses	$ 2,950	$1,288	$ 207	$1,523	$ (68)
Unexpected expenses					
Home repairs	$ 360	$ 90	$ 90	$ 90	$ 90
Automobile repairs	300	75	75	75	75
Medical expenses	300	75	75	75	75
Other	100	25	25	25	25
Total unexpected expenses	$ 1,060	$ 265	$ 265	$ 265	$ 265
Cash available for major purchases	$ 1,890	$1,023	$ (58)	$1,258	$ (333)

ters they are most likely to occur. Obviously, many expected expenses such as utilities and auto expenses also vary from quarter to quarter. It is important to distinguish between items that are expected and recur with regularity like the days of the week, and items that are unexpected and occur irregularly, like thunderstorms in spring. We all know there are going to be some thunderstorms. And we all know there are going to be unexpected expenses such as repairs, emergencies, or unusual buying opportunities. The question is when?

To get a better forecast of your expenses, classify them into "expected" and "unexpected" categories. Make your best estimate of yearly totals for unexpected expenses. Two good rules of thumb are 1 percent of replacement value for real estate maintenance, and 3 percent of replacement value for cars, appliances, and so on. If the things you own are older than average, you'll want to increase the percentages. Also allow about $250 per member of your household for unexpected medical expenses, assuming that everyone is *healthy*. People often fail to realize how many irregular unexpected expenses they regularly have. Failure to plan realistically for these expenses leads many people to believe they can afford items that in reality they cannot afford. It's like using up all your sick leave so you can attend the quarter finals of the international frog hopping contest—and then really getting sick.

When the yearly estimates for unexpected expenses are computed, divide by 4 and spread the estimates evenly throughout the year. Now you are ready to see how long your money months really are. Subtract the total of your expected quarterly expenses from your quarterly income. Hopefully your money is at least this "long" (which means that your "Excess cash before unexpected items" is positive). But in some periods it may not be. For instance, the person in our example will not have enough cash coming in during October, November, and December to meet "expected expenses."

Even this is not a complete look at the money calendar. Next you must subtract your "unexpected expenses." You may find some periods when you'll have plenty of cash for major purchases. But you'll see other periods when you'll run way behind. You need to plan for these.

Like any calendar, this one helps you see when things are supposed to happen so you can plan for them. The following are a few thoughts on analyzing your report:

1. If the total yearly excess cash figure is substantially positive, increase what you plan to save, invest, or put away for a major purchase so the money can work for you.

2. If the total excess cash figure is negative for the year, you must either cut expenses or increase income. Don't just do it on paper though; a real plan of action is necessary.

3. If the excess cash before unexpected expenses is positive, plan to put this money in savings; perhaps even a special account. The assumption is that while the money may not be needed the first quarter, it will all be needed at some time during the year, and you want it near at hand when the need arises.

4. If your excess cash is unbalanced, being positive in some quarters (like the first and third) and negative in others (like the second and fourth), plan to put the excess funds from positive quarters in savings to be drawn out during the negative quarters.

The quarterly (or monthly) cash calendar is a helpful tool for financial planning, but to get maximum value for your effort you must compare your actual experience with your estimates each period. Keep track of quarterly expenses in a manner similar to that described in Chapter 9. Each quarter, compare actual experience to estimated experience. Do *not* be alarmed or discouraged if your estimates are frequently wrong. Estimating errors are normal. Initially your estimating may be quite poor. But making quarterly comparisons will help you become a sophisticated estimator and will allow you to make timely financial adjustments, prevent fiscal strain, and control your finances so they work for you rather than against you.

Calendar months and quarters are very precise things; money calendars are not. Some electronic watches are programmed to give accurate dates for the next one hundred years. But personal finances can never be calendared that precisely. However, even though money calendars aren't precise a good one can help prevent too many Thursdays from coming on Tuesday and can help you avoid winding up with some months that have no weekends in them at all.

◇ 17 ◇
Where Should I Keep
My Money?

Today there is an increasingly fine line between investing your money for the future and finding a good place to keep your money for needs you have now or in the near future.

How you invest your money is important. A substantial portion of this book is devoted to that subject in Part V. But finding the right places to keep money you are not specifically investing is more important today than ever before.

It is more important today because today managing effectively means making every available dollar work as hard for you as it can.

And finding the right places to keep your money is more important today because there are so many places to choose from. Many of them are brand new financial products created especially for our times. Also, many of the old, well-known products are less useful today. You need to understand these financial products. Then you can determine which fit the various needs you have for money.

As just indicated there is a difference between investing and finding a good place to store your money. The concern in this part is only with money storage.

All of us need money to live. We need it for daily expenses like bus fare and lunch money. We need money for paying regular bills like rent and food. And we need money to meet unexpected emergencies like medical payments or appliance repairs. We need money we can get at conveniently, and we need the money stored in a safe place. Further, we do not want to be concerned that it will decline in value while it is in storage.

With these ideas in mind I will examine the financial products currently available for storing this kind of money. I'll discuss them in terms of what they are, and what they are not. I'll review their safety and convenience. And, of great importance, I hope to be able to help you understand how you can use these products to manage your finances better than ever before. Using these everyday products can give you a significant advantage in dealing with the 1980s.

The table on p. 124 offers a quick overview of the products to be discussed. The characteristics being compared are as follows:

◇ *Convenience:* Ease of making deposits and withdrawals.
◇ *User effort required:* Need for watching balances, keeping totals, and paying attention to other details.
◇ *Protection from loss:* Protection against market value fluctuations or a loss by the financial institution.
◇ *Protection against user misuse:* Protection against spending the money for unintentional purposes, or losing the funds, or misfiguring the balances.
◇ *Earnings:* The potential interest income paid in a year.
◇ *Purpose:* The normal use of money stored in this type of account.

Pocket Money

Characteristics: Very convenient; poor protection from loss; poor safety from user misuse; earns nothing.

Pocket money (including cash around the house) should be kept to a minimum. Money in your billfold tends to be perishable. It sometimes gets lost and it usually gets spent. Carry enough money with you to meet ordinary daily expenses. The modern advent of checking accounts and charge cards has significantly reduced the need to carry cash around.

Checking Account

Characteristics: Convenient; requires some user effort; excellent protection against loss; low safety from user misuse; earns nothing and may cost.

A checking account is a convenient and safe place to store the money you use for ordinary expenses.

Checking accounts are convenient because you can use your money whenever you want. Most business establishments will accept personal checks. They may demand you show two credit cards, a driver's license, and submit to a thumb print and a mug shot, but ultimately they will accept your check. Regardless of the

	Convenience	User effort required	Protection from loss
Pocket money (including cash around the house)	Excellent	None	Poor
Checking account	Very good	Some	Excellent
NOW accounts	Very good	Some	Excellent
Passbook savings	Fair	Some	Excellent
Money market mutual funds	Good	Some	Good
Investment checking accounts	Very good	Fair amount	Good but subject to investment fluctuations
Savings certificates (including All-Savers)	Poor	Some	Excellent

indignities you are subjected to, paying by check is usually quite convenient.

Checking accounts are also safe from loss. If your checkbook is accidentally lost, it normally isn't too serious. Forgery is rare and you are not held responsible even if your signature is forged. The bank has no right to honor checks without your personal signature. In turn, the bank can tag the merchant for the loss if he accepts a forged check. (See why your grocer asks for credit cards, driver's licenses, thumb prints, and mug shots?) Nor is there any meaningful risk that the bank will lose your money. No insured depositor has lost a dime due to bank failure since the Federal Deposit Insurance Corporation came into being back in the thirties. This is true even though there have been some spectacular bank collapses during that

Protection against user misuse	Earnings	Purpose
Poor	None	Small day-to-day needs
Low	None	Regular living expenses
Low	Fair	Checking and savings
Fair	Fair	Emergencies and identifiable future expenses
Low	Very good	Savings with checking
Very low	Potentially excellent	Investment with checking
Very good	High	Savings

time. So the risk of loss with a checking account is almost nonexistent.

Besides being convenient and safe, a properly handled checking account aids efficient money management. If deposits and withdrawals are faithfully recorded, you have an accurate figure of your balance at all times. Further, you have a precise record of your transactions, the amount, the purpose, and when they were made. Not only is all this information in your check register but, in addition, you get all your checks back at the end of the month. In most cases, cancelled checks are as good, or better, evidence of payment than receipts. This is a big advantage at income tax time.

Despite all their advantages, checking accounts also have their disadvantages. For instance, they can be too convenient. A checkbook can burn a hole in some folks' pockets just about as fast as a ten-dollar bill. And sometimes the hole is a lot deeper. Then there is the fact that people frequently get themselves into all kinds of red ink by writing checks against insufficient funds. Most of the time bounced checks are accidental. It turns out that the check writer has misfigured the balance, or hasn't figured it at all. Incidentally, writing checks against insufficient funds is illegal. Then there is always the financial wizard, like the person I knew, that called the bank and said "What do you mean I'm out of money? I still have some checks left!"

How much money should you keep in your checking account? Just what you need to work with during the month. Don't tie money up in a regular checking account that can be earning interest somewhere else.

Savings-Plus-Checking and NOW Accounts

Characteristics: Convenient, requires some user effort; excellent protection against loss; low safety from user misuse; earns a modest amount of interest.

Today new laws are allowing banks to offer checking accounts that pay interest, and savings institutions to offer savings accounts that offer checking. There are some technical legal differences between these new accounts and your old checking or savings accounts. But you needn't worry about the technical differences. You make deposits the same way, and people will still take your checks in the same way. You should use them and take care of them just like a checking account.

There is one key difference: when you get your statement each month you'll notice the bank or savings institution has added interest rather than deducted service charges from your balance. That's nice. So if you can, for the 1980s you should have a savings-plus-checking account rather than a simple checking account.

Of course, there is no free reindeer fry. The minimum required balance for these interest-bearing checking accounts is pretty big. Usually $1000 or $2000 or more is required. You may not be able to squirrel away that much money. Or you may not *want* to tie that much money up. These accounts pay interest at 5 percent to 5½ percent. You may have better opportunities for your money. So if you don't need a couple of thousand in your checking/savings account all the time, these accounts could cost you money.

Passbook Savings Account

Characteristics: Relatively convenient; little user effort required; excellent protection against loss; moderate protection from user misuse; produces moderate earnings.

Most passbook savings accounts are insured like most checking accounts and thus are very safe. But most passbook savings accounts are somewhat inconvenient to use. The passbook must be taken (or mailed) to the savings institution in order to make deposits or withdrawals.

The big advantage of savings accounts, of course, is the fact that they pay interest. Today, rates of 5 percent to 5½ percent are common on insured passbook savings. These are not high rates of interest today but, obviously, anyone would prefer to earn interest on the money they've got stored rather than to receive none.

The rates paid on savings accounts are the same as on NOW accounts. Why would anyone want a regular passbook savings account—which is only relatively convenient—when they could have a NOW account—which is very convenient? Well, a NOW account may be too convenient. Some people may not want to be able to write checks against all their savings. Some people need a little inconvenience to keep them from spending everything.

The money that should be kept in a savings account, therefore, is money you need for a specific purpose, at a specific time—money that must be safe, but money you don't want too easily exposed to your everyday spending habits.

Money Market Mutual Funds

Characteristics: Relatively convenient; some user effort required; safe from loss–but not insured; low protection from user misuse; produces high income.

One of the most startling phenomena of the past few years has been the explosive growth of money market mutual funds. Money in huge amounts has drained out of savings and checking accounts into these funds.

The reason for the heavy flow of money into money market mutual funds is that they are a product designed to meet the needs of the 1980s and the financial upheaval we all face.

You probably have wondered if you should use a money market mutual fund. And you probably should—if you can. And the only reason you might not be able to is that it usually requires an initial investment of anywhere from $1000 to $10,000 just to open an account.

Before you do open an account, however, you should know what a money market fund is—and what it isn't.

In the 1970s interest rates began to climb. Soon the interest rate that the government and major corporations had to pay for their borrowings was above what banks and savings institutions could legally pay their savers. If savers could only put their money directly with the government or major corporations, they could earn a lot more on their funds. But it requires large amounts of cash to deal directly with those large borrowers (millions of dollars to do it properly).

Very few ordinary people have millions. But ordinary people can get together, pool their funds in a mutual fund, and together they can have millions. The large mutual fund companies have seen this. Since they are in the business of running mutual funds it was natural they would start money market funds, and they did.

Thousands of ordinary people have poured millions into the funds. With the millions the fund managers can go directly to large borrowers and buy their short-term high-interest debt instruments. Then the interest can be paid to the ordinary people.

Who are the borrowers? There are many large borrowers—large corporations like Sears, General Motors, General Electric, and hundreds of others who have very large appetites for short-term borrowing. They can get these short-term loans from banks. Or they can get them from selling what is known as commercial paper. Commercial paper is a note. The company may borrow $10 million today and agree to repay it—plus interest—in 180 days, or thirty days, or next Thursday perhaps.

Another large class of borrowers is banks. They will borrow millions by selling certificates of deposit, or bankers' acceptances, or repurchase agreements. These are all short-term debt instruments which will be repaid with interest in anywhere from one day to one year.

Finally, there is the hulk of all borrowers—the federal government. The government's appetite for money is insatiable. As part of its borrowing program it sells short-term notes and treasury bills.

Money market funds buy notes from all the above with the pooled money of their investors. The interest on the notes accrues to the investors on a daily basis. Because free market interest rates fluctuate, the earnings on a money market mutual fund change every day.

Individual borrowers come in and out of the market depending on their needs. But total demand for money is fairly steady. For example, J. C. Penney may not need money for a few weeks and withdraws from the market. But at the same time someone like Deere Corporation may need to borrow more, and they will pick up the slack. This steadiness of demand is quite important. If no one needed to sell short-term debt instruments, the money funds would have nothing to buy and would be out of business. But there is no risk of that—there is always a borrower out there somewhere.

Investors' needs for cash change all the time too. Originally, money funds were thought of as a place for investors to park money temporarily while they were waiting to make more permanent investments in stocks or bonds. Originally, many people feared that all investors would try to get out of the fund on the same day. Massive liquidations could ruin a fund.

Experience proved, however, that money fund investors were at least as stable as borrowers. For every investor wanting to get out on a given day there was another investor wanting to put money in.

This stability of total borrowers and total lenders has been the key to the evolution of services offered by money market funds.

⬥ Since the original thought was of money awaiting more permanent investment, investors could only invest in fairly large chunks—say $1000 at a time, and withdrawals could take several weeks.

⬥ Then the fund managers allowed you to transfer from their money funds directly to one of their other mutual funds without delay.

⬥ Then the funds agreed to transfer money directly from the fund to your bank.

⬥ Then the funds began to allow checks to be written directly against your account like a regular checking account.

⬥ Today you can find money funds that accept deposits of all denominations, check writing in any amount, automatic bill paying, credit card transactions, automatic transfers, and more.

Today some money market funds are as convenient to use as the best checking accounts, more convenient to use than many savings accounts—and they pay interest. In recent years the interest they've paid has been quite high—more than investors could have earned in most alternatives.

With money funds so convenient and offering so much service and paying high rates of interest, why should anyone want a checking or savings account anymore? Well, many people don't seem to want their checking or savings accounts anymore. Money funds are offering very heavy competition. Many people are moving their dollars to money market funds. And these people are probably smart to move their money as long as they understand a few shortcomings the funds have:

First, the interest they pay changes every day, depending on the money markets. The interest on savings accounts is not volatile.

Second, the interest rate has been high, but it could plunge rapidly. It could wind up below savings accounts. Of course, you could liquidate your fund at that point and move your money elsewhere.

Third, they are not insured by any agency of the government. If a loss should occur you will suffer.

Fourth, the market value of nearly all funds has been stable, meaning $1.00 invested stayed $1.00. But theoretically the market value could fluctuate; $1.00 could become $0.98 or $0.95, or $1.05. It is not likely, but it is possible to lose money.

Fifth, it is possible a fund could be unable to meet withdrawals on request with cash. In that case they can delay your request, or send securities instead (which would be useless to most investors).

With all this, are they safe? Well . . . yes, we think so. Thus far there have been no losses. But they are not as safe as a government insured checking or savings account. It would require a massive financial panic or a sizeable fraud to result in much loss to participants of a good money market fund. These things are not likely—but they are possible.

Selecting a Money Market Fund

Once you've decided you'd like to use a money fund, selecting among the many can be a chore. There are hundreds available. They are offered by nearly all mutual fund companies and major brokers. They are not offered by banks or savings institutions because the law won't allow it yet. But if and when the law changes, they'll offer them too. And there is a good chance the law will allow banks and savings institutions to offer them very soon. Use the following criteria *in this order* to select your fund: (1) convenience and services; (2) safety; (3) expense; (4) investment return. To examine these criteria go to a large library or brokerage house. Ask to see their Weisenberger or Lipper Investment Company Services. Turn to the sections that describe money market funds and compare them.

1. *Convenience and service:* Can you deal with a nearby office where you can transact business in a hurry if necessary? Do they offer checkwriting? If so, can you write a check for any amount? Most have minimums of $500, but a few do not. Do they offer credit cards and/or bill paying services? A few do. Is there a large minimum required to open an account ($1000 is typical)? Are minimum deposits required? Automatic reinvestment of dividends, bank wire services, automatic withdrawal plans, Keogh and IRA plans are generally offered by all.

2. *Safety:* As previously indicated none are insured, none can absolutely guarantee no loss, all have fluctuating earnings. Still the risk should be small. You can reduce the risk further by buying a fund operated by a large, well-capitalized, experienced firm. Check the prospectus—they should plan to invest in paper rated A1 or P1 by Standard and Poors or Moody's rating service, or the equivalent. U.S. government obligations are the most secure. Foreign obligations are less secure and too many foreign sounding names in the portfolio is a telltale sign. Finally, avoid any fund whose share price has fluctuated at all in the past five years.

3. *Expense:* All funds charge management fees; they should be 0.5 percent or lower. All funds charge for expenses. The expense ratio should be 0.6 percent or lower—many will be more. This criterion will trim the field. Finally, a few charge a sales commission or load. Do not pay a sales commission.

4. *Investment return:* Believe it or not this is least important. Funds run with similar attention to quality of investment will have very similar investment results over time. The biggest difference in return will be the expenses they charge. Some funds consistently

get slightly higher returns by making lower quality investments. A money fund is not the place to reach for return—it isn't worth it.

As we look forward into the 1980s it becomes obvious that money market funds are changing the shape of the financial world. Once you understand what they are—and what they are not—you may want to let them change your financial world.

Investment Checking Accounts

Characteristics: Relatively convenient; a fair amount of user effort required; subject to normal investment fluctuations; very poor protection from user misuse; produces potentially high earnings.

There is a new invention on the market that may wind up doing everything today's checking accounts, NOW accounts, savings accounts, money market mutual funds, and investment accounts can do. With this concept you put all your investments and cash in one place with a securities broker. You'll probably need $20,000 just to open the account. The investments can be stocks, bonds, options, commodities, gold, or many other assets. Cash is also acceptable. The cash will be invested in a money market fund earning interest at prevailing market levels.

The broker will supply you with checks that look like any others. You will also receive a major bank credit card. When you write a check or use the credit card, the amount is deducted first from your cash held in the money market fund, and then, if you do not have enough there, you automatically receive a margin loan with your investments as collateral. New deposits pay off the loans first and are then invested in the money market funds.

The advantage in these accounts is that your money is always working as hard as possible and they are just as convenient as a checking account.

But this new financial technology is not for everyone. It takes $20,000 or more just to get started. Then great spending discipline is necessary or you'll wind up spending all your investments. There is still another very important difference: these accounts are not checking accounts with banks. That means they are not insured by the government, they are not examined by bank regulators, and the underlying assets change value all the time with market valuations.

This means you could see the value of your account decline suddenly and sharply when you least expect it.

Today these investment accounts are available only through a few large brokerage firms. But that appears certain to change. You can expect your bank to offer something of a competitive nature in the next year or so.

In the past the law has restricted banks from offering products like money market funds and investment checking accounts. But that is changing. Banks will receive more flexibility from the Reagan administration and they will use the flexibility to give you new products tailored to meet the financial challenges of the 1980s.

Use these new accounts if they are appropriate for you. They are the latest thing and they are great. But remember you will need more spending discipline than ever before. Now you can write checks against your savings, your investments, your future retirement, your kids' college, and anything else you might be saving and investing for.

Savings Certificates

Characteristics: Inconvenient; little user effort required; excellent protection against loss; good protection from user misuse; earns high income.

In recent years banking and savings institutions have offered new products which you may successfully use to help manage in the 1980s.

Today there are many savings certificates available. Most require you to tie your money up for three to ten years, which can be very inconvenient. Early withdrawal requires a substantial penalty. Certificates of this length should be considered investments rather than a place to keep your spending money.

Financial institutions do offer twenty-six-week savings certificates. These certificates pay interest that is pegged to the government treasury bill rate. In recent years that has generally been a more attractive rate than many small investors could get anywhere else.

The T-bill rate changes weekly. This means you can not be sure what rate you will get if you go to buy a certificate next week. But once you have purchased the certificate, the rate is fixed for the entire twenty-six weeks. These certificates are appropriate places to store money that you do not need for six months.

But if you withdraw your money before the twenty-six weeks, you will suffer a penalty in the form of interest reduction. However, you will not lose any of your principal.

This form of inconvenience and potential penalty is good discipline for many people. It helps them leave the money in savings, where they intended it to be.

The money is safe from institutional losses as well. If your certificate is purchased from a federally insured institution your money will be insured up to $100,000.

All-Savers Certificates

Characteristics: Inconvenient; little user effort required; excellent protection against loss; good protection from user misuse; earns high tax-free income.

This new and unique savings certificate deserves special mention. It is a creation of the 1981 Reagan tax package.

What is unique is that interest on the certificate is free from federal taxes. An individual can exempt up to $1000 ($2000 on a joint return) of interest from taxes.

Should you buy? The certificates are definitely worth your consideration if your marginal federal tax rate is 30 percent or more. (Depending on your state you may need a tax rate much higher than 30 percent to make All-Savers attractive. In many states these certificates are subject to state taxes. And in some states government treasury bills are not subject to state taxes. If one or both of these conditions exist in your state, All-Savers probably won't be attractive unless your tax rate is well over 30 percent. Maybe as high as 40 percent.)

Your tax rate is important because the interest rate on All-Savers Certificates is set at 70 percent of the government treasury bill rate. Other taxable certificates you can buy from the same bank or thrift institution will pay interest equal to the treasury bill rate. So, if your tax rate is *below* 30 percent you are better off buying the taxable certificate, and paying your taxes. And remember, tax rates will be lower in 1982 and 1983 than they were in 1981.

(A surprisingly large number of people dislike government and taxes so much that they will buy these tax-exempt certificates even though their tax rates are way below 30 percent. It makes them feel good not to pay taxes. But in these days of high prices when every dollar has to count, it can be an expensive form of vengeance.)

If your tax rate is over 30 percent you may want to consider an All-Savers Certificate. If you do you should know the following:

◇ The certificates are written for one year from date of purchase.

◇ There is a substantial penalty in the form of taxes and lost interest for early withdrawal. The penalty does not include loss of original principal.

◇ There is a $500 minimum purchase required.

◇ The certificates are insured to $100,000 by an agency of the government when the issuing institution is insured by the FDIC or FSLIC.

◇ A new rate is posted each month for certificates sold that month. (Once a certificate has been sold its rate is constant for the life of the certificate.) The rate is pegged at 70 percent of the treasury-bill rate established at the treasury's monthly auction.

◇ The pricing system leaves you a little room for strategy. The treasury auction is held the third Thursday of each month. You can learn the rate by following the financial section of any decent newspaper. Then you can calculate the new rate applied to All-Savers Certificates. But the new rate does not become effective until the following Monday. That leaves you all day Friday to figure out whether the new rate will be higher or lower. If higher, postpone your purchase to Monday. If lower, make your purchase Friday.

◇ Signing up is very easy. Just walk into any participating bank or thrift institution and ask; they will help you with the transaction.

◇ You can buy an All-Savers Certificate with cash, or you can use an existing twenty-six-week certificate if you own one. You will not be penalized for rolling the twenty-six-week certificate into the All-Savers.

◇ You can—but should not—overinvest. Only the first $1000 of interest ($2000 for a joint return) is tax exempt. But these levels should give you plenty of leeway. For instance, if the interest rate is 12½ percent, you can buy $8000 of certificates before exceeding the $1000-interest level. If you earn more than $1000 interest, the excess will be taxable.

⋄ Current legislation gives authority to sell the certificates only through December 1982. (However, many observers believe Congress will extend the program because it is so popular.)

Your interest in All-Savers Certificates should center on what they can do to help you manage better in the 1980s. Ask yourself if All-Savers make sense for you. Are you in the right tax bracket? Do you have money to tie up for one year? Do you have better investment alternatives?

These certificates are worth your consideration. They are one of the new products that can be a benefit in managing for the 1980s.

◇ 18 ◇
How to Use a
Checking Account (Correctly)

Most people are familiar with checking accounts. Some of the information contained in this chapter may not be new and useful to you. If so, I invite you to skip it. However, I suggest that rather than skipping it completely you skim it. There is a real possibility you will learn a few new things about your good old checking account.

A checking account is a great money convenience. It makes your money life easier. It allows you to pay most of your bills from the comfort of your home without needing to run all over town with a pocketful of cash.

A checking account is a marvelous invention that allows you to deposit money in a bank (probably by check) and then to use it anywhere in the world. And using it is easy—simply write a few numbers on a small slip of paper and sign it. Furthermore, your money is safe. It is far safer than cash.

A checking account is safe and convenient, but if you don't use it properly, a checking account can be trouble. The following procedures should be followed when handling checks.

Proper Endorsement

Nearly everyone receives a check at some time. In order to use the check, it must be endorsed. Be sure you endorse it properly, as follows:

1. Write your name on the back as it appears on the front.

2. With just your name on the back, the check becomes a bearer instrument. That means it is like cash. Anyone can pick it up and use it. Use this simple endorsement only if you are going to cash

the check. Don't endorse the check until you get to the checkout stand or teller's cage. Don't mail checks with this simple endorsement, and don't leave them where they can be stolen.

3. To deposit a check in your checking or savings account, write *For Deposit Only,* followed by your signature:

FOR DEPOSIT ONLY
Melvin of the Mountains

4. If you want to give someone a check made out to you, write *Pay to the Order of,* followed by his or her name, and then your signature:

PAY TO THE ORDER OF
Lilly Leprechaun
Melvin of the Mountains

5. When you endorse someone else's check, you are agreeing to cover the check yourself if for any reason the bank refuses to honor it.

Proper Writing

A check can be written on anything. Checks have even been written on pieces of scrap lumber. All that is required is an order signed by you instructing your bank to pay a specified amount out of your account. But scrap lumber is not convenient to carry around in your purse—checks are easier.

Part of the information is to fulfill legal requirements, part of it is for handling, and part of it is for convenience.

The parts to be most concerned about when writing a check are the legally significant items you must fill in.

Today, most checks include the following information:

1. *Date.* Be sure to date the check.

2. *Name of person or organization receiving the money.* If the check is made out to "Cash," it is just like currency and anyone can cash

Name(s), address and phone number of account holder(s)

Place to name person being paid

Numerical identification of bank

Amount in numbers

Date

Your check number

267

JOHN AND MARY DOE
120 MAIN STREET
ANYTOWN, USA 40036
(612) 555-0011

April 30 1982

$ 375.00

22-21
960

PAY TO THE ORDER OF *Rentco Company*

Three hundred seventy-five and no/100 ——— DOLLARS

Amount in writing

THE 1st NATIONAL BANK
1000 PARK BLVD.
ANYTOWN, USA 40036

Name of bank

memo *Rent*

Place to note what the check is for

John Doe

Authorized signature

⑈2200210⑈7 ⑈267⑈0101208221

Identifying machine-readable numbers:

Bank identification

Check number (optional)

Account number

it. It is unwise to leave this blank. Anyone could pick it up and write his or her own name in.

3. *Amount in numbers.* Always record the amount. Don't sign a blank check. Any amount could be filled in over your signature if you leave it blank.

4. *Amount written out.* Draw a wavy line in front of the amount. This prevents someone altering the amount by adding numbers in front. If the written amount and the numerical amount disagree, the written amount will be accepted.

5. *Authorized signature.* The check is no good unless it has an authorized signature. Any other signature is a forgery. Experts say the most difficult signatures to forge are clearly written, legible signatures.

6. *Notation of the purpose for the check.* This is purely a convenience for you and the person you are paying.

Properly filling out your checks can help protect you against problems and losses. But you must exercise care beyond proper writing. Don't leave your checks lying around in public places where they can be easily stolen. People do forge checks.

To some degree, you are protected against check forgery. Banks are not authorized to honor checks without authorized signatures. If they do, they must repay the amount to the account. In turn, the bank may be able to go back to the person who presented them with the check. For example, if a grocery store accepts a forged check, then presents it to the bank for payment, the bank can go back to the grocer. Now, all this probably means you won't lose any money due to forgeries. But if your name has ever been forged, just try cashing a legitimate check at that grocery store or perhaps any grocery store: They'll have your name on a list of accounts not to accept. Handle your checks carefully: you can avoid a lot of hassle by doing so.

There is a more common way of getting into hassles in trying to cash checks. The most common way is by writing checks against insufficient funds. Usually people make this mistake by accident: They make mistakes in adding, or a deposit doesn't clear in time, or their spouses write checks without communicating, or they forget to record a check, and so forth. Having checks "bounce" is not only a hassle, it is downright embarrassing. Worse yet, it is expensive. Both the merchant and the bank may charge you for handling the bad check. With good management, you can avoid this mistake.

Sometimes a check written against insufficient funds is no mistake. The writer knows he or she doesn't have the money when he or she writes the check. This is a crime; people can go to jail for bouncing checks. At a minimum, the bank account will be closed, and the individual's check-cashing privileges will cease.

Cashing checks in some ways is a privilege, because those who deal with you by check are trusting you. It is very convenient for you to pay by check. So it is worthwhile to follow good procedures and protect this convenient money privilege.

How to Balance Your Checkbook

The only way a checkbook can be balanced is with accuracy. In fact, accuracy is the whole reason for balancing a checkbook. When you balance your checkbook, you are trying to reconcile the amount your checkbook shows with the amount your bank shows. You have to make certain that everyone has been accurate and no one has made any mistakes.

Because you are far more likely than the bank to make a mistake, personal accuracy is important. If you keep your checkbook carefully as you go along, balancing your checkbook at the end of the month should be easy. Here are the three most important things to do in keeping your checkbook accurately.

1. Write down every check and deposit in your checkbook. Record these transactions as you make them. It is amazing how often thoroughly intelligent people write checks and then forget to record the amounts in their checkbook. Obviously, the balance in their checkbook will be wrong. To avoid missing an entry, it is a good practice to record the amount in the checkbook first, and then write the check.

2. Be sure that the amount you record in your checkbook agrees with the amount on the check or deposit slip.

3. Add and subtract carefully. The majority of inaccuracies are in simple arithmetic. It is a good idea to do the arithmetic on a ma-

chine. Today, calculators are so small and so inexpensive anyone can have one.

It's a good idea to keep your checkbook accurate as you go along. Try to balance your checking account as soon as the statement comes from the bank. If any errors have been made, you want to discover and correct them as soon as possible. The procedure is as follows.

First, *examine the statement*. Statements are organized by different banks in different ways, but they all have the same key information:

◇ *A date*. The date indicates when the statement was prepared.

◇ *A beginning or previous balance*. The previous balance is the same number that showed as the current or ending balance last month.

◇ *A summary of activity*. The summary will show the total amount of deposits and the total amount of withdrawals. Deposits are "credits" to the account. Withdrawals are "debits" to the account.

◇ *A current or ending balance*. This balance is the amount the bank showed in your account at the time the statement was prepared. This figure probably will not be the same as the current balance you show in your checkbook. The differences occur because of the time it takes checks and deposits to clear the bank. For example, if you write a check and drop it in the mail to a friend it will take days, maybe weeks, to clear the bank. Several days in the mail to your friend, several more days until he deposits it, a day or two for his bank to record it and present it to your bank for payment. You deducted the check when you wrote it. The bank deducts the check when they find out about it. They find out about it when it is presented for payment. The time lag results in different balances. The amount shown on your statement is not necessarily available for you to spend.

◇ *An item-by-item listing of all transactions in your account*. Some statements list the transactions chronologically. Some will list them in sequence by your check number. In either case, the date that is shown is the date the bank processed the transaction. It is not the date you wrote the check.

◇ *An individual listing of special charges*. Some charges may not have been recorded in your checkbook. These include service charges, cost of checks, automatic payments, safe deposit box rent, and charges for handling returned checks.

◇ *A section explaining all the codes.* Codes are used by the bank to identify various transactions.

◇ *A form to assist you in balancing your checkbook.* This form is usually on the back of the statement.

Second, *record all transactions in your checkbook.* The bank may have recorded transactions that you do not show in your checkbook, such as service charges, payment for checks, payments for safe deposit box, automatic payments, and special handling charges.

Third, *organize all the returned or cancelled checks.* Follow the sequence recorded in your checkbook.

Fourth, *note all transactions that have cleared.* Also note those that have not cleared. Go line by line down your checkbook. In the check register, there is a small column to check if the transaction has cleared. Actually, it is a good idea to note the month the transaction cleared in this column. This makes for easy future reference.

Fifth, *carefully list all uncleared transactions.* Your checkbook will show those checks have not yet cleared the bank. Use the form on the back of your bank statement for this list. Checks that are still out are recorded by number and amount. Deposits that haven't been credited are recorded in a separate section.

Sixth, *follow the instructions on the back of your statement.* The following is a typical example:

Checks not cleared		*Deposits not credited*	
426	$ 12.53	Sept 3	$612.15
431	1.80	Sept 7	5.35
432	707.00	Total	$618.50
444	75.00		
Total	796.33		

Reconciliation

1. Current balance (from front of statement)	$ 436.17
2. Add deposits not credited	618.50
3. Total Lines 1 and 2	$1,054.67
4. Subtract checks not cleared	796.33
5. Subtract Line 4 from Line 3. Total should be present checkbook balance	$ 258.34

As this person went through the checkbook line by line, he or she found six transactions that had not cleared the bank when the statement was made. There were four checks outstanding, totaling $796.33. There were also two deposits not credited, totaling $618.50.

Then the reconciliation form can be used to balance the account. The form works from the current balance, shown on the statement, to the current amount shown in the checkbook. You want to wind up with the checkbook amount, because it is the only amount that matters a great deal. The checkbook amount is the amount available to be spent. In this example, the checkbook balance is $258.34. The amounts are reconciled by adding deposits the bank hasn't yet received to the statement balance. These deposits are money you have that the bank doesn't know about yet. Then subtract from that total checks that have not yet cleared. These, of course, represent money you *don't* have. If all has gone well to this point, and you have worked accurately, your checkbook should balance easily.

Unfortunately, checkbooks only seem to balance easily in books such as this one. Often the amounts do not reconcile easily. Sometimes after hours of hunting for an error the amounts still do not reconcile. What most people want from a book is not an easy explanation of the information on the statement—they want an easy explanation of how to find the error to their checkbook. But there *is* no guaranteed way to find an error, because there are so many different kinds of errors. But there are some error-finding procedures that can be tried, as follows.

1. *Subtract the checkbook and bank balance.* This determines the amount of the error.

2. *Scan the checkbook and statement for similar figures.* These entries may be the culprit.

3. *If the error is divisible by 9, the problem may be a common reversal of digits.* For example, if 31 is recorded as 13, the error will be 18. The number 18 is divisible by 9, which gives you a clue to the problem. Furthermore, the result after dividing by 9 will be equal to the difference between the digits that were reversed. The error in our example is 18; and 18 divided by 9 results in 2; and 2 is equal to the difference between the digits that were reversed. The digits were 3 and 1; the difference between them is 2.

4. *If the error is 1, or 10, or 100, and so on,* a "1" probably wasn't carried during addition, or an entry was recorded wrong by 1. For instance, 25 for 24, or 100 for 110.

5. *If the error is 3, or 30, or 300* and if you used a ten-key calculator, the error may have been in working the machine. A common error is to depress the button immediately above or below the intended key. This will produce an error of 3.

6. *Check to see if the error could be a misplaced decimal.* For example, $25.00 recorded as $2.50, or $187.00 recorded as $18,700. Misplaced decimals are common when using an electronic calculator with a floating decimal point.

7. *Re-add everything in your checkbook.* Also re-add the figures in your reconciliation. Ask another person to recheck the figures. It is easy for one person to make the same error over and over again.

8. *Double-check to make sure you have recorded all the bank's charges in your checkbook.*

9. *Check to see whether you accidentally subtracted a deposit or added a check.* You can spot this error by dividing the discrepancy by 2. The result may give you a clue to the mistake. For example, a $112 deposit recorded as a check will produce a $224 error.

10. *Double-check the amounts recorded* in your checkbook, to be certain they agree with the actual amounts on the checks and deposit slips.

11. *Be sure your checkbook was in balance last month.* Errors in previous months will carry forward until they are corrected.

And after you have done all these things, carefully check to see if the bank made an error. Banks' errors are far more rare than yours or mine. But banks do sometimes make errors. To check for bank errors,

1. Make certain the bank accurately recorded the amount of each check and deposit. Each entry is listed separately, so it can be proven.

2. Be sure the bank didn't record a deposit as a check, or vice versa.

3. Be certain you can identify every entry on the statement as your own entry.

4. You might double-check the bank's addition and subtraction, but the bank's computers are very good at basic arithmetic.

By this time, everything should reconcile. Addition and subtraction are very exact sciences. If everything is done perfectly, the figures absolutely will balance. However, if after all this effort they still don't balance, then you have four choices: (1) go back and repeat all the procedures again, (2) hire an accountant (probably your spouse), (3) hang yourself with the adding machine tape, or (4) forget it. Sure, you can forget it, it's your money. Forgetting it isn't usually recommended, but if the error is small at some point it isn't worth spending more time finding it.

If you decide to go on living without ever finding your error, be sure to fix things so you won't run into the same error again next month. Make an error-adjusting entry in your checkbook so your checkbook balance reconciles with your statement's balance. For example, if your checkbook showed $2.91 more than the statement, make the following entry:

Date	Check description	Amount of check	Amount of deposit	Balance
				$261.25
10/17	To correct error never found	$2.91		258.34

Of course, you may be lucky and get to add a little to your balance. Be discriminating though—don't forget errors if they are significant.

The difficulty in reconciling your checkbook increases as the use of your checking account increases. For example, the following will probably complicate the balancing of your checking account:

◇ Heavy usage
◇ More than one person writing checks and making deposits
◇ Using your checkbook for accrual accounting (See Chapter 14)
◇ Writing checks, then holding on to them for long periods of time
◇ Automatic charges for savings or payments
◇ Automatic overdraft protection

This type of usage is not bad. It is good. But such usage will add to the complications of balancing your checkbook.

All things considered, the only way a checkbook can be balanced is with accuracy—*your* accuracy. It is worth taking the time to be accurate. After all, for the majority of Americans the checkbook is the key to personal financial management. For most families, the checkbook is the equivalent of financial records for a corporation. If you were running a corporation, you would insist on accurate financial records—financial records that balance.

◊ Conclusion ◊

How do we manage our money? We manage our money by controlling it, rather than letting it control us. We control money by avoiding such feelings as "I can't keep track of my expenses" or "I haven't got time for it" or "I can't understand it."

It is necessary to spend a few hours a month (more, when the system is initially being set up) to keep track of what we have, where we got it from and where it's going. We keep records, establish budgets, make "want" lists, try a money calendar, and make our money work for us.

Good management is the heart of a good financial plan. It is a prerequisite to the two final steps to freedom: dealing with (1) financial traps and (2) investing.

Part IV.
Dealing With the Great Financial Traps: Credit, Risk, and Retirement

Why do I refer to these as the great financial traps? Because beyond poor money management techniques, more people have found themselves financially trapped in these areas than all others put together.

All of us have to handle them in one way or another. We can't avoid them.

Credit

In order to survive in this modern world, we have to borrow. I don't know of anyone who's able to make it any more without some borrowing. It might be only a loan to get a car, or a mortgage to buy a house. Sometimes it's massive borrowing, to finance a new business. One way or the other, we all have to face borrowing decisions. How we handle our borrowing largely determines how well off we are financially.

Borrowing wisely can lead to peace of mind and, ultimately, to financial freedom. Being financially free doesn't necessarily mean you don't owe anybody anything. It can mean you owe a great deal, but that you have more than enough income to meet all your obligations and still to leave you plenty of money over and above to live comfortably as well as to have a large net worth.

But borrowing unwisely can lead to default, foreclosure or repossession, attachment or garnishment, and even bankruptcy. It can leave you totally trapped financially.

Insurance Risk

Are there any readers out there who aren't going to die? Or any who don't have the possibility of getting sick, or being disabled, or having an accident?

The answer has to be no. We are all exposed to risk—it is part of our lives. And in the modern world—with planes, cars, a hectic pace, even dangers from radiation and pollution—the risks may be far greater to each of us than in the past. We are all mortal and therefore vulnerable to risk.

How we deal with risk is important. If disaster strikes, and we are unprepared, we can be destroyed financially. No one can be financially free if he or she has not made some preparations for unexpected risks.

The answer, of course, is insurance. We all (or almost all) buy insurance to protect against such calamities. Insurance makes sense in the world in which we live.

However, there's such a thing as being too safe, just as there's such a thing as being not safe enough. Thus far in this book, I've discussed learning to cope with the forces at work in the 1980s, with personal financial problems, and with obtaining good money management and excess funds through budgeting and through wise borrowing. But what good is it all if one gets financially wiped out through a health disaster? Or as a corollary, if one spends too much of one's income overprotecting oneself?

In this section, I'll examine the kind and amounts of insurance people should have. How people meet this challenge goes a long way toward determining if they ever become financially independent.

Retirement

Finally, there is retirement. For many, retirement is the ultimate financial trap. You see, you can lose everything to unwise borrowing or unprotected risks, and still recover. But if you reach retirement with too little to live on, there is no way to recover and escape.

This is especially critical when we realize most retirees are hurt more by inflation than anyone else. They are hurt because they are on fixed incomes. The financial upheaval has trapped and buried many of this nation's senior citizens.

But what about you individually?

Will you individually prosper during your later years, or will you suffer?

I've heard people say, "I'm not worried about retirement. Somehow I'll have plenty of money by then to see me through."

I certainly hope it works out that way. But just in case there isn't that big reserve of wealth we had counted on for the future, shouldn't you begin retirement plans?

When is the time to start planning for retirement? The time is right now. It's never too early. Simply by mastering some skills in retirement planning at an early age, you can provide a net to catch you if you should fall at an age when increasing your income becomes physically impossible. In this section, I'll consider what everyone should know about retirement at any age.

These, then, are the three great financial traps that we all face: Credit, Risk, and Retirement. We cannot avoid them. We may think we're avoiding them by not bothering to learn about credit, risk, or retirement. But even doing this is handling these challenges—it's just handling them poorly.

And in the 1980s, handling them poorly will be more serious than ever before. That's why a large portion of this book is devoted to explaining in detail what each of these areas is, and what the risks of entrapment can be.

I have also included work sections for you so that you can analyze your own needs regarding credit, risk, and retirement. Because of the importance of credit, risk, and retirement, you will find some of the personal analysis sections quite detailed. I hope you will spend a few minutes with them. It has been my experience that they are very beneficial.

We have a choice—be prepared, or not. Given the importance of credit, risk, and retirement, I can't imagine anyone not wanting to be prepared.

◇ 19 ◇
What Good Is Credit?

What good is credit? It all depends on how well good credit is used. When credit is used properly, by people who can afford it, and it is used responsibly—then credit can work true financial miracles. Of course, if credit isn't used properly then it can require a true miracle to make finances work at all.

Credit is just about as miraculous an invention as money itself. Credit has contributed greatly to the high standard of living enjoyed in America. Because of credit many people have been able to buy things they might otherwise never have owned. Furthermore, credit allows many people to buy things when they need them, and to pay for them when they can. It is an interesting fact of life that typical families need to acquire most of their possessions when they are young and don't have much money. And most people need to acquire fewer possessions when they are older and have more money. Credit helps bridge the gap of this anomaly, and that in itself is a miracle.

A typical set of newlyweds, for example, is in no position to buy a car, a home, four rooms of furniture, and pay for a baby, all in the first few years of marriage. However, with good judgment they can enjoy some of these things while they are still poor, broke, struggling newlyweds. And they can pay when they are somewhat less poor, broke, and struggling.

The emphasis for newlyweds, or for anyone using credit, is good judgment. The key to good judgment in credit use is to borrow for things that should be purchased now but are better paid for later. Consider the following examples of things that "should be purchased now, but paid for later."

1. *Items that appreciate in value.* Items that go up in value are things such as homes, businesses, and investments. If you borrow for things that appreciate in value, the security behind the loan increases, and the item may return income. In some cases, the income may be enough to repay the loan and then some.

2. *You and your family.* An investment in you or your family can be one of the best possible uses of borrowed money. Borrowing for educational or career opportunities can increase your value tremendously. For example, consider the case of the man who borrowed to have his teeth straightened. The work created a noticeable improvement in his appearance and self-confidence. The self-confidence led to a noticeable improvement in his effectiveness as a salesman. His effectiveness in turn resulted in a noticeable improvement in his income. His higher income more than repaid the loan. Borrowing to invest in himself turned out to be one of the smartest moves this man ever made.

3. *Items that will lose their usefulness if you wait.* There was a family that planned to build a new home. The members were determined, however, not to go into debt for it. The house was specifically designed for the family. Each child was to have its own special bedroom, for example. However, it took so long to save the money and build the house that two of the four children were married and gone before it was completed. Within five years of the final completion of the home, the parents were all alone in their big, debt-free house, wondering if they should sell it. This family would have been justified in borrowing the money to build the home twenty years earlier, before the family grew too old to enjoy it.

Another family had a son who was a football star. The university he played for was halfway across the country. His parents were very proud of him. But unfortunately they never saw him play a game. They refused to borrow the extra money for the trip. And before they saved enough to go see a game their son's football career was over.

4. *Maintenance items.* If the refrigerator or the car breaks down, or a child gets ill, it is probably wise to borrow money to get things fixed. In fact, things that are not kept in good repair may develop more expensive problems later on. I knew a college student who needed brakes and tires on her car. She figured finances were tight enough already without borrowing extra money to maintain something such as the brakes, especially when she didn't drive very far anyway. But, as you guessed, she didn't have to drive very far—just through the corner traffic light one afternoon. Fortunately, no one was hurt seriously. But the car was demolished. Interestingly enough, the student who couldn't find the money to maintain her car found enough to buy another one.

5.*Items that are needed.* In modern America, most of us need certain things to function normally. We need places to live, we need cars, we need clothing, we need some appliances, and we need certain furnishings, for example. People are often justified in borrowing money to purchase needed items for which they haven't got ready cash. However, a reasonable individual might question whether most folks really need television sets, stereos, boats, motorcycles, fancy furniture, extended vacations, and so on.

6. *Items that will be unavailable in the future.* America is a land of plenty. Normally, if there is one item for sale there is another one exactly, or almost like it, close by. Some collectors and antique buffs could offer examples to the contrary. But as a general rule there is no rush to buy anything for fear there will never be anything like it again.

Usually the items we want to buy are available today and will be available tomorrow. What may be unavailable tomorrow is today's *price.* Occasionally the item you want goes on sale before you have all your money saved. The sale being referred to here is not just any sale, but one of those very special sales that come along every once in a while—one of those rare opportunities to buy something you need and want and are going to buy eventually anyway. The sale gives you a chance to save a lot of money if you are willing to borrow to complete the purchase. One family had been saving for a microwave oven. One day they received a call from a friend who, because of an order foul-up, could get a microwave for $75 less than the wholesale cost. The price was far below the price of similar models when they were on "sale" in the stores. It made sense for the family to borrow the money and take advantage of the bargain.

Although it is true there are many good reasons to use credit, good credit judgment must always be used. Good judgment must not be ignored no matter how important it seems to buy things now. Follow these rules of good credit judgment when considering getting a loan or when trying to decide if this is an item that really is better paid for later.

Rule 1. Be sure the things you are borrowing for really should be purchased now. Be certain all your arguments for needing to buy things now aren't just rationalizations. The rationalizations will be there next month when you want to buy something else. Unfortunately, so will the payments for the things you bought this month.

Rule 2. It is always more expensive to buy things with credit than to pay cash. The only time it is better to buy now and pay later is when there is no way to buy something now for cash. The exceptions to this rule are so rare and so theoretical they do not warrant discussion in this book. You must be charged for the use of someone else's money. The charge will come either in the form of interest and service charges or higher prices, or both.

Rule 3. Borrow to buy just what you need. On those occasions when borrowing is advisable, avoid borrowing a lot of extra money to buy a lot of extra things you really don't need. For example, suppose you absolutely need a car. Remember, what you need is basic transportation. If you must borrow to buy a car, then stick to the basics and avoid the luxury options. You have to borrow for the options as well as the transportation. The options, however, don't fit the definition of "should buy now but better paid for later."

Rule 4. Don't trade away your tomorrows for today. People sometimes forget that credit does not increase their incomes or the number of things they can buy during their lifetimes. Something purchased on credit today simply means something can't be purchased for cash, or even credit, tomorrow. Frequently, when people get to tomorrow they find out that the things they want to buy at that time are more important than what they already bought on credit yesterday.

Rule 5. Don't borrow if you can't afford it. Money that is borrowed must be repaid with interest. When debt repayments get so big people can't afford food, or clothing, or shelter, then they really can't afford to borrow. Unfortunately, by this time it is too late to do much to prevent getting overextended. The debts are already there. The only way to avoid borrowing more than you can afford is to stop borrowing while you can still afford it. (See Chapter 21, "How Much Should You Borrow?")

Rule 6. Know in advance how you are going to repay. Often people get excited about buying something, quickly take out a loan to make the purchase, and never even consider how they will repay the money. Some people seem to feel that "the money will come from somewhere." The money probably *will* come from somewhere— but snatching purses and holding up grocery stores is a less than desirable "somewhere." To avoid feeling that you will need to become an outlaw, look carefully at your future income and expenses. A salesperson may plan on repaying a loan with a bonus check. A student may plan on repaying school loans with a job after college. The business may plan to repay a factory loan with income from the investment. Of course, most loans will be repaid out of salary—future salary. The key is to make sure there is plenty of future salary to repay the loan, and to pay for everything else too.

Credit is one of those good inventions that, if properly used, can be good to the user. If credit is over used, then it is no good at all. As with taking medicine, there are rules to follow to ensure its effectiveness. When the rules are followed, it's amazing what miracles can result.

◇ 20 ◇
Where Can You Get a Loan?

You can get a loan on almost any corner. You can get a loan from the bank on the corner; the thrift institution around the corner; the stores at the shopping center that stretches from corner to corner; the gas station on the other corner; your credit union with an office in the corner; or in the comfort of your own home, where, if you like, you can sit in the corner. Modern America probably has more corners to get loans on than any society that has ever existed.

But citizens of our modern society run a risk of stopping at too many corners for too many loans. Eventually they find themselves cornered by too many debts and monthly payments.

To keep from being cornered by loans and monthly payments, you must treat debt the same way you treat anything else in your budget. You must decide objectively—away from the sales pressure—how much debt you want, what you want it for, and where you are going to get it. A brief review of the forms of credit available, their cost, convenience, and terms is helpful.

Classes of Loans

In *secured* loans, specified assets are used as collateral. Assets such as cars, furniture, and homes are frequently pledged as collateral. If the debtor fails to pay, the lender can take possession of the asset. People use secured loans because they can borrow far more money if there is collateral behind the loan. For example, many ordinary people can borrow $100,000—but only if they use their homes as security.

In *unsecured* loans, the only collateral for an unsecured loan is the borrower's signature. Unsecured loans are made only to the best credit risks. They tend to be smaller than secured loans. If the debtor fails to pay an unsecured loan, the lender can sue the borrower. The judge will probably force the borrower to sell off some assets to pay the loan.

157

Length of Loans

Short-term loans run less than a year. They are frequently small, un-secured loans.

Intermediate-term loans run one to five years. They are usually se-cured loans with installment payments.

Long-term loans run five years or more. They are nearly always secured loans, using property with a long useful life, such as a home, as collateral.

Types of Repayment on Loans

A *single-payment* loan is usually a small loan made to tide the bor-rower over for a short period of time. The entire loan plus interest is paid off at one time.

Rollover or renewable loans are really a series of single-payment loans. The borrower and lender agree in advance that each single-payment loan will be paid off with a new single-payment loan. This is called "rolling" or "renewing" the loan. Usually the lender re-quires that each loan be smaller until there is no loan. The advantage is flexibility to the borrower. He (or she) can repay large amounts when he's got the money, small amounts when he doesn't. Fur-thermore, he can keep rolling the loan over as long as the lender thinks he's a good credit risk. Usually he can increase the loan with-out difficulty if a new need arises.

In *revolving credit loans,* the lender establishes a maximum limit the borrower can borrow. The borrower then can borrow when-ever he (or she) wants until he has borrowed up to the maximum limit. All he must do to keep the loan current is pay off a portion of the balance each month: often only 10 percent. Interest is added on monthly.

Revolving loans are most often used by department stores and credit card companies. The advantage to the borrower is ease of use and flexibility. He (or she) can borrow when he wants, how much he wants, and frequently whenever he wants anywhere in the world. All he has to do is present his credit card. Furthermore, he can repay the entire loan, or just a portion, depending on his cir-cumstances.

Revolving loans have two distinct disadvantages. First, they are almost too easy to use. Many borrowers are tempted to overuse them. The stores don't help; they encourage the use of credit. There will be advertisements all through the store encouraging you to "charge it." The employees at the check stand are ordered to ask you before each purchase if you want to "charge it." Even the monthly statements you receive are frequently constructed in such a way that the only figure you can easily find is the minimum 10 percent payment. You may have to search all over to find out what your total balance is if you want to pay it all off.

The second major disadvantaage to revolving credit loans is expense. They tend to be the most expensive form of credit available. Interest rates range from 18 to 24 percent in most states. And some states have no ceilings at all. Rates like these may not seem high when the prime lending rate soars to more than 20 percent. But during most of the 1980s you can bet the prime rate will fall well below 20 percent. But you can not bet that the cost of credit card loans will fall at all. As with any other product or service, you must pay for ease and convenience.

An *installment* loan requires a fixed monthly payment for a fixed number of months. Installment loans are usually secured. The advantage of an installment loan is relatively large sums of money can be borrowed and on terms that the borrower can afford to repay. The disadvantages include the number of months or years the borrower may be tied down with payments, and the inflexibility of the loan. Installment loans are considered inflexible because a borrower unable to meet a few monthly payments on his (or her) customized Lear Jet will find it repossessed.

Purposes for Loans

Loans are made for so many purposes that it is possible to list only the most common here.

DURABLE LOANS

A durable is a car, a television set, a boat, a freezer, a bedroom set, and so on. Loans for such goods are of the installment loan variety. The borrower pays a fixed monthly payment for a specified number of months. Failure to pay can mean repossession of the durable. These loans are made by banks, finance companies, and credit unions. Interest rates are in the 12 to 24 percent range.

MORTGAGES

A mortgage is a loan on real estate. The most commonly used mortgage is for a home. Monthly payments are required for a specified number of months up to thirty years. Mortgages are usually long-term loans. Interest rates are in the 11 to 16 percent range. If a borrower fails to pay, his (or her) property can be foreclosed. A key difference in foreclosing on a home or repossessing a car, from a lender's point of view, is that a car can be moved—a home cannot. The law gives the borrower far more protection against foreclosure than against repossession. Mortgages are made by savings and loan organizations, thrift institutions, and commercial banks.

SECOND MORTGAGES
OR HOME IMPROVEMENT LOANS

Second mortgages are a cross between a durable loan and a mortgage. They are secured with the equity in a home over and above the first mortgage. They may run for five to ten years. Interest rates are in the 14 to 18 percent range. A common use of second mortgages is for home improvements, but there is a growing trend to use the money for other purposes, such as new cars. Second mortgages are made by savings and loans, thrift institutions, banks, finance companies, and companies specializing in second mortgages.

PERSONAL LOANS

Personal loans are made to cover a wide variety of needs. They provide cash for everything from a new baby to a new wardrobe. They provide cash for a trip to Tahiti or to consolidate all your other loans. Banks and finance companies are the principal sources of personal loans. Costs vary widely depending who is making the loan and to whom they are lending. Rates range from 12 to 24 percent. Personal loans are not usually secured. If the borrower doesn't repay, the lender must bring legal action to recover the money.

CHARGE ACCOUNT AND CREDIT CARD LOANS

A charge account loan is a loan made by a retailer for the specific purpose of making a purchase in their store. The borrower does.not receive cash, just merchandise. Loans of this nature are made by a wide variety of retailers, from gas stations to jewelry stores to restaurants. Banks are often in the middle of all this, with their bank cards. These loans tend to be the most expensive of all, with interest rates ranging from 18 to 36 percent.

STUDENT LOANS

A great deal of money is borrowed for school expenses. Many universities and private foundations make such loans. Banks are also a major source. The federal government will insure many student loans. Government insurance reduces the interest cost substantially. Costs are in the 12 percent range. Repayment terms are generous. Generally no payments are required until well after graduation, and many years can be used to repay after that. Student loans have become scarce because (a) their interest rates are not attractive to banks, (b) they have been abused by students who misuse the money and don't repay, and (c) the government is cutting its support. Feel fortunate if you can find one.

Sources of Loans

BANKS

Banks make most types of loans. Generally their loans are less expensive than those from other sources. Their credit standards are also generally higher than those of other sources. Many people do not like dealing with banks because banks seem cold and impersonal. Many banks are oriented to deal with big corporations. Often a bank's atmosphere reflects this orientation. However, despite this aura banks generally do seek the business of ordinary people and value their patronage highly.

SAVINGS AND LOAN,
AND THRIFT INSTITUTIONS

Savings and loan institutions deal primarily in mortgages on homes. Their rates and terms on mortgages are generally as good as any you'll find. However, things are changing. The thrift institutions are one of the real victims of the financial upheaval. Many won't survive. And, in the future, those that do survive will look and act more like banks than good old thrift institutions.

FINANCE COMPANIES

Finance companies principally make personal loans and durable loans for cars, and so forth. Their credit standards are not as stringent as a bank's, they deal mostly with individuals, and their rates are higher, too.

CREDIT UNIONS

Credit unions are generally sponsored by major employers or unions. Employees are thus able to open savings accounts that pay competitive interest rates. The credit unions in turn lend these funds to employees that need loans. Credit unions make personal and installment loans on durables such as cars. Frequently, the credit union is the least expensive place to borrow. The costs are low because the sponsoring institution often provides office space and personnel at little or no cost to the credit union.

RETAILERS

Stores and retail outlets have entered the lending business in a big way in the past two decades. Many major chains have their own finance subsidiaries. Others accept credit cards sponsored by banks. Rarely are retailers a source of cheap credit. Their advantage is strictly one of convenience and availability. After all, if you're browsing through the pet store and fall in love with a baby cobra for only $89.98 plus tax, it is very inconvenient to drop everything, rush to the bank, fill out twelve loan applications, wait a day for approval, and then rush back to the pet store to buy your snake. Instead, it is much more convenient just to reach for your credit card, buy your snake on credit, and take your chances on being bitten.

LIFE INSURANCE COMPANIES

Insurance companies are not really in the business of making loans directly to individuals. However, if you have a life insurance policy with cash value you can borrow against it up to the cash value of the policy. Often this is the least expensive source for a personal loan. It becomes very popular when interest rates are high. But don't die while you have the loan. The loan gets paid out of your life insurance benefits before your beneficiaries do.

MORTGAGE COMPANIES

As the name implies, mortgage companies specialize in first and second mortgages. Generally they resell the mortgage to interested buyers all over the country. Their advantage is that they may be able to take on an unusual mortgage or make a loan when everyone else in the city is out of money.

PAWNBROKERS

Pawnbrokers will lend anyone money and will accept personal items, such as diamond-studded pinky rings, as collateral. Their rates are very high. And if you don't repay on time they'll sell your ring to someone else's pinky.

RELATIVES, FRIENDS AND EMPLOYERS

Even though state laws theoretically cover all loans in practical terms, there really are no rules when it comes to loans from relatives, friends, and employers. Amounts, purposes, terms, and so on are wide open for negotiation. There is one important thing to remember—it won't be a true "arms-length" transaction. The relative, friend, or employer will make the loan not because of your credit worthiness, or because they are in business to make loans. They will make the loan because of your relationship. You should live up to every agreement and more, unless you don't mind wrecking that relationship.

LOAN SHARKS

Sources of loans are available on the streets of most big cities. The money comes from questionable sources. The interest rates are illegally high. And the collection tactics involve everything up to and including murder—your murder. Clearly, loan sharks are to be avoided at all costs, no matter how much trouble you are in.

Important Characteristics of Loans

Loans differ. They have important characteristics the borrower should be interested in.

COST

Cost is the interest rate you will be charged for borrowing the money. Besides interest, you may be charged certain fees for credit searches, loan initiation, and so forth. You should look at the lowest-cost loans, but you will have to pay something. Remember, there is no free borrowed lunch money.

EASE OF APPLICATION

Lenders naturally want to know a little about you. This has nothing to do with their personal sociability; they simply want to know if you're going to pay them back. Of course, *you* know you're going to pay them back, but they don't. So you'll have to fill out an application. Some credit applications can be pretty involved. Generally speaking, the complexity of the application procedure increases as the size of the loan rises.

CREDIT STANDARDS

Standards for giving credit vary considerably depending on where you borrow, how much you borrow, how long you'll keep the money, and what collateral you put up to secure the loan. Most places want to know about your job, how long you've worked there, and if you own your own home. They also want to know what kind of credit risk you've been in the past, so they'll ask for references. They will also check with local credit bureaus to see what other creditors have said about you.

FLEXIBILITY OF REPAYMENT

The terms of some loans are cut and dried. Others allow borrowers to repay a lot or a little, depending on how they are fixed for money that month. And with many loans, people can borrow more if the need arises.

BORROWING LIMITS

How much you can borrow is of great interest to most would-be borrowers. Most borrowers are restricted by their own ability to repay. That is, a lender will loan a person with a $20,000-per-year salary more money than the lender will loan a person with a $15,000 salary. But institutions also have limits. Regulatory authorities restrict the size of loans that institutions can make. The restrictions are based on the company's size and the type of institution it is. As a practical matter, most ordinary Americans don't have to worry about the limits on the lender.

LENGTH OF REPAYMENT

Frequently people who need to borrow want as long as possible to repay. Length increases with the size of the loan and the collateral. Often the useful life of the item being purchased is the key to length of the loan. A car loan might cover four years; a real estate loan might cover forty.

The following tables can serve as a convenient reference for determining where to look for what types of loans and what characteristics each has. Even though America seems to be a land where you can get a loan on just about any corner, it is important to go shopping at the right corner the first time.

Type of Loan and Place to Borrow

Places to borrow	Durable (auto)	Mortgage	Second mortgage home improvement	Personal	Charge account
Bank	X	X	X	X	X
Finance company	X		X	X	
Savings and loan, or thrift institution		X	X		
Credit union	X			X	
Retailer	X				X
Mortgage company		X	X		
Life insurance company				X	
Pawnbroker				X	
Relative, friend, or employer				X	

Types of Loans and Important Characteristics

Important characteristics	Durable (auto)	Mortgage
Cost	12%–24%	11%–16%
Ease of application	Moderate application form; minor credit check	Extensive application form; extensive credit check
Credit standards	Need job; no major past-due accounts	Difficult; need steady job, consistent work history; clean credit history
Flexibility of repayment	Limited	Limited
Borrowing limits	Based on value of durable; 75–90% of value normal	Based on value of property; 80% conventional; up to 95% possible
Length of repayment	Based on life expectancy of durable; 2 to 5 years typical	25 to 30 years typical

If You Can Get a Loan, Should You Take It?

Before you ask, "Should I take the loan?" ask, "Do I want to pay for it?" Loans cost money. Think of the cost as rent. When you use things owned by other people, you expect to pay rent. You can rent homes, television sets, cars, and tents, scuba diving equipment, and hospital beds. You can rent just about anything, including money. The money you borrow, after all, does belong to someone else. That someone else wants the money back, and then some. The "and then some" is the rent or interest on the borrowed money.

The rent on money makes things cost much more than their sticker prices. Let's say your eye has been caught by a turbo-powered snowmobile with a sticker price of $10,000. Let's say you

Second mortgage (home improvement)	Personal	Charge and credit cards
14%–18%	12%–24%	18%–36%
Moderate application form and credit check	Application forms and check vary but normally moderate	Easy application; little or no credit check
Need good home equity, job; no major past-due accounts	Varies, but need some way to repay, not necessarily a job	Need job and phone; consistent history of pay
Limited	Usually flexible	Can increase at will; repay 10% minimum or more
Based on equity in home; will lend to 95% of value	Varies with need; $2,000 to $3,000 typical limit	Predetermined limit; $300 to $2,000 typical
5 to 10 years typical	90 days up to 5 years	Perpetual; 8–10% minimum required monthly

don't have $10,000. The logical thing to do is get a turbo-powered snowmobile loan at 18 percent interest for forty-eight months. Your monthly payments will run $293.75, not including tax and insurance. But the real cost is $14,100, or $293.75 a month times forty-eight months. If the sticker price were $14,100, would you still be interested in the snowmobile? The difference in cost is over 41 percent. The 41 percent, of course, is the cost of renting the bank's money for four years while you race around the snow-covered landscape.

Your rent may actually work out to be less than 41 percent because the government will help you pay the rent so to speak. The government allows you to deduct interest from income taxes. If you are in a 25 percent tax bracket, your total after-tax cost would be $13,075. But even with the government's generosity, your cost is nearly 31 percent higher than if you paid cash.

Sometimes when people see how much the price goes up due to money rent, they decide to put off buying the item until they can pay cash. Sometimes, however, there isn't much choice. Sometimes you must borrow the money, pay the rent on it, and endure the higher cost. For example, let's say you're an Eskimo, and you really need a snowmobile so you can commute back and forth to the walrus hunts. Under these circumstances, you might readily fork out the $14,100 over four years, and figure the cost was worth it. But what about at the end of four years? Statistics on Eskimos and their snowmobiles are not readily available, but if they are like most other Americans, here's what they do. They wait until the snowmobile is paid off, and then they rush out and borrow the money to buy a new one. This doesn't mean the old snowmobile won't slide anymore. It probably means the snowmobile is not new anymore, and our Eskimo has become accustomed to making payments. If Eskimos do follow this pattern, they are making the same costly mistake many other ordinary Americans make: paying too much for transportation.

To see how much mistakes like this can add up to over time, look what would happen if the Eskimo decided not to trade in his (or her) snowmobile at the end of four years. Assume, instead, that he decided to get the after-burner repaired on his old one, suffer the humiliation of having the oldest snowmobile on the iceberg, and drive it for another four years. Suppose instead of paying the $293.75 a month, including interest for a new snowmobile loan from the bank, he paid $293.75 a month to his own savings account at the bank and let them pay him interest. At the end of the next four years, he could go out, buy a new snowmobile and probably have money left over. In fact, if he can earn 10 percent after taxes (which he can, even in Alaska), he will have about $17,978 in his snowmobile savings account at the end of four years. Of course, inflation might increase the cost of new snowmobiles. Suppose they inflate 10 percent a year. The cost will rise from $10,000 to $14,641. Even with inflation, that should leave him enough to buy a new snowmobile, with options such as an automatic driver defroster, and still have more than $3300 left over. Furthermore, once he gets going in this pattern he can be a cash snowmobile buyer forever.

Whether to borrow or not to borrow depends on whether you need the item in question badly enough to justify paying substantially more than the sticker price. If you can justify paying all that money rent, then probably you should get a loan. But before you get a loan, make sure you look at the real cost of "buy and borrow" versus "save and wait." If you don't, you might get snowed in the process of buying your new snowmobile.

Can You Shop for a Loan?

Not only *can* you shop for a loan, but you *should* shop for a loan. You should shop for a loan just as you shop for everything else. You shop when you want to buy a home, a car, or a rare fish. You look for the features you like best about the product and the best price. And so it is if you are going to finance a home, a car, or a rare fish. You should look for the features you like best about the loan and the best price. Generally, the bigger the purchase, the more you shop. Generally, the bigger the loan, the more you should shop. Shopping for a loan may not be as much fun as shopping for rare fish, but it can be more fun when making the payments for the fish.

Some people don't know they can shop for loans. Some people don't know that the lender isn't doing them a personal favor to make them a loan. Some people don't know lenders *want* to make loans. In fact, some people don't know that lenders are practically begging them to come in and get loans. Lenders beg you through radio and TV advertising. They beg you in unsolicited pieces of junk mail advertisement. And if you are really worth begging, they'll send a loan officer to your house and beg you in person. The banks want your personal loans. The thrift institutions want the mortgage on your home. The finance companies want the lien on your car. The furniture stores want to give credit on their sofas. The department store wants you to use its charge account. And the small loan company wants to make you a bill consolidation loan so you can pay everyone else off.

Why is everyone so generous? Profit, that's why! Extending credit can be very profitable to the lender. It is profitable for two reasons. First, you will buy more and, second, they will charge you interest. Some stores make as much money loaning money to people to buy things as they do selling the things in the first place. In reality, everyone's generosity isn't generosity at all—it is simply profitable business.

Because everyone wants to improve his profits by making you a loan, it makes sense for you to consider your own self-interests and be choosy. You owe it to yourself to shop around before you

owe everyone else. If you do shop around, you may owe less in the
end. Consider the following examples.

EXAMPLE 1

The Robinzine family was in the market for a mobile home. They
fell in love with a model sold by several dealers. That was great as
far as Bob Robinzine was concerned. Bob favored himself as a
pretty fair trader, and he was. He played two dealers against each
other, and eventually he got a price of $12,125, which was $2,050
off list and at least $200 lower than he could have gotten without
shopping.

With the price finally negotiated, the dealer told Bob that financing could be arranged right there. That pleased the Robinzines. Little did they know it pleased some other people, too. It
pleased the finance company, which finally got the loan at a 16 percent interest rate. It also pleased the dealer, who got a $150 kickback
from the finance company. The Robinzines took a loan of $10,913 or
90 percent of the price. They wound up paying $182.80 a month for
ten years or $21,936.00 over the life of the contract. They were
happy with the deal they had made.

Bob Robinzine was so happy with the deal he had made that he
couldn't resist telling all his new neighbors at the mobile home park
about it. It made him even happier to find no one had gotten a bigger discount on their home. Bob continued to be happy until one
neighbor pointed out that Bob had only gone halfway in his shopping. The neighbor had shopped for a loan, as well. He had contacted four different lending institutions and finally got a loan for 12
percent from a bank. He showed Bob that if Bob had done the same
thing, his payments would have been $156.56 a month and his total
contract would have been $18,787.52 instead of $21,936. Bob paid
$3,148.48 too much for financing, which was more than he saved
haggling over price. Bob isn't so happy any more.

EXAMPLE 2

Al and Judy Newman were out to buy a color television set for
Christmas. The set they picked cost $600. The store would let them
have it without paying anything for ninety days. The Newmans intended to use their tax refund to pay for the set, so the ninety days
was attractive. However, they'd had experience with such things before. They asked for a lower price for paying cash immediately. To

start with, they were told "no." But Al knew somebody's money was tied up in that television set. He also knew that somebody would be paying interest on the money for ninety more days. He also figured that somebody must be the man he was talking to. Apparently he was right, because eventually the owner knocked $36 off the price. Al borrowed the money from his credit union the next day and repaid the credit union with his tax refund. The interest came to $11.72 for the time he had the loan. They only saved a little over $25, but $25 is $25 as far as Al was concerned.

EXAMPLE 3

For years, Richard and Karen Vaughn had planned to build a home of their own. They figured they could do much of the work themselves. They acquired property, they acquired plans, and they spent many happy hours mentally enjoying their dream house.

Then came a major setback. Richard dropped by the savings and loan institution one day to see about getting a mortgage. The Vaughns had $7000 in an account there. However, despite the size of their account the savings and loan institution turned him down flat. The loan officer said that in the first place the Vaughns needed some type of construction loan to pay the bills while the house was being built. Permanent mortgages were only made on completed properties. Not only had Richard Vaughn been unaware they needed such a loan, but the loan officer told him their institution wouldn't even consider giving a construction loan to the Vaughns. The only people the savings and loan institution made construction loans to were established builders. The loan officer said that too many people building their own homes didn't finish them on time, or spent more money than they were supposed to, or didn't meet specifications, and so on. Richard Vaughn was a refrigeration mechanic, not an established builder.

Never had the Vaughns been more depressed. But after a while the logic of what the loan officer had said sunk in, and the Vaughns allowed their dream to die.

The issue lay dormant for more than six months until a friend asked why the Vaughns never talked about their house any more. The friend knew very little about building but a lot about finance. After a long discussion, the Vaughns put together a loan proposal and showed it to four different institutions. Two simply said "No way," but two others accepted it. This left the Vaughns with the happy problem of choosing the best loan.

Like the Robinzines, the Newmans, and the Vaughns, you should shop for loans too. You should shop in order to get lower rates, lower prices, better terms, or just to get the money at all. As you shop for loans, be guided by these rules:

1. Remember that the lenders want to make you a loan if they can—it is their business.

2. Be willing to shop around.
   a. If the loan is pretty standard—such as a car loan, for instance—you can learn a lot in a hurry just by calling lenders on the phone and asking for their rates.
   b. If the loan is complicated or unusual, make a typewritten loan proposal and present it in person. Include information on:
      ◇ The need for the money
      ◇ How it will be repaid
      ◇ Your personal financial statements
      ◇ Your personal background, occupation, age, family status, credit references, and health

3. Read all the fine print in your loan agreement, and understand what each clause means. Do not be embarrassed to make the loan officer explain each unfamiliar term. Better to ask a stupid question now than pay for a stupid mistake later.

4. Don't rush. There is no need to accept the first loan offered to you.

5. Don't be discouraged if you are turned down. Try to determine exactly why you were turned down.
   a. Perhaps the institution temporarily was out of money to lend. Go elsewhere or come back later.
   b. Perhaps the loan is not the type usually made by that institution. Try elsewhere.
   c. Perhaps the lenders felt your loan proposal wasn't compelling. That's only their opinion. Improve your proposal and try elsewhere.
   d. Maybe your credit worthiness is not sufficient for the institution. There are generally other lenders with more liberal standards.
   e. Maybe you really shouldn't get the loan. Face the fact, and make other plans.

6. Seek advice. Be particularly persistent if you know others who have received similar loans. Ask how and where they got them.

Shopping for a loan may not be as much fun as shopping for other things. No one ever got excited by window shopping at a bank. But if you are the kind of person who doesn't like to pay full retail price for homes, cars, or rare fish, why pay full retail price for a loan?

◊ 21 ◊
How Much
Should You Borrow?

You should borrow only what you can afford to repay. Credit is a service you must pay for if you want to use it. Like anything else people buy, those who have money can get the most. People who don't have money can't get any. It seems perverse, but those who need a loan the most are the least likely to get one. Banks and finance companies don't like to make loans to people who can't repay them. Of course, their attitude is completely selfish. But their selfishness keeps some of their would-be customers from borrowing money unwisely and winding up bankrupt.

Unfortunately, there is so much competition among lenders to make loans that you cannot always rely on their selfishness to keep them from making you a loan you shouldn't have. There are many bad loans made these days. In fact, you may have to do the lenders a favor and refuse to let them make you a loan. You may help both of you avoid winding up bankrupt.

To determine when you really should say "no" to a loan, analyze your income and your equity. Your income is the source of dollars with which you will repay the loan. Your equity is the source of security behind the loan. If anything goes wrong with your income, your equity must be liquidated and sold to repay the loan. Here is a detailed approach for analyzing your income and equity.

Income

Total income is generally not the issue. Discretionary earnings available to repay debt is the issue. The following is a simplified illustration. Family A earns $1250 a month ($15,000 a year) while family B earns $2500 a month ($30,000 a year). These figures suggest how much more debt family B can afford than family A. In this case twice as much income may be able to support more than four times as much debt.

	Family A	Family B
Monthly income	$1,250	$2,500
Less basic living expenses	1,055	1,623
Discretionary income	$ 195	$ 877

The reason the wealthier family can afford four times as much debt is because basic living costs do not increase as much as income—at least, they shouldn't increase as much. Basic living costs are things such as food, clothing, rent, insurance, medical, etc. What money is left over can be used for discretionary purposes, such as debt repayments.

The amount of income is not the only income issue. Stability of income must also be considered. A family that is subject to strikes, layoffs, and other income interruptions should borrow less than a family earning the same income without these uncertainties. It is very hard to estimate your personal exposure to income stability. People frequently let their enthusiasm for buying cloud their objectivity about their own circumstances. For example, one man wanted to borrow to buy a new power saw. He assured his reluctant wife there was plenty of work right then, so his checks would keep rolling in. But two weeks later, when she wanted a washer, he was sure there was a layoff just around the corner.

Grade yourself in the following four areas of income stability: (1) employer stability, (2) personal stability, (3) payment stability, and (4) emergency preparedness. The questions associated with each area are intended to assist you in properly analyzing your stability. For comparison, try imagining the answers three or four of your friends in different occupations would give to these questions. Hopefully, as you consider your job relative to others, you'll see a pattern develop that will help you be more objective about your own circumstances.

1. *Employer stability.* If your employer is subject to changes in profits and revenue, so are you.
   What kind of industry do you work in?

   _____

   Does business fluctuate with the economy, or the seasons? The grocery business is stable, for example; the building and construction business is unstable.

What kind of company do you work for?

Does their business reflect industry trends?

Is it among the first to have orders cancelled when business in the industry declines?

Do they lay employees off when work is slow, or do they try to hold on to them?

Is the company sound financially?

Very stable (1)   Stable (2)   Average (3)
Unstable (4)   Very unstable (5)

2. *Personal stability.* If you are subject to strikes or layoffs, then your income is unstable.
Is your personal position stable?

Are you subject to strikes?

Is your office subject to closing?

Are you working on a job or project that will come to an end soon?

Can funds for your job be removed due to politics?

Is new technology taking jobs?

Are you protected by seniority, or are you subject to being bumped?

Are you a top employee, whom the firm is anxious to keep, or have your reviews been poor?

Are you happy with your job, or is there a chance you'll get disgusted and quit?

Do you work for yourself? If so, what happens to your income if you are sick or can't work?

Are you in good health?

Very stable (1)   Stable (2)   Average (3)
Unstable (4)   Very unstable (5)

3. *Payment stability.* If the amount of your checks is variable, your income is unstable.
Are you on commission that depends on sales?

Is a major portion of your income in the form of bonuses or profit sharing?

Are parts of your income due to overtime payments or temporary travel allowances?

Very stable (1)   Stable (2)   Average (3)
Unstable (4)   Very unstable (5)

4. *Emergency preparedness.* If you are unprepared for an income interruption, you are in an unstable position.
What kind of emergency security do you have?

Are there other sources of income you can rely on if your main source ceases?

Are you eligible for generous supplementary unemployment benefits or other forms of aid?

Do you have substantial savings to fall back on?

Very stable (1)   Stable (2)   Average (3)
Unstable (4)   Very unstable (5)

If your responses add to 4, then you are in a good personal position to borrow. But if you score 20, you would be smart to borrow nothing and pay cash for everything. If you are in the middle, like most people, you can do some borrowing—but don't get overextended. You are bound to have your fair share of surprises.

Whether your income is stable or unstable, it is a terrible feeling to be overextended. If you have borrowed more than you can afford to repay, you will slowly but surely fall farther and farther behind until there seems to be no financial way out. If you've overborrowed on your income stability, you are vulnerable to a sudden shock. Your income could stop, and you might not be able to pay your bills. In this case, your creditors may cooperate for a while, but when you do get back to work you may be too far behind to catch up. And the things you bought won't bring you any happiness while you are struggling to make the payments on them.

Equity

The most important thing in repaying debts is income. Sometimes, however, the income isn't enough. Sometimes the only thing left to do is sell something to get the cash to pay the bills. Selling things to pay bills is always emotionally hard to do. It can be tough financially, too. It is especially tough if you don't have anything to sell.

If something must be sold, the first item to sell is the one you borrowed money to buy. It is important, therefore, not to borrow more than the item is worth. Sometimes the item is worth more than the loan when you buy it, but the item may depreciate in value so fast that the loan may soon be more than the value of the item.

1. *Homes.* Conventional loans equal 80 percent of the appraised value. Because homes tend to appreciate in value, it is possible to get financing up to 95 percent of the home's value. If the home must be sold to pay off the mortgage, chances are good it will bring more than the outstanding balance no matter when it is sold.

2. *Cars, boats, recreational vehicles, and so on.* Loans are frequently at 90 percent or more of the value on these big-ticket items. However, these high-ratio loans are risky when it comes to the equity in them. Items such as cars and boats go down in value, not up. Generally, they go down faster than the loan. For example, a $6000 car may be worth only $4500 one year after driving it off the showroom floor. But a $6000 forty-eight-month loan would probably still be worth $5100 after one year. There would still be $600 of debt left even if the car were sold to pay off the loan. Of course, the loan repayment will eventually catch up with the depreciation. After four years, the car is worth something, but the loan is paid off.

3. *Appliances, television sets, and so on.* These items typically cost between $100 and $1000. Loans can usually be arranged to cover 100 percent of the purchase price. Here the item is probably not worth

enough to pay off the loan for two-thirds of the life of the loan. Sometimes the appliances wear out completely before the loan is paid off.

4. *Clothes, soft goods, services, and so on.* There is no equity at all in these items. For all practical purposes, soft goods and services cannot be resold to repay loans.

The borrower must be concerned about equity because he (or she) should be concerned about what he would do in an emergency. If an emergency develops and the borrower can't raise the money to pay off the loan by reselling what he bought, then he might have to sell off something else that he already owns. Selling things you don't want to sell to repay debts is an unhappy situation at best.

The easiest way to avoid unhappy situations is to avoid borrowing more than you can afford. Credit, after all, is a service to the consumer who uses it. It is a product to the lender who sells it. Credit has a definite cost. And, as with any other service you buy, you shouldn't try to buy more credit than you can afford. Many Americans can't afford the debts they already have. Many Americans should have been smart enough to start saying No to the lenders years ago.

◇ 22 ◇
Suppose You Can't Pay on Time?

If you don't pay on time—you'll wish you had. If you don't pay on time, you will really have a feeling of being trapped. Today credit is so easy to get that it is easy to get too much. And when you get too much, it can really give you a pain that feels like indigestion, insomnia, headache, and ulcer all rolled into one.

People get a pain when they get too much credit and get behind on their payments because they can't forget about all the money they owe. The reason they can't forget about all the money they owe is because the people they owe it to won't let them forget. If you've never been hounded by a bill collector, you might wonder what happens. If you have been hounded by a bill collector, then you already know what happens—but probably wish you didn't.

What happens depends a lot on whom you owe the money to. Approximately fifteen to thirty days after your payment is due, most organizations will send you a form letter. Generally the letter has been sent out by a computer. The computer will personalize the letter to make you think it was written just for you. It will say things like "Dear Mr. Slopayee, Just a friendly reminder. . . . You apparently overlooked . . . and please disregard if payment is in the mail." The next note will be sent about ten days after the first. It will be firmer in tone but will still be sent out by the computer. It will say, "Your account is seriously past due. . . . Don't jeopardize your good credit rating. . . ."

This series of letters will continue until you are two or three months past due. At that point, most firms will have a human being call you on the phone. The caller will call you at home, at work, and at your country club if he or she can track you down there. The calls will embarrass you, upset you, and make you angry. This is OK as far as the firm is concerned. The firm's objective is to get some kind of immediate payment from you and an agreement to pay the rest. Unfortunately, sob stories do not work well at this point. First of all, the person on the other end of the line has heard dozens of sob stories, many of them undoubtedly better than yours. Second, the caller is just an employee.

The callers may personally feel you need the money more than their company, but they know that kind of thinking will get them fired. Then they'll have bill collector problems of their own. Besides, these collectors rarely are in any position to answer complaints, make adjustments on inferior merchandise, or change the terms of your loan. Do them and yourself a favor—don't blame them for your problem.

If you reach this point with a utility or a service company of some type, and still don't pay, the company will cut your service off. Other companies without that leverage may refer your case to a bill collection agency.

The collection agency may start the letters all over again. They may send a collector out to see you. If you felt intimidated, humiliated, and insulted by the phone calls, wait until a bill collector shows up at your doorstep. Again, all the previous comments about the collector just doing a job apply; but it is hard to believe some bill collectors don't love every minute of what they do, because they do it so thoroughly. They do it for 40 to 60 percent of what they can collect from you, so they'll try pretty hard to collect.

The company may refer your account to a lawyer. The lawyer may or may not be of concern. Whether the lawyer is a concern or not depends on whom you owe for what, and how much. If you owe a small amount (say, under $250), or the debt isn't for something that can be repossessed, or if the debt is owed to somebody like the pet-of-the-month club, then you need have no real fear of legal action being taken against you. The lender will figure that legal action would be too expensive for what would probably be recovered.

The lawyer *may* be of concern, however, if you owe a lot, or if you owe money on something valuable. If you owe a lot of money, the lawyer will probably try to garnishee your wages. This is a form of legal action. If your wages are garnisheed, your employer will be forced to take a percentage of your paycheck and send it directly to your creditor. Most people hate to have their employers get involved in their personal financial problems. Many people fear their employers will fire them because of the garnishment. Technically speaking, it is illegal to fire you for the garnishment. But some companies would probably figure out a reason to fire you anyway.

Of course, the lender prefers not to garnishee your wages. Consequently, if the lender has a lien on something valuable, such as your car or your home, when a lawyer gets involved, look out. There are some legalities involved in repossessing your property or foreclosing on your home. The lawyer knows about all the legalities—that's what he or she is there for.

Lawyers rarely force you into bankruptcy. It is expensive to file bankruptcy proceedings. Furthermore, lenders know they probably won't get much out of your bankruptcy. If they can't collect from you directly, they will probably just write you off as a bad debt expense. Nearly all companies have reserves for bad debts. They build bad debt expenses right into their selling prices, which they must pass on to their legitimate customers. At this stage, the way they handle the loss is not much different from the way they handle the expense of shoplifting, forgery, and general thievery. It is all part of the cost of doing business. But companies who do not carefully control their bad debt expenses will wind up bankrupt themselves. So don't expect them to give up easily.

The companies won't give up easily. They won't give up until they've driven you nearly insane. However, as already stated, they probably will stop short of forcing you into bankruptcy, because it is not profitable for them to put you in bankruptcy. There are some other things reputable firms will stop short of doing, too. For example, they will not hire a couple of gorillas in striped suits to beat you to a pulp, nor will they bomb your house, nor will they force you to sell your kids into slavery. Some financially frustrated people make take great comfort in this knowledge. In fact, some folks may figure they might as well become pseudo-deadbeats because the penalties are not very great. A pseudo-deadbeat is an ordinary basically honest human being who wants to pay his (or her) bills—but can't. At least he thinks he can't. But while modern laws protect pseudo-deadbeats from debtors' prison, there is still an awful price to pay. The price of emotional strain is high, and simply reading about it doesn't do it justice. It is far worse to live through. Furthermore, by the time you get to this point you may have seen your waterbed repossessed and carried out the front door, your electricity turned off, and your VISA card publicly seized and cut to shreds at the checkout stand of your favorite drugstore.

This humiliation is not all you'll suffer. You'll also suffer damage to your credit reputation. You will certainly lose the right to borrow again from the particular lenders you haven't paid. Furthermore, those lenders will notify their credit bureau. And with today's modern computers, notifying one credit bureau is like notifying credit bureaus all over the country. If you apply for credit somewhere, the new prospective lenders will get the full story from the credit bureau. And the credit bureau tells only one side of the story—the lender's. Not paying your bills can make it very tough to get another loan you may need badly.

Obviously, the best thing to do is avoid getting into the jam altogether. However, if you are already in a jam, consider the following list of the important do's and don'ts.

1. *Stop borrowing.* Sometimes a bill consolidation loan can help, when prescribed and administered by a qualified financial counselor. The thing to really avoid, however, is frantically borrowing a few extra dollars just to make a couple of payments to someone who is really on your back. This action may buy you a little time, but very little. Worse yet, it doesn't cure the problem. In fact, it only digs you in deeper. It's like taking aspirin to cure cancer.

2. *Don't write bad checks.* Knowingly writing checks against insufficient funds is a crime for which you could be put in jail. Legally speaking, however, failure to pay your bills is not normally a crime.

3. *Call the lender before he (or she) calls you.* When you see you are in a jam and can't pay, contact the lender before he or she contacts you. Explain the problem and the solution. Reputable lenders will go along. They prefer not to hound you or to write you off.

4. *Be honest.* If the lender catches you lying about your circumstances, he or she will feel completely justified in being as tough on you as he can. Furthermore, he'll never believe another thing you tell him. Honesty is particularly important when you call him first. Whatever you tell him you are going to do from that point on, make sure you do it.

5. *Pay something.* Most lenders will not go beyond the letter-writing stage if the account stays active. "Active" means that at least partial payments are being received regularly on the account, and the outstanding balance is consistently declining. Sending even $5 when the payment should be $50 is often enough to keep the account active.

6. *Don't become depressed with worry.* Sometimes people worry so much about their bills they become terribly depressed. The depression may cause a lot of other problems including poor work performance, loss of job, domestic difficulties, poor health, and inability to figure out what to do about any of them. And the worse these

problems become, the harder it will be to pay your bills. So before you worry yourself to death, remember there is only a limited amount the lender can and will do to you.

Most people who can't pay their bills wish they had. Most people who can't pay their bills wish they had never gotten the loan to begin with. Most people who don't get loans, especially loans they can't repay, are happy. For these smart people, the closest they'll ever come to understanding the bill collector's function in our modern society is to read about it in this book. What is in this book is all the understanding anyone really needs if he or she plans to be financially free.

◇ 23 ◇
What About Credit Cards?

Credit cards are probably the most convenient form of credit ever devised. The use of credit cards will become even more widespread in the 80s than in the 70s—if possible. They are:

- ◇ *Easy to get.* Most applications take less than five minutes to complete.

- ◇ *Convenient to use.* Simply present the card at the cash register and sign the credit slip.

- ◇ *Good anywhere.* You can use your credit card, where honored, all over the world without further identification.

- ◇ *Good anytime.* You can use your credit card as long as you can find a place open.

- ◇ *Safer than cash.* They can be identified with specific owners—cash cannot.

- ◇ *Convenient to pay.* An itemized statement comes once a month giving you a complete record of your purchases.

- ◇ *Helpful in a tight spot.* There are times when you really need something, but don't have any cash.

Credit cards do have some disadvantages. The disadvantages may outweigh all the advantages for many people such as the following.

Credit Addicts

For people prone to credit addiction, carrying a credit card around is like an alcoholic carrying a bottle of booze around. There is only one solution for credit addicts—they must not have any credit cards whatsoever.

Social Spenders

For people who are not technically credit addicts, but who are prone
to overspend a little, the ready availability of credit encourages them
to overspend a lot. And if a drunk has an accident, who cares if he
or she is an alcoholic or just a social drinker? Such people must restrict credit card purchases to very specific predetermined things.
For example, they may decide to use credit cards to buy gasoline,
because the risk of abuse is low. They may, however, refuse to use
cards in department stores, where the risk of abuse is high.

Credit Card Amnesiacs

People who are prone to forget how much has been bought with
credit cards will find huge holes developing in their budgets. Just
when they think they are a few dollars ahead, the credit card statements come. But such people have forgotten how much the statement will be for. Frequently, the statements absorb all the extra dollars they thought they had, and more. Nearly all people are prone to
credit card amnesia. The amnesia syndrome is more serious when
more than one member of the family is carrying a credit card. Credit card amnesia can be overcome by keeping a running total of credit
card purchases and deducting them from the checking account balance as purchases are made (see Chapter 9).

Unaware Consumers

People who fail to realize the hidden costs associated with credit
cards can spend too much for things they buy. Credit cards are convenient, but the convenience is not free. Establishments that accept
credit cards must pay the credit company a fee every time people
use such cards in their stores. Fees are charged by VISA, Master
Card, American Express, Diner's Club, Carte Blanche, and all the
gasoline credit cards, for example. These fees vary between 3.5 and
6.0 percent of the purchase. The merchants must pass on these fees
to you in the form of higher prices. But things are changing. You
may be able to buy more cheaply for cash. You may occasionally see
signs offering you a reduction in price if you pay cash rather than
use a credit card. The reduction represents the fee the store would

otherwise pay the credit card company. In most of the country, you can already find discount service stations that sell their gas for less but accept nothing but cash. You should look for opportunities to avoid the hidden costs of credit cards. The savings can be significant.

Naive Borrowers

People who use credit cards as a source of loans pay the highest interest rates allowed by law. Nearly all credit cards allow you to pay just a portion of your total bill in any given month. The balance carried over to the following month has a 1½ to 3 percent finance charge tacked on. The amount depends on local law. The charge seems small. Usually it is just a few cents. It is small because it represents the charge for only one month, and usually the amount of money involved is small. However, the interest rate works out to be 18 to 36 percent on an annual basis. You can borrow money cheaper than that almost anywhere. The obvious solution to the credit card problem is to keep your account current. Resist the temptation to stretch out your repayments. If you must purchase something with your credit card that can't be repaid in a month, sometimes your best strategy is to get a loan from a bank, pay off the credit card, and pay the lower interest to the bank.

Speaking of getting a loan from a bank, beware of the loan actuator and overdraft privilege often associated with credit cards. These are simply extensions of your credit card and carry the same high interest rates. You can spot loan actuators and overdrafts by the fact that information and forms on starting one up come with your credit card statement. But the loan you want is the kind you get by getting out of your easy chair, going to the bank, and applying for a personal loan.

Careless Card Carriers

Careless people may wind up paying for things they didn't buy. Some people do not realize they are legally responsible to pay for whatever is purchased with their credit cards *no matter who used the cards*. Sometimes this becomes a big problem in families. Sometimes a son, a daughter, or a spouse borrows the card and runs up a lot of bills. Naturally, such experiences do little to promote family harmony. And sometimes credit cards get into the hands of nonfamily members. Sometimes the cards are lost or stolen. Even under these circumstances, the owner is liable for the purchases. The credit card owner could wind up paying for the jolly time some thief had using his or her cards. Nearly all credit card companies relieve you of your liability as soon as they are notified your card has been lost or stolen. It is important, therefore, to keep a list of all your credit cards in a safe place. Record the card numbers, the expiration date, and the phone numbers or addresses of the companies to contact in case your cards are lost. As added protection, low-cost insurance against unauthorized use of your credit cards can be purchased from major auto insurance companies, auto clubs, or even the company that issued the card itself.

The credit card is a masterpiece of modern monetary technology. It brings more convenience to the ordinary buyer than any other monetary invention has ever done before. But, as with most powerful new technologies, greater education, discipline, and maturity is needed to use the credit card than the system it replaces. Youngsters were easily taught to guide the oxen teams that pulled pioneer wagons westward. But only mature, well-trained pilots are allowed to command today's modern jet airplanes. No federal agency requires specialized training for credit card users, as it does for pilots. But everyone who holds a credit card owes it to him- or herself to learn all there is to know about owning one of these newfangled contraptions. The knowledge can help avoid costly misuse.

◇ 24 ◇
What Is Risk?
What Is Insurance?

Risk has a number of uses in a financial book. In this section, risk refers to an unexpected financial loss.

What, then, is insurance, and what does it have to do with risk?

Insurance is a transfer of risk. It involves paying someone in advance to pay for your losses and misfortunes. It involves trading losses. You trade a loss you are not sure you are going to have for a loss you are absolutely sure you are going to have. Losses you are not sure you are going to have are things such as fires, accidents, and premature deaths. The losses you trade, which you are sure you will have, are insurance premiums. Why would anyone pay an insurance premium to cover a loss he or she may never—in fact, *probably* will never—have? Because the uncertain loss might be a huge loss, a loss way beyond your ability to handle loss. But the insurance premium is a small loss, a known loss, a planned-for, budgeted, and liveable loss. That's insurance.

To see how this insurance and all these losses work, think about your lawnmower. Think how you would like to replace your lawnmower with a new riding lawnmower complete with bucket seat, mag wheels, and eight-track stereo tape player. Such a lawnmower would cost enough to clip your budget pretty well. So naturally, after forking over all that green money to buy the mower, you would hate to lose it. And while you don't think there are any marauding mower thieves lurking around your yard, you can never be completely sure. After all, losing that mower would trim you financially. So what should you do? You should get your lawnmower insured.

Insuring your mower is where the trading of losses comes in. You are afraid your lawnmower could be stolen, destroyed, stapled, spindled, or mutilated in some way. Sure, it seems like a small chance, but if it did happen the loss might be more than you

189

could handle—financially. So you agree to trade the uncertain loss to an insurance company for the certain loss of an insurance premium. Every six months, or year, you will pay the insurance company a premium. Most people figure the premium is a loss because it is money out of their pockets. But although it is a loss, it is a known loss. The cost of the premium is set in advance. The premium is small enough to budget for and handle. Insurance is trading a manageable, known loss for a potentially huge, unmanageable loss that could occur at any time without warning.

The insurance company is a big organization. It can handle the loss of your machine and not get mowed down, because it is collecting premiums from lots of mower owners. Some are going to get cut off by mower rustlers, or other forms of pestilence, but most will not. Because most people won't suffer a loss, the insurance company can charge everyone a low premium. Let's say this fancy mower cost $1000. Let's say an average of one mower in 1000 will get snatched. The insurance company can charge you, and 999 of your neighbors, a premium of $1 for theft insurance. Actually the insurance company has to charge more than $1. It has other costs to cover out of the premium. It must pay for its clerks, salespeople, and the company president. It must pay for offices, stationery, and the computer. It must pay insurance premiums of its own. Insurance companies have lots of overhead to pay for out of the premium they collect, and they need to make a little profit as well.

Consequently, mower premiums may run $2 instead of $1. This means the company will collect $2000 from 1000 mower owners. For every 1000 mower owners, the company will have to replace one mower worth $1000. If the insurance company handles things right, the $2 premium should work out to be a good deal for the company.

The $2 premium is probably a good deal for you the mower owner as well. A $1000 loss, coming when you least expect it and are least prepared for it, could really cut your grass. But a $2 premium is something you can live with, plan for, manage, and handle. Consequently, the insurance protection is something you probably should get.

You probably should get the insurance unless you don't need insurance. After all, paying for insurance you don't need is a waste of money. There are two reasons for needing insurance. First, it may be required by some outside person. The outsider may be the law or the company where you got your mower loan. It is normal and proper for outsiders to require insurance. The law may require you to carry liability insurance, for example. Liability insurance will pay innocent people if they or their property are accidentally injured by your mower, or if your mower runs amuck and cuts down all your neighbor's prize petunia plants. The finance company also may require you to carry insurance. Because it has accepted the mower as security behind the loan, it wants to be sure the mower is insured against theft or damage.

Outsiders may require you to carry insurance to protect people other than yourself. But you may also need insurance to protect yourself—or maybe you don't. So far, we've assumed that losing a $1000 lawnmower would be nearly catastrophic for you, but that may not be true. Perhaps you can deal with all or part of the loss without difficulty. If you are in a position to stand some loss without difficulty, you should not buy insurance to cover that amount. *Not* insuring yourself is done by using deductibles or self-insurance. It can also be done by neglect—which is the wrong way, of course.

To determine how much to self-insure, or find out how large a deductible you can handle, ask yourself one simple question: "How big a loss can I handle unexpectedly without causing financial hardship?" If you feel that losing $1000 tomorrow morning—or any morning— would not cause you to suffer "financial hardship," then you probably shouldn't insure the mower at all. If you answer that the biggest loss you can handle is $25, then buy an insurance policy with a $25 deductible. That means you'll pay the first $25 of any loss, and the insurance company will pay the rest.

The reason for writing deductibles is to save money by paying lower insurance premiums. Small losses are the most frequent and the most expensive for the insurance company to handle. Therefore, they can reduce the premium substantially if you take responsibility for the small losses and they take responsibility only for the large ones. For example, suppose you want damage insurance on your mower. In considering the premium, the insurance company may conclude there is only a remote chance of your mower being run over by a steam roller while parked in your driveway, or being trampled by a herd of angry elephants in your garage, or being accidentally driven over a cliff in your backyard. The premium to cover these potential catastrophic losses may only be $1.89. However, there may be a fairly good chance of a fender being dented by your son playing Demolition Derby, or the racing stripes being scratched by your wife parking the mower next to your Mercedes, or the pearl-studded shift lever knob breaking off in a four-wheel drift around the maple tree. These losses are small. They may cost less than $50 to repair. But if the insurance company has to send a person out to verify the damage, get three competitive bids for repair, fill out seventeen different forms in quadruplicate, and send you a check, the administrative costs alone could be three times higher than the damage. (It actually costs $25 or more for the company to simply create a file on your case.) The insurance company must charge a pretty healthy premium to cover all these costs. Perhaps the premium will run $12.61. Obviously, the premium on small losses is steep. But if you can handle the small losses, the premium will be small—that is why you should use deductibles when you can.

Some people do not like to use any deductibles. They want the whole loss covered by insurance. They figure that in the end they will be money ahead. But they are wrong. The odds are always against you. Remember—the insurance company must charge enough to cover the losses, the overhead, and make a profit. That means that unless you are prone to having extraordinarily bad luck in life, you will always wind up paying more in insurance premiums than you'll collect. Therefore, the only reasons to insure are because some interested outside party, such as the law or the bank, makes you insure, or because you cannot afford to suffer the large potential financial loss.

Insurance is a way to get rid of losses you don't want and can't handle, and to trade them for losses you don't want but can handle. Insurance is a way to ride your mower, work in your yard, and live your life without the nervous worry that you'll be unexpectedly flattened financially.

◇ 25 ◇
Auto and Homeowner's Insurance

Some of our biggest personal risks are associated with our automobiles and our homes. Unexpected property or liability losses associated with either of these can be financially destructive.

Automobile Insurance

Automobile insurance usually involves several different coverages all packaged together in one policy, with one premium. Some coverages are optional, some are not.

PERSONAL LIABILITY INSURANCE

Personal liability insurance is usually required by law. If you are at fault in an accident that injures another person, it is your legal responsibility to compensate that person for injuries. You do not have to be issued a citation by the police to be found at fault. The insurance will pay for ambulances, doctors, hospitals, missed work, pain and suffering, and everything else you could be held liable for. If a person is killed, the insurance will compensate his or her estate for the death and pay all the funeral expenses.

Your insurance will pay up to the limits of the policy. If your liability exceeds those limits, you must pay. Limits are usually referred to as 10/30, for example. Under these limits, the insurance company will pay up to $10,000 for any single person and up to $30,000 per accident.

To see how personal liability insurance works, suppose you have limits of 10/30. (As you will see, everything in this story is typical of everyday situations—except the coverage. It should be much higher.) Suppose that you are truckin' along and affectionately lean over to give your wife a kiss and, while nibbling on her ear, you plow into the back of a dune buggy loaded with women from the neighborhood garden club. Suppose there were three injuries to garden clubbers. The first lady suffered paralysis of the hair follicles when her hair abruptly stood on end. It isn't clear how this happened. It might have been the fright of the accident, or it might have been the shock at the language you used. Regardless, it is your fault, and it cost $12,000 for a special Parisian hair transplant. Your liability insurance will pay only the first $10,000, your limit per person. Your pocketbook will have to come up with the other $2000. A second lady dislocated her tongue. So $5000 worth of tongue massages were required to restore her speech. Your insurance will cover the entire $5000. The last lady received a severe injury to the first knuckle of her great toe. And although a team of fifteen doctors could not detect the injury, the jury awarded her $10,000 for pain and suffering damages. Her lawyer, who got 50 percent of the settlement, convinced the jury she was just about to launch a new career. She planned to be the first fifty-year-old woman to break into professional football as a place kicker for the Pittsburgh Steelers. Naturally, with the pain in her toe all those dreams have vanished. The insurance company paid a total of $25,000 in claims, and you are lucky there wasn't a fourth lady. If there had been a fourth injury, the claims might easily have exceeded your $30,000-per-accident limit. In that case, you'd probably have been stuck for the difference.

PROPERTY DAMAGE LIABILITY INSURANCE

Property damage liability insurance is required by law in most states. This coverage pays for damage done by your vehicle to the property of other people. Limits are stated as a flat figure, such as $10,000. For instance, let's assume that when you hit the dune buggy it was pushed into the rear of a seventeen-year-old Cadillac hearse now being used as a delivery truck by a guy who sells basketball poles. During the collision, the hearse's right front hub cap flew off, crashed through the window of a jewelry store, and tipped over a display of imitation crystal goblets on loan from the Museum of Unnatural World Wonders in Moscow, Idaho. You are going to wind up owing a lot of people for a lot of things. You'll owe for repairs on the dune buggy, the hearse truck, the jewelry store, and the goblets. Let's assume each one's damage comes to exactly $3000, or a total liability of $12,000. Your property liability insurance is for $10,000. That means the insurance company will pay each person $2500, and you'll have to pay the rest.

NO-FAULT INSURANCE

No-fault insurance is required by law in many states. In many accidents, it is difficult, time-consuming, and expensive to determine who was at fault. Court dockets have become jammed with liability suits. Often innocent people must wait years for settlement of their injuries. To streamline this system, a new insurance concept has been born—no-fault. Under no-fault, each injured person is paid by his or her own insurance company, regardless of who was at fault.

For illustration, assume for a minute the dune buggy was backing up at 52 miles per hour down a one-way street through a school crossing at the time of the mishap. Under this assumption, you may not have been entirely at fault just because you were speeding, failing to watch the road, and driving in a reckless manner. So the whole case will go before the judge to see who's at fault, and that might take four years or longer (no exaggeration, unfortunately).

In such cases, the lawyers have fun and the judges have fun, but many innocent people do not have fun. These innocent people sit around with smashed-up cars and smashed-up bodies wondering if their bills will ever get paid. Something has been needed to clear the pipelines—no-fault insurance.

In this case, for example, many of the garden clubbers' damages would be paid immediately by the company who insured the dune buggy. Likewise, your damages would be promptly paid by your insurance company. All these payments will be made without any attempt to prove who was at fault. A lot of people have trouble understanding no-fault insurance intellectually. They can't see the justice in letting some screwball driver who is clearly at fault get off scot-free. And the reason they can't understand it intellectually is because it *doesn't* make any intellectual sense, it only makes practical sense.

Practicality only goes so far, however. In most states, no-fault limits are low. In many states, no-fault only covers property damage; in others, only personal liability. Every state is different. If damages exceed the no-fault limits, then you are back to the old tort liability system, trying to figure out who was at fault, and spending years in court doing it. In the 1980s we may see the federal government pass a national no-fault regulation to standardize the situation.

One thing should be made clear. No insurance relieves a person of criminal charges brought by the state. The state may prosecute you, fine you, and even jail you if you were breaking the law, regardless of whose insurance company pays what. By the same token, the state's failure to issue you a citation does not mean you won't be held liable for the accident.

COLLISION INSURANCE

Collision insurance is required by lenders but not by law. Collision pays accident damages to your car if you are at fault. It also pays if the other driver is at fault but is not insured. It is smart to carry collision insurance.

To see how collision insurance works, let's assume you were clearly at fault for the dune buggy disaster. It is unlikely your own vehicle would escape all that devastation unscathed. Let's assume your gold-plated Robert Redford hood ornament got a broken nose. What good is Robert Redford with a broken nose? Your collision insurance will pay to have it fixed again.

COMPREHENSIVE INSURANCE

Comprehensive insurance is required by lenders, not by law. This coverage will pay for damage to your car that is not the result of a collision. It will pay for loss from theft, or fire, or damage from falling objects, or rocks hitting the car, or riots, and so on. It is wise to have comprehensive coverage.

Let's assume that while you're waiting for the police to finish the red tape a hailstorm unleashes its fury on your car. Let's say the hailstones dent your green metallic finish so the whole car looks like a giant pickle. Let's also assume that when you and the garden clubbers turn your backs to answer the police officers' questions, a gang of neighborhood kids attack your car. In exactly 4 minutes and 12 seconds, they steal your high-performance transmission, your low-mileage V8 engine with customized cam, and your chrome-plated mag wheels, leaving you four very nice cinderblocks in exchange. (These kids are so fast they should work for the pit crews at the Indy 500.) You may wish they had stolen the whole car, but fortunately you never leave the keys in it. Also fortunately, your comprehensive coverage will pay for the hail damage and the thefts.

MEDICAL COVERAGE

Medical coverage is entirely optional, but good coverage to have. This coverage takes care of your medical bills, or those of your family, if you are injured in an accident that is your fault. For instance, suppose the dune buggy accident causes you to bite off your wife's ear lobe, on which you were nibbling. Your wife needs somewhere to hang earrings. So plastic surgery is the answer, and that's expensive. Thank goodness for the insurance company, again.

TOWING INSURANCE

Towing insurance is entirely optional. It covers towing expenses if your car must be towed for reasons other than a collision. For example, after all this suppose you finally arrive home to find the battery of your second car is dead. Investigation reveals your sixth-grader used it to power her science fair display. Your insurance will pay the cost of towing the car to the service station.

About this time, you'll be glad to let your insurance agent pressure you into buying all that extra coverage he (or she) sold you. His company, however, is not going to be very happy. And when they get this call from you, reporting your accident, you can count on your insurance rates going up even if you agree to quit kissing your wife in the car.

Of all the coverages mentioned, only the liability and/or the no-fault coverages are required by law. All the rest are up to you or the company that loaned you the money for the car. How much coverage you should carry depends on your ability to pay for unexpected losses out of your pocket. Most people feel that $50 or $100 is their limit. Hence, deductibles in these amounts are good ideas.

The law won't let you write deductibles on your liability insurance. Furthermore, you shouldn't skimp on liability coverage. The law may require you to carry 10/20/5, or $10,000 per person, $20,000 per accident, and $5,000 property liability. But with the cost of everything today these limits are way too low. Consider 100/300/50, or $100,000 per person, $300,000 per accident, and $50,000 property liability. The additional cost is relatively small—a few dollars a year.

The higher limits don't cost much, but they could be very important. The dune buggy accident, for example, was obviously fictional, but the following story is not. A middle-aged woman, a model driver who had never had an accident, was travelling 55 mph down a four-lane road. Suddenly a cat darted in front of her. She reacted without thinking and swerved into a gasoline truck. The impact caused the truck driver to lose control. He hit a railing, sending the truck over the side down on to a busy street below. The resulting explosion and fire left seven dead, fourteen injured, and a good portion of a city block burned. The liability ran into the millions. It all happened so quickly—and it could happen to anyone. The woman herself was not hurt, but, as you can imagine, that didn't make her feel much better.

Homeowner Insurance

If you own a home, you should have homeowner insurance. In fact, if you still have a mortgage on your home, the lender requires you to get insurance.

The lender requires insurance on your home to ensure that the collateral doesn't disappear due to fire, or wind, or snow, or theft, and so on. These perils are just a few covered by homeowner insurance. There are many more. Determining how many more can be a little complicated. There are five basic homeowner forms. In most cases, you want to buy the broadest coverage, or so-called "all-perils" coverage. That means your home is insured against every kind of peril imaginable unless the peril is specifically excluded. Some homeowner forms are "named-perils" coverage. Under "named-perils" coverage, you collect only if you have a damage from something specifically named. The average person can read a "named-perils" contract and it may sound fine. But a layperson may fail to see all the things that could cause damage but are not covered. "All-perils" insurance takes care of that. Then, if your home is destroyed by a giant sea monster, you don't need to worry about whether your insurance will cover it or not.

It is impossible to list all the perils covered by an "all-perils" contract. However, the following are the most important: fire, lightning, wind, hurricane, tornado, hail, explosion, riot, vandalism, burglary, freezing pipes, bursting water heaters, and electrical damage.

There are some important perils no homeowner policy covers. They include flood, backed-up sewers, earthquake, war, and normal wear and tear. Flood and earthquake insurance can usually be obtained by buying a separate policy and paying a higher premium.

In many areas, flood insurance is only available through the federal government. Ask your agent for further information.

It is hard to imagine all the perils, pestilence, and hazards that can befall your humble dwelling. And it's hard to imagine all the things in, on, under, and around your dwelling that can be damaged. If something can be damaged, you probably need insurance. Fortunately, the homeowner policy imagines most of them for you. Typical homeowner policies have the following coverages:

1. *Dwelling.* This includes your house, your attached garage, your screened-in porch, even the gas line in your backyard, and so on—everything directly connected to your house.

2. *Appurtenant structures.* This includes buildings on the property not directly attached to your house. Such structures include your detached garage, tool shed, and doghouse.

3. *Unscheduled personal property.* This covers such incidentals as clothes, beds, tables, and scrapbooks. It includes tools, couches, clocks, and canning supplies. It includes everything incidental to living in your home, or being a guest there. In fact, it includes so many things that you need an inventory. If a fire, tornado, and explosion all hit your house tomorrow, could you remember everything that was in it? How about the silver-plated snail forks you got for your wedding? How about that cherished self-portrait of your father-in-law you've got hanging in the broom closet? How about the raccoon coat you wore in college? If you really had to sit down and make out a list of everything you own, you would certainly miss lots of useful items like these—and you may forget about some pretty important things, as well. An inventory is invaluable. But even the best inventory is no good to you if it is burned up, blown away, and exploded beyond recognition like everything else. Keep it in a safety deposit box.

Personal property insurance covers items whether they are at home or not. If all your clothes are stolen from a hotel room in a faraway city, your homeowner insurance will reimburse you for their value, but not for your embarrassment.

4. *Scheduled personal property.* If you have very expensive personal belongings, you need *scheduled personal property* insurance. The only difference is that you make up an inventory of your jewels, your furs, your coin collections, and so on at the time the insurance is written. These items are specifically valued and scheduled, usually for an extra premium.

5. *Additional living expenses.* If a disaster makes your home un-livable, this coverage will pay for the increase in your living ex-penses for motels, meals, and so on. The company pays until you are settled in your repaired or new home. But watch our for the limits here. You'll have a tough time living if you really have to live on these amounts.

6. *Family liability.* This coverage will pay for any bodily injury or property damage for which you may be held liable due to an ac-cident at your home. If you borrowed your neighbor's tuxedo, for example, and it was burned in a fire at your house, it would be cov-ered. If a bill collector trips on a broken step, your liability insur-ance will pay to fix his or her broken bones (it may not be able to do anything about fixing his or her personality, however).

7. *Guest medical insurance.* This pays for medical bills to your guests who are injured in an accident in your home, even if you are not held legally liable.

Please note: Homeowner insurance will *not* pay medical expenses for you or your family even if you are hurt while some form of in-sured calamity is occurring. If the roof suddenly caves in on your head, the insurance company will pay for repairs to your roof but not for repairs to your head.

Now, to see how all these wonderful coverages work, imagine for a moment that your wife Gwendolyn and you, Joe Sptfz, are sound asleep in your cozy little castle when suddenly a freak puff of wind blows the whole east wing down. The spire crashes through the roof of the stable, frightening the dickens out of your prize thoroughbred horses. The 134 guests in the east wing all suffer in-juries ranging from loss of sleep to good-sized goose eggs. As you and your frightened household rush from the castle, you acciden-tally drop the drawbridge on a reporter from a local newspaper who is already on the scene seeking some sensationalism for tomor-row's paper. The impact knocks her into the moat and ruins her new electronic watch.

The problems continue. You call to inform your son, who is in Harvard Business School. As he rushes down the hall to answer the pay phone, a sneak thief steals into his room and swipes his prize collection of autographed sweat socks. Due to the damage of your castle, you must temporarily find other living quarters. Given your everyday living standards, it is necessary to take over the top four floors of the Waldorf Astoria Hotel in order to barely subsist while repairs are being made. Fortunately for you, you are insured. Fortunately—because it seems that due to a string of bad luck you only have $5 or $10 million left to see you to the end of the month.

Assuming that all the limits of your policy are high enough, just about everything will be covered. The east wing will be rebuilt. The spire will be put back on top of the roof. The damaged equipment in the dungeon will be restored. The candelabras, coats of arms, paintings, and suits of armor that were destroyed will be replaced. The jousting arena where all the stones fell will be cleared, and the horse stable will be fixed. However, insurance may not cover the cost of a private Boeing 747 jet to ship your horses to Hilton Head Island for therapeutic rest and relaxation. So think twice before you make the reservations—maybe they could fly coach this time instead of first class.

Your 134 guests will be cared for. The cost of 134 ambulances, 134 hospital rooms, and 134 attending physicians will all be covered.

Your liability insurance will pay for the bodily injuries to the half-crushed, half-drowned reporter. It'll fix her watch too, so she can keep track of time while she's recuperating.

As for your son's sweat socks, they will be difficult to replace, especially with authentic sweat. Hence, a direct cash settlement will probably be agreed on.

Naturally, the bills at the Waldorf, including rooms, meals, and service, will all be paid for.

Fortunately, you and Gwendolyn were not injured. After some adjustment, you are able to view the whole experience philosophically.

You may or may not live in a castle, or be married to anyone named Gwendolyn, but if you own a home you certainly want it insured. Homeowner insurance may be your best form of preventive maintenance.

What Should You Know about Buying Auto and Home Insurance?

Most automobile and most homeowner insurance policies are basically the same, regardless of the company you buy them from. But the cost and the service may vary substantially from one company to another. So if you know the basic coverages are about the same everywhere, then you should buy insurance based on lowest cost and best service.

Buying insurance based on lowest cost and best service is so logical, you'd think everyone would use this criterion. But not everyone does. There are probably three reasons why people don't use it:

◇ *Ignorance.* They don't know there are differences in cost and service. Hence, they buy from the first salesperson they meet.

◇ *Intimidation.* They feel intimidated buying a product they don't understand and don't want but are forced to buy. Under these conditions, people tend to buy from the first place they can.

◇ *Habit.* They've always dealt with the same company, maybe because their parents did.

Buying out of ignorance, intimidation, or habit is not likely to lead to the best purchase. Educating yourself and shopping around will. This section can help educate you—the shopping around you must do yourself.

All big insurance companies have roughly the same loss experience. Their internal efficiencies can, however, vary substantially. This can mean some companies have greater costs that must be passed on to you.

But the biggest cost difference, company to company, is their cost of marketing the product to you. Many insurance companies use independent agents (non-company employees) to sell their insurance. Other companies use direct marketing (where the salesmen are company employees).

As a very rough rule of thumb, insurance through an independent agent carries with it somewhat higher cost but better service than a direct marketing force provides.

These generalities, however, do not always hold true. The way to shop for price, then, is to call a number of independent and direct agents. In auto and home insurance, the policies are very similar, so comparisons are reasonably easy.

Shopping for service is a difficult matter. It is hard to know how good the service will be until you have a claim. What you can do is ask friends what experiences they've had. Most people feel it is worth paying a little more if an agent really helps you structure an insurance program that is right for you, and works hard to help you solve any claims you have.

Something else you should know about auto and homeowner insurance is that it's changing—for the better.

There have always been two very distressing things about insurance.

The first distressing thing is that ordinary people couldn't understand the big words and legalese in the policies. Half the time it was hard to tell what you were really insured for. Often you only discovered what you were not insured for when you had a claim.

Fortunately, the companies are redoing their policies in plain English. Now most people can understand them if they try.

The second really distressing thing is that frequently you received a lot less money on a claim than you thought you would. If your four-year-old TV burned up, your homeowner insurance covered the loss. But it paid you only the depreciated value of the TV, which might be $150. With comparable new models selling for $400, you still wound up with a pretty good loss.

Now policies are being written with new-for-old replacement clauses. These clauses, which apply most importantly to homeowner insurance, would replace your old TV with a new $400 TV.

It's a change for the better in these inflationary times. But before you thank your insurance agent for his goodness, remember the new policies cost more.

Once you've shopped and bought, don't just forget shopping forever. Shop again, every time your premium comes due. Rates change all the time. You may find that the low-cost seller one year is not the low-cost seller the next year. It is very easy to change insurance companies. Therefore, unless you have some kind of special relationship with your salesperson, why shouldn't you keep your insurance costs at a minimum? And learning how to get the best service for the lowest dollar is the most important thing you should know about automobile and homeowner insurance.

◊ 26 ◊
Should You
Have Health Insurance?

You should have health insurance only if you are mortal. If you are not mortal, then you are not subject to illness and mishap, and you don't need insurance. How do you test to see if you are mortal? Pinch yourself. If you feel pain, you are as mortal as the next person. And if you're mortal, you need health insurance. (If you don't feel pain, it's probably already too late to insure against what's wrong.)

You need health insurance because you are the most valuable asset you have. You're more valuable than your car, your house, or anything else you insure. If you, or one of your family, break down, you must get fixed, right away, without question, without consideration of cost. At least, you won't consider cost at first, but later you'll realize how expensive it is to get fixed these days. It's not uncommon for a simple overnight stay in the hospital to run $200 to $500 for doctors, nurses, drugs, tests, and so forth. Such expenses are enough to make anyone sick. And enough such expenses can ruin the best financial plan.

Health insurance can help you avoid financial sickness. Fortunately, a large majority of Americans have some form of health insurance through their employers or unions. Many others are covered by Medicare or various other governmental programs. But these programs may be insufficient. You would be smart to look into the details of your plan, to see if you need to buy supplemental coverage. A typical plan might require you to pay a deductible. That means you pay the first $50 or $100 of any medical bill. Then it might require co-insurance, which means you pay 20 percent of everything over your deductible and the insurance company pays 80 percent. Suppose you had a group plan at work with a $50 deductible and 20 percent co-insurance. Suppose you slipped in the bathtub and broke your sacroiliac. Suppose the bill from your family doctor came to $150. You would pay $70, and the insurance company would pay $80.

Bill	$150
Deductible	− 50
Insurable	$100
Company's share	× 80%
Company's payment	$ 80

Bill	$150
Company's payment	− 80
Your payment	$ 70

If you had gone to a sacroiliac specialist instead of your family doctor, the bill might have been $1000, in which case you would owe $240 and the insurance company would owe $760.

Bill	$1,000
Deductible	− 50
Insurable	$ 950
Company's share	× 80%
Company's payment	$ 760

Bill	$1,000
Company's payment	− 760
Your payment	$ 240

An unexpected $240 can *really* be a pain in the back.

The co-insurance type policy does have the advantage of automatically adjusting for inflation—many policies do not. Some policies have fixed limits. With a fixed limit, the policy will pay a predetermined amount for a specified injury. Though they are increasingly rare, some policies pay a fixed amount for specified treatments. For example, a broken sacroiliac may have a $50 limit. Or a night in the hospital may have a $50 limit. No matter how the policy is fixed, you will probably find the coverage less than satisfactory in these inflationary times. Take the broken sacroiliac, for example. Suppose the limit is $50. If the bill turns out to be $150, you'll owe $100.

Bill	$150
Insurance limit	− 50
Your payment	$100

But if inflation and specialists run the bill up to $1000, you get stuck for $950.

Bill	$1,000
Insurance limit	− 50
Your payment	$ 950

Talk about breaking things!

Fixed-limit plans not only fail to offer you any protection against inflation—they frequently don't offer you any protection at all. One big deficiency in policies of this type is that you are not covered if your particular ailment isn't specifically named. So if you break your sacroiliac, and it is not named, you are hurting in more ways than one.

Areas of coverage you'll specifically want to understand no matter what type of policy you have include:

⋄ *Dependent coverage.* Are your spouse and children covered? Who is considered a dependent? Many policies will not cover babies until they are fifteen days old, for example.

⋄ *Pregnancy coverage.* Frequently policies treat pregnancy differently from anything else covered. This may include miscarriage and other pregnancy problems.

⋄ *Mental illness coverage.* Policies often pay less for mental illness than physical illness, although it's hard to understand why.

⋄ *Dental coverage.* Most policies don't pay dental bills, but more plans are including them all the time.

⋄ *Major medical coverage.* Major medical is an important coverage that is frequently inadequate. All policies have maximum limits. Medical expenses exceeding these limts are borne completely by the sick and afflicted person. Some major medical limits are as low as $10,000 or $25,000. It may sound as if it would take a pretty expensive illness to use up $10,000 or $25,000, and with a little luck you will never be that sick. But such medical expenses are not at all uncommon these days. If you should happen to run up a major bill, with only minor coverage, your recovery from the financial setback may be tougher than the recovery from your illness. Additional major medical coverage is not very expensive, and is well worth it. Plan to buy at least $250,000 in major medical coverage.

Once you've read your policy and understand what it does and doesn't cover, you can decide whether you need to buy additional supplemental coverage. But remember that the purpose of health insurance is the same as all other forms of insurance. Its purpose is to transfer risk that you can't afford to assume to the insurance company. You probably can afford to assume the risk of a $50 medical bill, but a $50,000 bill would be a whole different matter. Therefore, resist the temptation to spend your insurance dollars on coverage that will take care of the small nuisances, although admittedly they are frequent. It would be much smarter to increase your limits on the upper end, to make sure you are well covered in the event of a major problem.

I knew a man who was buying group health insurance for himself and his employees at a small company. He found that he could buy a policy with a $25 deductible but an upper limit of only $10,000. For the same premium, he could buy a policy with a $100 deductible but a $50,000 upper limit. He thought how annoying it was every time someone in his family went to the doctor and ran up a $45 bill. He also had a hard time imagining how anyone could spend $10,000 for medical expenses. So he bought the low-deductible policy.

A year later, one of those $45 trips to the doctor revealed an enlarged prostate gland that had to come out. The operation didn't sound too awesome: a few days in the hospital, ten days at home, and then as good as new. And that's the way it started, but complications set in. Shock caused his kidneys to stop working. After fifteen days, intensive care, teams of medical specialists, two more emergency operations, kidney dialysis, and hosts of new procedures, the doctors saved his life. But then it was three more weeks in the hospital, and nearly two months of recovery at home, plus another major operation one year later to repair all the internal damage caused by the frantic attempts to save his life the first time.

The $10,000 insurance money didn't even make a good down payment on the total bill. The doctors didn't volunteer to give him any royalties on the books they wrote about his medical history-setting case, either. Still, the guy is glad to be alive, except for those times he thinks about how much it all cost.

Group Health and
Health Maintenance Organizations

Today most health insurance is sold in the form of group insurance. There are some important cost savings for the insurance company in dealing with a group. It has one place to send the premium invoice, one place for the salesman to visit and one place to call in handling claims.

Another significant advantage to the company in group policies is it gets a statistically average loss experience. As you can imagine, the most likely buyer of individual health insurance is the person who thinks he has some health problems. Usually he does. This means more losses to the company. In a group everyone joins—the sickly and the healthy—so the company has a predictable loss experience.

Because of the lower costs associated with groups the companies can provide the coverage at substantially lower cost than through individual policies.

You should obtain your health coverage through a group if possible—and it should be possible. Groups are everywhere. Your employer, your union, your club, your church, any organization you belong to might be a group.

There are many insurance companies who write group health. The most prominent is Blue Cross and Blue Shield. The concept behind Blue Cross and Blue Shield is interesting. When you need medical care you give your doctor or hospital your Blue Cross/Blue Shield number. The doctor or hospital then submits the bill directly to Blue Cross and Blue Shield who in turn pays them directly. They cut out the middleman in this case—the middleman being you.

You should appreciate being cut out; it saves you effort. And it should save everybody money. In actual practice other insurers have been forced to lower their rates and improve their efficiencies to be competitive. And they've succeeded.

One thing to remember. Whether the insurance company sends the bill directly to the doctor or to you, you are responsible for paying the bill. You cannot tell your doctor you aren't paying because the insurance company hasn't paid you. That's not his problem.

A word about health maintenance organizations (HMOs). This is a promising new concept that should help fight your medical inflation. Here a group of doctors and hospitals will affiliate with the HMO. They are not an insurance company. They do not incur much of the overhead associated with an insurance company. The doctor is reimbursed directly from the HMO. In some cases his reimbursement is more like a salary for belonging as opposed to payment for individual services.

As a member you pay only a monthly premium. You do not receive any bills for your medical attention. You may go to any of the doctors in the organization you like. The expense efficiency of an HMO is substantial. This helps reduce costs all the way around.

An HMO is particularly good for families with young children that are prone to making lots of trips to the doctor for sniffles and such. They are also very good in encouraging preventive medicine. Regular physicals cost the patient nothing extra—so people tend to get them.

The HMO concept is spreading. But today many people complain that (a) they do not have a broad choice of doctors, (b) they receive impersonal medical treatment, and (c) the participating doctors are overloaded, making it difficult to get an appointment.

The accuracy of these complaints will vary from HMO to HMO. But you can see how an HMO could take on some characteristics of socialized medicine. If that should happen it will be a shame. The service will decline and the cost will rise.

◇ 27 ◇
Disability Insurance

Somewhere between temporary illness and death is disability. Disability is being too ill or physically impaired to work any longer.

Disability is frequently the biggest gap in a person's personal insurance program. What if tomorrow you suffered a stroke, or broke your back, or had a heart attack and couldn't work for a long time—perhaps never again? In many cases, disability is financially worse than death. When you die, you cause no more expense after the funeral. With disability, you must still eat and be cared for. In fact, your care may be very expensive.

As you analyze an insurance policy, or your current coverage, ask the following questions:

1. *What would it cost my family and me to live if I were disabled?* This is obviously a key question in order to determine the amount of coverage you need.

2. *In the policy you are considering, what is the definition of "disability"?* Some policies do not pay unless you are totally disabled and cannot perform any useful service. Others pay even if you are forced to leave your profession but can still earn some money at another job.

3. *Does the policy cover mental breakdowns and nervous disorders?* Many do not, but such disabilities are common.

4. *What type of proof of disability is required?* Some policies ask questions doctors refuse to give definite answers to. For example, they may want the doctor to certify that you can do no useful work. The doctor's best medical opinion may be that you should not, but he (or she) may be unwilling to put his (or her) professional reputation on the line that you can do *no* useful work.

5. *How long must you be out of work before you are considered disabled?* Many policies require six months out of work. That is a long time without a paycheck.

6. *How does the policy treat supplemental forms of income you may be entitled to such as workmen's compensation?* Many policies reduce what they pay by the amounts received from other sources.

7. *How long do the benefits extend?* A disabled person may outlive any fixed dates such as ten years or age sixty-five. Your expenses will continue even if your insurance does not.

Disability insurance may seem expensive, but you should not overlook or do without it. Healthy young adults stand a far greater chance, statistically, of suffering disability than premature death.

◇ 28 ◇
Life Insurance

Actually, life insurance is not life insurance at all, it's death insurance. It pays the people you want paid, called *beneficiaries,* in the event of your death. That's important, because I can't imagine anyone feeling financially free if their loved ones will be left destitute and trapped when they die.

Basically, life insurance is like all other types of insurance; that is, it is a transfer of an uncertain economic loss for a certain loss. In this case, you are trying to relieve your loved ones of an economic risk and to transfer that risk to an insurance company. The company will gladly take your risk—for a premium, of course. In return for the premium, your beneficiaries receive money if you die.

Eventually you *are* going to die—no one ever gets out of life alive. Your death is a certainty, but a premature and untimely death is an uncertainty. That's where the risk comes from. When you die, your loved ones lose a lot. They lose your love, your companionship, your friendly smile, and they lose your economic contribution to the family. Certainly love can't be measured in dollars and cents, but groceries, house payments, and clothes can. And although this may sound cold and mercenary, a family that loses its breadwinner has suffered a real economic loss. Sometimes the loss of a loved one results in financial hardships that linger long after the funeral is over.

Historically, these hardships have often been associated with the loss of a husband and father. Increasingly, however, economic loss is also associated with the death of a wife and mother. This is particularly evident where the wife is employed and makes an important contribution to the family income. But even in cases where the mother is at home, and not supplying an income, her loss is a hardship. Employing sitters to care for the children, domestics to clean the house, and taxis to shuttle a busy family around is expensive. Life insurance to offset the loss of the leading lady in the family is a good idea. Moreover, many women *are* the sole breadwinners in their families.

Some economic losses associated with death have nothing to do with income; for example, funeral and burial expenses. It's not cheap to die these days. Many families are also faced with sizable estate tax payments. The government wants a share of the inheritance from most estates over $250,000 in size. This figure will increase to $600,000 by 1987. Sometimes legal fees are necessary to straighten out the will and estate. There may be many costs associated with dying, and the survivors tend to view them all as economic losses.

Offsetting and transferring losses is what insurance is all about. In this regard, life insurance is like any other kind of insurance. But life insurance does have some unique differences from other kinds of insurance. Frequently these differences lead people to buy the wrong amount of insurance. First, life insurance is not required by law or by anyone else. Consequently, it is easy to ignore, and it is easy not to buy. Second, there is no easy way to determine accurately what the economic loss resulting from the death of a loved one will really be. You can easily figure out the potential loss if your car is taken, but you can't easily figure out the potential loss if your life is taken. Third, this is the one insurance you can buy as much of as you want. Your purchase doesn't have to bear any relationship to real economic loss. If you insure a house for less than its value, you may discover there are actually hidden penalties for buying too little insurance. But if you buy more insurance than the house is worth, the company will only reimburse you for the actual damage, no matter how much insurance you have. With life insurance, however, you can buy as little or as much as you want.

Buying the right amount of life insurance is important, no matter who's being insured. If too little is purchased, hardships develop. If too much is purchased, money is wasted that should be spent for family happiness while everyone's still living. The following do's and don'ts will help you choose the correct amount of insurance:

⋄ *Do* take the need for life insurance seriously.
⋄ *Do* carefully analyze your needs.
⋄ *Do* insure against economic loss only, the loss that your survivors cannot afford to assume.
⋄ *Don't* just pick amounts out of thin air. Numbers such as $10,000 or $100,000, or even $1,000,000 are just impressive

numbers that may bear no relationship to your circumstances.

◇ *Don't* buy an excessively large policy just to flatter yourself into feeling rich.

◇ *Don't* try to make the insurance benefit a monetary present to cheer up the bereaved.

◇ *Don't* make yourself worth more dead than alive.

Your life insurance salesperson can help you figure out how much insurance to buy. But remember that your salesperson makes money selling insurance, so don't count on his or her objectivity entirely. He or she wants to sell you as much insurance (or premium) as possible. To keep from buying more life insurance than you really need, you may have to think for a while about the questions your salesperson will ask. This way, you will come up with your own answers, rather than the answers he or she would like to lead you to. Consider the case of the Simpsons.

George was thirty-five years old; Shauna was thirty-two. He was a bookkeeper making $22,000 a year. Shauna worked part-time at a gift shop, making $5000. They had three children, ages twelve, ten, and six. The Simpsons owned a home currently worth $80,000. The outstanding mortgage was $50,000. The house payment was $475 a month. Property taxes and insurance increased that to $610. They owned two cars. One car was paid for; on the other, they paid $176 per month. They owed a finance company $82 per month for some furniture they had purchased.

The following table shows three columns. The first shows the insurance salesperson's questions to them. The second shows the Simpsons' initial answers. The third column shows the answers they came up with after thinking things over for a few days. The difference in their answers was based on a hard look at what they really wanted to insure against. What they really wanted to insure against was the family falling into poverty, need for welfare subsidies, and degradation if George were to die. They realized that death is an unhappy and unwanted experience for everyone. They also realized the odds were heavily against George's premature death. In fact, the odds were so heavily against his death they soon came to think it might be better for Shauna to make some reductions in her standard of living in the unlikely event that George did die, than to make some needless reductions in their standard of living in the very likely event that he lived.

Salesperson's Questions	*Initial Responses and Cost*	*Reconsidered Responses and Costs*
1. You would want Shauna and your children to live in this house, wouldn't you?	1. Yes. Annual cost for staying in current home, including maintenance and utilities: −$8,822	1. No. The family could live in an apartment or smaller house. Annual cost including utilities: −$7,200 Earnings from equity in home, invested at 6% after tax: +$1,800
2. You would want your children's college education completely paid for, wouldn't you?	2. Yes. Annual savings needed to pay for college: −$4,000	2. No. We're not putting that much away for their school now. Many kids work their way through college. Our kids can help, too. Annual cost: −$2,000
3. You could probably get by with one car, but you would want Shauna to have the new one, wouldn't you?	3. Yes. Annual payments: −$2,177 Maintenance, gas, oil, etc.: −$1,200	3. No. The old one doesn't look like much but it runs fine. Maintenance, gas, oil, etc.: −$1,350
4. Your costs for food, clothing, health care, recreation, personal, and miscellaneous should stay about the same, shouldn't they?	4. Yes. Annual cost: −$7,000	4. No. Almost, but there would be one less person, and cuts could be made in many places. Annual cost: −$6,700
5. Do you have some special needs to provide for? For example, care of aged parent, a child	5. Yes, we have planned to have Mom live with us, and it would be nice to leave a donation to	5. No. If George dies, Mom will have to live with Shauna's brother. It seems inappropriate to make

with special prob-
lems, a gift to
a charity?

the church. Savings
needed annually:
                           −$1,000

an unusual gift to the
church at that time.
Annual cost: $0

6. You would want
Shauna to be able to
meet the time pay-
ments, wouldn't you?

6. Yes. Annual
cost: −$984

6. Yes. Annual
cost: −$984

7. You wouldn't want
Shauna to have to
work at all, would
you, especially with
all the extra
burdens she would
have?

7. No. Annual
income: $0

7. Yes, she could
work. In fact, in a
real emergency, she
could work full time.
But it would be best
if she kept working
part time. Annual
income: +$5,000
Annual work-related
expenses: transpor-
tation, clothes,
meals, etc.:   −$1,000

8. If you died,
Shauna would be eli-
gible for Social
Security benefits as
a widow with depen-
dent children.

8. Annual
benefits: +$8,500

8. Annual
benefits: +$8,500

9. You wouldn't want
Shauna to have to
spend the $5000
savings, would you?

9. No. It would be
good to have an emer-
gency fund. Interest
on savings: +$275

9. No. It would be
good to have an emer-
gency fund. Interest
on savings: +$275

10. This is the in-
come Shauna will
need every year in
order to achieve your
goals. (Add Lines 1
through 9.)

10. Annual income
needed: −$16,408

10. Annual income
needed: −$3,659

11. The estate you
need to leave Shauna
through life insur-
ance is found by

11. $16,408 divided
by 6% = $273,467

11. $3,659 divided
by 6% = $60,983

dividing Line 10,
her annual needs,
by an estimated
after-tax investment
rate—say, 6%

| 12. I know this looks like a lot of money, George, and we haven't even considered inflation yet. I would increase it. | 12. $300,000 of term insurance. Annual premium: $1,107.00 per year ($92.25 per month) | 12. $75,000 of term insurance. Annual premium: $276.75 per year ($23.06 per month) |

In this abbreviated example, George and Shauna found that their life insurance needs could range all the way from $300,000 to $75,000, depending on how they answered the salesman's questions. That's a considerable difference. The cost could vary too, all the way from $1,107 a year to $276.75. Some people find they don't absolutely need any insurance. In fact, the Simpsons could conclude they didn't need life insurance if they assumed Shauna would work full time. However, it is unusual to need no life insurance. *Most families will find they need some life insurance.*

To find out whether you need life insurance or not, complete the more detailed analysis given in the next section. As you complete the analysis, give the best answers for your family. The amount each family needs depends on its own answers. Who is to say which set of the Simpsons' answers is correct? No one but the Simpsons. Each family is different. But each family can give better answers if its members give *their own* answers for their own needs and avoid letting the salesperson give *his or her* answers for their needs.

Life insurance may be properly thought of as death insurance. Death is something people ought to insure against because people can't be sure when they will die. And there *will* be a loss associated with death. That loss is something people should try to do something about before they die. They sure can't do anything about it after they die. People should try to transfer the risk of loss elsewhere. Unfortunately, far too many thoughtless people wind up transferring the risk and loss to their already bereaved loved ones. This is unfortunate, because they could transfer the risk to an insurance company that is more than willing to assume it—for a premium, of course.

◇ 29 ◇
How Can You Analyze
Your Life Insurance Needs?

Analyze your life insurance needs carefully. A careful analysis can help you buy the right amount of insurance for your needs. Careful analysis of your needs requires a pencil, the worksheet on p. 219, a little time, and some thinking—especially some thinking.

Your thinking, and the worksheet, will help you analyze two types of economic loss your family might experience if you or your spouse, or both of you, should die. First, survivors' living expenses; second, cash needs at the time of the death. Your family may not have enough income to live properly if there is a premature death. Every family's definition of "living properly" is different, as we have already noted. Your family may also find itself without sufficient cash to meet expenses that arise from a death. In extreme cases, families have been forced to sell homes and possessions to raise enough cash to pay estate taxes.

As you complete this analysis, you may find some questions hard to answer. However, a good guess is better than no answer at all. Furthermore, you will realize that even the partially right answers keep changing all the time. So it is a good idea to reevaluate this analysis every few years to see if your needs have changed.

The first step in analyzing your life insurance needs is to estimate what a death in your family would cost and whether there is enough money to cover the costs. Maybe some life insurance is desirable to meet the cash needs at death.

If Line 13 is positive, your estate has sufficient liquidity to pay costs associated with a death. If Line 13 is negative, you need life insurance to provide the difference. Without life insurance, the difference must be made up by selling such assets as your home or business or by the survivors going into debt.

After the survivors have finally paid off all the bills and taxes that may be associated with a death in the family, they must worry

Resources Available to
Meet Cash Needs at Death ˆ

	Assuming the death of			
	Spouse 1	*Spouse 2*	*Both spouses*	*Line*
Cash, checking, savings	_____	_____	_____	1
Certificates	_____	_____	_____	2
Stocks, bonds	_____	_____	_____	3
Other	_____	_____	_____	4
Total (add lines 1–4)	_____	_____	_____	5

Cash Needs at Death

	Assuming the death of			
	Spouse 1	*Spouse 2*	*Both spouses*	*Line*
Funeral and burial costs	_____	_____	_____	6
Legal fees for probate and estate management, etc.	_____	_____	_____	7
Debt repayments[2]	_____	_____	_____	8
Special gifts and bequests	_____	_____	_____	9
Estate taxes[3]	_____	_____	_____	10
Other	_____	_____	_____	11
Total (add Lines 6–11)	_____	_____	_____	12
Net cash available after death expenses (excess or deficiency) Subtract Line 12 from 5.	_____	_____	_____	13

If excess, record on Line 14. If deficiency, record on Line 56.

[1] Be sure to list here only those assets that you are willing to have used to pay death expenses.

[2] In most cases, the home mortgage, and other joint debts, need not be paid off if one spouse dies.

[3] If you are wealthy you may be subject to estate taxes. The new tax law makes some important and favorable changes in estate taxes. First, beginning in 1982 a surviving spouse can inherit everything from a deceased spouse's estate, without tax, no matter how large the amount. (Previously, if the deceased's estate was more than $425,000, the surviving spouse could face some stiff taxes before receiving the inheritance.) Second, the tax thresholds are rising dramatically from estates where there is no surviving spouse. In 1981 estates in excess of $175,000 are subject to tax. In 1982 that threshold increases to $225,000 and it rises each year until 1987. In that year estates below $600,000 in value will not be subject to any estate tax. Estate tax law is complex. If your estate, including the value of your home, is near these thresholds you should consult a lawyer or tax advisor.

about finding enough money to stay alive themselves. So the next step in your analysis is to estimate what income survivors can expect. Begin this portion of the analysis by looking at the assets that survivors can invest and earn a return on.

Investable Assets[1]

	Assuming the death of			
Assets	Spouse 1	Spouse 2	Both spouses	Line
Net cash available after death expenses (Line 13). Record excess only. If deficiency, record zero here.	_____	_____	_____	14
Cash, savings, certificates, bonds, stocks, notes not recorded on Lines 1–4.	_____	_____	_____	15
Profit sharing	_____	_____	_____	16
Business equity	_____	_____	_____	17
Home equity (if home is sold)	_____	_____	_____	18
Equity in real estate investment	_____	_____	_____	19
Other investments	_____	_____	_____	20
Personal property (items that can be sold—cars, furniture, collections, etc.)	_____	_____	_____	21
Other	_____	_____	_____	22
Total (add Lines 14–22)	_____	_____	_____	23

Liabilities[2]				
Personal loans and notes	_____	_____	_____	24
Other liabilities	_____	_____	_____	25
Total (add Lines 24–25)	_____	_____	_____	26
Net investable assets (subtract Line 26 from 23)	_____	_____	_____	27

[1]These assets include only those which can be used to generate income to meet survivors' living expenses. Do not include assets that are sold to pay death expenses.

[2]The assets should be shown as net equity; that is, assuming all associated loans are paid off. Do not include liabilities here that must be paid off before the estate can be settled.

Normally Line 27 will be positive. These funds are available for investment to earn income for the survivors to live on. If Line 27 is negative, additional income must be provided beyond the survivors' regular living expenses to satisfy the obligations.

At this point, you must estimate what the survivors' living expenses will be. The following worksheet has a column for current cost. This can guide estimating costs in the event of a death.

Survivors' Living Expenses

Expenses	Current family expenses	Assuming the death of Spouse 1	Spouse 2	Both spouses	Line
Food					28
Personal care					29
Clothing					30
Mortgage or rent					31
Utilities					32
Transportation (including auto payments, maintenance, insurance, gas, oil, etc.)					33
Medical (including insurance payments)					34
Education (including savings for future tuitions)					36
Child care					37
Entertainment					38
Time payments					39
Taxes					40
Other					41
Total (add Lines 28–41)					42

Next you must determine the sources of income survivors will have to meet the expenses of Line 42. Generally there are three key sources of income for survivors: the survivors' own salaries, Social

Security benefits, and the investable assets left in the estate. Investable assets are where Line 27 becomes important. The amount on Line 27 represents the investable assets the survivors will have to live on. Because the survivors may have to live on this money for a long time, it is important they not have to spend it. All they should have to spend is the earnings from the assets.

The assets on Line 27 will be quite different for everyone who completes this worksheet. Therefore, the level of earnings the assets generate will also be quite different. Each person should make an effort to estimate the earnings from his or her individual assets—this book cannot do it for you. But for those assets you cannot individually determine, use an estimated *after-tax* earning rate of about 7 percent (.07). Multiply those assets whose earnings you cannot individually determine by 7 percent (.07).

Survivors' Source of Income
(After Taxes)

| | Assuming the death of | | | |
	Spouse 1	Spouse 2	Both spouses	Line
Net investable assets (Line 27)	————	————	————	
Earnings on investable assets (determine according to individual asset earning rate or multiply Line 27 × .07)	————	————	————	43
Spouse 1 after-tax income	————	————	————	44
Spouse 2 after-tax income	————	————	————	45
Other family members' income	————	————	————	46
Annuities	————	————	————	47
Trusts and inheritances	————	————	————	48
Assistance from friends or relatives	————	————	————	49
Other income	————	————	————	50
Social Security	————	————	————	51
Total income (add Lines 43–51)	————	————	————	52

Call your local Social Security office for further information. In general, Social Security will pay a surviving spouse with dependent children 75 percent of their deceased spouse's benefit. In some cases, the spouse will receive 100 percent of the deceased spouse's benefit when the survivor reaches age sixty-five. Also see Chapter 34 "Social Security." You may not want to count on a full Social Security benefit.

The figures on Line 52 are important. They are the estimated income survivors will have in the event of death(s) in the family. To see if it is enough, you must compare it with the survivors' living expenses from Line 42.

	Assuming the Death of			
	Spouse 1	*Spouse 2*	*Both spouses*	*Line*
Total survivors' living expenses (Line 42)	_____	_____	_____	
Subtract total survivors' sources of income (Line 52)	_____	_____	_____	
Survivors' income excess or deficiency (record only the deficiencies on Line 54)	_____	_____	_____	53

If Line 53 is positive, the survivors theoretically will have enough money to live on, and extra life insurance is not needed.

If Line 53 is negative, the survivors will not have enough to live on and will need additional income. The additional income could be secured through the purchase of life insurance. The question is "How much life insurance?" When considering this question, remember that you do not want the survivors to actually have to spend the insurance benefit itself. If they spend the actual insurance benefit, they may run out of money long before they run out of a need for money. They could spend years of their life destitute and on welfare.

To avoid survivors' running out of money, you want a big enough insurance benefit so they can invest it and live off the earnings.

To estimate the required life insurance amount needed, divide the total deficiency on Line 53 by an estimated after-tax earnings rate—perhaps 7 percent (.07). With today's high interest rates, 7 percent after tax may seem too low. But there is no guarantee that today's high rates will last as long as the survivors will live. Note that 7 percent is higher than long-term historical experience.

	Assuming the Death of			
	Spouse 1	*Spouse 2*	*Both spouses*	*Line*
Income deficiency from Line 53 (if Line 53 showed an excess, record zero here)	_____	_____	_____	54
Divide Line 54 by 7% estimated investment rate (after tax)	.07	.07	.07	
Total needed to provide for survivors' living expenses (the number will be negative)	_____	_____	_____	55

You are now ready to determine your total life insurance need. The need arises from cash needed to pay death expenses (Line 13) and the total dollars needed to meet survivors' living expenses (Line 54). For there to be a need, there must be a deficiency, hence both numbers will carry minus signs.

Life Insurance Need

	Assuming the Death of			
	Spouse 1	*Spouse 2*	*Both spouses*	*Line*
Net cash available after death expenses, from Line 13. Record only deficiencies. If excess, record zero here.	_____	_____	_____	56
Add total needed to provide for survivors' living expenses (from Line 55—this number will be negative)	_____	_____	_____	57
Total face amount of life insurance needed (this number will be negative)	_____	_____	_____	58

Line 58 is the grand total. This number is the deficit that must be made up through life insurance. Compare this amount with the amount of insurance you now own. You may need to buy more, or you may already own too much.

Whether you personally have too little or too much, there are four important observations about the analysis just completed.

1. *These numbers are estimates.* Using estimates may make you uncomfortable. But do not allow your discomfort to lead to inaction. There is no precise way of figuring how much survivors will need. Your actual experience could vary 10 to 25 percent from your estimate. An estimate is far better than nothing at all.

2. *Your circumstances and assumptions will change.* You should work through this exercise every year.

3. *This analysis makes no adjustment for future inflation.* What may be adequate insurance for survivors' living expenses today may be woefully inadequate five or ten years from now.

4. *You probably got different answers from each of the three columns.* Buy sufficient insurance to meet the needs of survivors in the most difficult circumstances. For instance, both spouses may currently have good incomes, meaning that little insurance is necessary if one of them dies. But what about the children if both parents die?

A careful analysis of your life insurance needs requires a pencil, the preceding worksheets, a little time, and some thinking. It's important to put these all together—right now. Once you're gone, it's too late for pencils, worksheets, time, or thinking.

◇ 30 ◇
Term versus Whole-Life

This chapter deals with the two basic types of life insurance: term and whole-life.

Term life insures you for a specific period of time, such as one or five years. At the end of the term you must either renew or be without insurance.

Whole-life (also known as ordinary-life, or straight-life) insures you for your whole life, not just a specified period.

Term life insurance is the most basic and least expensive form of life insurance. It is growing in popularity because families can buy large amounts of term insurance at affordable rates while they are still young and need life insurance most. For example, in the early 1980s $100,000 of term life insurance would cost a thirty-five-year-old man approximately $210 a year. But $100,000 of whole-life insurance would cost approximately $1360 a year, or more. Rates for women are lower because they live longer.

Obviously the cost is substantially different. There are several reasons:

First, term insurance covers you only to the end of the term. If you are thirty-five, odds are you will *not* die before age thirty-six—so the premium can be low. But each year the cost of term insurance rises because your statistical chance of dying increases. At age sixty-five the cost of a $100,000 annual term policy for a man might have risen from $210 to $2780 or more.

The whole-life policy is written with the expectation that it will be in force when you die. The whole-life policy is expected to pay off, the term policy is expected not to pay off.

Second, whole-life premiums are level for the duration of the policy. In order to provide constant insurance protection at a constant premium from age thirty to one hundred, for example, the company must overcharge the young person and undercharge the old person. This is because statistically speaking old people are more likely to die than young people.

Third, term insurance is less costly because it provides only basic insurance protection. Whole-life provides insurance and it also builds a cash value. You may borrow the cash value of your policy—usually at very favorable rates—or you may cash in your policy and receive a check for the cash value. A cash value is not true savings, nor does it accumulate as fast as investments. It has some characteristics of savings and investments but it is an expensive way to accumulate them. Part of your whole-life premium dollar goes into building these inefficient savings.

Fourth, whole-life policies cost more because the salesperson receives a much higher commission for selling a whole-life policy than a term policy with the same face amount of insurance.

There are many variations of these basic forms of insurance. The important variations of term insurance are:

Level Term Insurance. Statistically speaking the risk that you will die increases each minute you live because you're getting older. Theoretically, the insurance company should constantly be raising your insurance premium to offset the increasing risk of your dying. Of course, no one would find a policy that raised its premium every few minutes very attractive, so insurance companies write policies that guarantee level premiums over the term. The most popular terms are one, five and ten years. At the end of the term the policy must be renewed—at a higher premium, of course.

Renewable Term. After buying a term policy, your first thought is probably that you hope to live to see the end of the term. If you do you will certainly want to renew the policy, even if the premium does go up. But suppose you become uninsurable during the term? Suppose the company says, "We're glad you lived to the end of the term, too, but we can't take another chance on you." What would you do then? Well, "then" is too late to do anything. The thing to do is get a guarantee to begin with that you can renew, no matter what. Today renewable features are almost standard, but they are worth it.

Decreasing Term. Once you've paid for the renewable feature, you can be sure you can keep buying life insurance protection. But the guarantee that you can buy it doesn't guarantee you can afford it. The cost of basic insurance keeps rising, remember. As illustrated above, a man may pay $210 for $100,000 of life insurance at age thirty-five, but he will pay in the neighborhood of $2780 a year for the same policy at age sixty-five. A woman will pay less at both ages.

A lot of people may find premiums like that too steep for their old age. Besides they may not need $100,000 of insurance when they are sixty-five and the kids are raised. Decreasing term insurance meets these changing needs. With decreasing term, the amount of insurance coverage decreases each time the policy is renewed and the premium is adjusted to stay constant. For example, if a man paid $210 when he was thirty-five for $100,000, he could still pay $210 when he was sixty-five and get $7550 worth of insurance. Coverage of $7,550 may be enough at that time.

There are also several variations of whole-life policies. But first it is important to understand the substantial variations between similar whole-life policies themselves.

Each premium dollar you pay is divided among four purposes: sales commissions, company overhead and profit, insurance reserve, and cash value accumulation. Each policy may use different assumptions for these, producing great differences in premium cost. For example, in the early 1980s the premium for $100,000 of whole-life insurance may vary from approximately $1000 to $1700 a year for a healthy thirty-five-year-old man. And initial premiums are only part of the story. Depending upon cash value accumulations and other assumptions the relative cost of two policies may change over the years.

Sales expenses, overhead, and profit may vary from company to company as you can imagine. But presumably these are legitimate costs for which you receive services. If you receive the full service of the company, you probably have little complaint and should expect little reduction in these charges.

However, variations in your premium dollar due to insurance allocation and cash values may be of concern. The concern is that most whole-life policies cost you too much.

The company puts a portion of each premium dollar into a reserve to pay insurance benefits. The reserves are invested in bonds, mortgages, real estate, stocks, etc. How much they need to put in the reserve depends to a large extent on how much they assume they will earn on the investments. As the earnings assumptions increase, your insurance premium declines. And this has occurred. A new policy today may cost 50 percent less than an identical policy ten or fifteen years ago. But regardless of the change in assumptions most experts feel the insurance companies still use investment assumptions that are too conservative—and this costs you money.

There is a similar problem with respect to cash value accumulations. Some people view the cash value accumulation as a form of savings or investment. The more rapidly these build, the lower the ultimate cost of your insurance. Today, many companies are still using investment return assumptions of 4 or 5 percent. These rates are very unattractive in today's environment.

Cash value accumulation may seem like an attractive feature of a whole-life policy—and it could be if the assumed investment returns were higher.

One of the attractions is the ability to borrow the cash value. These loans generally carry lower interest rates than loans available anywhere else. Today 8 percent is typical, but on older policies the rates may be as low as 5 percent or 6 percent. However, if you die while the loan is outstanding the loan will be paid off first and your beneficiaries will be paid off second. But, of course, if you had borrowed elsewhere and then died, your estate would probably have had to use a portion of your life insurance benefit to pay the debt anyway. So, if you need to borrow, and you have some available cash value, you should look closely at borrowing against it.

Borrowing is not the only way to get hold of the cash value of many policies. Generally the holder can "cash in the policy." Cashing in means you stop paying your premiums, fill out some simple forms, and the company will send you a check for the cash value of your policy. The cash value is very roughly the excess premiums they've accumulated against your policy. Of course, cashing in your policy will leave you without life insurance protection. Obviously, you should cash in your policy only if you no longer need the coverage, or you are switching to a better form of protection. Never cash them in just to meet pressing financial obligations.

I will deal more with cash values as an investment and the whole-life cost problem later when I discuss the purchase of term versus whole-life.

Two popular variations of the basic whole-life policy are:

Limited Pay Life. Limited pay life, or twenty pay life, or paid up at sixty-five life, etc., is a common variation. With ordinary whole-life you can plan to pay premiums for your whole life or at best until you are ninety or one hundred years old. If you faithfully pay your premiums your insurance will be in force when you die. But not everyone wants to pay premiums his whole life. Many people don't want to pay premiums when they are sixty-five or seventy-five or eighty-five or older. Limited pay life policies are worked out so you pay only twenty or thirty years, or until you are sixty-five. After that you pay no more premiums, but your insurance is still in force.

To work out this limited pay arrangement, the company must charge you more excess premium when you are young and not likely to die. By charging a larger excess premium when you are young, the company can invest more. By investing more, they can build an adequate reserve and stop charging you premiums before you are a hundred. It's great not to have to pay premiums when you're a hundred, but don't kid yourself into thinking this is some special deal the insurance company has worked out just for you. The "more" they will charge you means "much more." If you are a thirty-five-year-old man and you want $100,000 of insurance, you might pay $210 a year for term, $1360 for ordinary whole-life, and $1970 a year for a limited pay policy that is paid up in twenty years. That is a considerable difference.

Single Pay Life. This is a form of limited pay life. As the name implies one large payment is made at the outset and then the policy is paid up for life.

Endowment. This is the ultimate in a life insurance policy. Not only does it protect your family in the event of your premature death, it protects you in your old age if you live. It protects you by paying you money back when you are old. Most policies endow at age sixty-five. Some endowment policies will send you a lump sum of cash on your sixty-fifth birthday. Some will send you a monthly check for the rest of your life. Some will send you or your beneficiary a check for a given number of years. Regardless of how the cash comes, the policy holder really appreciates getting it, even if he didn't appreciate paying for it.

Endowment policies might almost be thought of as "living insurance" whereas most life insurance is really "death insurance." Endowments are living insurance because they insure you against the highly likely risk of living, while providing some protection against dying. If you do live you'll need money.

There are two broad categories of endowment policies: fixed and variable rate. With a fixed rate policy your return is guaranteed. With a variable rate policy your return depends upon investment performance. A fixed rate policy is similar to a bond; the variable rate is more like a stock.

Some people believe they will come out better in the long run buying a variable rate policy. In a fixed rate policy the insurance company must quote you a rate they are willing to guarantee for perhaps thirty years. As you can imagine they must be conservative in their quote. With a variable rate policy they can do their best to get high investment returns and pass the results (good or bad) on to you.

Which policy is best probably depends on future inflation. If I didn't persuade you early in the book that inflation would be slow, if you believe it will stay high and go higher, then variable rate should be best. If inflation does moderate substantially in the 1980s then today's high yielding fixed rate policies should prove most attractive.

As with most policies that combine insurance and savings, many experts are critical of the cost and generally poor investment returns characteristic of annuities—and so am I. However, there is one variation worth looking at, a product designed for the 1980s—the tax deferred annuity.

If you are in a high income tax bracket a tax deferred annuity may make sense. On the surface, the product will look like a high yield mutual fund. But because it is legally defined as an annuity you can defer taxes on the investment earnings until you withdraw them.

In the 1980s you get more flexibility on withdrawal. Traditional annuities don't pay off for a fixed number of years, or until a certain age, or until you die. But these new annuities have a lot more withdrawal flexibility. In fact, the IRS is beginning to question whether they are really annuities at all. Until the IRS says they are not (which they may never say) go ahead and use them. They are a good way of building investment dollars.

Giving guidelines on potential annuity returns is difficult because guaranteed returns vary greatly. For instance in October of 1981 fixed rate annuities were available with guaranteed rates ranging from 15 percent down to 4 percent. As a guideline, look for a guaranteed rate near the thirty-year government bond rate. You can find the quoted rates on government bonds in the financial section of major newspapers.

The variations and combinations of life insurance policies are numerous. You can get anything from basic life insurance protection to a tax deferred investment program. Many offer benefits like insurance still in force when you are too old to be insurable, benefits like not having to pay insurance when you are retired and can no longer afford to pay insurance, benefits like getting money back from the insurance company. These are good benefits but remember *you must pay for them.* Nothing in this life is free—including old age and death.

Should I Buy Whole-life or Term Insurance?

Whether you should buy whole-life or term depends upon your personal financial self-discipline. Most financial advisors would tell you to avoid whole-life insurance as you would avoid the bad part of town on payday. They would say whole-life is too expensive. They would say whole-life is a better deal for the company than it is for you. They would say you should buy inexpensive term insurance and invest the difference between the premiums. And what they say would be right if only people would invest the difference. But a lot of people don't. A lot of people don't have the financial self-discipline to invest the difference.

The difference can be substantial, because whole-life insurance costs a whole lot more. Suppose you are male, thirty-five years old, and concerned about life insurance (it works even better if you are female because insurance rates are lower). Suppose you think you need $100,000 of life insurance now and would like an estate of at least $100,000 when you die. You could rush out and buy whole-life insurance and pay $1360 a year for the rest of your life. Then when you died your heirs would collect $100,000.

As an alternative (a better alternative) you can buy annual renewable term and invest the difference. Your term policy will cost you $210 initially. The difference available for investment is $1150. As you grow older the cost of your term insurance will rise, meaning you will have less to invest each year. In fact, somewhere around age fifty-eight your term insurance will cost you more than the $1360 you've been spending for insurance and investing. At this point you probably need less than $100,000 in life insurance, and your investments should be worth more than $75,000. In total you have a potential estate well in excess of $100,000. So, the logical thing may be to continue paying $1360 and take a reduction in the amount of your insurance.

The charts on p. 233 illustrate this situation. Their comparisons will help you to see how you might stand at various ages along the way. Note that your total expenditures for insurance and investments are the same. But term and investing the difference have done a great

Comparison:
Whole-life versus Term and Investments
Whole-life

Age	Annual premium	Annual investment	Insurance protection	Accumulated cash surrender value*	Accumulated investment	Total death estate
35	$ 1,360	$0	$100,000	$ 0	$0	$100,000
45	1,360	0	100,000	11,000	0	100,000
55	1,360	0	100,000	30,400	0	100,000
65	1,360	0	100,000	47,200	0	100,000
Total	$40,800	$0	$100,000	$47,200	$0	$100,000

*Accumulated cash surrender values are not available to be used unless they are borrowed or the policy is surrendered.

Term and Investments

Age	Annual premium*	Annual investment*	Insurance protection	Accumulated cash surrender value	Accumulated investment (10% return)	Total death estate
35	$ 210	$ 1,150	$100,000	$0	$ 0	$100,000
45	414	946	100,000	0	19,280	119,280
55	1,075	698	100,000	0	63,165	163,165
65	1,360	0	48,920	0	164,454	213,374
Total	$22,396	$18,404	$ 48,920	$0	$164,454	$213,374

*Total payments to insurance and investment equals $40,800 or $1,360 per year.

deal more for you. (The table assumes you can earn 10 percent after tax on your investments over the years—which you should be able to do.)

1. In the event of death your estate is $100,000 with the whole-life policy. With the term it rises from $100,000 to $213,374 by age sixty-five. This represents $48,920 of insurance still in force and $164,454 of accumulated investments.

2. If you need money along the way you can borrow against the cash surrender value of your whole-life policy. With the term

you can borrow, or spend, or whatever makes sense. You have considerably more flexibility with term and a greater amount of money to work with.

3. When you reach sixty-five you are not through making insurance payments with whole-life. If you want to you can cash in your policy for $47,200 and do without insurance. With term you may also cancel your policy but you will have $164,454 to live on.

These numbers clearly show what most financial advisors would tell you, which is: you'd have to be nuts not to buy term and invest the difference, unless you don't invest the difference. If you buy the term with all kinds of good intentions, but invest the difference in cars, vacations, orthodontists, drapes, entertainment, etc., you will wind up without an endowment. For people without financial discipline "buy term and invest the difference" is not a good idea.

There are other negatives to "invest the difference" as well. The negatives are:

1. (Again) Many people do not invest the money, but spend it as they go along instead. Then they wind up with nothing for retirement or to pass on.

2. The money may be invested unwisely and lost. The 10 percent after-tax rate used in the examples above is conservative today and can be achieved without risk by buying insured savings certificates. Other investments may have even greater potential returns, but the risk will also be greater. Further, there is no guarantee today's attractive rates will persist for thirty or forty years. If the investor takes too many risks he may lose it all. The whole-life policy, on the other hand, is guaranteed.

3. The investments may be put in good but illiquid assets. Then when the money is needed for current living expenses it may be difficult to sell.

4. The accumulated investments may get tied up in probate court at your death. Life insurance can reduce or eliminate those complications.

So what should you buy, whole-life or term? The answer is you should definitely buy term and invest the difference—but beware. The right decision is not always the smartest decision. Unless a person really will invest the difference, and invest it wisely, the smartest decision may be whole-life.

◇ 31 ◇
Variable and
Universal Life Insurance

The whole-life insurance policy has some important deficiencies, as discussed in Chapter 30. Those deficiencies look more serious as investment returns increase on things such as money market mutual funds, savings certificates, bonds, and stocks. Insurance companies are beginning to realize the world has changed. They must offer products that are more competitive for our times.

Important New Insurance Products

Two brand new offerings that are apparently more competitive are variable life and universal life insurance.

These products are so new that at this time they (1) are offered by only a handful of companies, but many others are studying them; (2) are not yet comparable from company to company; (3) can't even be found in the rate books; (4) are not well understood by most insurance people; (5) still have some important unanswered questions regarding their tax and actuarial viability. Despite the uncertainties associated with newness, you should know about these new financial tools.

To understand these new offerings, recall that all whole-life insurance offerings are made up of two parts—basic insurance protection, and savings or investment accumulation called *cash value*. It is the low amount of investment accumulation, or cash value buildup, that bothers most financial people about whole life. In some cases, the investment returns on the savings portion are as low as 4 percent—not very competitive today.

Variable and universal life policies are also made up of insurance protection and investment accumulation. But in these offerings the policyholder participates very directly in actual investment experience.

Participating in actual investment experience has an important additional benefit to the policyholder—the investments accumulate without tax.

To illustrate, assume you want $100,000 of life insurance protection and something accumulated for your estate. As discussed in Chapter 30, you can buy a whole-life policy for $1360 a year. Or you can buy a term insurance policy for $210 a year and invest the $1150 difference. As shown in Chapter 30, you should come out way ahead in the end by buying the term and investing the difference.

Unfortunately, as you invest the $1150 each year you will generate some taxable income. For instance, if you buy a 13 percent savings certificate and if you are in a 23 percent tax bracket, you will only wind up with a 10 percent return after taxes.

When the insurance company invests the difference for you, however, you do not pay taxes—at least until you take the money. Now your investment compounds at 13 percent, not at 10 percent. For example, the $1150 invested every year and compounding at 10 percent would become $189,168 in thirty years. But if there were no taxes, and the money could compound at 13 percent, that same $1150 would be worth $337,179 at the end of thirty years— substantially more than you would earn paying taxes along the way. Of course, there will be taxes to be paid on some of the $337,179 when you finally take it, but the taxes are deferred for many years.

Tax-free investment accumulation has always been a feature of whole-life offerings. But when the returns were only 4 percent, who cared? Variable life and universal life may convince you to care.

Variable Life

A variable life policy works as follows. Suppose you place the $1360 you are willing to spend for insurance and investment in a variable life contract. The insurance company will deduct certain commissions and expenses, pay for the death insurance portion of the policy, and then invest the difference. It will establish a figure such as 4 percent as the standard investment return. Hopefully it will do better than 4 percent. Assume, for example, that in the first year the company earns $100 more than the 4 percent rate would imply. This excess $100 will be used to buy additional paid-up life insurance. That means that both your insurance coverage and cash values will increase to reflect these excess earnings.

Year after year, as investment experience exceeds the 4 percent assumed rate of return, the excess earnings are used to buy additional paid-up whole-life insurance. In years where investment experience is below the 4 percent level, your cash value will be reduced to reflect the shortfall.

Over time, your investment experience should exceed 4 percent. Therefore both your basic insurance coverage and your cash values will increase. For instance, if the investment experience is typically 10 or 11 percent, your basic insurance coverage might expand from $100,000 to $190,000 in twenty years. And your accumulated cash value might be in excess of $80,000.

There are a number of advantages to variable life insurance:

⋄ You receive a far more competitive investment return than you can get with a traditional whole-life policy.
⋄ Your basic insurance protection increases without additional premium on your part. The value of this benefit is limited to unusual situations. Normally a person's need for basic insurance protection declines as he or she grows older. However, in situations where your estate values are growing, meaning your potential estate tax liabilities are growing, and your assets are somewhat nonliquid—such as land or art—then this growing insurance coverage is a very valuable feature.
⋄ Your cash value is increasing at a competitive rate.
⋄ You can borrow against your cash value at favorable rates.
⋄ The policy has a fixed premium. Many people need the discipline of a fixed premium to make themselves save.

Universal Life

The universal life policy works as follows. Once again, assume you want savings and $100,000 of basic life insurance protection, and are willing to pay a premium of $1360 a year to get them.

The company will place your payment in a side fund. From this fund, it will deduct expenses and enough money to buy $100,000 of term insurance for you. Your side fund will appreciate or depreciate with investment experience.

When it comes time to make your payment again, you have several choices. You can pay in the same amount, you can pay more, or you can pay less—perhaps nothing.

Your insurance will not lapse if you do not make a payment. The company will deduct the necessary premium from your existing side fund. It will keep doing so as long as you have money in your side fund. Only when your side fund runs out of money will your insurance lapse. You may be able to go years without paying for insurance, if you want.

You have another option available, too. You can vary your insurance coverage by notifying the company. The company will simply increase, or decrease, the deduction from your side fund accordingly.

Your side fund accumulates without paying taxes. This can be a real advantage, because you may be able to pay for your insurance with before-tax dollars. Most people have to pay for their insurance (and everything else) with after-tax dollars. That means you earn money, pay your taxes, and then with the after-tax dollars you buy insurance. So if you are buying $210 of term insurance, and if you are in a 23 percent tax bracket, you must earn $273 before taxes to meet the payment.

If you have a universal life policy, however, you may buy the insurance with before-tax dollars. Because the plan qualifies as an insurance policy, you pay no taxes until you withdraw more than you've put in. Assume you've built your side fund up to $2100. Assume the side fund earns 10 percent return or more. Assume your insurance cost is $210. At this point, you could let your investment income pay your insurance and theoretically you wouldn't have to put in any more money.

The universal policy has other flexibilities. You can withdraw money from your side fund without paying loan charges and maybe without paying taxes. (The IRS views a withdrawal of cash value as a loan and not income, but this issue is still being studied for universal life policies.)

The universal policy has these advantages:

- ◇ Your savings accumulate without tax.
- ◇ Your savings earn at a competitive interest rate.
- ◇ You can skip payments without your life insurance lapsing.
- ◇ You can withdraw money from your fund without interest or taxes.
- ◇ You can change your insurance coverage as your needs change.
- ◇ You receive a payment schedule, which provides some inducement to make payments. (However, because you can reduce, delay, accelerate, or skip payments these policies may

not provide enough structure for people with poor financial discipline.)

At the present time, universal life seems to be better than the whole-life insurance offerings on the market.

Variable life and universal life seem to be superior to typical whole-life offerings—they are definitely worth your consideration. Furthermore, they are fairly competitive with buying term insurance and then investing the difference. They are competitive, first, because they provide some discipline, which helps people actually make the payments. And, second, the savings portion accumulates tax free.

DRAWBACKS

There are, however, a number of drawbacks, and if you are a fairly disciplined investor, you may very likely do better buying term insurance and investing the difference.

Tax Status. So far I have been stressing tax advantages. But there are two serious unanswered tax questions for these new offerings. The first concerns insurance company taxes. In a normal whole-life policy, the company guarantees 4% return on the cash value. But if the company actually earns more—and all companies do—the excess flows into their surplus account. Money flowing into the company's surplus account is subject to corporate taxes. In variable and universal policies, the company is trying to pass excess earnings on to you, not to the surplus account. At this point, it believes the Internal Revenue Service (IRS) will not force them to pay corporate taxes on the excess earnings. But the issue is not resolved. The companies are trying to offer investment funds that look like life insurance policies. Some experts believe the IRS will not accept this concept and will apply taxes as they would with any whole-life policy.

If the IRS interpretation is unfavorable, some companies have options to shield the earnings from taxes for a while. But their options are limited, especially for mature companies. Eventually they would be forced to reduce your earnings by their tax rate.

Second, the issue of your personal taxes on the products may not be completely resolved. At this time, it appears the savings can accumulate without taxes because the savings are an insurance product. The minimum earnings guarantee on the policies makes the savings an insurance product.

However, if over time these policies start to look more like investments than insurance, the IRS will try to impose some taxes. For the moment the policies look safe, but the government is watching the situation.

These two tax issues create a "Catch 22" dilemma. If the policies are really new wrinkles of traditional insurance policies, then the company should be liable for taxes on excess earnings. But if they are not insurance policies, then they are investments or mutual funds. In this case, the investor should be liable for taxes on earnings.

The insurance companies are trying to get favorable treatment on both issues. We will have to wait and see.

Expense. Variable and universal policies are not cheap. The companies have added heavy loads (graduated payments) and expense deductions.

It is difficult to be specific at this point about costs, because of the current lack of standards. But watch out for a first-year load of 20 percent or more. This means that you could make a $1360 payment—then the company could deduct $270 to pay commissions and selling expenses, and then another $210 or more to pay basic insurance costs. You could wind up with more than 35 percent of your first-year payment going somewhere besides investment. And loads in subsequent years continue to be high—perhaps 6 to 29 percent.

The cost of the term insurance portion of the policy is more expensive—perhaps 20 percent more expensive—than comparable coverage purchased only as a term insurance. (Although I have used similar rates in my examples for comparison, you may find actual costs higher than the illustrations in this book.)

Finally, the company charges fees and expenses for managing the money and maintaining the account. These expenses can run to a hefty 1.25 percent of your cash value. The expense is deducted before any earnings accrue to you.

In total, when you examine the loads, commissions, fees, expenses, and high term insurance costs, you can see that the insurance company plans to make a healthy profit and pay its salespeople well. Some analysts expect competition to squeeze these expenses somewhat in the future.

Investment Earnings. The investment rates earned on the savings portion are competitive, but in most cases they are far from attractive. Typical returns are 8 to 12 percent, which are still well below what many competitive forms of investment return.

Complexity. A general problem in the life insurance business is the difficulty laypeople have in understanding the policies and comparing one to another. Variable and universal policies are even more complex and difficult than normal policies. Therefore, buyers have a greater risk of being sold something they don't really need and can't really use, by a salesperson who likewise may or may not understand the policies.

Large Policies. These policies are sold in fairly large amounts—say $100,000 of basic life insurance. This can raise your premiums to several thousand dollars a year. You may not want that much insurance.

These new policies represent an important trend worth watching and worth knowing about. The new state of the world is forcing the insurance industry to catch up and offer policyholders a better deal. Today only a few companies are offering these new policies in any form. But their use will spread.

If you need life insurance (and most people do) and if you need to invest for the future (and most people should), and if you like the discipline of a payment schedule (and it helps most people), and if you like investments that accumulate tax free (and everyone does), then you are a candidate for a variable or universal life policy.

◇ 32 ◇
What Is
"Participating" Life Insurance?

Participating life insurance is a concept that allows policyholders to participate in the favorable mortality experience of the company, and to a small extent in the profits. Sounds like a great idea— policyholders get back some of the profits the company made from them.

Participating in the profits of an insurance company is an idea that comes from the concept of mutual ownership. Mutual insurance companies are owned by the policyholders, although many stock insurance companies do offer participating policies. Everyone buying a policy from a mutual company becomes an owner, a kind of stockholder in the company. Of course, it is common for companies to pay dividends to their owners out of the profits. So the policyholder-owners of the mutual insurance companies receive dividends from the profits.

What's more, a dividend is usually fairly well assured, which is not true in a regular company. Insurance companies selling participating policies can assure dividends because the companies are practically guaranteed to earn profits. The near guarantee of profitability occurs because the policyholder pays a substantially higher premium for a participating policy than for a nonparticipating policy. Therefore, the company can earn a substantially higher profit than normal. So the company can pay a dividend. With a little luck, the dividend might almost equal the overpayments the policyholder made in the first place.

The general concept of participating insurance seems to make some sense. What's disturbing is why the premiums have to be so high. Many insurance companies have proven they can charge far lower rates, make a decent profit, and still pay a reasonable dividend to their owners. Many companies proving this point are the same companies that also write participating insurance. About one-third of the insurance companies in this country write both participating and nonparticipating policies. All these companies charge more for their participating policies—about 34 percent more. This percentage is a substantial difference as far as most people are concerned.

Perhaps most people wouldn't be concerned about the difference in premiums if the dividends they received made up the difference, and a little more. When that occurs, the total cost of the insurance is favorable. But often the dividends don't result in a lower total cost. On balance, there is no indication that people who buy participating policies save money on their insurance costs.

In fact, the company actually charges a premium larger than it needs, then holds the excess premium for twelve months, and then sends it back to the policyholder at the end of the year. In some ways, this process is similar to what the government does. The government withholds too much tax from your paychecks, then sends you a refund in April.

As with your tax refund, you can do several things with your dividend checks. You can take your refund in cash, or apply it to next year's taxes, or buy government bonds with it. You can take your dividend in cash, or apply it to your premium, or buy more insurance, or leave it with the company and let it collect interest. The interest it will collect today is usually 7 percent. This percentage is lower than the 9 to 14 percent and more you can get by purchasing savings certificates from a bank.

Not everyone has enough will power to save money at a bank. For many people, big tax deductions from their paycheck are a form of forced savings—not a good one, but still a form of savings. Excessive participating insurance premiums can also be a form of forced savings—not a good one, but still a form of savings. If you need the discipline of a government deduction or an insurance bill to force you to save, then maybe the higher premiums of participating insurance are for you. If you don't need that kind of discipline, you probably don't need participating insurance.

◇ 33 ◇
Shopping for Life Insurance

You should only shop for life insurance if you are interested in saving money. If you don't care about saving money, then sit tight—the life insurance will come shopping for you.

And it often does seem as if the insurance is shopping for you. Insurance salespeople find you everywhere you stop for breath. There are salesmen at family reunions, town meetings, and championship hog-calling contests. There are prerecorded phone calls that interrupt your Chinese checkers game. There are junk mail offerings for free sky-diving lessons and a sales pitch with no strings attached. There are newspaper ads next to your favorite obituaries. You find you can buy life insurance through your work, through your club, even through your old college fraternity. And if you don't belong to a group, some enterprising insurance person will invent a group for you so you can buy insurance. Life insurance is available everywhere.

There are a lot of insurance companies—at least 1900 in the United States. Each one is a little different. Furthermore each company sells slightly different policies. You could consider hundreds of thousands of different policies before making a decision.

These thousands of choices can make life insurance shopping one of the most frustrating tasks in financial planning. Unfortunately, the task is so frustrating most people don't know where to begin and, consequently, never get started. So, while people are sitting around not getting started, the insurance comes shopping for them. Therefore, most people wind up having insurance "sold" to them, rather than "buying" it. When a product is "sold" rather than "bought," the odds of getting the right product for you are poor, but the odds of you getting the right product for the salesperson are terrific.

To raise your chance of buying the right product for you, and letting the salespeople worry about themselves, you must start by analyzing your needs. Be sure to complete the analysis found in the Chapter "How Can You Analyze Your Life Insurance Needs?" (p. 218). What would the economic impact in your home be if you, or your spouse, or even one of the children died tomorrow? Hopefully your analysis will give you a reasonably good estimate of your insurance needs.

With this estimate in mind, ask yourself if your insurance needs will be increasing, constant, or decreasing in the future. Generally, insurance needs increase if you are young and your family and other obligations are still expanding. They tend to decrease as you pass through middle age and your children move out on their own. Your life insurance needs may disappear completely when you retire. Remember, you want to insure only against that economic loss you, or your estate, cannot risk suffering.

Your economic risk of dying will change, but so will your economic risk of living. What will you do if you don't die on schedule? Will you have enough income to live in dignity? (See the section on retirement later in this book.) Retirement is an important thing to think about when shopping for life insurance. Many life insurance policies, called *annuities,* have retirement benefits built into them. As explained earlier, you can generally provide for your retirement better through the purchase of term insurance and investing the difference in premiums than through buying an annuity. But if you are one of those people that save money the way the federal government does, a whole-life annuity policy may be just the thing for you.

When you have a good idea how much insurance you need now, how much you'll need in the future, and whether you want a term, a whole-life, or an annuity policy, you are ready to shop for the best price. One resource to use in shopping is the following table. This table gives a rough idea of what two popular policies might sell for, on the average, during the early 1980s.

The premium costs are shown as annual premium for $1000 of face amount of life insurance. For example, if you are age thirty-five and want to buy $100,000 of insurance, it will cost you:

$$100 \times \$2.10 = \$210 \text{ per year for term}$$
$$100 \times \$13.60 = \$1360 \text{ per year for whole life}$$

Annual Insurance Cost
per $1000 of Insurance

Age	Term (Annual renewable)	Whole-life (ordinary)
25	$ 2.06	$ 9.05
30	2.07	10.99
35	2.10	13.60
40	2.70	17.08
45	4.14	20.91
55	10.75	33.73
65	27.80	57.99

These policies are two of the most popular and widely sold policies in America. The prices in the table are reasonable approximations of average costs today. But actual costs can vary from these averages 20 percent and more either way. For example, of one hundred leading companies examined, costs for roughly comparable term policies for a thirty-five-year-old man ranged from $1.41 per $1000 to $3.67 per $1000. For whole-life, the cost for a thirty-five-year-old man ranged from $10.30 to $16.64 per thousand. Clearly, it is worth your while to do some shopping. Interestingly, the firms that were at the extremes in one age group were not usually at the extremes in all groups.

This table may help you avoid buying some of the extremes. Unfortunately, there are so many companies and so many policies that this book cannot begin to deal with them all. The A.M. Best Co. does at least begin to deal with them. The Best service includes annual comparisons of companies, their policies, their premiums, and their financial strengths. The Best service can be found in most good-sized libraries. Use the Best service to identify several insurance companies that seem to offer competitive premiums. Of course, as with anything you buy, you can't assume that the cheapest is always the best buy, but lowest cost is a good place to start looking for the best buy.

Take the yellow pages of the phone book to the library with you. This will help you identify which of these competitive companies write insurance in your area. You'll need the yellow pages to call some of the companies, too. As you work through *Best's,* you will probably have questions about each company. It's a good idea to call a few of the most likely candidates. Ask for the manager, rather than a salesperson. Tell the manager you don't want to see a salesperson yet, you just want some information. Usually he or she will be willing to answer questions for you about the company's policies, rates, and procedures, and naturally he or she will try to convince you that that company is the best to buy from. While you have the manager on the phone, be sure to ask if the firm offers any special rate reduction programs. Companies are introducing new concepts to keep up with the financial evolution of the 1980s. One of the most popular is rate reduction for nonsmokers. There is also a trend in the industry toward indeterminate premium policies. These provide a guaranteed maximum rate, but a lower, adjustable rate based on favorable loss and mortality projections.

In the end the best company to buy from will probably be the one that offers the best price on the best coverage you want. Service from the company is important. But service is all pretty much the same if you are analyzing your own needs. Beyond financial analysis, all that is left for the company to do is send you a request for your premium when the time comes, and send your beneficiaries a check for your mortal departure when that time comes.

Speaking of departures, some people wonder if they will outlive the company. Is the company solid? This consideration is critical for someone buying life insurance. Fortunately, today it is not a great concern. Life insurance companies are pretty carefully supervised by the states in which they sell. However, on rare occasions problems do occur. And it is particularly important to be alert right now to see if the financial upheaval of our times has uprooted your company. Best's service can help again. This time get *Best's Insurance Reports*. This service rates the financial stability of the various companies.

All this searching to find a company you are interested in needn't take a long time. You can do a lot in a few hours if you are organized. Even if you spend more than a few hours, the time is well worth it. You could easily save yourself enough money to buy an expensive new car, and more, over your lifetime.

Once you've identified a company you consider a viable candidate, call and invite a salesperson to your home. By the time this particular salesperson arrives on your doorstep, you will be a very sophisticated life insurance buyer. This will put you in a good position to control the meeting, rather than vice versa. Then rather than having the policy that's best for the salesperson "sold" to you, you will be in a good position to "buy" the life insurance that's best for you. After all, being in control of your insurance dollars is a key step in gaining your personal financial freedom.

◇ 34 ◇
Planning to Retire

Retirement can be thought of as an asset—an asset like a home, a car, a television set, or any other asset you may own and consume during a lifetime. It may be the ultimate asset in achieving financial freedom because this asset is usually consumed by senior citizens. Everyone not already a senior citizen is a prospective senior citizen. A good retirement is a valuable asset. It can add quality and dignity to your standard of living during an important time of your life. A poor retirement can be thought of as a trap. It can result in degradation during an important time in your life. Like most assets, a good retirement costs money. But, unlike most assets, it must be paid for in advance. It definitely cannot be used now and paid for later.

Because a retirement must be paid for in advance, it is logical to decide what kind of retirement you want in advance. In modern America, retirements tend to range from standard government-subsidized models to elaborate luxury models loaded with all the options. Naturally, the luxury models cost more. The challenge is to decide how luxurious a retirement you are willing to pay for. After all, a luxury retirement tomorrow could mean a stripped-down standard of living today.

There are three steps in determining the retirement you want and can afford:

1. Analyze the cost of retirement

2. Determine the value of "involuntary" retirement payments

3. Calculate the amount of "voluntary" retirement payments

Retirement Cost

It is useful to get an idea about the range in retirement costs. The worksheet on p. 251 can help you estimate retirement costs. (And

249

you can use the blank worksheet at the end of this section to estimate the cost of your own retirement.) Most normal retirement options people consider are listed on this worksheet. There are two cost columns: Under "Maximum," record the cost of the option you really want and desire. Under "Minimum," record the lowest cost you could get by with and still preserve your dignity. For example, your maximum desire might be retirement in a lovely four-bedroom home that gives you plenty of room when the grandchildren come to visit. But if that proves too expensive, as a minimum you may be willing to live in a nice one-bedroom apartment and let the grandchildren stay in a motel. However, a dilapidated room in a skid row hotel where the grandchildren would be mugged when they came to visit may be beneath your dignity.

Another example might be assistance to the children. You may want to help them with their college expenses. It may not compromise your dignity, however, if the kids must work and help put themselves through school. But your personal dignity may be destroyed if your kids must skip college altogether and support you. When considering maximums and minimums, therefore, future feelings are important considerations. Feelings of desire are associated with maximum costs; feelings of dignity are associated with minimum costs.

In estimating costs, project your mind forward in time to the age of your retirement. Try to imagine what your wants and needs will be at that time. Consider your circumstances. For example, your home may be paid for, your recreational pursuits may change, and your health may be poor. After you have a good mental picture of your wants and needs at retirement, record the estimated costs of your anticipated expenses. Use today's prices—an inflation adjustment will be made later. *Please note:* The figures used in the example are for illustration only. They are responses that a typical prospective senior citizen might give, but these figures are not intended to be used to fit *you* exactly.

The figures you fill in for these columns should represent your personal estimates of yearly retirement expenses. Unfortunately, the cost of just about everything tends to rise—including retirements. To adjust these figures for future inflation, refer to Table 1 at the end of this section. The far left column is the number of years until you anticipate retiring. The numbers along the top are potential inflation rates.

Estimated Annual Retirement Expense

		Maximum	Minimum
1.	Retirement options		
2.	House mortgage	0	0
3.	Rent	$ 7,000	$ 5,000
4.	Utilities	1,200	800
5.	Maintenance	200	0
6.	Property taxes	0	0
7.	Food	1,800	1,300
8.	Personal care	600	400
9.	Clothing	800	300
10.	Cleaning and laundry	200	100
1†.	Furniture	500	0
12.	Transportation		
13.	Automobile payments	2,000	800
14.	Automobile expense (gas, oil, insurance, maintenance)	2,400	800
15.	Bus, train, or other routine travel	0	0
16.	Health care (not covered by insurance)	900	900
17.	Entertainment	1,000	100
18.	Hobbies	1,000	100
19.	Travel	4,000	0
20.	Contributions and gifts (including assistance to relatives)	3,000	0
21.	Other	2,500	1,200
22.	Total estimated retirement expenses	$29,100	$11,800

Assume, for instance, the prospective senior citizen in our example anticipates retiring in thirty years. Furthermore, assume that he (or she) thinks inflation will average 4 percent during that thirty years. He recognizes that inflation has been much higher in recent years. But he uses 4 percent because long-term inflation in the United States has been 2 to 4 percent. He thinks inflation may decline to near normal levels over the next thirty years. (Other columns are provided so that you can select your own estimated inflation rate if you don't agree with this prospective senior citizen.) Reading down the 4 percent column to the thirty-year line, our prospective senior citizen finds the number 3.24. This index number implies that it will cost more than three times as much to live thirty years from now as it does today. To convert that sobering implication to a dollar figure, multiply the estimated maximum and minimum retirement costs in Line 22 by 3.24. These maximums and minimums give a decent estimate of the annual income our prospective senior citizen will need during his retirement. (Incidentally, Table 1 also shows that at a 10 percent rate of inflation for thirty years it will cost more than seventeen times as much to live as it costs today!)

Estimated Future Retirement Expense
(Inflation Adjustment)

	Maximum	*Minimum*
23. Total estimated retirement expenses (Line 22)	$29,100	$11,800
24. Inflation index (Table 1)	× 3.24	× 3.24
25. Total estimated future retirement expense	$94,284	$38,232

At this point, most prospective senior citizens agree that retirement, even at minimum levels, will be expensive. Furthermore, to be certain there is no confusion, it is worth stating that these future cost figures represent what the prospective senior citizen will spend every year of her retirement, at least. It will not be enough for our prospective senior citizen to retire with a mere $38,232 in the bank. Thirty years from now, that $38,232 will only support her for one year—at minimum standards. Moreover, our prospective senior citizen doesn't know how many years she will need her retirement income, because no one knows long he or she will live.

To be confident your retirement income will last as long as you do, you must accumulate investments and savings today that will earn for you during your retirement. These investments must be sufficient to let you live off the earnings they generate without dipping into the investments themselves. If they are not sufficient, you may be forced to liquidate your investments just to live. Liquidating investments to live is like a farmer eating his or her entire harvest during the winter, and failing to hold back anything for seed. When the following spring rolls around, the farmer will discover he or she is out of business and faces starvation.

There are two classes of earning investments available to help avoid financial starvation during retirement: involuntary and voluntary. As implied by the name, there are some things that can be thought of as earning investments that we accumulate "involuntarily." Social Security is an example. Payments are made to Social

Security whether we like it or not. Voluntarily accumulated investments are things such as savings, securities, real estate, and so on. These are accumulated only if payments are made voluntarily. Involuntary investments are going to be made regardless, so the big question is "What do you need to accumulate voluntarily to ensure a good retirement?" You can estimate your voluntary needs by first analyzing your involuntary investments. Then subtract your involuntarily accumulated investments from your total needs.

Involuntary Investments

The major forms of involuntarily accumulated investments are Social Security, or government retirement benefits, and employee pensions. Other involuntary investments may include veterans' benefits, disability benefits, and assistance from family and friends. Still others may be applicable to your special circumstance.

Pension benefits are an important source of involuntary retirement income. In many cases, your employer makes contributions directly to a pension account without making visible deductions from your paycheck. Pension plans vary widely. Some pay a fixed predetermined retirement benefit. Others pay a benefit that depends on your earnings or inflation or some other factor.

If your pension is adjusted for inflation, you must make an adjustment in your estimate. Refer to Table 1 for the proper index number. In this example, assume the pension is not adjusted for inflation, so the index is 1.00.

All employer plans must be adjusted for taxes. You will have to pay income taxes on the benefits as you receive them. Perhaps the best estimate of future taxes is to estimate what taxes you would pay if you were receiving the benefits today. Apply this tax rate to your future benefit.

In order to make a reasonable estimate of your potential retirement benefits, you should speak to your employer regarding the details of your plan. When you do check with your employer, be sure you are getting the details of a pension or annuity plan; that is, a plan that makes periodic payments during retirement. Many employers have profit-sharing plans, which make lump sum distributions when you retire. These plans are considered later.

Nationally, Social Security is the most important involuntary retirement asset. Most workers are covered by Social Security, or government pensions, or railroad retirement pensions. If you are not covered by Social Security, you should figure out what you *are* covered by. Workers make involuntary payments into the system through deductions from their paychecks, so look at your paycheck to find out what is being taken from it.

Most people born after 1928 will receive full Social Security benefits if they work at least ten years before they are 65. The basic Social Security benefit changes with inflation, so examples tend to get out of date. For purposes of this example, assume the basic benefit is $6400. Nonworking, dependent spouses are eligible for 50 percent of their spouse's benefit. Spouses who have worked for ten years or more are eligible for full benefits, of course. There are many exceptions and special situations in the Social Security program. It is a good idea to call your local Social Security office for more information on what your benefit would be if you were retiring today.

It is a good idea to read chapter 34 of this book on Social Security. There are some important changes taking place that may affect your Social Security benefit.

Today Social Security benefits are indexed to inflation. This means that the benefit will rise with the cost of living. In estimating your Social Security benefit at retirement, therefore, you must multiply, by an inflation index, the benefit you would receive if you were retiring today. Again, refer to Table 1 at the end of this section, and select the inflation rate you expect between now and retirement. Then follow down the column to the number of years until you turn sixty-five. That index number will help you make a reasonable estimate of what your Social Security income will be during retirement.

After gathering as much information as he (or she) could on income from involuntary assets, our prospective senior citizen's figures look like the ones on p. 255.

In this case, the prospective senior citizen estimates his (or her) company's pension program will pay him $9500 a year when he retires. The benefits are not adjusted for inflation. He will have to pay income taxes on his pension. In this case, let us estimate taxes at $1500. He also thinks he will qualify for a Social Security benefit of $6400, and his spouse will receive 50 percent of that amount, or $3200, for a total of $9600. This must be adjusted for inflation. Our prospective senior citizen uses the same inflation adjustment he used to determine his needed retirement income. He has no other sources of involuntary retirement income.

Annual Involuntary Retirement Income

	Col. A: Benefit today	Col. B: Inflation adjustment	Col. C: Future benefit
26. Involuntary retirement income taxable			
27. Pension benefit	9,500 ×	1.00	9,500
28. Employer-provided annuity	0 ×		0
29. Other	0 ×		0
30. Total before taxes	9,500		9,500
31. Less taxes	1,500		1,500
32. Total after taxes	8,000		8,000
33. Add involuntary retirement income nontaxable			
34. Social Security benefit	9,600 ×	3.24	31,104
35. Other	0 ×		0
36. Annual involuntary retirement income	17,600		39,104

In this example, our prospective senior citizen estimates he will have an annual retirement income of $39,104 coming from the government and his employer (Line 36, Column C). In theory, the money will be available when he retires, without any special effort on his part.

After completing his calculation of involuntary retirement income, he compares the figure to his estimated income needs as follows:

	Maximum	Minimum
37. Estimated involuntary retirement income (Line 36, Column C)	$39,104	$39,104
38. Less estimated future retirement expense (Line 25)	94,284	38,232
39. Additional retirement income needed	−$55,180	+$ 872

Eureka! Our prospective senior citizen can live during retirement—at minimum levels at least. Not only can he (or she) live, but the estimates show he'll have $872 a year to spend any way he wants. Of course, $872 doesn't leave much margin for error if, for any reason, his thirty-year estimates are wrong. But the point is that many senior citizens *can* live off their involuntary sources of income. In some cases, it isn't absolutely necessary to set anything aside voluntarily. However, to get an idea what it really means to live on Social Security and pension, ask yourself the following question: "How would I and my spouse enjoy living on Social Security and our estimated pension today?" If you would be satisfied with that, then you could probably be happy living on involuntary income when you retire. But if you think you want a retirement asset with a few more luxuries than Social Security and pension will buy, you must spend some time determining how many investments you should accumulate voluntarily.

Voluntary Investments

If you are among the great majority of Americans who want more than a Social Security retirement asset, go back and look at your maximum retirement income needs after involuntary income. The prospective senior citizen in our example must earn $55,180 a year more than his Social Security and pension will provide. This means the prospective senior citizen should voluntarily accumulate enough investments to provide $55,180 a year in additional income. Perhaps the best assumption that can be made right now is that during retirement the senior citizen's accumulated investments can earn 9 percent (.09) before taxes and perhaps 7 percent (.07) after taxes. (These returns look too low in today's financial environment. But remember our prospective senior citizen is looking out thirty years. It is best to stay conservative.) At an earnings rate of 7 percent, the prospective senior citizen must retire with a nest egg of $788,286— over three-quarters of a million dollars—calculated as follows:

		Maximum	Minimum
40.	Additional retirement income needed (Line 39—reverse the sign, if no retirement income is needed; that is, if Line 39 was positive, record zero)	$ 55,180	$ 0
41.	Divide by after-tax investment rate	.07	.07
42.	Total voluntary investments required	$788,286	$ 0

Three-quarters of a million dollars is a lot of money for most people. In fact, it might seem like an overwhelming sum to be raised voluntarily. But for many prospective senior citizens, much of the investment will be accumulated accidentally. Accidental investments are things such as homes, business equity, and company profit sharing. They are called *accidental* because, in most cases, the primary reason for putting money into them is not to build a retirement fund.

Home ownership is a good example. Most people buy homes for the enjoyment and comfort they bring throughout their lifetimes. They would probably buy homes regardless of the retirement implications. The fact that the home appreciates in price and becomes a valuable retirement asset is almost an accident. A dental practice is another example. A dentist nurtures a good practice to make a good living while he or she is active. The fact that the practice has value and can be sold when the dentist retires is almost accidental.

Accidental investments aren't quite the same thing as involuntary investments, but they have a great deal in common. Both tend to build up value automatically in the normal course of everyday life. However, accidentally accumulated investments are not required. After all, no law forces a person to buy a home or build a business.

Examine the accidental assets you are accumulating, and estimate their retirement value. Subtract that value from the total retirement assets needed. This will help you see how much you need to accumulate intentionally. Be a little careful about what you include as accidental assets. You may spend a lot of money during your lifetime on a matchbook collection. Indeed, your matchbook collection may be so unique that it will be worth a fortune by the time you retire. But if you are not willing to sell your matchbooks and live off the proceeds, the collection is not an earning investment at all. A home is a bit different. Even if you do not want to sell your home when you retire, at least you can continue living in it and avoid paying rent.

Accidental Voluntary Investments

43. Home equity at retirement	$120,000
44. Profit sharing (ask employer)	20,000
45. Private business	0
46. Other	0
47. Total accidental investments	$140,000

Intentional Voluntary Investments

		Maximum
48.	Total voluntary investments required (Line 42)	$788,286
49.	Less accidental investments (Line 47)	140,000
50.	Total intentional investments required	$648,286

These figures show that the prospective senior citizen in our example must intentionally accumulate investments worth $648,286 in the next thirty years to enjoy his (or her) desired retirement. Intentional assets are things such as savings, stocks, bonds, insurance annuities, and real estate investments. They also include voluntary participation in government-sponsored programs like the Keogh Plan and the Investment Retirement Account (IRA) law. In determining what your monthly payments toward retirement must be, the final steps begin with Table 2 at the end of the section. Table 2 is based on compound value techniques. Invested earnings tend to grow over time. A dollar invested today will grow in value and be worth more than a dollar invested thirty years from now. Table 2 assumes that the investor intentionally invests money at a constant rate during his or her working life. This consistent investment might be considered monthly payments toward his or her retirement asset. The column at the far left of Table 2 is the number of years until retirement. The line at the top is estimated earnings rates on assets.

For the prospective senior citizen in our example, the rate of 7 percent after-tax earnings for thirty years has been selected. Reading down the 7 percent column to thirty years, we find the divisor of 1,219.97. When the prospective senior citizen divides the retirement assets he must accumulate intentionally by this divisor, the resulting number is the monthly payment he must make throughout his working life.

Monthly Payment on Retirement Asset

		Maximum
51.	Intentional investments required (Line 50)	$648,286.00
52.	Compound interest divisor (Table 2)	÷ 1,219.97
53.	Monthly payment required	$ 531.40

Finally, our prospective senior citizen has a figure he can relate to. If he can only make monthly payments of $531.40 and invest them at 7 percent after tax from now until he retires in thirty years, he can buy the luxurious, option-filled retirement of his dreams.

Unfortunately, monthly retirement payments of anything like $531.40 appear to be way beyond the means of most prospective senior citizens. At this point, many people become alarmed. They are alarmed to find out how much retirement can really cost. Frequently, one of three unfortunate attitudes, described as follows, grow out of this alarm.

The "It's Hopeless" Attitude

Overwhelmed by the magnitude of the problem, the prospective senior citizen becomes depressed and gives up. Feeling that he (or she) does not have enough current income to save anything, he decides to forget it and save nothing. He usually concludes rather matter-of-factly that he will spend his old age in poverty and degradation. Deep down inside he doesn't believe he'll wind up destitute. But the problem is he really *may* wind up destitute. But when today's depressed prospective senior citizen actually becomes a senior citizen, scrimping for every penny, the "It's hopeless" attitude of years earlier may not seem like such a good attitude anymore.

The "Lots of Time" Attitude

Startled by the potential impact on his (or her) current standard of living, the prospective senior citizen chooses to procrastinate and delay his retirement payments. He is persuaded he should do it— someday, but not now. There are two fallacies in such thinking. First, it generally isn't any easier to begin saving next year, or the year after, than today. There always seem to be demands on a person's current income. Second, it is a mathematical fact that the job gets harder to accomplish as time goes on. In the example that has been used, the prospective senior citizen needs to accumulate $648,286 in thirty years (Line 50). This will cost $531.40 a month (Line 53) if he gets started right away. But assume he procrastinates five years and then starts his payments. Now he only has twenty-five years until retirement. Instead of a mere $531.40 per month, he will have to make payments of $800.28 ($648,286 ÷ 810.07) to reach his goal. And if he delays ten years, the monthly tab rises to $1244.48 ($648,286 ÷ 520.93). Like anything else you pay for, the longer you can stretch out your payments, the smaller the payments are. Spend some time with Table 2: It makes a powerful case for starting your retirement payments as soon as possible.

The "I've Got to Save Every Dime" Attitude

Panic-stricken by the size of the problem, this prospective senior citizen may deny himself every current luxury in an attempt to be secure in the future. Unfortunately, through overreaction, he (or she) may miss much of the enjoyment that he can only experience today, while he is young.

None of these attitudes is appropriate. With the problems and costs carefully laid out, the wise prospective senior citizen will conclude that, whatever he does, he should do *something,* and the sooner the better. He will make intelligent trade-offs. He will try to assess how much of his standard of living he is willing to give up today for security and enjoyment tomorrow. He may properly conclude he can forgo some desired retirement options, such as travel. He may decide he would rather take a family vacation with his kids when he's forty than a cruise around the world by himself when he's seventy. He will try to get as much out of life today as possible and still leave himself something for tomorrow. The wise prospective senior citizen will use good judgment in his trade-offs, leaving himself a little margin for error. After all, about the only thing left in the "minimum" column was dignity, and if anything goes wrong between now and retirement he may not even have that.

Work Sheet for Estimated Annual Retirement Expense

		Maximum	Minimum
1.	*Retirement options*		
2.	House mortgage	_____	_____
3.	Rent	_____	_____
4.	Utilities	_____	_____
5.	Maintenance	_____	_____
6.	Property taxes	_____	_____
7.	Food	_____	_____
8.	Personal care	_____	_____
9.	Clothing	_____	_____
10.	Cleaning and laundry	_____	_____
11.	Furniture	_____	_____
12.	Transportation	_____	_____
13.	Automobile payments	_____	_____
14.	Automobile expense (gas, oil, insurance, maintenance)	_____	_____
15.	Bus, train, or other routine travel	_____	_____
16.	Health care (not covered by insurance)	_____	_____
17.	Entertainment	_____	_____
18.	Hobbies	_____	_____
19.	Travel	_____	_____
20.	Contributions and gifts (including assistance to relatives)	_____	_____
21.	Other	_____	_____
22.	Total estimated retirement expenses	_____	_____

Estimated Future Retirement Expense (Inflation Adjustment)

		Maximum	Minimum
23.	Total estimated retirement expenses (Line 22)	_____	_____
24.	Inflation index (Table 1)	×_____	×_____
25.	Total estimated future retirement expense	_____	_____

Annual Involuntary Retirement Income

	Col. A: Benefit today	Col. B: Inflation adjustment	Col. C: Future benefit
26. Involuntary retirement income taxable	_____	_____	_____
27. Pension benefit	_____ ×	_____	_____
28. Employer-provided annuity	_____ ×	_____	_____
29. Other	_____ ×	_____	_____
30. Total before taxes	_____		_____
31. Less taxes	_____		_____
32. Total after taxes	_____		_____
33. Add involuntary retirement income nontaxable			
34. Social Security benefit	_____ ×	_____	_____
35. Other	_____ ×	_____	_____
36. Annual involuntary retirement income	_____		_____

Voluntary Retirement Investments Required

	Maximum	Minimum
37. Estimated involuntary retirement income (Line 36, Column C)	_____	_____
38. Less estimated future retirement expense (Line 25)	_____	_____
39. Additional retirement income needed	_____	_____
40. Additional retirement income needed (Line 39—Reverse the sign, if no retirement income is needed; that is, if Line 39 was positive, record zero)	_____	_____
41. Divide by after-tax investment rate	_____	_____
42. Total voluntary investments required	_____	_____

Accidental Voluntary Investments

43. Home equity at retirement   _____
44. Profit sharing (ask employer)   _____
45. Private business   _____
46. Other   _____
47. Total accidental investments   _____

Intentional Voluntary Investments

	Maximum	Minimum
48. Total voluntary investments required (Line 42)	_____	_____
49. Less accidental investments (Line 47)	_____	_____
50. Total intentional investments required	_____	_____

Monthly Payment on Retirement Asset

	Maximum	Minimum
51. Intentional investments required (Line 50)	_____	_____
52. Compound interest divisor (Table 2)	_____	_____
53. Monthly payment required	_____	_____

Table 1. Inflation Adjustment Index

Expected inflation rate

Number of years	2%	3%	4%	5%	6%	8%	10%
1	1.02	1.03	1.04	1.05	1.06	1.08	1.10
2	1.04	1.06	1.08	1.10	1.12	1.17	1.21
3	1.06	1.09	1.13	1.16	1.19	1.26	1.33
4	1.08	1.13	1.17	1.22	1.26	1.36	1.46
5	1.10	1.16	1.22	1.28	1.34	1.47	1.61
6	1.13	1.19	1.27	1.34	1.42	1.59	1.77
7	1.15	1.23	1.32	1.41	1.50	1.71	1.95
8	1.17	1.27	1.37	1.48	1.59	1.85	2.14
9	1.20	1.31	1.42	1.55	1.69	2.00	2.36
10	1.22	1.34	1.48	1.63	1.79	2.16	2.59
11	1.24	1.38	1.54	1.71	1.90	2.33	2.85
12	1.27	1.43	1.60	1.80	2.01	2.52	3.14
13	1.29	1.47	1.67	1.89	2.13	2.72	3.45
14	1.32	1.51	1.73	1.98	2.26	2.94	3.80
15	1.35	1.56	1.80	2.08	2.40	3.17	4.18
16	1.37	1.61	1.87	2.18	2.54	3.43	4.60
17	1.40	1.66	1.95	2.29	2.69	3.70	5.05
18	1.43	1.70	2.03	2.41	2.85	4.00	5.56
19	1.46	1.75	2.11	2.53	3.03	4.32	6.12
20	1.49	1.81	2.19	2.65	3.21	4.66	6.73
21	1.52	1.86	2.28	2.79	3.40	5.03	7.40
22	1.55	1.92	2.37	2.93	3.60	5.44	8.14
23	1.58	1.97	2.47	3.07	3.82	5.87	8.95
24	1.61	2.03	2.56	3.23	4.05	6.34	9.85
25	1.64	2.09	2.67	3.39	4.29	6.85	10.84
26	1.67	2.16	2.77	3.56	4.55	7.40	11.92
27	1.71	2.22	2.88	3.73	4.82	7.99	13.11
28	1.74	2.29	3.00	3.92	5.11	8.63	14.42
29	1.78	2.36	3.12	4.12	5.42	9.32	15.86
30	1.81	2.43	3.24	4.32	5.74	10.06	17.45
31	1.85	2.50	3.37	4.54	6.09	10.87	19.19
32	1.89	2.58	3.51	4.77	6.45	11.74	21.11
33	1.92	2.65	3.65	5.00	6.84	12.68	23.23
34	1.96	2.73	3.79	5.25	7.25	13.69	25.55
35	2.00	2.81	3.95	5.52	7.69	14.79	28.10
36	2.04	2.90	4.10	5.79	8.15	15.97	30.91
37	2.08	2.99	4.27	6.08	8.64	17.25	34.00
38	2.12	3.08	4.44	6.39	9.15	18.63	37.40
39	2.17	3.17	4.62	6.71	9.70	20.12	41.15

Number of years	2%	3%	4%	5%	6%	8%	10%
40	2.21	3.26	4.80	7.04	10.29	21.73	45.26
41	2.25	3.36	4.99	7.39	10.90	23.46	49.79
42	2.30	3.46	5.19	7.76	11.26	25.34	54.76
43	2.34	3.57	5.40	8.15	12.25	27.37	60.24
44	2.39	3.67	5.62	8.56	12.99	29.56	66.26
45	2.44	3.78	5.84	8.99	13.77	31.92	72.89
46	2.49	3.90	6.08	9.43	14.59	34.47	80.18
47	2.54	4.01	6.32	9.91	15.47	37.23	88.20
48	2.59	4.13	6.57	10.40	16.39	40.21	97.02
49	2.64	4.26	6.83	10.92	17.38	43.43	106.72
50	2.69	4.38	7.11	11.47	18.42	46.90	117.39

Table 2. Compound Interest Divisor

	Estimated investment rate			
Number of years	5%	7%	9%	11%
1	12.27	12.39	12.50	12.62
2	25.19	25.68	26.19	26.71
3	38.75	39.93	41.15	42.42
4	53.01	55.21	57.52	59.96
5	68.01	71.59	75.42	79.52
6	83.76	89.16	95.01	101.34
7	100.33	108.00	116.42	125.69
8	177.74	128.20	139.86	152.86
9	136.04	149.86	165.48	183.18
10	155.28	173.08	193.51	217.00
11	175.51	197.99	224.17	254.73
12	197.67	224.70	257.71	296.83
13	219.11	253.33	294.39	343.81
14	242.60	284.04	334.52	396.22
15	267.29	316.96	378.41	454.69
16	293.24	352.27	426.41	519.93
17	320.52	390.13	478.92	592.72
18	349.20	430.72	536.35	673.93
19	379.35	474.25	599.17	764.54
20	411.03	520.93	667.89	865.64
21	444.34	570.98	743.05	978.43
22	479.35	624.65	825.26	1,104.28
23	516.16	682.19	915.18	1,244.69
24	554.84	743.90	1,013.54	1,401.35

Number of years	5%	7%	9%	11%
25	595.51	810.07	1,121.12	1,576.13
26	638.26	881.02	1,238.80	1,771.15
27	683.19	957.11	1,367.51	1,988.72
28	730.42	1,038.69	1,508.30	2,231.48
29	780.07	1,126.17	1,662.30	2,502.33
30	832.26	1,219.97	1,830.74	2,804.52
31	887.12	1,320.56	2,014.99	3,141.68
32	944.78	1,428.41	2,216.51	3,517.85
33	1,005.40	1,544.06	2,436.95	3,937.56
34	1,069.12	1,668.08	2,678.06	4,405.83
35	1,136.09	1,801.06	2,941.78	4,928.30
36	1,206.50	1,943.65	3,230.25	5,511.22
37	1,280.50	2,096.55	3,545.78	6,161.59
38	1,358.29	2,260.50	3,890.91	6,887.23
39	1,440.06	2,436.30	4,268.41	7,696.83
40	1,526.02	2,624.81	4,681.32	8,600.13
41	1,616.37	2,826.95	5,132.97	9,607.95
42	1,711.35	3,043.71	5,626.98	10,732.39
43	1,811.18	3,276.13	6,167.34	11,986.96
44	1,916.13	3,525.36	6,758.39	13,386.70
45	2,026.44	3,792.60	7,404.87	14,948.41
46	2,142.39	4,079.16	8,112.02	16,690.85
47	2,264.28	4,386.43	8,885.49	18,634.92
48	2,392.40	4,715.92	9,731.51	20,803.95
49	2,527.08	5,069.23	10,656.90	23,223.99
50	2,668.65	5,448.07	11,669.10	25,924.07

◇ 35 ◇
What You Should Know
About Retirement Plans

In order to know anything about your financial freedom during retirement, you should know about your employer's retirement plan. You should know if you have a retirement plan (a pension, profit sharing, or other retirement plan). You should know how much your plan will pay. And you should know how long you have to stay with your employer or union to get your benefits.

There are very strict laws requiring employers to tell employees all about their retirement plans. Unfortunately, no laws require employees to listen or understand. Some employees aren't even sure what a retirement plan is.

A retirement plan is money your employer keeps paying you long after you've retired. Some years ago a concept developed that employers shouldn't give their employees all their compensation immediately in the form of wages. Part of it should be held back, invested, and given to them after they retire. Because many American wage earners don't put anything aside for old age, retirement plans are a good idea.

There are a few things you should know about your retirement plan:

1. *Does your employer offer a retirement plan?* There is no law requiring an employer to provide a plan. Most large employers do, but hundreds of thousands of employers do not.

2. *If you do have a retirement plan, what type of plan is it?* Profit-sharing plans are most common. An amount of money is set aside for you every year depending on corporate profits. Pension plans are next most common. With a pension, you receive benefits according to a predetermined formula. Usually the formula is not dependent on company profits. There are also thrift plans where the employer matches your savings, and ESOP's where the employer gives you company stock, and others.

267

3. *When do your benefits vest?* This means how long do you have to work for your employer before the employer is obligated to pay you benefits out of the retirement plan? For example, typical vesting in a pension account is ten years. This means if you quit before ten years you may not get any pension from that employer. Under current law, once your benefits have vested, your employer must pay you a pension—even if you quit and go to work somewhere else. Usually you will receive any vested profit sharing immediately if you leave.

4. *When do payments begin?* Typically you will receive your benefits after you reach age sixty-five and you retire.

5. *How much will your benefits be?* Usually the size of your pension will depend on how long you have worked for the employer or union and on how much you were paid. Profit sharing benefits usually depend on how profitable the company has been, and how well the money was invested.

6. *How will your benefits be paid?* Most pensions are paid in monthly payments from the time you turn sixty-five until you die. Usually these payments are made regardless of how much other money you might make while retired. Some plans pay a single lump sum.

7. *Will your benefits stop when you die?* Some plans keep paying your spouse as long as your spouse lives.

Why do you need to know all this information? After all, your retirement is probably many years away. You need to know because you need to plan for that retirement now. You are the one who needs to get this information. You can't get the answers out of this book because every employer or union has a different plan, and many employers don't have a plan at all. To find out about your retirement plan, talk to your employer's personnel department or your union's business agent.

You know what your wages are, to the penny. But do you know what your pension is? To help spark your interest in your pension, consider this—many people will receive more money from their employers after they retire than they received from their employers all the years they were working. That's something worth knowing about.

◇ 36 ◇
IRA and Keogh
Retirement Plans

This chapter discusses two independent retirement plans for people who work for themselves or have no other retirement plans.

What Is IRA?

IRA sounds like an acronym for some militant organization, but it's not. IRA stands for Individual Retirement Account. It is the government's attempt to help you save money for your old age. And recently the government made its attempt even better.

The government made IRA better by increasing the amount you can save and by vastly expanding the number of people who can participate.

Previously only people whose employers did not provide an employee retirement program could have an IRA. Now, with the passage of the Reagan tax package, beginning in 1982, everyone can have an IRA. You can have an IRA even if you already participate in an employer sponsored retirement program.

Why should you want an IRA? Here's the deal. The government will let you invest $2000 a year individually (or $2250 for a couple with non-working spouse) and deduct it from your taxes. That's how the government helps. They let you save your own money, tax deferred. Furthermore, they will not charge you tax on the interest or dividends your IRA investment earns either. At least they won't charge you tax right away. When you retire and use the money, they'll tax you. By then, however, you'll probably be in a lower tax bracket.

Some people may ask, "Is it worthwhile to have an IRA?" Is it worth it?! If you are thirty-five and faithfully put $2000 a year in a tax-free IRA and earn 10 percent on it, you'll have $328,988 when you turn sixty-five. The following table shows how your money would accumulate over the years. A 10 percent return doesn't look very high, and it's not. You'll learn how to do much better than 10 percent during the 1980s by reading this book. But the table goes out thirty years. It's hard to know what investments will be earning in the year 2082. Sometimes it is wise to keep projections on the conservative side.

Year	Amount invested	Accumulated value
5	$10,000	$ 12,210
10	20,000	31,875
15	30,000	63,544
20	40,000	114,550
25	50,000	196,694
30	60,000	328,988

Remember—the government has helped you by not charging you taxes on your investment. Suppose you took the same $2000 and saved it, but not in a tax-free IRA. First, since you must take the money out of your regular income you would be required to pay taxes on it before you could save it. If you are in the 30 percent tax bracket, that cuts your investment to $1400, with $600 going to the government for income taxes—before you could start investing. Then you would have taxes to pay on the earnings your investments generated. So, instead of earning 10 percent you would effectively earn only 7 percent after tax. Here's how the numbers work out.

Year	Amount invested before income taxes	Accumulated value invested	after taxes
5	$10,000	$ 7,000	$ 8,051
10	20,000	14,000	19,342
15	30,000	21,000	35,181
20	40,000	28,000	57,395
25	50,000	35,000	88,549
30	60,000	42,000	132,245

The total of $132,245 is still a lot of money, but it is obviously quite a lot less than the $328,988 accumulated the IRA tax-free way.

Of course, the IRA tax-free way only goes so far. (Just how generous do you think the government's going to be with your money, anyway?) You will have to pay full ordinary income taxes when you take the money out of your IRA. But, even though you will have to pay taxes later on you should still come out way ahead with an IRA.

In our example the IRA accumulates $328,988 in thirty years, the non-IRA account only $132,245. But taxes have already been paid on the non-IRA. Still, there is a significant advantage to the IRA.

	IRA	*Non-IRA*
Accumulated amount (A)	$328,988	$132,245
Tax rate (B)	30%	0%
Taxes due (C)	$98,696	$ 0
Net accumulation (A−C)	$230,292	$132,245

Obviously, an IRA is something you should take full advantage of. If you are married, your full advantage may be $2250. Assume your spouse is a homemaker without separate income. Under these conditions, you can probably put an extra $250 a year into your IRA for your spouse.

Another way of taking full advantage of IRA might be through an IRA rollover. If you leave an employer and receive a lump sum payment from that employer's pension or profit-sharing fund, you probably qualify for an IRA rollover. You can take the lump sum payment and, within sixty days, put it in an IRA. Again, the big advantage in doing this is saving taxes. The lump sum payment you received is subject to taxes. However, if you put it in an IRA rollover account, the government will not tax you until you draw the money out.

Starting an IRA is easy. There are some records and bookwork, of course, but many firms are anxious to do this for you, free. These are the same firms that want to keep your IRA money. IRAs may be invested in savings accounts, savings certificates, bonds, stocks, mutual funds, insurance annuities, and other investments. The organizations that sell these investments and provide the free bookkeeping are banks, credit unions, savings and loans, brokerage houses, mutual fund organizations, insurance companies, and so on. Just call any of these companies; they can explain all the details, send you literature, and even open an IRA for you, if you want.

In fact, under the new laws many Americans will find the easiest place to have an IRA will be at work. Many large employers will offer IRAs through payroll deductions. These deductions will probably be invested in an employer sponsored pension, profit-sharing, or thrift plan. It will be a very convenient way for you to invest.

Naturally, there are some restrictions you will want to know about. The most important is that you can't get your money back out of an IRA until you are 59½ years old. At least, you can't get it out easily. If you withdraw all or some of your money before you are 59½, you may lose a lot of interest, or you may have to pay a 10 percent penalty. Remember, the government thinks it is doing you a big favor letting you save money tax deferred for your retirement. So they figure they'll do you another big favor and make it very costly to draw your money out early. Actually, for most people, the penalty *is* a big favor. It forces them to exercise some financial discipline, ensuring there will be something in the account when they turn 59½.

There is an exception to the early withdrawal penalty. If you become disabled and cannot work, you can withdraw the money without penalty.

Assuming you do reach 59½ in good health, then you can withdraw your money. You may take it out in a lump sum, in periodic installments, or any way that suits you. You will have to pay taxes on the money as you withdraw it, of course. The government's goodness only goes so far.

Another thing that only goes so far is how long you can leave your money in an IRA. You must start using the money by the time you are 70½. The government would like to see you use your IRA during your own lifetime.

IRAs are definitely worth looking into and joining if you qualify. The IRA is bent on preserving some of the American way of life for you. So join in good conscience. And when you do join, pay your dues every year. It's the only way to get the full benefits membership can bring.

What Is Keogh?

Keogh is a retirement plan that was established by special federal law. Keogh is meant to look out for those people who nobody else looks out for—the self-employed. There are millions of self-employed people who prefer to work for themselves. And most people who work for themselves work pretty hard. But regardless of how hard they work, even self-employed people must eventually retire. And when the previously self-employed do retire, they will need to live off the earnings they made while they were still working.

Retirement circumstances among the self-employed vary far more than among regular workers and salaried employees. Some self-employed people have built substantial businesses and find themselves worth millions at retirement. Some self-employed people have not built much of anything and may feel like they *owe* millions at retirement. Statistics show that most do not enter retirement worth millions. In fact, so many wind up with so little the government has created a program to encourage self-employed people to save. That program is Keogh.

Keogh is similar to IRA in that dollars can be put into savings and investments before any taxes are paid on them. Putting dollars in before you pay taxes means that when the income tax form is prepared, gross income is listed at the top. Then contributions to Keogh are subtracted. So no taxes are paid on the Keogh contribution, or on the earnings generated by the investments.

This tax-deferred contribution feature is very important. The following table shows how much faster investments build up in a Keogh account than in regular after-tax savings and investments. Keogh is also like IRA in that the government just increased the amount that can be invested. In the case of Keogh the limit has been raised from $7500 to $15,000 a year up to a maximum of 15 percent of income.

Like IRA the tax-free feature is the key to Keogh. The table assumes $15,000 of pretax income is available for investment. It also assumes a 40 percent tax rate. This means income taxes must be paid on the $15,000 before it is available for investment into the non-Keogh account. That is a net of $9000. Also assume the investments will accumulate at 10 percent a year for 30 years. Again, taxes are paid on the non-Keogh earnings as they go along, so the effective investment return is 6 percent. (Incidentally, 10 percent doesn't look like a particularly good return in today's environment. But these assumptions are for 30 years. Things could be quite different in the future.)

Notice how much steady investments can mean, especially if you don't have to pay taxes as you go along. Tax deferral is important. You wind up with more than twice as much in your Keogh account 30 years from now—even after you pay your taxes—as you do in your non-Keogh account.

To be eligible, you must be self-employed or a major owner in a small firm. Doctors, dentists, lawyers, contractors, druggists, tree surgeons, barbers, art brokers, and junk dealers are only a very few examples of small businesspeople who may qualify for Keogh. If

Year	Keogh total investment	Account accumulated value	Non-Keogh total investment (after tax)	Account accumulated value after tax
5	$ 75,000	$ 91,575	$ 45,000	$ 50,733
10	150,000	239,055	90,000	118,620
15	225,000	476,580	135,000	209,484
20	300,000	859,125	180,000	331,074
25	375,000	1,475,205	225,000	493,785
30	450,000	2,467,410	270,000	711,522

Taxes (30 Years − Rate 40%)				
Net Accumulated	(986,964)			0
Investment	$1,480,446			$711,522

you do qualify, you may open a Keogh account with a bank, an insurance company, a savings institution, a mutual fund, a brokerage house, and so on. These firms will help you establish the Keogh and will do most of the bookwork for you. All you must do is come up with the money. The amount of money you are allowed to come up with is 15 percent of your earned income—up to a maximum of $15,000 a year.

You may have to come up with more than $15,000 a year. If you have employees, you may have to include them also. If you have full-time employees with three or more years of consecutive service, you must contribute for them when you contribute for yourself. Full time is described as 1000 hours or more per year. You must contribute for them a percentage of their salaries that is equal to the percentage of your income that is invested. For example, assume you have earned income of $40,000 and plan to contribute 12 percent, or $4800 to Keogh for yourself. Assume also you have two employees, earning $18,000 and $10,000, respectively. Here is what your Keogh contributions would look like:

	Income	Contribution as percentage of income	Contribution
You	$40,000	12% (optional)	$4,800
1st employee	18,000	12% (required)	2,160
2nd employee	10,000	12% (required)	1,200
Total contribution			$8,160

The percentage you contribute for yourself is optional, but once that is established, the percentages you must contribute for your employees are fixed.

Funds you put into Keogh for yourself must remain there until you turn 59½. Furthermore, you must start withdrawing the money at least by age 70½. You will be penalized by the government if you withdraw either too early or too late. Not being able to withdraw your money also means you can't pledge it against a loan. The exception to this rule is disability. If you become disabled, you can withdraw early without penalty.

With a little luck, you'll reach 59½ alive and without disabilities. With a little more luck, you'll reach age 70½. Between ages 59½ and 70½, you must begin to withdraw your Keogh money. You may take it in a lump sum, or periodic payments, whichever suits you. However, you will have to pay taxes as you withdraw the money. Because you will probably be in a lower tax bracket by then, the burden should not be as great. And, after all, the government did let you invest your money as if it really were yours, and not theirs, all those years.

Regardless of whose money it is, Keogh is a good plan for self-employed people. Even those who are self-employed must retire sometime. And if you are self-employed, the odds are you'll recognize that Keogh is a good deal. Most people who like to look out for themselves recognize a good deal when they see one—even when it's sponsored by the government.

◇ 37 ◇
Social Security

At the time of writing of this book the Social Security system of the United States is facing serious long-range difficulty. If you are more than ten years away from retirement, it is unwise to assume that you will receive full Social Security benefits as currently described.

In the opinion of many well-qualified observers, the system will be unable to meet its statutory payment of benefits by the mid to late 1980s. Unfortunately, the system is not adequately funded. Benefit payments have exceeded income. The cushion is not sufficient to pay future benefits.

This problem is compounded by the current birthrate, which is historically low. This condition has existed since the 1960s and is continuing at this time. Furthermore, life expectancy is improving. Demographically, a large number of people will eventually be retired and will have to be supported by a small group of younger workers. It currently seems unreasonable to assume these younger workers will be able to support the demands of the Social Security program from normal tax sources. These demographic forces are already in place. They represent people already born, or not born. There is *no* possibility of reversing the demographics.

The Reagan administration seems willing to look at this political time bomb. Options are few and painful. They include the following:

1. *Increases in Social Security taxes.* Social Security taxes are already uncomfortably high for workers and employers alike. Furthermore, current legislation calls for additional increases, to levels some people think are burdensome and oppressive. Increases beyond current legislation would seem difficult to obtain.

2. *Using income tax revenues for Social Security.* In my opinion, this option will be used to some extent in the future. However, help from income taxes may be limited. Demands on general taxes are already excessive. The government is currently running large deficits each year, with little relief in sight.

3. *Delay of benefits.* In my opinion, delays in retirement benefits from Social Security are inevitable. Congress has passed legislation forbidding companies to force employees to retire before age seventy. A natural following step to this legislation is to delay full Social Security benefits to age sixty-eight or seventy.

4. *Reduction of benefits.* In my opinion, paid benefits from Social Security will be reduced in some manner. There are several options. One is to reduce the anticipated adjustments for inflation. Another possible method of reducing benefits is to link them with private pension funds. Today the benefits from many private funds are partially reduced by the Social Security benefit. In the future, pensioners may find the opposite; that is, Social Security benefits may be reduced to reflect private pension benefits. This move would probably be accompanied by legislation forcing private industry to offer improved pension funds. Congress will find it easy to require the private sector to do what the private sector has never been willing to require of itself—namely, provide adequate funding.

Other likely possibilities include elimination of benefits to dependents over age eighteen where one parent is deceased; elimination of minimum benefits for workers who earned only a partial benefit; or elimination of so-called double clipping for workers who qualify for Social Security and federal pension by working part of their careers in both private industry and government.

5. *Seizure of private pension assets.* Some experts predict the government will solve its problems by seizing the assets of today's private pension accounts to fund the Social Security system. Anything is possible. However, the logistical, legal, and political problems of such a move are enormous. This drastic step seems unlikely to me.

In my opinion, the system will not be disbanded altogether, but it will be changed. Benefits will not be eliminated entirely, but they will be reduced. Future retirees cannot count on as much help from Social Security as current retirees can. It is not possible to predict accurately how or when these changes will occur. Therefore, all examples used in this book are based on existing legislation. But the message is clear—people who are planning their future retirements must plan on acquiring more of it themselves, even more than the worksheets in this book imply.

◇ 38 ◇
Should You Make a Will?

There's an old saying, "You can't take it with you!" But it should go on to say, "So you should decide where to leave it!" You will leave something behind—even if it's only your sacred remains and a pile of bills. Because you can't take it with you, you really ought to make some decisions where you're going to leave it. Those decisions have to be made while you still have it. And they should be made right away, because none of us knows how long we'll have any say in the matter. That's why you need a will.

Leaving a will is a little like leaving a list of instructions for the babysitter. If you do not leave instructions, the sitter will have to make all the decisions about putting the kids to bed and feeding the dog. Without knowing what you want, he or she will do what he or she wants to do—which may not please you.

If you do not leave a will, the Grand Supreme Babysitter of us all will decide what to do with your kids, your dog, and your everything. The Grand Supreme Babysitter, of course, is the government. Each state has its own set of probate laws for making babysitting—or should we say *estate sitting*—decisions. These probate laws are administered by the courts. Fortunately, most of the laws are quite reasonable. But the laws are very rigid, even worse than a strict babysitter. And the decisions made under the law may not please you a bit.

Consider these simple examples of decisions you might not like. If you die without a will, state law may dictate that your assets be divided one-third to your spouse and two-thirds to your children. This may not please you, especially if you leave an almost destitute spouse while the largest portion of your assets goes to your employed, self-sufficient kids. Also, if you die without a will and have no children, the law might divide your assets between your spouse and your parents. In fact, if you and your spouse die together, your interfering in-laws, who constantly nag at you about not getting

278

ahead, could wind up getting everything they never gave you credit for having.

Relatives aren't the only ones who may get more of your estate than you want. The Grand Supreme Babysitter may take a share too. Under the law, the government may be entitled to a share called *estate taxes*. Under the new tax law estate taxes for most estates will be nothing at all. But people with large estates ($225,000 in 1982 rising to $600,000 in 1987) may wind up paying estate taxes. And if you die without a will, you may wind up giving the baby-sitter much more than is necessary.

So if you have any feelings whatsoever about where you want your things to go after you've gone, you'd better put your feelings down in writing—now. And even if you think you don't have any feelings, you ought to have, because the court certainly won't.

Some people really believe they don't have any feelings about what they want done with their property after they die. Although it seems silly, here are some reasons why people don't have opinions, or haven't expressed their opinions in a will.

⋄ *I never thought about it.* When people are busy living, they find it easy not to take time to plan for dying. But no one ever gets out of life alive, no matter how busy one is. Death is inevitable, so you might as well plan for it.

⋄ *I don't like to think about dying.* The subject of death isn't a pleasant one—especially when it's your own death. Besides feeling that death is a morbid topic, some people believe that talking about dying, or making plans for dying, will some-how cause them to die. Of course, that is not true. Making a will doesn't mean you are going to die, any more than having a fire drill means you are going to have a fire.

⋄ *I don't own very much.* Maybe you're not wealthy. But if you have anything at all, you should express your wishes about where it will go. Cars, homes, furniture, even personal be-longings such as pictures and papers, are all important to you and to your family. Furthermore, you may have some minor children. It is important to indicate who will be responsible for them. If you don't express your feelings about your chil-dren's custody, the court will make the decision for you.

⋄ *I can't decide.* Sometimes people can't decide. Sometimes they can't decide because they don't want to hurt anyone's feelings.

If all your kids desperately want to inherit your handmade ukulele, you have a dilemma. But isn't it better to force yourself to make the decision now? You can discuss it with them now, while you are alive. A rational discussion *now* is better than letting a family-splitting feud get started over your ukulele after you die.

◇ *I don't care.* Some people take the attitude that after they're dead and gone they won't care what happens to things they couldn't take with them. But your survivors will care, and you don't want to leave them in a mess. Their messes can run all the way from having inadequate support because your property went elsewhere, to lawsuits between family members trying to get what they think belongs to them. Family bitterness arises far more often than most of us imagine, even in formerly close families. And it's a tragedy that can easily be avoided.

◇ *I'm too young.* Death isn't reserved just for senior citizens who have lived a long and useful life. It is more expected when people are elderly, to be sure; but people of all ages die. In fact, the unexpected nature of premature death makes a will even more important. A young parent who dies usually leaves more loose ends than an elderly person, simply because he (or she) wasn't planning on dying. A will can easily tie up lots of loose ends.

◇ *My spouse has a will.* Many wives take the attitude they don't need a will. They reason they don't personally own much, and their husbands have wills. But wives need wills too. For one thing, they certainly have personal possessions that are important. Beyond their personal possessions, they may also wind up inheriting their husbands' property. Unfortunately, they may not have it long enough to write wills before they also die. In fact, they may only own it for a few minutes. For example, assume a husband and wife are killed in a common disaster. It can be proved that she died last. All her husband's assets would go into her estate, according to his will. But if she does not have a will, her estate will be handled entirely by the court. So the property may wind up in places neither she nor her husband wanted.

◇ *Procrastination.* This uniquely human failing afflicts almost as many people as death itself. Unfortunately, no one can procrastinate death. Fortunately, unlike death, we can overcome procrastination with will power.

There must be lots of other reasons why people do not make a will. More than 50 percent of the adults in America do not have wills. Most of their reasons are probably as bad as the ones just given. There are, however, many good reasons to have a will. For example,

◇ To express your desires about the disposition of your property: to whom and how much
◇ To express your desires about the guardian of your children
◇ To provide financially, as best you can, for your loved ones
◇ To reduce taxes and other costs at your death
◇ To help avoid bitterness and disharmony among loved ones

Once you've finally decided to make a will, it is important to do so properly. There is more to making a will than leaving instructions for the babysitter. For example, few babysitters require two witnesses to your signature—unless you have very unusual kids. Although making a will is a little more involved than a list of babysitting instructions, it is no more involved than going to the doctor for a routine physical. Lawyers are professionals, just like doctors. They are no more overwhelming than physicians. The time spent in the lawyer's office is about the same. The cost of $35 to $100 is similar. And it doesn't hurt a bit to draw up a will. Here are the steps:

1. *Choose a lawyer.* As with choosing a physician, you want a professional, somebody that knows what he or she is doing. Estate laws are complex. To make sure your will complies with all the laws, you need an expert. If you do not already have a family lawyer, choose one the way you choose a physician—ask your friends. Or, as a good independent source, you can look in the yellow pages under "Lawyer Referral Services." This is a service of your local bar association, and it is free. The association will help you find a competent lawyer.

2. *Make a complete list of everything you own.* Obviously, many items can be lumped together and do not need to be listed separately, such as furniture, or family records.

3. *Decide whom you want to inherit your property.* It is a good idea to talk this over with the people who will be named in your will. You might be surprised to find out how some of your loved ones feel about things. Frequently there are strong opinions about personal items such as wedding rings and scrapbooks.

4. *Decide whom you want as executor of your estate.* The executor will be responsible for your assets when you die. Under law, he or she is required to pay off your debts and distribute the assets according to the provisions of your will. Normally the executor will be someone outside your immediate family—someone not named for an inheritance in your will. If your estate isn't complicated, you can probably choose a friend. It should be someone whose judgment you respect and who is close enough to you to understand your wishes. But there are problems with friends. For one thing your friend may die before you do. Second, estate administration is a lot of work. You may not want to unload your estate problems on a friend. You may prefer to unload it on a bank or law firm. They are experts in handling estate matters—and the bank doesn't die. Whatever you do, it is good advice to ask your friend if he (or she) is willing to be named as executor. Most friends will say yes because they don't know what they are getting into. Most banks or law firms do know what they are getting into and they will say yes because they want the business.

5. *Decide whom you want as guardian for your children.* Some people can't bring themselves to make this decision. They find fault with every guardian they consider. But even if the decision is a tough one, isn't it better for you to face up to it than leave the court to decide with whom your kids will live? Once you have decided in your own mind whom you want as guardian, then ask that person's permission to name them. It creates real problems if your friend's wife suddenly finds out she has inherited your kids—and she doesn't want them.

6. *Decide what type of burial you want.* If nothing else, everyone has to be disposed of in some way. You can save your family lots of grief and possibly expense by leaving your instructions in your will.

7. *Take all your lists and decisions with you to the lawyer.* He or she will help you express your decisions properly in a will. It is impor-

tant that they be legally clear and conform to all applicable laws. These are the only type of instructions the Grand Supreme Babysitter will pay much attention to.

After the lawyer has helped you make a proper list of instructions, it is important to keep it up to date. You wouldn't use the same list of instructions to the babysitter year after year. Things change. Your kids get older and have different needs. The same is true about wills. Also, the things you own change. The following is a list of changes that may occur in your life. Each would be a good reason to update your will.

⋄ Change in marital status
⋄ Birth or death of a child
⋄ Change in needs of inheritors
⋄ Meaningful increase or decrease in assets
⋄ Change in business relationships, such as formation of a partnership or small business
⋄ Change in your desires or opinions

Changes in your will are easy to make, but you have to go back to a lawyer. The government is very fussy about instructions. You can't just cross out a sentence and write a new instruction in the margin. It has to be properly worded, witnessed, and so on.

Sometimes you'll have enough changes to justify making a whole new will. Again, making a new will is easy to do. Only the last set of instructions will be used. However, if you do make a new will it's a good idea to gather up all the old wills and destroy them. If you don't, confusion could arise. Imagine the frenzy of your poor babysitter if she found contradictory sets of instructions in every room in your house.

Perhaps worse than finding several lists of instructions is finding no instructions at all, especially when you really did go to the trouble of making them. It is important, therefore, to keep your will in a safe, convenient place. Your home is the most convenient place, but it isn't very safe. At home, your will could accidentally be lost, stolen, or destroyed. Many people like to keep the originals on file with their lawyers. Some put the originals in a safe deposit box. These places are safe, but not convenient. Safe deposit boxes can be especially inconvenient if no one is around with authority to get into your box. Probably the best idea is to keep several copies in places where survivors are likely to look. Then attach notes indicating where the original is safely kept.

After you've taken every precaution to make sure your list of instructions can be found, it may irritate you to discover that the Grand Supreme Babysitter may not follow your instructions after all. Like babysitters in real life, the courts are sometimes faced with conditions you didn't entirely anticipate before you left. In those cases, the babysitter must use her best judgment—regardless of what your instructions say. Fortunately, these circumstances are rare. If you've left a good set of instructions, they will probably be followed completely.

Because "You can't take it with you," it is wise to make sure you've figured out where you're going to leave it. Your list of instructions to the Grand Supreme Babysitter is very important, because you never know when the babysitter will have to come. And after she has come, you won't be able to call home and see how everything is going.

◇ 39 ◇
The Personal Trust

A trust, according to one unabridged dictionary, is "the obligation arising from the confidence, reposed in a person (called the *trustee*) to whom the legal title to property is conveyed for the benefit of another (called the *cestui que trust*) that he will faithfully apply the property according to such confidence."

This definition will strike most people as being difficult to grasp at first. And if the definition of a trust seems hard to understand, the laws dealing with trusts are even worse. But even though the definition is ambiguous and the law is complicated, the average person can and should at least understand what a trust can do. Actually, the concept of a personal trust is easy to understand. Once it is understood, the usefulness of a personal trust for many people becomes obvious.

To understand what a trust is, consider the following unlikely example of a man who designs and builds a race car. He may be concerned about what will happen to the car when he dies. Therefore, he may write into his will provisions for a trust that becomes effective on his death. The trust will be made effective by transferring the car's ownership—title and all—to a trustee. The trustee may be a bank, a friend, or perhaps a professional car driver.

Assume that in this case the trustee is a professional driver. The driver will become the legal owner of the car—and he (or she) won't even have to pay for it. But he will have to agree to do certain things the builder wants done. In fact, he must do everything the builder wants, the way the builder wants, and when the builder wants. For example, the driver may agree to race the car, and to wash it regularly, and to make sure it is tuned up. The builder is trusting the driver to do all of these things. The driver, in turn, will be paid a fee for his work, and the whole arrangement will be backed up with the force of law.

Perhaps not many car builders do this. But many other people do. People who own property do it—everyday property such as

285

stocks, bonds, real estate, businesses, and other assets—possibly even such assets as race cars. The procedure is known as "establishing a trust." The property owner is called the *donor* or *giver* or *creator*. He or she willingly gives the ownership rights to his or her stocks, bonds, or other property to a second person. This second person is called a *trustee*. The property owner is literally and legally trusting the second person to take care of his or her property the way the owner wants. In modern America, the second "person" is frequently a financial institution, such as a bank or trust company. The trustee or bank takes title to the donor's property. Then, according to the donor's instructions, the trustee administers the property for the benefit of a third person, called the *beneficiary*. The beneficiary may be a spouse, a child, a charitable organization, and so on. For a property owner to give his or her property to a bank or a trustee, and go to all the trouble of setting up a trust, you can imagine that trusts must offer some special benefits. And they do offer benefits, such as the following.

Protection

Protection usually means protection of the property from the beneficiary him- or herself. Many beneficiaries do not have the maturity to care for the property the donor wants to give them. For example, the race car builder may want his son to wind up with the car, eventually. But Dad thinks it's crazy to turn a race car over to a teenager. So he gives it to someone else, like a qualified race driver. Then he trusts the driver to take good care of the car until Junior grows up. A lot of people feel the same about their property. Dad may feel that if the kids are given all his money before they grow up, they may fritter it away on light-minded living. To ensure there will be something left when they reach a ripe old age such as twenty-five, Dad may give the property to a bank. The bank will hold and administer the property in a trust until the kids grow up.

Sometimes taking care of the property requires special expertise that even mature adults do not have. For example, a man may own a substantial number of stocks. He may want his wife to have them when he dies. But his wife may not know anything about stocks. He may fear that if the stocks are left in her care she will fall prey to financial charlatans who'll give her bad advice. To protect his wife and the stocks, he may establish a trust and let the bank take care of them for her. Of course, all women can and should learn to handle their own finances, and that would be the best solution here, too. But many women have in fact never learned to deal with money. If you are a woman, learn to do so now. If you are a man, encourage your wife and daughters to do so. This book can help.

Proper Distribution

Through trusts, property owners can be sure their property will go where they want it to go, when they want it to go there. This will be true even when they die. For example, consider the case of the race car builder who wants his son to get the car, but not until the son is mature enough. The builder may not want to leave the decision about his son's maturity to someone such as a probate judge. Through a trust, Dad can decide, while he is still alive, when he thinks Junior will be mature enough. The builder may feel his son won't be ready for this particular car until the son is ninety-one. Through a trust, the builder can arrange to have the car held that long, if he wants. However, if the only thing a builder leaves to express his wishes is a will, his son may get the car as soon as the builder dies. And, who knows—the kid may be only seventeen at that time. Consider another example: The builder may want his daughter to get the trophies. But he might worry that they will be used as flower pots if his father-in-law, who thinks racing is foolishness, somehow gets control of them. The builder, knowing his father-in-law, may fear he will contest the will in court and somehow get control of the trophies. He can avoid that potential problem by establishing a trust while he is still alive. By putting the trophies in a trust, he will technically remove them from his estate when he dies. Because they are not part of his estate they won't be subject to any dispute in probate court.

These same principles apply to any property owner that wants to be sure where and when his or her property gets distributed when he or she dies. Take a farmer who wants her farm to go to her daughter at age twenty-one. But the farmer has an ex-husband whom she dislikes. She is afraid he will somehow convince the probate court he is the rightful heir to the property despite what her will says. It's not far-fetched at all. But she can avoid this uncertainty through a trust.

Security

Security refers to security of the beneficiaries. There is a certain security for a surviving spouse, for example, to know that a given sum of money will come in every month. He or she can plan for it and set a budget accordingly. This is frequently better than getting huge sums when earnings are good but receiving nothing when times are bad. For example, the car builder may arrange to have the race car prize money paid to his wife in "even" monthly installments. She may prefer this to big lump sums when the car wins, followed by months of nothing when the car loses. The agreement with the trustee can be drawn in such a way that the beneficiary can be secure in the knowledge that the money is coming.

Avoiding Probate

Sometimes settling a property owner's estate in probate court becomes quite involved—even if there is a will. Portions of the property may need to be sold to pay taxes or creditors. This must be done before anything can be given to the heirs. Furthermore, the deceased owner can't be sure which assets the court will choose to sell. In the case of our builder, he can be sure the car won't be sold if he puts it in a trust. When the trust is established, the title is transferred to the race driver. At that time the trust owns the car, and it is no longer part of the builder's estate. Consequently, the probate court can't touch it and the son will eventually get the car as planned. (Of course, this concept can only be pushed so far. The court will not allow you to leave all your creditors with nothing but your obituary. The court might dissolve the trusts if it appears they were created to help you avoid your financial responsibilities.)

Continuity of Operation

Frequently, when a property owner dies, things get tied up in probate. Then some things that should get done might not get done, such as buying or selling stocks. It may be clear that one of the stocks is going down in value, but no one may have the ready authority to sell it. Moreover, creditors must be notified of the property owner's death and given a chance to file claims. During this sometimes drawn-out procedure, there may be a lot of confusion about who gets and does what. There have even been cases where the surviving spouse couldn't drive the family car for months because it was tied up in probate court. If our builder still owns his race car when he dies, for instance, the court may not let the car be raced until after the will is settled in probate court. The judge will want to be sure he or she knows who really owns it. He or she will also want to know that the taxes have been paid on it, and that there are no outstanding bills for things such as spark plugs and hubcaps. While everyone is waiting for the court to satisfy itself, the car may be losing a chance to win the "Indy 500."

These delays can be particularly damaging if a small business is left with no clear indication of who has authority to run it. Who signs the checks? Buys the inventory? And makes up the payroll? Many small businesses have been shut down and finally liquidated because of probate. And this can happen regardless of the wishes of the deceased or the survivors. Such problems can be avoided through a trust. If the race car is in trust when the builder dies, it will not be subject to probate. That way it can be driven in Indianapolis even if the builder's will is being read in Little Rock on the same day.

Avoiding Taxes

Actually, no one avoids taxes completely. But property owners can sometimes delay or reduce their taxes. There may be a choice between several taxes. With good planning, the property owner can choose to pay only the smallest ones. Consider income taxes, for example. If the car builder is wealthy, he may find that most of the prize money is going to Uncle Sam. If, however, he establishes a trust while he is still alive and arranges for the winnings to go to his wife, who is not in a high tax bracket, maybe Uncle Sam won't get quite as much.

Avoiding Creditors

The creditors that are being avoided may be either the creditors of the donor or the beneficiary. Perhaps, after signing the car over to the driver, the builder may get himself hopelessly in debt trying to build the world's fastest canoe. The builder's canoe creditors cannot sue him and get the car to pay his canoeing debts, not even if the builder dies. However, this would not be the case if the builder ran up the debts before he put the car in trust.

The builder's son may have debts, too. If the builder simply gave the car to his son, or willed it to him at death, then Junior's creditors could sue and get the car. But the creditors can't touch it as long as it is held in trust for Junior. In fact, a stipulation of the trust might include Junior's being free of debt before he can get the car.

There are perhaps dozens of other good reasons for establishing trusts. A major consideration in the establishment of most trusts is whether the trust should be revocable or irrevocable. A revocable trust allows the property owner the option to change his or her mind at some time in the future before he or she dies. He or she can perhaps take the property back, name someone else as beneficiary, or change the trust in some other way. With an irrevocable trust, the owner usually gives up any right to change his or her mind in the future. This is not a minor decision. None of us knows how long we will live. If the trust is irrevocable, we do not know for how long we have given up the right to change our minds.

Why would anyone give up the right to change his or her mind? The answer is, taxes! If a revocable trust is established, the government will consider that all the earnings on the property still belong to the donor while he or she is alive. Consequently, the earnings will be taxed at a high tax rate. If the trust is a qualified irrevocable trust, however, the government will agree that the earnings belong to the beneficiary. Then the earnings will be taxed at the beneficiary's lower tax rate. In the past, many irrevocable trusts were set up to take advantage of the lower taxes on gifts than on inheritances. However, recent tax laws have changed that possibility. People may be willing to give up the right to change their minds for other reasons, too. It is possible, for example, a charitable beneficiary can qualify for additional funding from outside sources only if a major gift from some generous person is a certainty. An irrevocable trust may satisfy the requirements.

For many people, the question is not revocable versus irrevocable trusts. It is "Do we need a trust at all?" Trusts are not needed by all families. In this regard, trusts differ from wills in personal estate planning. Everyone should have a will, but not everyone needs a trust. The great majority of people leave behind a house, a few family heirlooms, and a lifetime of happy memories. In such cases, a trust is probably not necessary. People who need trusts usually have some of the following characteristics:

⋄ They have large net worths. President Reagan's new tax law raises these amounts substantially. If a husband and wife have a joint net worth of $225,000 in 1982, or if they are likely to have a joint net worth of $600,000 by 1987, a trust may be useful. Net worth includes equity in home, value of life insurance, as well as businesses and other investments.

⋄ They want to leave money to minor children, mentally retarded people, or others currently incapable of properly administering the property.

⋄ They own property titled in several different states.

⋄ They want to leave philanthropic gifts and want the gifts dispersed over a number of years.

⋄ They are in the 40 percent tax bracket or higher.

⋄ There are circumstances where an interruption of operation or income would be detrimental.

⋄ There is a business involved.

⋄ There are circumstances where liquidation of specific parts of the estate at death is undesirable.

If any of these characteristics describe you, perhaps a trust is in order. Note that age is not a requirement. People needn't be approaching retirement when they think about trusts. They must just have a need for one. If you have a need for one, you should be aware that trust law is very complicated. The services of a qualified expert are absolutely necessary. Most banks have trust departments and can offer competent advice. The legal work must be done by a lawyer, however. If your circumstances are very complex, you may need to retain a lawyer specializing in the field. Through the use of expert advice, you can set up a trust that is best for your circumstances.

Once you have set up your trust and it's running well, you can sit back and relax. No more concerns that at the end of your personal race your chief mechanic will sue to get your engine, or that your pearl-studded steering wheel will be sold at auction to pay for your last tuneup. You won't even need to worry about who'll wax your car after the race. All this can be described in your trust.

◇ Conclusion ◇

It has been my hope in this section to help readers identify areas of personal vulnerability to credit, risk, and retirement traps. Far too often I have found people assuming an attitude that "it always happens to the other guy, never to me." Well, what do you think the other guy is assuming? He (or she) is assuming it will happen to you. And it might.

So a little caution with regard to your use of credit, your handling of risk, and your preparation for retirement is appropriate.

Please notice I have not recommended extreme preparations. There are certainly those who would advise absolutely no debt even for a house, burning your credit cards, carrying a million or more in insurance, and spending absolutely nothing today so you have something tomorrow. Such an extreme position is not financial freedom.

But there are also large numbers of people who—through their actions—take the extreme opposite position. They exercise no caution. They may feel nothing bad can happen to them, or they may not understand. Either way many of these are in for a very unpleasant surprise at some point. To achieve financial freedom, wisdom and balance are needed.

Part V.
Investing for
Financial Freedom

Ultimately in order to be financially free, we must invest. The first four parts of this book make investing for financial freedom possible.

Understanding the world of the 1980s and ourselves, managing our money efficiently, and avoiding major traps allows us the flexibility to invest. Good investments lead to greater financial flexibility and finally total financial freedom.

But investing can hurt. It means you must take some money you are currently spending and put it aside for the future. It means diverting some income from current consumption. But if you follow the principles in the first four parts of this book, it should not be so difficult.

It is important to get started, and to invest well. The following table illustrates the effect that both time and rate of return can have on your money.

Future Value of $10,000 Invested Today

Rate of Return	10 years	20 years	30 years
5%	$16,289	$ 26,533	$ 43,219
10	26,937	67,275	174,449
15	40,456	163,664	662,114

You don't have to be a financial whiz kid to see that you earn much more financial freedom earning 15 percent for 30 years than earning 15 percent for 10 years ($662,114 versus $40,456). Furthermore, anyone can see how much better it is to earn for 30 years at 15 percent than 30 years at 5 percent ($662,114 versus $43,219). You need to get started, and you need to do it well.

But I know these are tall orders: getting started with all the pressures on us today and doing it well with all the complexities of the investment world. That's what this book is about.

This part of the book is about helping you understand the complexities of the investment world. There is much in this part. It is the longest in the book. But I hope you will find it interesting. I have compiled tables for quick comparison of investments. But quick comparisons are not enough. I have also explained most of the commonly available investment vehicles and how they work in detail. Understanding what you are investing in is the best defense against making a mistake.

I have also devoted considerable time to the potential pitfalls of all these forms of investments. Far too often I read books, hear lecturers, and see sales materials that only tell one side of the story. And hearing just one side can lead to many financially heartbreaking problems.

There is such a serious tendency in this country to tell just one side of the story that the government has passed some strict laws requiring both sides to be told. The most visible evidence of these laws are the prospectuses that must accompany most new offerings.

But people don't read things like prospectuses. I can understand why. They are written in legalese. Well, this book isn't written in legalese. I hope you will read it with care.

I hope something else. I fear in my attempt to illustrate potential pitfalls you may conclude I don't like investing in anything. Nothing could be further from the truth. In fact, properly used and understood I like (and have actually used) nearly all these investment types. They can all work for financial freedom.

I'll close this introduction to investing with a word of warning that I feel very strongly about. *Do not let yourself get sucked into popular fads.* Every professional investor knows that all forms of investments go through cycles. By definition, an investment is at the high point of its cycle when most people are enthusiastic about it. And by definition an investment is at the low point of its cycle when most people are pessimistic about it.

If there is any one principle in this book that can really make you rich it is the one just given. If you can really understand what it means and apply it by buying at the bottoms of cycles and selling at the tops of cycles, you will do well in investing. And the more enthusiastic everyone seems, the more "sure-fire" the investment appears, and the better it performed last year—*the more skeptical you must be.*

Investing is fun, exciting, and rewarding, and it leads to financial freedom.

◇ 40 ◇
What Are Investment and Speculation?

Investing: The use of one's ability to attract scarce economic resources for purposes other than current consumption with the intention of receiving future financial gain through income and/or appreciation of value.

This definition makes some important points:

1. *"Ability to attract scarce resources."* Not all your savings and investments must come from your weekly paycheck. Sometimes you can invest using other people's money. Your home is the best example of this. With a down payment of $20,000, you might be able to buy an $80,000 house using someone else's $60,000 for the mortgage. If the house goes up 10 percent in value to $88,000, you have made an $8,000 profit on the $20,000 you invested—that's 40 percent on your money. Incidentally, you can often attract more of the world's scarce resources (money) for investment purposes than for current consumption. Just try borrowing $60,000 for a trip to Disneyland, for example.

2. *"Current consumption."* People don't always have as much choice on how they spend their money as they would like. If the paycheck barely covers the basic necessities of food, shelter, and clothing, then investing is nearly out of the question. There are many things they spend money on that are not true basics. But many things, such as television sets, new cars, big homes, and expensive vacations, are more than "basic necessities": they are luxuries. There is nothing wrong with luxuries. But they are not investments. They will not do us any good later on, during retirement. Most of us, therefore, are constantly faced with the decision not between investing and basics, but between investing for the future and consuming some luxury today.

296

3. *"Intention."* This is more important than might be thought, for two reasons. First, we sometimes delude ourselves about why we spend money. A good coin collection, for instance, will probably appreciate in value. But be honest with yourself, you probably have no "intention" of selling it. So it is not an investment at all—it is a hobby. Second, money might be put into a venture with the "intention" of making more money. But in the end the venture may wind up losing the whole bundle. Your father-in-law would claim you were not investing at all, you were gambling. But the definition maintains that you were investing. Unfortunately, this investment turned out to be a "bad investment." (Perhaps your father-in-law would agree with this, too.)

4. *"Future financial gain."* This might be dividends and interest you plan to receive while your money is invested. The gain may also be the "appreciation" in value you hope your investment will achieve. Future financial gains, however, do not refer to simple "preservation" of value. When your main concern is to preserve and protect your money, you are simply saving, not investing.

The definition of an investment can be clarified by examples of things that are frequently referred to as investments but that often are not investments.

- ◇ Cars, television sets, appliances, stereos
- ◇ Furniture (including antiques)
- ◇ Most types of insurance
- ◇ Many forms of savings accounts
- ◇ Checking accounts
- ◇ Jewelry and collections
- ◇ Houses (under some circumstances)

Chapter 41, "Choosing The Right Investment" lists a large number of items that usually are investments. Strangely enough, there are some overlaps; some items, such as "houses," appear on both lists. Where you personally list them depends on your "intention."

Speculation

Understanding what speculation is can be important so you can avoid it. Simply stated, an investor is speculating when the amount he or she stands to make from an investment isn't enough to offset the financial and/or emotional loss he or she could possibly suffer.

The amount you stand to make versus the loss depends somewhat on the odds. If you are betting on the toss of a coin, you have one chance in two of winning. If each bet is $1.00 and you win $2.00 every time heads comes up, your odds are exactly even. In theory if you play all night you'll take home the same amount you came with.

Suppose, however, the odds change. Say you can get in the game for a mere $1.00 and you will receive $100,000 if you win. But assume you only have one chance in 200,000 of winning. Would you still play? Lots of people would, even though the odds are terrible—lotteries and raffles are very popular. The risk of losing $1.00 isn't that worrisome. But mathematically the odds are very much against you, so this game is speculation. And if you play long enough, odds are you'll lose all your dollars.

Straight mathematics is not the only consideration. Your aversion to the risk of losing is also important. Aversion to risk is your emotional reaction to losing. For example, you may say that, even if your odds are fair, you work too hard for your dollars to risk losing even one flip of the coin. But suppose someone raised the odds. Say you would win $4.00 if heads comes up but you only risk losing $1.00 if its tails. The odds are very good, so you might risk your milk money. In fact, the odds are so good that you could make a fortune playing all night long.

Other people might be willing to play with these good odds even if the minimum bet were higher, like $100 or $1000. But at some point everyone gets very risk-averse and will refuse to run the risk of losing even once. Suppose the minimum bet was $1 million. Let's say you had one chance in two of winning $4 million. That's a lot of money and those are great odds. But you have one chance out of two of losing your $1 million. Losing $1 million would probably mean going completely bankrupt. The emotional pain of losing is so great you will not play even though the odds are strongly in your favor.

All this tells us some important things about speculation. First, a speculation for one person could be a great investment for another. The Rockefellers may have no qualms about risking $1 million on the flip of a coin—you probably do. Second, potential losses are far more than just financial, they are also emotional. Emotional considerations must be carefully considered when assessing risk. Finally, whether an expenditure of money is a speculation or an investment is a function of the way things are expected to be when the expenditure is made. They are not a function of how things finally turn out. Rank speculations sometimes make a lot of money. The summary is that the speculators will be losers over time. They will lose either financially, or emotionally, or both.

Why would anyone "speculate," then? There are three reasons: greed, stupidity, and laziness.

1. *Greed.* This is the most important reason by far. In fact, it is usually part of the other two reasons. Greed is a human "emotion." This makes it extremely tough for most of us to clearly understand and deal with in ourselves. We conjure up great mental images of wealth and power, and soon we are so involved with our "get-rich" daydreams that we ignore obvious risks and plunge in. All too often, the results are pretty bad.

2. *Stupidity.* This arises in two ways. Sometimes we are just plain stupid. We fail to use the best asset we have: good common sense. We make investments that clearly do not have much chance of working. If we were to stop and really think about it, we would see the problems in advance.

   A more honest form of stupidity is ignorance. Here we simply do not know enough about the subject to ask the right questions or to understand the answers.

3. *Laziness.* This occurs when the information is available but we do not take the time to dig it out and understand it. It becomes easy to accept someone else's one-liner opinion and to avoid thinking for ourselves.

Because human weaknesses are present in all of us, this section and maybe the whole book will have achieved its goal if you make it a habit to consider the following questions when analyzing a possible investment. If you must give the wrong answer one or more times, the odds are pretty good that your "investment" is really a "speculation."

1. Are you counting on someone dumber than yourself to buy the investment from you at a price higher than you paid? Put another way, what incentive will he or she have to buy when your good judgment says it is time to sell?

2. Do you thoroughly understand how the investment will make

money for you? Is it supposed to go up in value? If so, what will cause that to happen? Is it supposed to pay a big dividend—if so, how?

3. Do you understand how your investment is priced? Is there a way to establish a true value not only now but when you plan to sell? If you do not understand how your investment is priced, then how can you be sure you are not paying too much?

4. Does the success of the investment depend on the occurrence of complex events completely outside your control (such as getting a patent and then financing)? Remember, the chain is only as strong as its weakest link. When it comes to investments, each time you add another link you increase the probability that one link will be weak.

5. Must the investment be sold before a specific time in order to work? For example, do you lose all your money if you don't exercise a certain option on time?

6. Does the potential return seem to be *very* large? Be particularly careful if at the same time the risks seem small. There are very few "sure-fire" investments!

7. Will you have to borrow heavily to make the investment?

8. How serious would it be if the investment fell in value or cut its dividend for a while? Would it wipe you out?

9. Is your possible loss great? Is it as much as 100 percent, or more?

10. If everything went wrong, would the loss create a serious financial strain on you?

11. Would failure of the investment cause you severe mental anguish? Would it damage a valued relationship with a relative or friend?

In summary, there is nothing wrong with taking risk. All investing involves some risk. Many "deals" with high risk are worth taking and are very appropriate for some investors. But investors should be sufficiently informed so that they know exactly what they are getting into, and know that they can afford it. If they handle it well over time, the odds say they'll be "winners."

Special Notice to
Those Considering Investments

Although the following pages should serve as a good introduction to investing, I do not intend them to be the final word. There are many individuals and companies out there just waiting to prey on the newcomer. Therefore, before making any investment, you should first seek the advice of your attorney, your accountant, or your personal financial advisor.

◇ 41 ◇
Choosing the Right Investment

You should choose those investments best suited to your needs.

There are all kinds of investment possibilities, from stocks to art. An important consideration, then, is finding the right investment to meet your specific needs. Investing is like buying a pet. Your first problem is to figure out what kind of animal you can live with. Like pets, investments have different personalities and characteristics. Some are easy to care for, others require substantial work. Some will work for you, others will just sit and look pretty. Some may guard you against intruders but may turn and bite you if you're not careful. Studying the personalities and characteristics of available pets or investments is the first step for all potential owners.

The following table shows major classes of investments and important characteristics about which investors should think. The list may look exhaustive, but it's not. In fact, it could be much longer. I've had to make some generalizations, but I hope the list is useful in total. This table may also prove useful for future reference. Someday it may help call to mind a key question you should ask before investing. After all, who wants to wind up buying an elephant when what you really want is a pet to sit on your lap while you watch TV?

Explanations of the Table Columns

These descriptions of terms are intended to help you interpret the table.

1. *General suitability for average investor.* This column represents a reasonable assessment of the overall desirability of the investment for the average person. The assessment includes judgment regarding the chances the investment will actually accomplish what the investor wants. Describing an "average investor" is probably impossible. But for the purpose of this

book, think of an "average investor" as married, with two to four children, a total family income of $18,000 to $30,000, and a household head twenty-five to fifty years old with somewhat limited time and interest to devote to investments. Investors not meeting this description aren't excluded—their financial needs are simply a little different, so the suitability criteria may vary.

2. *Appreciation capability.* This criterion rates the investment's potential to increase in value. A high rating doesn't guarantee the investment will go up; it only means that this type of investment *can* go up.

3. *Volatility risk.* This term describes how rapidly and how often the investment's value might be expected to change. Extremely volatile investments may go up or down 30 to 50 percent in a single week.

4. *Current income.* "Current" means one year or less. "Income" is cash received in the form of dividends and interest without selling the investment.

5. *Ease of entry.* This factor describes the ability of the average investor with average knowledge and contacts to purchase the investment. The column also offers a rough guideline for the minimum initial investment required to get started.

6. *Ease of exit.* Sometimes it's easy to buy an investment, but it's difficult to get your money back when you want it. Sometimes the value declines substantially if you want to liquidate prematurely. This column describes these phenomena.

7. *Protection against inflation.* Some investments tend to rise in value with inflation, thus protecting the investor's buying power. Other investments do not rise. This column rates inflation-hedging potential.

8. *Protection against emotional decisions.* Many investors are their own worst enemies, buying or selling emotionally at highly inopportune times because of "fear" or "greed." Some investments have built-in safeguards against emotionalism. Others accentuate emotionalism by their very nature. This column considers the nature of the product, the availability of good advice, or the potential for a "sales pitch" to stimulate an investor into an emotional decision.

9. *Personal effort required.* Frequently investors look only at the profit opportunity and fail to adequately consider the work involved. This column rates the personal effort necessary to achieve success with the investment.

10. *Tax advantages.* Many tax advantages are associated with certain investments. This column describes them in general terms.

Major Classes of Investments and Their Characteristics

	Col. 1 General suitability for average investors: Excellent Good Fair Poor	Col. 2 Appreciation capability 5 years: Excellent=100%+ Good=50–100% Fair=15–50% Poor=0–15% None	Col. 3 Volatility risk—6 months or less: Extreme=100%+ High=50–100% Average=15–50% Low=0–15% None=0%	Col. 4 Current income or yield: High=14%+ Good=9–14% Fair=6–9% Poor=0–6% None=Negat
Common stocks				
Blue chips	Good	Good	Average	Fair
Secondary (e.g., traded American Exchange)	Fair	Excellent	Average	Poor
Speculative (e.g, traded over-the-counter)	Poor	Excellent	High	Poor
Mutual funds				
High growth	Good	Excellent	Average	Poor
Long-term appreciation	Excellent	Good	Average	Fair
Income and growth	Excellent	Fair	Low	Fair
Income	Good	Poor	Low	Good
Money market	Excellent	None	None	Good
Preferred stocks	Fair	Poor	Low	Fair
Savings				
Checking account	Excellent	None	None	None
Passbook account	Excellent	None	None	Poor
Savings certificates	Good	None	None	Good
Credit union	Excellent	None	None	Poor
Debt instruments				
Short-term (certificates of deposit, etc.)	Good	None	None	Good
Government bonds	Fair	Poor	Low	Good
Municipal bonds	Poor	Poor	Low	Fair
Industrial (high quality)	Fair	Poor	Low	Good
Industrial (low quality)	Poor	Fair	Average	High
Government E-Bonds	Poor	None	None	Fair

(Continued)

Col.5 Ease of entry and normal minimums: Excellent Good Fair Poor	Col. 6 Ease of exit: Excellent Good Fair Poor Bad	Col. 7 Protection against inflation: Excellent Good Fair Poor None	Col. 9 Protection against emotional decisions (buy/sell): E=Excellent G=Good F=Fair P=Poor NA=Not applicable	Col. 9 Personal effort required: Extreme Modest Some None	Col. 10 Tax advantages: CG=Capital gains potential I=nontaxable income S=Depreciation shelter D=Tax deferral Potential
Good $5,000	Good	Good	F/F	Some	CG
Good $2,000	Good	Good	F/F	Modest	CG
Good $1,000	Good	Good	P/P	Modest	CG
Good $500	Good	Good	F/F	Some	CG
Good $500	Good	Good	F/F	Some	CG
Good $500	Good	Fair	G/G	Some	Modest CG
Good $500	Good	Poor	G/G	Some	None
Good $500	Good	Poor	G/G	Some	None
Good $1,000	Good	Poor	G/G	Some	Limited I + Modest CG
Excellent $25	Excellent	None	NA/NA	None	None
Excellent $5	Excellent	Poor	NA/G	None	None
Good $500	Poor	Poor	E/E	None	None
Excellent $5	Excellent	Poor	NA/G	None	None
Fair $5,000	Good	Poor	G/G	Some	None
Good $10,000	Good	Poor	F/F	None	None
Fair $10,000	Fair	Poor	F/F	Some	I
Good $10,000	Good	Poor	F/F	Some	None
Fair $10,000	Fair	Poor	F/P	Modest	Possible CG
Good $50	Poor	Poor	E/E	None	None

	Col. 1	Col. 2	Col.3	Col. 4
Life insurance				
Whole life	Fair	None	None	None
Term	Good	None	None	None
Variable annuity	Good	Fair	None	None
Options				
Buying	Poor	Excellent	Extreme	None
Writing	Poor	Good	Average	Good
Commodity futures	Poor	Excellent	Extreme	None
Precious metals				
Bullion	Poor	Good	Average	Negative
Coins, jewelry, etc.	Poor	Good	Low	Negative
Real estate				
Home	Excellent	Good	Low	Negative
Income property (personal management)	Fair	Fair	Low	Fair
Limited partnership (professional)	Fair	Fair	Low	Good
Farms and ranches	Poor	Fair	Low	Poor
Raw land	Poor	Fair	Low	Negative
Recreational	Poor	Poor	Low	Negative
Oil/gas partnerships	Fair	Good	Low	Good
Cattle ventures	Fair	Fair	Low	Good
Rarities and collectibles (art, antiques, etc.)	Poor	Fair	Low	Negative
Private business	Fair	Fair	Low	Fair
Diamonds	Poor	Good	High	Negative

Col. 5	Col. 6	Col.7	Col. 8	Col. 9	Col. 10
Good $200	Poor	Poor	F/F	None	None
Good $100	Good	None	F/F	None	None
Good $500	Poor	Fair	F/F	None	Limited CG
Good $500	Fair	Good	P/P	Extreme	D
Fair $10,000	Fair	Good	P/P	Extreme	None
Good $500	Fair	Excellent	P/P	Extreme	D
Poor $10,000	Fair	Excellent	F/F	Some	CG
Fair $500	Poor	Excellent	P/F	Modest	CG
Fair $15,000	Fair	Excellent	G/E	Modest	CG + S
Fair $5,000	Fair	Excellent	G/G	Extreme	CG + S + I
Fair $5,000	Poor	Good	F/E	None	CG + S + I
Fair $25,000	Poor	Good	F/F	Extreme	CG + S + I
Fair $1,000	Poor	Excellent	F/F	Some	CG
Good $500	Bad	Fair	P/E	Some	CG
Fair $5,000	Bad	Fair	F/E	None	D + I
Fair $5,000	Bad	Fair	F/E	None	D
Poor $500	Poor	Excellent	P/E	Extreme	CG
Poor $25,000	Bad	Good	F/E	Extreme	Varied
Poor $500–$25,000	Bad	Fair	P/E	Some	CG

Having looked at a brief chart comparison of many of the investment potentials, let's now take a closer look to determine which is most likely to lead to financial freedom.

◇ 42 ◇
Making Money in Stocks

The stock market is as unpredictable as a tornado, it has the attention span of a two-year-old child, and it is as determined as an enraged bull. The stock market is in constant, forceful motion! Once you understand this point, you'll find the market as easy to love as a pet tiger.

Making money in the stock market means understanding the stock market. It means getting to know what stocks are and how the mechanics of buying and selling them work (including costs). It also means learning where the risks are and how high they are, and whether or not the potential rewards justify the risks.

I want to be complete in my approach. I am assuming that some readers may know little about stocks. Therefore I am going to begin with an elementary explanation of what stocks (and the stock market) are. Those who already understand these areas may want to skip to the next chapter, where I discuss more sophisticated principles of trading. (But if you do skip, you may lose out on some critical bit of information that you somehow never acquired before!)

Common Stock

Common stock is ownership. It is ownership in a corporation. It can be sold, transferred, and given away. And it may exist without direct managerial involvement on the owner's part.

To see how such ownership works, imagine that your cousin Dino has an idea for a great new business. He's going to open a service station. To be different, he plans to offer service—as well as gas. He has only one problem—money. It takes lots of money to make money in service stations. Cousin Dino needs $10,000 to get things going. He can invest $2000 personally. That means Dino must raise $8000 somewhere else. You are part of the "somewhere else." You are seriously considering buying $1000 of common stock in Dino's service station. When you do, you'll be a part owner in the business.

Here's what you'll get for your $1000.

OWNERSHIP

You will own 10 percent of the business. Dino will own 20 percent. Other stockholders will own the rest.

VOTING RIGHTS

You will get the right to vote on the board of directors, the by-laws, the auditors, and so on. You will not get the right to hire the company managers. The board will hire the managers, who in turn will actually run the company. The managers may be stockholders, they may even be board members, but they need not be. The board doesn't have to hire you, for example. In this case, the board will probably hire Dino to be the president of the corporation. Dino will also probably pump most of the gas. Being president of a corporation isn't always glamorous.

LIMITED LIABILITY

You are usually liable (responsible) for the things you own. That is, if an innocent person is hurt by your property you must pay. The same thing is true for companies. If you are the sole proprietor of a service station, and your part-time helper accidentally fills a Jaguar's gas tank with water and the radiator with gas, guess who's liable? You are. The Jaguar's owner can sue you personally for the loss.

Personal liability is also an issue with most partnerships. In fact, in a partnership you may even become liable for the nonbusiness debts of your partners. It's a good idea to keep close tabs on your partners. As a stockholder of a corporation, you are not liable for the debts of other stockholders. You are not even liable for the wrongful acts of the company or its employees. The Jaguar's owner could sue the corporation for damage to her car, but she could not sue you personally as a shareholder. That's a relief for people who own stock in big corporations such as GM. Some companies are always being sued.

LIQUIDATION RIGHTS

If the board ever decides to close the station down and sell everything, you are entitled to 10 percent of what's left—that is, what's left after all the creditors are paid off. Practically speaking, boards rarely liquidate companies unless the company is going bankrupt. And if the company is going bankrupt, there probably won't be anything left for stockholders after all the creditors are paid off.

DIVIDENDS

If the company prospers and earns a profit, the board may pay dividends. Dividends are one way to make money on your investment. The dividends average 2 to 8 percent of market value for well-established ("blue chip") companies.

TRANSFERABILITY

Ownership in a company is ownership of property. You have a legal right to sell your property. Not only can you sell, but you can give your ownership away, and you can pledge it against a loan. In fact, the ability to transfer ownership may be the most important feature of all. Most stockholders don't think much about voting, liquidating, or even liability. Most stockholders are only interested in making money. Part of that money comes from dividends. But usually the most money is made (or lost) when the stock is sold. If all goes well, the stockholders can sell their ownership interest for more than they paid for it. This makes transferability the most important ownership right of all.

Common stock is particularly well suited to transfer of ownership. The stockholder's ownership is represented by a piece of paper. The paper is a certificate showing how many shares are owned. If you want to sell your ownership, just sell the certificate.

Selling your ownership in a sole proprietorship or a partnership is far more involved than simply selling the certificate. You may have to inventory everything and divide up the typewriters, paper clips, and old tires. You may have to draft reams of legal documents before you can sell out. Clearly, selling a stock certificate is much easier.

None of your rights as a shareholder guarantee you'll make money. In fact, many people are not sure how owners make money in stocks, anyway. As already indicated, there are two ways of making money: (1) dividends and (2) price appreciation. Dividends are the easiest to understand. Let's go back to Dino's service station. If it is well run, and if gas and oil are sold for more than their cost, the station should make a profit. Some of the profit may be retained in the business; such profits are called *retained earnings*. Retained earnings are reinvested back in the company to help it grow. For example, the retained earnings may be used to install a car wash. Hopefully the car wash will attract more customers and result in more profits.

Those earnings not retained in the business are paid to the owners. Most service station owners depend for their livelihoods on the stations' earnings. For stockholders, the earnings paid out are called dividends. Whether the dividends represent a stockholder's livelihood or not depends on the stockholder. Usually they don't, but dividends do represent real, green, spendable dollars, and stockholders love them.

PRICE APPRECIATION

The second way to make money in a common stock is *price appreciation*. The price appreciates because the value of ownership increases as the company grows. For example, General Motors was once a small company. Perhaps it wasn't much bigger than Dino's service station. Can you imagine buying 10 percent of GM for $1000 when it was a tiny company? Today 10 percent of GM is worth billions.

GM has grown to its present gigantic size by reinvesting in the business. The earnings kept increasing, which allowed the company to pay bigger dividends and to retain more. As GM retained earnings, it built more plants, which meant greater earnings, bigger dividends, and even more retained earnings. So ownership in the company became increasingly valuable. Soon, investors who were not current owners wanted to get in on the action. They saw all the increases and wanted to become shareholders.

Generally, the only way to become a shareholder of GM, or of Dino's service station, is to buy shares from someone who is already a shareholder. If more investors want to buy than want to sell, the value of the shares will increase. If the reverse occurs, the value will decline. This means the value of the shares may change much more often than the book value of the company changes. What counts most is not the assets, or the earnings, but what everyone thinks the company is worth.

To see how this works, think of Dino's service station. Imagine that things have gone well, and $5000 has been reinvested in the business. So the total investment has risen from $10,000 to $15,000. You still own 10 percent. On paper, your investment has risen in value from $1000 to $1500. Then some good news arrives—a new roller derby rink is going to be built farther down the road. A new rink means more traffic, more cars, and more sales. None of this has actually occurred, but the perceived value of ownership goes up.

Your sister-in-law is one person who thinks the value of ownership has gone up. She wants to buy your shares. She is willing to pay not $1500, but $3000. You say you'll think about it. While you are thinking about it, American Motors announces experimental work on a car that runs on air pollution. The implications are obvious: There's enough air pollution to run cars for years. No one will need gas from Dino's station. Frantically you call your sister-in-law to accept her offer of $3000. But your sister-in-law is no longer interested at $3000. Now her offer is $750—one-half of the book value. The market value of Dino's station first rose (+300 percent) and then dropped (−75 percent), but nothing has actually happened to Dino's business. The same customers are stopping today as were stopping yesterday.

The point is clear—two values are attached to ownership. The first is the market value. The market value changes with the demand for ownership. The demand may be influenced by changes in fundamentals. Or it may be influenced by changes in emotion. But regardless of what it is influenced by, it does change.

The second value is related to asset value, or book value, or real worth of the corporation. It is related to machines, inventory, and customer goodwill. It is related to what everything could be sold for. Over time, the market value of the stock will tend to move toward this real or intrinsic value.

These values are worth thinking about. If you plan to be an owner for a long time, the real value of the company is your most important concern. But if you plan to sell your ownership sometime, market value becomes important. In fact, when the time arrives that you absolutely must sell your stock, the only price that will matter will be the prevailing market price.

Common stock is ownership. Owners take risk. They are not guaranteed a profit. Owners are not even guaranteed they'll get their money back. But they *do* get an opportunity. Ownership of common stock is an opportunity.

How the Stock Market Works

To understand the stock market, you need to realize there are always at least four different movements at work:

◇ *Trading fluctuations.* No one makes money on these except employees of the New York Stock Exchange (maybe).
◇ *Technical moves.* These are the feeding ground for greedy speculators, most of whom will lose their shirts in the end.
◇ *Market cycles.* This is the favorite arena for the professional investor and top-flight amateur investor.
◇ *Long-term market trends.* There is hope! The lay investor can do well here.

The following deeper look at these movements may be valuable.

TRADING FLUCTUATIONS

Some time, wander down to a local brokerage house and watch the "tape" for a while. The "ticker tape" reports trades, as they are made, on various stock exchanges. At first you won't be able to read the tape. Don't worry; you can lead a very rewarding life even if you never learn to read the tape. Each trade starts with the ticker tape symbol of the stock, such as IBM (for International Business Machines) or GM (for General Motors), or X (for U.S. Steel). Many ticker symbols don't make any more sense than X for U.S. Steel. If you want to become a serious tape watcher, you'll need a list of symbols to help you translate for a while.

The rest of the trade notation carries information about which stock exchange the transaction took place on, the number of shares in that trade, and the price. For example,

PRD   M   20   23^3

This is Polaroid, the camera company. The trade was on the Midwest Stock Exchange. The trade was for 2000 shares (multiply whatever amount shows by 100 to determine the actual amount). The price was 23^3 per share. The small, raised "3" is "⅜." Stocks trade in eighths, for some reason. So the total cost of this trade was $23.375 × 2000 = $46,750, plus commission, which isn't reported. Another example is

MCD   52^7

This is McDonald's Corporation, lovingly referred to as "Hamburger." The trade was on the New York Stock Exchange. You know that because there is no exchange designated. Trades are always on the New York if not designated. There were 100 shares traded. Again, you know this because nothing else is designated. It is always 100 shares if nothing is designated. Finally, the price was 52⁷, or 52⅞, or $52.875 per share.

Now that you know how to read the tape, pick out any stock that's trading actively. You'll notice that it changes price more often than your son changes his mind about what he's going to do when he grows up. These frequent changes are the result of a stream of buy and sell orders arriving on the floor of the stock exchanges from all over the world. If buys come in faster than sells, the price goes up. If sells come in faster than buys, the price goes down. If you are like most people, in a few hours you will get a "feel" for the stock you're watching. You will feel you can predict with pretty fair accuracy whether the next trade will be up or down. Your first impulse will be great excitement. You'll think of Las Vegas, where you could get rich predicting numbers. Forget it. You'll never make any money in the stock market doing this. In fact, you'll probably lose your job if you sit there too long.

TECHNICAL MOVES

"Short run" is a very imprecise term. The short run may be a few days or several months. These short-run moves are frequently "technical" in nature. Stocks build up pressure for what is called a "break-out," the way a volcano builds up pressure for an eruption. A handful of investors begin accumulating the stock. Then something, such as a bit of news that might normally be considered insignificant, sets the stock off. The investors who are accumulating accelerate their purchasing. Others are attracted to the move itself, and suddenly the stock is erupting. It may move 10, 20, or even 30 percent in a few days. Similar and sharper movements occur on the down side. These moves are more a result of several investors getting the same idea at the same time than of any fundamental change at the company. For this reason, the move is called a "technical move." Investors who catch these technical moves can make a great deal of fast money.

Everyone dreams of "getting rich quick" by catching these technical moves. Investors imagine themselves buying stocks just before they break out, riding them up 30 percent, then switching to another stock just before it breaks out, and so on. In theory, it is possible. However, instead of getting rich, most people trying to play the switching game go broke. They go broke because the moves occur at random without warning, and they move rapidly. Few people can spot a move in an individual stock quickly enough to do anything about it. Almost no one ever moves from stock to stock and is consistently right. The movement itself attracts the attention of most investors. Initially they react with skepticism. Soon, however, all the "Waffling Wandas" say to themselves, "There really must be something happening," and on they climb—right near the top of the move. Short-run technical movements are veiled with the allure of instant wealth. But the painful reality for most investors is persistent disappointment.

MARKET CYCLES

As a general rule, all stocks tend to go "up" or "down" with the overall stock market. In fact, individual stocks are so influenced by the general market that even investments in poor companies usually make money when the whole market is going up. Likewise, even good stocks tend to lose money when the whole market is going down. The broad stock market, like individual stocks, experiences "trading fluctuations" and "short-run technical moves," but real market cycles go for many months, maybe years. Because market cycles are broad and continue for a long time, top-notch investors feel they can take advantage of them. Market cycles can be more certain than "technical" moves. Stocks can be bought and held while the cycle is going up, and sold when the cycle is going down.

During market cycles, nearly all stocks are carried along, but the expert investor knows certain stocks will become "fashionable" and will emerge as leaders that outperform the rest. The expert tries to maximize his or her performance by identifying these leaders. Leaders are usually stocks that a broad group of investors believe have unusually good fundamentals. The fashionable stocks are not always fundamentally the best stocks. Frequently some of the best stocks are overlooked. So it isn't easy to identify which ones will be the leaders. But in a broad up cycle nearly all stocks will do well. Investing with the market cycle can help overcome some mediocre decisions about which will be the most fashionable stocks.

Investing with the market cycles is not as glamorous as short-term trading. With short-term trading, you can jump in and out of stocks each week, which will give you plenty of stories to swap. But investing with the cycles can pay off handsomely through consistency. Notice, however, that the term *expert* investor is used in discussing market cycle investing. Stock "fashions" really are not easy to spot. And the market cycles themselves, although long-lived, change so subtly that a "rookie" can fail to realize they have turned downward. If you can afford to spend lots of time reading about investments, and if you have a fairly good understanding about how other people think, then market-cycle investing might be a good arena for you. If not, read on.

LONG-TERM MARKET TRENDS

The long term means years, probably ten years or more. Several market cycles with different stock leadership may come and go. In this time frame, most stocks will perform in line with their fundamentals. If a company is well run, growing, and in a profitable business, you can be almost sure of making money. The difference between long run and market cycle investing is timing. In the long run, investors are willing to accept some lengthy periods when their stock will be out of fashion and go nowhere. They are willing to wait because they know a good stock will attract enough investors to do well in the long run. Of course, investors can potentially make more money investing in market cycles. If successful, investors will never experience lengthy pauses when no one cares about their stock. But market cycle investing requires plenty of effort. Many investors actually do just as well—and sleep much better—when investing for the long term.

Sleeping well and investing for the long term are worthwhile goals—and this book can help. After all, with all the movements in the stock market you want to be sure that when you move, you move in the right direction.

◇ 43 ◇
A System for
Beating the Stock Market?

There is no simple system for beating the stock market. Furthermore, you should beware of sure-fire schemes promising that you can.

There are thousands of formulas, systems, and schemes that are supposed to beat the market. They proliferate because everyone is anxious to find a simple way of getting rich, just as Ponce de Leon was anxious to find a simple way of staying young. His exploring was made possible by discovery of the "New World," a vast expanse of uncharted land where the "Fountain of Youth" just might be found. Today's stock market exploration is made possible by invention of the computer. This remarkable machine can analyze tremendous amounts of previously uncharted data wherein the secret to riches just might be found. Some systems for "beating the market" look very sophisticated. Some systems aren't worth anything. Some can help you pick the right time to buy a stock that looks attractive fundamentally. But no system yet has been discovered that is consistent enough to bet your money on blindly. Here's why.

First, the stock market is constantly changing its mind about what it's worrying about. Modern market explorers are looking for a set of measurable conditions that always precede a move in the market. With the aid of a computer, they can explore correlations between the stock market and such conditions as interest rates, corporate profits, and trading volume. The permutations and combinations of possible correlations are staggering. The designer keeps adding conditions and running correlations until the formula shows that every time certain conditions existed *in the past,* the stock market made a move. The assumption is that when the same conditions exist in the future the market will make the same move. Unfortunately, the assumption is wrong. The market is always changing its mind about what it's worrying about.

To illustrate this changeability, suppose the computer has made the unique discovery that the market has always gone up in relationship to the length of Russian squirrel fur and the number of sunspots during the summer season. (Unfortunately, this isn't as facetious as it sounds.) Armed with this knowledge, the designer sallies forth to convince all his or her friends to invest, too. Into the computer go all the data on squirrel fur and sunspots. Out comes the prediction—the market is going up! Everyone rushes to buy. Then thud!—the market drops into the basement. Today the market is worried about live births of Australian yaks, not squirrel fur, and the computer wasn't programmed for yaks. Such fickle-mindedness makes computer predicting a hazardous business.

Even if someone does find a magic formula, it will only work as long as no one else knows anything about it. Common sense tells you that if Ponce had found the Fountain of Youth there wouldn't be enough for everyone in the world to have a drink. Common sense also tells you that if everyone tries to buy or sell on the same computer signal the job just isn't going to get done. After all, the stock market only works if there are approximately equal numbers of buyers and sellers. So even if a perfect system could be devised, as its popularity and fame spread its workability would decline.

Yes, if only *you* have been told about this spectacular system, you could make some money. But why would *you* be told, and no one else, especially when there are some huge financial institutions capable of paying millions for such a wonderful system? Anyone smart enough to invent such a terrific system is also smart enough to know where he or she can get the most money for it. And, with all due respect, that is probably not from you.

Even though there is no simple magic system, there are legitimate timing services available. People who work with and develop these formulas are called "technicians." When the formulas are properly interpreted, they can be helpful in deciding whether the market or an individual stock is in a position to make a move. Assuming that the interpretation is favorable and assuming that you like the fundamentals—the economy improving, for example—then you are well advised to buy. However, reputable technicians freely admit they are often wrong in their interpretations and that buy and sell decisions should not be made based on formulas alone.

Here are some skeptical questions to ask yourself if you are approached about investing on the basis of a system or formula.

1. *How does it work?* A reputable system can be explained and will make sense.

2. *How long has the system been working in actual practice ("real time," as it is called)?* A newly invented system is unproven and can't be trusted even if there are data showing that it would have worked in the past.

3. *Who else uses this system?* Are they sophisticated investors?

4. *Why is the system being offered to you?* Be particularly careful if your contact is a stranger to you.

5. *Has a book been written about it?* A cynic would probably say that many authors make their first million dollars hitting it lucky in the market and their second, third, and fourth millions selling their books.

6. *Are you receiving information on the system first hand?* Be careful if your information is coming by way of your cousin from his roommate, who got it from an old girlfriend's husband.

7. *Are you being asked to invest blindly?* Don't invest with only the formula's signals to go on and no fundamental examination of the investment itself.

Ponce de Leon wandered in vain through the jungles, looking for a fabulous fountain to make himself young. Many investors grow poor wandering through data looking for a fabulous system to make themselves rich.

How Can You Know Whether the Stock Market Is Going Up or Down?

You can't know whether the market is going up or down. But you *can* develop a point of view and learn to be right more often than wrong.

The best way to make money in the stock market is to buy stock in good, strong companies and to hold the stock for the long term. However, during short periods, such as six months or a year, individual stocks are heavily influenced by the general trend of the market. Obviously, if you consistently buy when the market is down and ready to go up, you can give yourself a running start.

Many people would like to get their running starts by listening to someone else's point of view on the market. This grows out of the popular delusion that hidden somewhere in a palatial office, deep within the canyons of Wall Street, is a gnome who knows every move the stock market will make. And all an investor need do to get rich is speak to a market "expert" who is in touch with the gnome and thus find out "what the market is going to do."

The awful truth is that no one knows for sure what the market is going to do, because there are no gnomes. There aren't any in Wall Street, none in Zurich, not even in Olathe, Kansas. Some investors' faith in the whole capitalist system may be shattered to learn this truth. But most people handle the blow about as well as they handled the news about Santa Claus and the Easter Bunny.

Because there are no gnomes, and because the "experts" are just people who work hard developing a viewpoint, you should learn how to do the same for yourself. After all, it *is* your money, and *you* are as smart as the next person—once you understand a few basic concepts, such as

1. The crowd is always wrong.

2. No market trend ever lasts forever.

3. The market is always early.

4. The mood of the nation drives the market.

5. The odds make the difference.

THE CROWD IS ALWAYS WRONG

Logic tells you the market is at its peak when most investors are bullish, or optimistic. Likewise, it's on the bottom when most investors are bearish, or pessimistic. When nearly everyone is buying and no one is selling, the demand for stocks will exceed the supply and stock prices will be up. As investors change their opinion and become sellers, the market will begin to roll over and go down. Eventually, when nearly everyone agrees the outlook is terrible and everyone is selling, prices will be way down.

There is no way to know for sure how each of the millions of people who are interested in the market individually feels, but by reading and listening you can develop a viewpoint about how unanimous the general bullish or bearish thinking is. Remember to be far less persuaded by what you are hearing than by the number of people you are hearing it from. When everyone else seems to agree, you go and do something different—the odds will be in your favor.

NO MARKET TREND LASTS FOREVER

In the stock market, what goes up must come down, and then back up, and then back down, and so on. When you see how it has gone up and down in the past, you'll realize how advantageous it is to buy when the market is down. Forget about buying right on the bottom—that almost never happens. But you can develop a viewpoint and improve your odds of buying when the market is low by asking such questions as "Which way has the market been going within the past six months? In the past year? How fast is it moving? Is the market up or down? Is its trend accelerating or dissipating?" Remember, no matter where it is now, it is absolutely certain that it won't stay there forever.

THE MARKET IS ALWAYS EARLY

There is no doubt that stock prices are influenced by the economy. But if you wait to see the economy turn bad before selling, you will be late; your stocks will already be down. The market generally begins major moves, either up or down, six to nine months before a change in the economy is apparent. In fact, the market leads the economy so consistently the government uses it as a leading indicator of business activity. Hence, when things appear bleakest and before anyone will talk about recovery, your viewpoint should be shifting to the buy side.

THE NATIONAL MOOD DRIVES THE MARKET

The most important influence of all on the stock market is the general optimism or pessimism of the country. Not necessarily just about the market or the economy, but about conditions in general: politics, weather, even family conditions. When people are happy, they are willing to spend their money; when they are depressed, they hold back. Eventually, all this shows up in stock prices.

Make a mood chart. Ask yourself, "How do my neighbors feel?" (Don't analyze yourself—you're too smart to be representative.) Pay more attention to what your neighbors are *doing* than to what they are *saying*. Are they spending money, buying cars, planning vacations, recarpeting the living room? Their actions give clues to their feelings about job security, future income, even the state of world politics. Rate their mood from +10 to −10. Ask, "How did they feel six months ago? A year ago?" Next ask the toughie, "How do I think my neighbors will feel six months and a year from today?" Remember, the market is always ahead of the economy. So when your estimated ratings six and twelve months from now start showing 8's, 9's, and 10's, either positive or negative, it is time for you to shift your viewpoint. Resist the temptation to wait until complete euphoria or depression have swept over the country and +10 or −10 shows up on your current rating. By that time, the market will already be started going the other way.

THE ODDS MAKE THE DIFFERENCE

Because there is no secret formula for knowing "what the market is going to do," successful investors play the odds. In the Las Vegas game of Twenty-One, players try to get cards totaling as close to 21 as possible without going over. If their total is closer to 21 than the dealer's, they win. The rules dictate that the dealer must draw when his or her total is less than 16 and must stay at 16 or more. A skillful player watches the game proceed. If the low cards play early, for example, and the odds shift to the player's favor, he or she bets heavily. When the odds shift in favor of the dealer, the player makes a minimum bet. The player may lose any single hand, even when the odds are in his or her favor. But by consistently betting heavily when the odds are favorable, he or she will win.

Only on rare occasions will all these indications give clear signals at the same time. The reason to force yourself to examine these factors carefully is to help you develop a viewpoint. A viewpoint is nothing more than an opinion regarding the odds existing in the market at any time. You will find that your viewpoint is generally contrary to conventional wisdom. Your friends will snicker, your children will cry, your dog will growl at you. And to make matters worse, just as in Twenty-One, you will lose a few hands even when the odds are in your favor. Those losses may cause you to distrust yourself. But if you consistently bet heavily when the odds are in your favor, you will get the running head start you want and eventually wind up a big winner.

◇ 44 ◇
How to Avoid
Paying Too Much
for Stocks

Buy stocks on sale—if you can.

Whenever an investor buys a stock, then watches it go down, he (or she) figures he's paid "too much." And his "figuring" would be right if he had known in advance the stock was going down. Unfortunately, without a crystal ball he couldn't know. So the real question is "Did he pay a fair price at the time he bought the stock?"

Sometimes things *do* go down in price after we buy them. For example, when was the last time you stopped by your corner grocery store and bought a case of pickled grasshoppers to munch on while watching the wrestling matches? Then, only two days later, you found the store running a big sale on pickled grasshoppers. Sure, it's too bad you missed the sale, but the grasshoppers were still worth the price you paid for them. You wouldn't have been unhappy about the price you paid if you hadn't seen the sale price.

Stocks go on sale, too. Frequently they go on sale without warning. Sometimes they go on sale right after you've made a big purchase. With a little work, you can improve your chances of paying a fair price for your stocks, and with a little luck you may even get a few of the sales.

Price, obviously, is the key to a good buy. But the quoted price of a stock doesn't mean much by itself. What you really want to know is how many dollars of earnings you are buying for the price. A price of $3.95 for pickled grasshoppers doesn't tell you much. You need to know how many pounds of grasshoppers you are getting for the price. Because pounds per dollar is what grasshopper freaks look for, it stands to reason that earnings per dollar is what stock market freaks focus on. The correct terminology in the case of stock is "price-earnings ratio" (P/E ratio).

The price-earnings ratio is calculated by dividing the current quoted price of the stock by the earnings per share. If you don't trust yourself to make the calculation, you can read it right out of the paper for stocks traded on major exchanges. The stock quotation section of widely circulated financial papers like *The Wall Street Journal* and *Barron's* have a column for the P/E ratio.

Naturally, you want to pay the lowest price-earnings ratio possible. If all stocks were equal, you could glance down the column, pick out the stock with the lowest P/E ratio and buy it. Unfortunately, all stocks are not equal. Just as a pound of pickled grasshoppers may be worth more than a pound of candied ants, the earnings of some companies are considered more valuable by the market than the earnings of others. Generally the reason for the difference is the different outlook for future earnings.

It is often difficult to compare earnings outlooks among companies; consequently, it is difficult to compare their P/E ratios. An easier approach is to compare the stock's price-earnings ratio today with its price-earnings ratio in the past. Stock prices change daily. Therefore the stock's P/E ratio can vary considerably. But over time, the price-earnings ratios of most stocks do establish a range. To get a good feel for that range, you need at least ten years of P/E ratio history for the stock. This information is readily available from many sources. Two easy ways to get information are to call a stockbroker, or to consult Standard & Poor's or Moody's stock services at your local library. Once you have ten years of high, low, and average data on the stock, ask yourself where today's price-earnings ratio stands. Does the stock seem to be selling high or low? Has the long-term P/E ratio been trending up and down or sideways? If the long-term trend continues, where will today's P/E ratio fit? Is the stock expensive, or does it appear to be on sale relative to its own history?

Stocks also develop a normal relationship relative to the general stock market. To get a feel for this relationship, compare the historical P/E ratio range of the stock you're considering with the market itself. Here is a history of price-earnings ratios for the Dow Jones Industrial Averages:

Decade	Extreme high	Average	Extreme low
1950s	20.9×	13.7×	6.4×
1960s	23.0×	18.0×	12.0×
1970s	17.3×	11.6×	5.8×
1980s*	8.6×	7.4×	6.2×

*1980, 1981, 1982.

Ask yourself if your stock usually sold higher or lower than these figures. Where does the stock stand today? This comparison will give you an indication of how the stock is selling today.

As you can see, if the stock is selling at a low price-earnings ratio compared to its own history and compared to its normal relationship with the market, you should be very interested. If the stock looks expensive, you may want to delay purchase until it goes on sale.

A cheap price alone is not sufficient reason to buy a stock, any more than a cheap price is a reason to buy pickled grasshoppers. You may not like pickled grasshoppers. Throughout this chapter, we have assumed that you really like the stock you are considering. Liking the stock in the long run is important. Remember—stocks only go on sale when most people *don't* like them. If you don't have a long-run outlook, you could be swayed by the crowd and miss the sale. Your corner grocer only runs inventory reduction sales when very few customers are coming in and he or she is awash with pickled grasshoppers. If you really like grasshoppers, you should buy cases of them when no one else wants them and they are on sale. Then, when the great grasshopper famine strikes and everyone wants grasshoppers, and the grocer's shelves are bare, you'll be curled up in front of your television set with a mouthful of the tasty morsels. You might even consent to sell your good friends some of your grasshoppers—at a tidy profit, of course.

What Are the Best Stocks to Buy?

The best stocks to buy are the stocks that will make money for you over the years!

There are thousands of stocks. Sorting through them all to find the best stock is like driving every car in Chicago to find the best car. Simply wanting a stock that will go "up" is like wanting a car that will "run." Thought must be given to such things as cost, maintenance, and comfort.

There are two steps in buying a car or a stock—becoming aware of what's for sale, and making a final selection among thousands of possibilities. In theory, all this could be done on a gigantic computer. But in actual practice, very few "cream puffs" or "stock steals" are discovered by using computers.

Most investors become aware of stock ideas through friends, brokers, or personal familiarity with the company. This type of stock awareness may not sound very sophisticated, and it isn't. But as a practical matter, for most investors it's not all that bad. However, after the investor becomes aware of a stock he (or she) needs to investigate it to be sure it fits his personal criteria. If not, he should keep looking. After all, who wants to get stuck with a compact car when you've got four kids and a St. Bernard to haul around.

If you are an average investor, you probably do not want to spend every waking minute thinking about stocks and every sleeping minute worrying about them. If you are an average investor, your major reason for buying stock is probably (or at least should be) to build value for the long term. If you are an average investor, your Number One criterion should be to find stocks you can buy and hold. You want stock that will increase in value over the years. This type of stock can be called "buy and hold" stock.

"Buy and hold" stocks have a big advantage over "buy and sell" stocks—stocks that are purchased for a quick rise and then sold. The advantage is time. Time is on your side in "buy and hold" stocks. For example, if things go bad right after you buy the stock, time may run out on the reason for the quick move in your "buy and sell" stock. But you can nearly always count on coming out ahead in the long run if you own a good "buy and hold" stock. Time allows the company to grow and strengthen. Time is on your side. In the long run, time can help neutralize many short-run mistakes.

Two classes of stocks best fit the "buy and hold" criteria. They are growth stocks and high-yield stocks. Before considering the special characteristics of growth or yield stocks, apply these preliminary tests to any stock you become aware of:

⋄ Sales should exceed $100 million. This might sound big, but hundreds and hundreds of companies are bigger.

⋄ The stock should be listed on the New York or American Stock Exchanges. Most truly great companies are listed.

⋄ The company should have been in business ten years or more. A business history less than ten years is not sufficient to prove the company can survive in a world of intense competition.

Assuming the stock meets these preliminary tests, then examine it in greater detail to see if it is a true "buy and hold" stock.

GROWTH COMPANIES

The key question is "Can the company grow rapidly?" It should be able to double sales and earnings over the next five years. This is a

15 percent growth rate, and hundreds of companies will achieve it. With a little effort on your part, you can answer this key question yourself. To get at the answer, ask the following specific questions. (You can obtain the information you need directly from the company by writing for an annual report, or from your stockbroker, or from either the Standard & Poor's or Moody's stock services, which are found in many large public libraries.)

⋄ Does the company have the opportunity for growth? Look at the product or service it offers. Is it a new and rapidly growing market, or is it mature? Is it virtually alone in the market, or does it have tough competition? Is it an industry leader, or is it a minor factor? Is it protected from competition by patents, proprietary technology, unique marketing, or control over vital resources? Ask yourself if your neighbors or the company you work for would purchase from this firm. You should be able to gain enough understanding of what the company does to answer these questions yourself. If not, don't buy the stock.

⋄ Has the company at least doubled its sales and earnings in the past five years? If it hasn't done so in the past, you must question whether it can do so in the future.

⋄ Has the growth been consistent? Sales should have increased every year for ten years. Earnings should not have declined in more than two of the ten years, and never declined more than 25 percent.

⋄ Can the company finance its future growth? The company's retained earnings should be at least 15 percent of shareholder's equity. Calculate this by subtracting dividends paid from net income. This figure represents earnings retained in the company for growth and expansion. Divide the retained earnings by the shareholder's equity or the book value of the company. The resulting figure should be at least equal to your expected growth for the company—a minimum of 15 percent. Do this calculation for the past three years to determine the trend.

YIELD STOCKS

There are two key questions here: Does the company pay a dividend equal to an 8 percent yield or more? And can it keep up the pace? (Yield is calculated by dividing the yearly dividend by the current stock price.) Answer the following specific questions:

◇ Is the company in a large, well-established industry? If the industry is mature, its growth is expected to be slow. (This is all right.)

◇ Is the company an important factor in its industry? Generally speaking, it is best if the company is one of the two largest companies in the industry.

◇ Has the company paid out at least 50 percent of its net earnings in dividends in each of the past five years?

◇ Has the company cut its regular dividend in the past ten years? It should have maintained or steadily increased its dividend over the years. Occasionally bonus or special dividends are paid. These should be ignored unless the company pays the bonus dividends nearly every year.

◇ Have sales and earnings tended to increase? Sales decreases should not have exceeded 20 percent in any year during the past ten years. Earnings should not have declined more than 50 percent during the same period. Sales and earnings should have shown a tendency to grow during the last five or ten years.

Often the price of a yield stock tends to remain fairly stable for long periods of time. However, because an 8 percent yield is substantially higher than the yield on most stocks, you can count on the market eventually discovering it, just as you can count on a teenage boy eventually discovering girls. In the meantime, while you are waiting for the discovery to take place, you collect a good cash dividend (on the stock, not the teenager).

Growth and yield stocks are not the only possibilities for making money in the stock market. However, potential investors, like potential car buyers, do need systematic approaches with predetermined criteria to select from the thousands of possibilities and to live with this selection. In my opinion, buying and holding growth or yield stocks will give the average investor many carefree miles and a good resale value at the end.

◇ 45 ◇
What Is
Preferred Stock?

Preferred stock is so named because it has a preferred position of security over common stock. Preferred stockholders stand ahead of common stockholders in several key areas:

◇ Preferred stock has a stated, fixed dividend. The corporation gives firm assurances the dividend will be paid. Holders of common stock receive no such assurances.

◇ Preferred stockholders receive all their dividends before common stockholders receive any.

◇ Preferred stockholders are paid off before common stockholders if the company is sold or liquidated.

However, in some very key areas preferred stockholders are not in a preferred position:

◇ Preferred stockholders usually do not have the right to vote for members of the company's board of directors. Nor do they vote on other corporate matters.

◇ Preferred stock usually does not share in the increase in wealth of the corporation.

◇ Preferred stock has a preferred position when it comes to security, but it does not have a preferred position when it comes to ownership, and that is important.

Preferred stockholders have one additional preferred position, a position provided by federal tax law. The first $25,000 of dividend income received from preferred stock is tax free. But it is tax free only if the stockholder happens to be a corporation. Individuals don't get this advantage, for some reason. So if you are an individual, not a corporation, this favorable tax treatment may not mean much to you.

The fact that you can't get in on the tax-free dividends doesn't exactly mean you shouldn't be interested in preferred stocks. They still offer features that are attractive to many individual investors. They generally offer high yield, a predictable dividend, and greater price stability than common stock. Many investors prefer these features to ownership features. For such investors preferred stock is preferable.

◇ 46 ◇
All About Mutual Funds

A mutual fund is a common pool of money. Many people who don't know each other put their hard-earned money into a common pool. Then somebody else decides what to do with their money. All this is for the common good of the people. Sounds like communism, doesn't it? But it's not communism—it's capitalism. In fact, mutual funds probably have made capitalism possible for more people than any other financial concept.

The concept is this: A fund is organized. The fund is a legal corporation. This corporation, however, doesn't make, sell, or provide anything. Usually the corporation doesn't even have any paid employees. All it has is assets. The assets come from the people who buy shares in the corporation.

Of course, a corporation with just assets and no one to run it isn't much good. So the shareholders of the corporation contract with a professional money manager to invest the assets. Usually the professional money manager does not become an employee. In fact, usually the professional money manager is a whole company, not a single person. It is important to know that legally the money management firm is an entirely separate corporation from the fund corporation. The only legal relationship between the two is through a management contract. The contract can be canceled by either corporation any time they want.

Hopefully neither party will want to cancel. Hopefully the professional manager will invest the assets in such a way that the shareholders will make a nice return on their investments. Returns on investments are the key to capitalism and to mutual funds. In fact, the reason investors put their money in a mutual fund is because they believe they can make a higher return in the mutual fund than by investing themselves. And, generally speaking, they can. Here's why:

◇ *Affordable investment.* Buying stocks and bonds directly can require a lot of capital. Typical round lots of stock (100 shares) may cost $5000. A round lot of bonds may cost $10,000. The majority of Americans can't afford such investments. By contrast, an initial investment in a typical mutual fund may be $500, and subsequent purchases can be for almost any amount. These lower dollar amounts make investing affordable for many Americans.

◇ *Diversification.* Diversification is a good investment principle. Without diversification, investment risks are high. A well-diversified portfolio of stocks should have thirty stocks or more. At $5000 per round lot, that could cost $150,000. Diversification is more affordable through a mutual fund. Every share in the fund already represents ownership in a fully diversified portfolio.

◇ *Professional Investment Management.* Hiring a professional money manager is prohibitively expensive for most individuals. Minimum fees at typical investment counseling firms are $1000 per year or more. But by pooling assets with other investors, you can come up with millions of dollars. That is enough to hire a top-notch money manager without costing any single investor very much.

◇ *Constant attention.* Part of the service the shareholders receive is constant attention. Someone is paying attention to the fund all the time. Prices are checked, trading decisions are made on a timely basis, dividends are received, coupons are clipped, corporate reports are read, proxies are voted, and on, and on. Some individual investors don't attend to these matters on a timely basis, which isn't good.

◇ *Bookkeeping.* Many individual investors have terrible financial records. The money manager will keep track of all the buys and sells, total holdings, costs, and taxes. Near tax time each year, all fund shareholders get statements showing the tax consequences of their investments.

These mutual fund aspects are of tremendous advantage to the vast majority of Americans—Americans who want to be capitalists but really can't afford to be capitalists directly. By pooling their resources with other small and medium-sized investors, they can (and have) become some of the most powerful investors in the world. It's not communism. It's investing for one's own future, and that's capitalism.

Open- and Closed-End Mutual Funds

In an "open-end" fund, investors buy and sell shares directly with the fund, not with other shareholders. There is no limit on the total number of shares the fund can have outstanding. In a "closed-end" fund, investors buy and sell shares with other shareholders, not with the fund. There is a limited number of shares the fund can have outstanding.

To the investor, the biggest difference between open and closed-end funds is the way the price of the investor's shares is determined. In an open fund, the price of the shares equals the market value of all the assets divided by all the shares outstanding. A $100 million fund with 10 million shares outstanding has a price of $10 per share. And $10 is also the net asset value per share. The value of the shares varies directly with the value of the assets in the fund. The price is unaffected by new buyers or sellers of the fund. New buyers or sellers mean more or less assets and more or less shares. It does not affect the price of the shares.

In a closed fund, the price of the shares depends on the number of buyers and sellers for the shares, not on the value of the assets. It is possible to have a situation where $100 million with 10 million shares outstanding has a share price of not $10, but $12, or $8, or some other price. The share price may differ from the net asset value because of investors' hopes or fears. Their hopes or fears cause them to be buyers or sellers. If there are more buyers than sellers, the price goes up. If more sellers than buyers, the price goes down. And possibly none of this movement reflects actual changes in the net asset value of the fund.

Naturally, the shareholder is interested in the price of the shares. So he or she should be interested to know that closed-end funds tend to be more volatile (changeable) in price than open-end funds. Some investors may not like volatility. They should avoid "closed" funds. Some investors may want to take advantage of anticipated changes. They can possibly profit by buying closed funds. Which fund is most suitable for you depends on you, your objectives, and your investing skill.

The following comparison gives more information on the differences and similarities of open and closed funds.

	Open End	*Closed End*
Pricing	Net assets divided by total number of shares outstanding	Free market action; demand to buy or sell shares
Market for shares	Directly from the fund through a securities broker, or mutual fund selling organization	From other shareholders through securities brokers using stock exchanges
Share price	Varies directly with the total of all assets owned by the fund	Is influenced by the value of assets owned by the fund but may sell at a premium or discount to the value
Volatility	As volatile as the fund's assets	Generally more volatile than the fund's assets as shareholders anticipate changes
Commissions	May pay a commission when buying the fund of up to 8.5%; no commission on sales	Will pay a regular stock exchange commission on all buys and sells; actual commissions vary with size of purchase; will usually be less than open end
Marketability of shares	Guaranteed market to buy or sell shares at any time in any amount	No guaranteed marketability; could experience difficulty in buying or selling large amounts
Size of fund	Varies with amount invested and value of assets	Varies only with value of assets
Shares outstanding	No limit	Limited
Shareholder services	Recordkeeping of purchases and sales; tax notifications; dividend notification	Dividend and tax notification

Load and No-Load Funds

The dictionary says a "load" is a burden. Many mutual funds have "loads," and to some people those loads are burdens. The load on a mutual fund is a sales commission. You pay the commission when you buy shares in the fund. Typically, the load equals 8.5 percent, and it is included in the purchase price of the shares. You will find the fund quoted in the financial papers this way:

	NAV	Offer Price
ZIP Fund	10.00	10.93

In this quote, "offer price" is the price at which you can buy the fund today. NAV is the net asset value of the fund; it is also the price at which you can sell the fund today. Notice you pay $0.93 more to buy than you get when you sell. That $0.93 is the load. It equals 8.5 percent of the offer price ($0.93 ÷ $10.93 = 8.5%). You pay for having the fund sold to you.

Today there are many "no-load" funds. No-load funds don't have an 8.5 percent sales commission tacked on the front. Their quotes are listed this way:

	NAV	Offer Price
ZAP Fund	10.00	NL

The offer price is not listed because it is the same as the net asset value. Every dime you spend is invested. Nothing goes to pay sales expenses.

Without a sales commission, however, there are no salespeople. You have to sell the fund to yourself. You write the company directly and ask it to open an account for you. It will handle your account through the mail. Mail doesn't cost very much, so it doesn't have to charge you a burdensome load.

Whether a load is a real burden or not probably depends on what the burden is and on what benefit you will get from it. This is also true of mutual fund loads. The 8.5 percent sales commission can be a burden unless you get some real service for it. If the salesperson or broker gives you some real help, then the load may not be a burden—it may be a bargain.

Some services you may receive that can make the load a bargain include financial counseling, estate planning, financial objective determination, fund selection, and market timing. If you need these services, a fund salesperson or a broker may be able to help. And if someone helps, he or she deserves to be compensated. The compensation comes out of that load. So the load can turn out to be a real bargain.

The load will be a burden rather than a bargain if (1) you don't need the services, or (2) you aren't getting the services. Many people do not need the help of a salesperson in setting financial goals and selecting a mutual fund. They shouldn't pay a load. Many others are paying a load, but never receive any service from the salesperson. They shouldn't be paying a load, either. If you fit either of these categories, consider a no-load fund.

Considering a no-load fund isn't entirely easy. Remember, there is no salesperson. No one knocks on your door to tell you about no-load funds. The best way to find out about no-load funds is through the Wiesenberger service or some similar service. You may also learn of no-load funds through ads they run in the financial sections of newspapers. You can also spot them by running your eye down the mutual funds quotes in the financial pages. Unfortunately, the quotes don't tell you who to write for information. Finally, of course, you can learn about no-load funds from your friends.

If you work at it, you can find many different no-load funds. Maybe you can find a no-load fund that fits your financial needs. If you find such a fund, buy it. There is no sense carrying a heavy load on your fund if you don't need it. After all, why strain yourself?

Understanding the Fund

Choose a mutual fund with which you can be compatible. It is possible that a mutual fund could be your major investment. It is possible because each share of a mutual fund represents a diversified portfolio, a professional manager is constantly working to achieve good investment results, there are funds for almost every investment objective, and mutual funds are specifically designed for small and medium investors. Because of all these factors, you may not need any other investments besides a mutual fund. Of course, you'll still want a checking account, a savings account, and life insurance. But a mutual fund could be your major investment. And if it is your major investment, you certainly want to be compatible.

Compatibility begins with you. You must determine what your true investment objectives are. Do you want growth? Do you want income? Do you want stability of principal? Do you want some combination of these? You can find a mutual fund that also has these objectives. The following is just a sample of the fund objectives you can choose from.

◇ *Money market fund.* This is a good place to invest cash. You can get the cash back whenever you want and earn interest in the meantime. The interest rate varies with money market conditions. These funds are very safe, and theoretically the share price should not fluctuate. (For a complete discussion of money market funds, refer to Chapter 17.)

◇ *High-quality bond fund.* Such funds have a high degree of safety plus a fairly high yield. The share price is relatively stable, with only minor fluctuations. There is little chance of loss due to default of a bond.

◇ *Maximum-yield bond fund.* These funds give the highest current income available. There is a modest amount of price fluctuation. And there is some chance of loss due to default, although not great.

◇ *Municipal bond fund.* Such funds have the same objectives as other bond funds except these are invested in municipal bonds. Therefore, the dividends they pay are exempt from federal income taxes. The objective is high after-tax income. These funds are best for high-tax-bracket investors.

◇ *Balanced fund.* A combination of bonds and stocks is called a balanced fund. The objective is to achieve good income and good appreciation of principal. The share-price fluctuation should be moderate.

◇ *Long-term appreciation fund.* The principal holdings are common stocks with long-term growth possibilities. Income is desirable but is only a secondary consideration. Above-average share-price fluctuations are likely.

◇ *Appreciation fund.* Such funds seek to achieve maximum appreciation. Principal holdings are common stocks with near term-price appreciation potential. The fund may buy and sell stocks rapidly to benefit from short-term swings in the stock market. Furthermore, the fund may invest in less seasoned or speculative companies thought to have substantial appreciation possibilities. Current income is of little consideration. Share price fluctuations will be high.

◇ *Leveraged funds.* The objective is maximum appreciation. These funds will do the same things as appreciation funds. In addition, they can borrow money to buy stock, or they can sell stocks short. Hopefully, these actions allow such funds to take greater advantage of market swings. Current income is of little or no concern. Share price fluctuations are potentially extreme.

There are also many specialized mutual funds. Funds may specialize in technology stocks, or insurance stocks, or in energy stocks, or in pollution stocks, or in low-grade bonds, or in options, or in just about anything you can imagine. There are mutual funds dedicated to almost every known investment wrinkle—and maybe a few that aren't known.

The way to begin choosing among so many funds is to know what your own financial needs are. Assume, for example, that

⬦ You have some extra cash that you will need to spend some time soon—use a money market fund.

⬦ You are extremely worried about the stock and bond markets and want all the protection you can get—use a money market fund.

⬦ You are retired, and you need all the income your investments can give, and then some. You must spend some of the investments themselves—use a high-quality bond fund.

⬦ You are retired and can earn enough on your investments to live, but you could always use a little more—use a maximum-yield bond fund.

⬦ You are investing for the future and believe that high-yielding investments will accumulate value most rapidly. You also believe common stocks are risky or do not have much long-term appreciation potential—use a maximum-yield bond fund.

⬦ You are in a high tax bracket but like high cash dividends—use a municipal bond fund.

⬦ You are forty-five or fifty-five years old and are thinking about retirement. You can't afford to take a lot of risk, but you do want some stock appreciation potential—use a balanced fund.

⬦ You have many uncertainties about the economic and financial world. You think it is wise to receive a high current yield, but in case things get better you don't want to ignore stock appreciation potential—use a balanced fund.

⋄ You are in your thirties or forties, have a little money for investment, and want to build for the future. You don't need income from your investments right now—use a long-term appreciation fund.

⋄ You are optimistic about the future. You believe the economy will grow in the next two years. You feel common stocks will appreciate—use a long-term appreciation fund.

⋄ You are in your twenties or thirties, you have some money to invest, and you hope you might actually strike it rich and retire early. You can take some risk and can still sleep at night—use an appreciation fund.

⋄ You have many investments and can afford to speculate—use a leveraged fund.

There are many more compatibility circumstances that can be imagined. Only you can decide what your needs are. Don't fall in love with the idea of getting rich without effort. Ask yourself if you can live with the peculiarities of your fund—such as volatility. After all, what good is it to marry the best-looking person in the world if you can't stand his or her personality?

Which Mutual Fund Should You Choose?

Finding the right mutual fund means finding the fund that's most compatible with you. Determining your own compatibility needs is the first giant step. Knowing your own needs will help you concentrate on that group of funds with objectives that fit your needs. And it will help you from falling in love with a good-looking fund that you could never live with in the long run. But even with your own needs firmly in mind, you still need to know who the potential candidates are and what their personalities are like. What you need is some type of "little black book."

There are several services that might be thought of as "little black books" for mutual funds (actually, most of the books aren't black, and none are little). These services give all kinds of information on mutual funds, such as names, objectives, past performances, available services, and addresses. All "little black books" have addresses. You need the addresses so that you can contact the funds you are attracted to for more information. Two of the best services are

Wiesenberger National Services
(Division of Warren, Gorham & LaMont, Inc.)
870 Seventh Avenue
New York, New York 10017
(212) 977-7453

Lipper Analytical Distributor, Inc.
74 Trinity Place
New York, New York 10006
(212) 269-4080

You can find one or both of these services at large public libraries. They are also found at libraries associated with universities that teach business administration. Or you can find them at many brokerage houses. Any of these sources should let you consult their services free. Of course, the broker will probably try to sell you something while you are there. But just take a little sales resistance along, and you'll enjoy your visit.

Hopefully you'll also enjoy browsing through the service books. While browsing, consider the following criteria for selection of your mutual fund.

◇ *Objectives.* Look only at those funds with objectives compatible with your own. There should be many candidates.

◇ *Size.* Try to limit yourself to funds with assets between $50 million and $300 million. If the fund is much smaller, that may be an indication that it never sold very well or is declining through liquidation. These can be signs of difficulty. If the fund is too large, the manager's investment flexibility may be limited.

◇ *Investment advisor.* Select a fund that has an investment advisor managing at least $1 billion. You may need to look at all the funds the firm manages and add up the assets. You want an investment advisor of this size so you can be satisfied it is large enough to have a full staff of investment professionals.

◇ *Turnover.* Turnover is a measure of how much buying and selling was done in the fund last year. Frequently, the number is reported in these services. Look for numbers between 15 and

60 percent. Turnover much lower than 15 percent may imply inaction on the manager's part. Turnover much higher than 60 percent may imply excessive and costly trading.

◇ *Load.* The load is the sales commission. After all this work, you may not feel you need the service of a salesperson. If you don't, don't pay for it. Consider buying a no–load fund.

◇ *Open or Closed.* Determine whether the fund is open or closed and which type you want to buy. Generally you will want to look at open-end funds. If the fund is closed, you should also study the portfolio itself. You must decide whether you think the fund is likely to attract additional investors. The additional investors are the ones who will cause the price to rise.

◇ *Approved.* Not all funds are approved for sale in all states. Not being approved in a specific state means only that the fund has never bothered to go through the red tape of becoming approved. That in turn means the fund has no marketing effort in the state. Rarely does nonapproval mean anything is wrong with the fund. But wrong or not, you will have to look at funds approved in your state.

◇ *Performance.* Performance is the most important consideration of all. Your whole purpose in considering a fund is to achieve some kind of investment performance. Unfortunately, future performance is also the most difficult consideration of all. The only clue to future performance a layperson can use is past performance. But future performance isn't always like past performance. However, a record of consistently good performance may show that the fund manager has a workable investment strategy.

Most services group funds according to investment objective. Then they rank the funds according to performance. Measuring against similar funds with similar objectives is far better than measuring against some market index. Indexes have no particular objective.

The funds are usually ranked according to total return. Total return means that dividends and appreciation are added together. Concentrate your investigative efforts on funds in the top third of their groupings. And, if the data are given, you should prefer funds that have been consistently above average for the past five or ten years. However, avoid last year's top fund. Unfortunately, history shows the top funds don't persist in that spot. Almost inevitably they are ready for a tumble.

After you've considered all criteria, you should have eliminated nearly all the names. Don't be alarmed. Eliminating names is what you've been trying to do. In fact, you may have eliminated all the names. If so, ease your criteria a little. Then, having cut the field to a very few names, you can choose the fund you feel best about. Write to the fund, or its distributor, and ask for more information. Better yet, call the distributor directly. Tell the distributor you are interested in opening an account. They will send you literature, forms, and a prospectus. Read the prospectus, even though it looks very dull. The prospectus, which is required by the government, will tell you a great deal about the fund and the people who manage it.

Once you've followed all these steps, you can be satisfied you've done everything possible to achieve a happy, compatible relationship with your mutual fund. Of course, mistakes are still possible. But a careful, disciplined approach should yield happy results. Then, as with any valued relationship, be patient and long-suffering. There are bound to be times when you'll be unhappy and want to divorce yourself from the situation. But try to give things plenty of time to work. Hopefully, in the end, everyone will live happily ever after.

◇ 47 ◇
Buying Options

Let's say you like your neighbor's stock and want to buy it, but you want a little time to see which way the stock market is going first. And let's say your neighbor is willing to sell you her stock. In fact, she's even willing to give you a guaranteed price. Furthermore, she's willing to give you six months to make up your mind. She does want to be paid something right away for granting all these privileges. If you complete the deal, you have purchased a "call option." It gives you the option to "call" for the stock if you want it. To pursue this example, assume the following:

1. The stock is currently trading on the New York Stock Exchange for $47.

2. The guaranteed purchase price of the stock is $45. This price is known as the "exercise" or "striking" price.

3. You have six months to exercise your option. It need not be six months; you and your neighbor could pick any date. The date you pick is the *expiration date*.

4. The money you pay for the option is called a *premium*. It is the cost of the option, not the cost of the stock. In this example, assume that the premium is $4.50 per option. This price is just an example; premiums fluctuate constantly. They vary with the price of the underlying stock as compared to the exercise price. And the premiums tend to diminish as the expiration date gets closer.

5. The amount of stock you are talking about is 100 shares.

With these facts and definitions in mind, we can see how this call option might work out for you, the buyer, or for your neighbor. In order for you to make a clear profit, the stock will have to trade above $49.50 some time before that expiration date ($45.00 exercise price plus $4.50 premium).

If it does trade above $49.50, you will make money—possibly lots of money. But if the stock goes down, you may lose everything.

	Possible Outcomes			
	1	**2**	**3**	**4**
Price on expiration date	$ 60.00	$ 49.50	$ 47.00	$ 40.00
Value of 100 shares	6,000.00	4,950.00	4,700.00	4,000.00
Cost of exercising option to buy at $45	4,500.00	4,500.00	4,500.00	4,500.00
Gross profit on exercising option (if negative, you will not exercise the option to buy)	1,500.00	450.00	200.00	0.00 (Won't exercise)
Less premium already paid	450.00	450.00	450.00	450.00
Net profit (or loss)	1,050.00	0.00	(250.00)	(450.00)
Return on original investment	133% Profit	0% Profit	(−56%) Loss	(−100%) Loss

Your reward or risk in this little example ranges from +133 percent to a complete −100 percent loss. It should be noted however, that there is no upper limit on the profit. For example, you might get really lucky; the stock might soar to $99. At $99, your return on the original investment would be a fantastic 1000 percent. The sky's the limit.

There is a limit, however, on how much you can lose. Unfortunately, the limit is everything—100 percent of your investment. And most unfortunately, people lose everything more often than they make a quick 1000 percent. Option buying is a speculative way to invest.

Options buying is a speculative way to invest, but options writing can be a conservative way to invest. For every buyer, there must be a writer. In this case, your neighbor is the option writer. She is the investor willing to sell you the stock. And she is the investor that receives the premium you paid. Many option writers are conservative investors. They are not trying to make a quick 1000 percent. They hope to achieve a consistent return of income and moderate appreciation on their stocks. Such investors believe a consistent return produces the best results over the long run.

Here's the situation from your neighbor's viewpoint: The stock is currently at $47, the exercise price is $45, there is a fixed expiration date, and she receives a premium from you of $4.50 per share optioned.

Writer's Results if Option Is Written

	Possible Outcomes			
	1	*2*	*3*	*4*
Price on expiration date	$ 60.00	$ 49.50	$ 47.00	$ 40.00
Cash received from exercised option	4,500.00	4,500.00	4,500.00	0.00 (buyer will not exercise)
Value of stock still held	0.00	0.00	0.00	4,000.00
Cash received from premium	450.00	450.00	450.00	450.00
Total value of cash or stock	4,950.00	4,950.00	4,950.00	4,450.00
Value of original stock at $47	4,700.00	4,700.00	4,700.00	4,700.00
Profit (or loss) on original value	250.00	250.00	250.00	(250.00)
Percent profit (or loss)	5.3%	5.3%	5.3%	(−4.3%)

Writer's Results if Option Is Not Written

Value of stock if held	$6,000.00	$4,950.00	$4,700.00	$4,000.00
Value of original stock at $47	4,700.00	4,700.00	4,700.00	4,700.00
Profit (or loss) on original value	1,300.00	250.00	0.00	(700.00)
Percent profit (or loss)	27.7%	5.3%	0.0%	(−14.9%)

All these numbers are just examples, but they are typical. Notice how writing the option reduces both your neighbor's risk and reward. When the stock went to $60, she made 5.3 percent. If she had not written the option, she would have made 27.7 percent. However, if she is able to make 5.3 percent on her stocks, and if she can do it every six months or so, and if she can do that in Outcomes 2 and 3 as well as in 1, she will do very well. She will probably wind up earning 10.0 to 12.0 percent on her portfolio for the year, and she can achieve 10.0 to 12.0 percent with much more consistency than 27.7 percent. Your neighbor might think that consistency is pretty good.

Options writing not only improves your neighbor's chances of making some money, but it also reduces her risk of losing. Under the worst outcome in our example, the writer only lost 4.3 percent. She would have lost 14.9 percent if the option hadn't been written. For many investors this reduction in risk is very attractive.

Because option writing is conservative investing, most writers *aren't* your neighbors. Many writers are large, professionally managed portfolios such as pension funds and college endowments. Sometimes the writer is an individual with a large concentration in a particular stock. Curiously enough, most writers are writing options on stocks they really don't want to sell. The most sophisticated thinking today argues that options should only be written on stocks the owner likes. That thinking sounds a little backward. The very act of writing an option exposes that stock to the possibility of being taken away. And if it is taken away, it will be done when the option buyer wants, not when the option writer wants. That's a strange kind of exposure to create for a stock you like.

The reason conservative investors write against stocks they like is because they definitely don't want to write against stocks they don't like. If you own a stock, don't like it, and think it will go down, you should sell it outright. You should not fool around wasting time writing options on the stock. Furthermore, experience shows that most stocks do *not* get called away. So there is a good chance you'll wind up owning the stock after the option has expired. You don't want to wind up owning a stock you don't like.

Not all writers are worried about their favorite stock being called away. And not all writers are conservative. Some option writers are every bit as speculative as the option buyers. The speculative writers are those who are writing "naked" options. This is not a subtle way to sneak sex into this book. Some investors write options on stock they don't own. This is known as "naked" writing. The "naked" writer receives the premium from the buyer, as before. Then, if the stock doesn't go up and isn't called away, the writer simply pockets the premium. He (or she) never invests a dime of his own money. However, if the stock does go up, the "naked" writer has to scurry around to buy the stock. He must cover his option. If the investor finds himself in this predicament, he can wind up losing a great deal of money.

Because buyers and writers may not be neighbors, they need a place to get together. In recent years, flourishing option exchanges have sprung up. Premium quotes for the options on many stocks are carried daily in leading financial papers. If you don't have a willing neighbor, you can pick up the phone and buy or write an option through a broker. It's as easy as buying or selling a stock.

You may not want to buy a "call" option to purchase stock. You may prefer to sell your neighbor one of your stocks instead. If you've got a very accommodating neighbor, you can work out such a deal. Such a deal is known as a "put" option. And you really don't have to bother an accommodating neighbor. You can buy a "put" on the option exchanges.

Why would you want the right to sell or "put" your stock to someone? Well, it might help you limit your loss on a stock you are afraid will go down. Or you might buy a "put" on a stock you don't even own. Then you're speculating there will be a price decline. For instance, if the stock is $47 and you buy a "put" at $45, you will be in great shape if the stock drops to $40. If you own the stock, you'll exercise your "put" and sell it to your neighbor at $45. This restricts your loss to $2 a share. If you don't own the stock, you'll rush out and buy it at $40, and then "put" it to your neighbor at $45. He or she loses $5 immediately on the transaction. You, in turn, get the $5. This might be known as the Golden Rule of investing—"Do unto your neighbor that which makes the most money for you."

There is almost no end to the creative ways in which you can use "Do unto your neighbor" or unto anyone else you can find on the option exchange. You can be an options buyer, or an options writer. You can be speculative or conservative. But you shouldn't do any of them unless you know what you're doing. All options strategies require skill, judgment, and substantial investment sophistication. Options may work into your personal investment program. But don't work them in until you've gained the sophistication you need. Unfortunately, this book is a simple introduction at best. It cannot begin to give you the knowledge required. But if you are intrigued, there are many books devoted entirely to the subject of options. There are good books available in bookstores, at libraries, and through your securities broker. If you're interested, you should learn more. Because if you don't learn enough, your neighbor might just "do it unto you." The option is up to you.

How Does an Option Work?

An option works by giving the investor a choice and time to decide which choice to make. It's like an option play in football. As the play develops, the quarterback can either choose to run with the ball himself or toss it to someone else. The quarterback doesn't need to make a final decision until he sees what the defense is going to do. By waiting to see what the defense is going to do, he can make the choice that will gain the most yardage.

The stock market also has options. The decision maker, or financial quarterback, may acquire an option on a stock. The option gives him (or her) the right to buy or not to buy the stock. It also gives him some time to make his choice. He doesn't need to make a financial decision until he sees what the stock market is going to do. By waiting to see what the market is going to do, he can make the choice that will gain the most financial yardage. Consider the following example. Imagine there is a company called Lovely Socks, Inc. Lovely Socks makes powerful detergents for fumigating sweat socks. The stock is trading at $50 a share. Follow an option from the point of view of a buyer and a seller.

OPTION BUYER

Say you are a quarterback who likes football, clean sweat socks, and speculative investing. Say you've amassed a fortune of $1000 that you want to invest in Lovely Socks, Inc. You could buy 20 shares of stock with your $1000. Or you might be able to buy a call option on 1000 shares. The call might give you the right to buy 1000 shares of Lovely Socks at $55 any time between now and the Super Bowl game six months away. For that option, you must pay the current owner of the stock a premium of $1 a share today, or $1000.

Now, on the surface, paying $1000 today for the right to buy a $50 stock at $55 doesn't seem like a good deal. But you would gain potential control over 1000 shares, not 20, and you would get six months to watch the market and decide what to do. Here are two of the many possible outcomes.

Outcome 1. You have a winning season. You not only get to the Super Bowl, but you also personally score the winning touchdown. Next day you get more good news: Lovely Socks, Inc. is trading at $70 a share. You exercise your option to buy the 1000 shares, and then you sell the shares immediately.

Buy 1000 shares at $55	$55,000
Sell 1000 shares at $70	70,000
Gain on sale	$15,000
Less initial premium	1,000
Net profit	$14,000

You made $14,000 on the transaction and only invested $1000 to begin with. If you had purchased the 20 shares directly instead of the option, your $1000 investment would have given you a profit of only $400.

Original purchase of 20 shares at $50	$1,000
Current value of 20 shares at $70	1,400
Paper profit	$ 400

You sure called the right play that time.

Outcome 2. You take an unwise chance on the first play of the season and break your leg. Your team goes on to lose fifteen straight. You wind up watching the Super Bowl on a black and white TV, and the team you bet on gets clobbered 85 to 0. Somehow you're not surprised to see Lovely Socks trading at $35 the next day. Your option is worthless. No one would pay $55 a share for a stock that's worth $35.

Gain on *not* exercising option	$ 0
Less initial premium	1,000
Net (loss)	$(1.000)

Losing all the money you had available for investment is not fun. You have a better idea now why buying options is considered speculative. If you had bought the twenty shares of stock instead, you would have a $300 paper loss. However, you would still have the stock. It would be worth $700, and there's a chance it would go back up. Who knows, it could recover faster than you will.

Original purchase of 20 shares at $50	$1,000
Current value of 20 shares at $35	700
Paper loss	$ (300)

The buyer of an option does have the right to wait and see how things develop. But despite this advantage, options are speculative. Usually the buyer will either make a lot of money, or lose a lot of money. There isn't much in between.

OPTION WRITER

For every option buyer, there must be an option seller, or writer. In this case, let's assume it's the football coach. Over the years, he has agreed to help advertise Lovely Socks detergent by pacing up and down the sidelines during games in his stocking feet. The company pays him for his promotional efforts in common stock. Over the years, the coach has accumulated a lot of Lovely Socks stock from the promotions. Over the years, he has also accumulated a lot of colds from wet feet.

Despite the wet feet, the coach likes the stock at $50. However, if the price were to move up to $55 he would be willing to diversify his holdings somewhat. So he writes an option on 1000 shares. He receives $1000 today and puts that in the bank. The $1000 becomes income that no one can take away. Then he waits for the outcome.

Outcome 1. The team is practicing hard, playing great, and using plenty of Lovely Socks detergent. By Super Bowl time, the stock is trading at 70^0. Naturally, the coach feels a twinge of remorse—he sells his stock for a mere $55. But the coach is a pro. He knows it's a good diversification. He knows the stock may now be overpriced, and he knows this is a good discipline to make him sell. "Play conservative and get the points on the board" has always been his motto. Obviously, he couldn't know in advance the stock was going to 70^0. So he satisfies himself with the $5 plus the $1 on the option. Together they add up to 12 percent from where he started. And the coach knows that consistently making a certain 12 percent is like "5 yards and a cloud of dust"—it's the way to win in the long run.

Outcome 2. Things are going well, just as before. Suddenly it is discovered that Lovely Socks detergent is also good for controlling bad breath and impulsive swearing. The stock jumps to $70. This is new information. As an impulsive swearer, the coach can't be philosophical about selling his stock at $55. Now he figures the stock is still a good buy at $70. He thinks Lovely Socks might go to $120 on this new opportunity to fumigate mouths. He probably will swallow hard and buy 1000 more shares to replace the 1000 he optioned away. He is going to lose $14,000 in *replacement cost,* but he still made $6000 in *selling the option.*

Original value of 1000 shares at $50	$50,000
Cash received from sale of 1000 shares at $55	55,000
Cash profit from sale	$ 5,000
Add premium received	1,000
Option profit	$ 6,000
Cash received from sale of 1000 shares at $55	$55,000
Current replacement cost of 1000 shares at $70	70,000
Gross opportunity cost lost	$15,000
Less premium received	1,000
Net replacement cost	$14,000

Outcome 3. It is one of those seasons for the coach. His team loses every game on a fluke. Flukes like his all-pro tackle running into the wrong end zone with a recovered fumble. Or the field goal kicker's shoe coming off and flying through the uprights, instead of the ball. And so it is with Lovely Socks, Inc. Athletes are not fumigating their socks as they should. The lights in the locker rooms are turning green from the fumes, but sales still lag. The stock drifts down to $35. But the coach is a firm believer in "Wait till next year!" and holds on. He's sorry to see his stock drop to $35, but he's glad he wrote the option. He has a paper loss of $15,000 on the stock. But he also has $1000 of cold cash in the bank. And he wouldn't have had the cash if he hadn't written the option.

Value of 1000 shares at $50	$50,000
Value of 1000 shares at $35	35,000
Paper loss	$15,000
Cash received from premium	$ 1,000

Outcome 4. The team is bumbling along. Things are going so bad they even lose practice games with the song leaders. Then it

happens—the coach gets fired. Suddenly real disaster strikes. The government announces it has been testing Lovely Socks detergent. They fed rats forty-three boxes of detergent a day. This demonstrates the skill of the experimenters—it's not easy to feed that much detergent to a rat. The results are clear: The detergent killed every one of them. (The rats, not the experimenters.) The tests didn't prove conclusively that eating Lovely Socks detergent causes cancer because all the rats died before the tests were complete. But a warning label on the box will be required. The stock plummets to 35, and the coach knows it's going lower. It's going lower not because of the cancer scare, but because the government is going to stop testing. It seems that the government has been Lovely Socks' biggest customer.

This is the position the coach really didn't want to get into. He has an option written on a stock he doesn't like anymore. He has three choices:

1. He can wait until the option expires unexercised, then sell the stock for whatever he can get.

2. He can sell the stock right now anyway and hope it doesn't go back up. If it recovers, he might be forced to rebuy the stock at high prices to make good on his option.

3. He can buy the option back through an option exchange. Then he can sell the stock. Buying the option under these circumstances will cost much less than $1000. This means he'll be able to keep some of his original premium.

The coach has had a loss, but the loss could have been worse. The coach is glad he wrote the option.

Writing the option has been a conservative strategy. It cushioned the losses when they occurred. It provided extra income when nothing occurred. And it resulted in modest gains when price rises occurred. Writing options won't make the coach rich quick, but they'll help in the long run.

People who take options seriously spend a lot of time learning how options work. And no one should fool around with options unless they take them seriously. Most people playing in options are professionals. If you want to get into options, plan to become a pro. If you don't, you may have roughly the same experience as trying to play quarterback for the Dallas Cowboys when all your previous experience was touch football with the kids.

◇ 48 ◇

Investing in Bonds

A bond is a loan. It's a big loan. It's a long-term loan. It's a loan to a big corporation, such as American Telephone & Telegraph, or to a big government such as the United States. And it's a loan made by a lender such as you. Why would the world's largest corporations and governments be coming to you for a loan? Because you have the money they need.

You might not agree that you've got money to lend. You might even say that making loans to Uncle Sam and Ma Bell has never crossed your mind, not even in your wildest financial fantasies. But you probably made the loan anyway. If you own anything like a life insurance policy, or a car insurance policy, or if you participate in a pension plan, or own shares in an income-oriented mutual fund, or have a checking account, you have probably made loans to the government, to AT&T, and many other big borrowers. Financial institutions such as insurance companies and banks buy corporate and government bonds—with your money. So in effect you own the bonds, and you've made the loans.

Many people prefer to make their loans in person. They can do so by purchasing bonds directly. It is perfectly possible for you to buy corporate or government bonds yourself. Simply call your securities broker and place an order.

Characteristics of Bonds

Before you place that order, however, there are a few things you should know about bonds. Consider the following characteristics:

◇ *Instrument of indebtedness.* A bond is an instrument of indebtedness. The corporation is borrowing money from investors. It will use the money to build plants, to buy equipment, or to run the company. It agrees to repay all the money, plus interest, sometime in the future.

353

◇ *Interest rate.* The company will pay interest on the money it has borrowed. The interest rate is known as the "coupon rate." The coupon rate is determined by money market conditions at the time bonds are sold. Once the coupon rate is determined, it never changes.

◇ *Large loans.* Bond issues generally represent very large loans. Amounts of $20 million, $50 million, or $100 million are commonplace.

◇ *Bond certificates.* The loans are so big no single financial institution can handle the entire loan. Therefore, the loan must be broken down into small pieces called *bonds.* The bonds are then sold to many investors. The normal denomination is $1000 per bond.

◇ *Coupons.* Often the actual bond certificate has a number of coupons attached to it. In order to get the interest you should be paid, you must physically clip off the coupon and mail it in. Typically, one coupon should be sent each six months.

◇ *Free market.* Individual bond certificates can be bought and sold in the free market. If an owner wants to sell them, he or she can call a securities broker, who will find a buyer for them. For investors, this is one great advantage bonds have over ordinary loans. Most ordinary loans are not very marketable. Your car loan at the bank, for instance, cannot be bought and sold on the New York bond exchange.

◇ *Price fluctuations.* As with any item trading in a free market, the price of bonds fluctuates. Fluctuations are caused by supply and demand for the bond. The price must adjust to balance these forces. Fluctuating prices mean that a seller can make a profit. Of course, it also means he or she can suffer a loss. It all depends on the price of the bond at the time of sale.

◇ *Free-market interest rates.* The most important factor causing price fluctuations are free-market interest rates. Because the coupon rate of a bond is fixed, its price will fluctuate to reflect changing market interest rates. A bond with a 7 percent coupon rate is worth less than a bond of similar quality but with an 8 percent coupon rate. Market interest rates change constantly. Interest rates rise or fall, depending on the number of lenders and borrowers in the marketplace. When market interest rates rise, bond prices fall. When interest rates fall, bond prices rise.

◇ *Quotes*. Because bonds fluctuate in price, brokers naturally make quotes on them. But quotes aren't the real price. For instance, if you ask about the price of a bond and are told it is 99, you will have to pay $990 to buy it, not $99. The basic price of all bonds is 100. This basic price is also known as *par*. A bond selling at 100 is really selling for $1000. Usually bonds do not sell in nice round numbers. There may also be a fraction on the end of the quote. For example, a quote of 83 3/16 really means $831.875 (3/16 = 0.1875).

◇ *Quality ratings*. Some borrowers are better credit risks than others. Bonds from good credit risks are of higher quality than those from poor credit risks. High-quality bonds have lower yields than low-quality bonds. Large borrowers are rated according to quality by Standard & Poor's and Moody's services.

◇ *Length*. These loans usually run for a long time before they must be paid off. Ten or thirty years is typical; fifty years is still seen. The time a bond has to run until it matures and is paid off is described in terms of length. Short maturities are seven to ten years or less. Intermediate maturities are ten to twenty years. And long maturities are twenty years to forty years and beyond. Long bonds usually sell to yield a higher interest rate than short bonds.

◇ *Call provisions*. Many bonds have a provision that allows the borrower to pay off the bonds early. The provision is known as a *call provision*. Borrowers only *call* the bonds when it is favorable for them. That usually means it is less than favorable to the lenders. Consequently, most lenders do not want to have their bonds called and paid off early. So lenders try to get as much call protection as possible. Typically, bonds can't be called for five to ten years after they are originally sold. Even then, the company must buy them back at more than they sold them for. If the company sold them for $1000 a bond, for instance, the call price might be $1080.

◇ *Sinking funds*. Most ordinary loans require periodic repayments. So do most bond issues. The repayments are called *sinking funds*. They work differently from your car payments.

The sinking fund payments may not even start for ten to fifteen years after issue. Then the company will pay off some of the bonds each year.

Bonds can be excellent investments. Chances are you already own some indirectly through a financial institution and don't even know it. But just in case you've got an extra $10 or $20 or $100,000 burning a hole in your pocket, you might want to buy bonds directly. Just think of the satisfaction you'd get in making a loan to some needy company like Ma Bell!

Pluses and Minuses of Owning Bonds

As with any investment, there are advantages and disadvantages in owning bonds. Some advantages are as follows:

◇ Bonds pay consistent interest.
◇ The yield on bonds is usually higher than on common stocks or on savings accounts.
◇ Bond prices are generally less volatile than stock prices.
◇ In the event of bankruptcy of the borrower, the bondholders get paid off before stockholders do.
◇ Bonds are generally less risky than nearly all other investments except savings accounts and certificates.

Bonds also have some disadvantages. Many of these disadvantages may be more properly called *misconceptions* on the part of some investors.

◇ Bonds are poor hedges against inflation. Neither the interest payments nor the value of the bond will be increased to keep up with inflation.
◇ Bonds do fluctuate in price during the life of the bond, unlike savings accounts. Many people do not understand that bond prices fluctuate.
◇ Bonds are hard for small investors to buy. *Small* bond purchases are $10,000. Many ordinary purchases are in the millions of dollars.
◇ Bondholders do not participate in the growth of the borrower, as a stockholder does.
◇ Reselling some bonds can be difficult.

⋄ In some cases, the bondholder must go to the trouble of physically detaching a coupon every six months and mailing it in order to receive an interest payment.

Whether these items are advantages or disadvantages depends on you. It depends on your financial objectives. If you are looking for an investment providing a fixed income, relatively low risk, and more price stability than a stock, then bonds may be your answer.

◇ 49 ◇
What Determines
Bond Prices?

Buyers and sellers determine bond prices. If there are more buyers than sellers, the price goes up. If there are more sellers than buyers, the price goes down. The price of a bond keeps moving until it settles at a price where the buyers and sellers are in equilibrium. But just about the time the price attains equilibrium, usually a new buyer, or a new seller, comes into the market and price changes again. The prices of actively traded bonds are being determined all the time.

That buyers and sellers determine price is obvious. The real question is "How do rational investors determine at what price they will become buyers or sellers?" There are many variables. The most important variables are interest rates, quality, and length. The following sections explore these variables in detail.

Interest Rates

Interest rates are the most important variable in bond prices. Interest is the cost of borrowing money. Thousands of borrowers in the market are borrowing millions of dollars all the time. Likewise, there are thousands of lenders lending millions of dollars all the time. But sometimes the number of borrowers increases. As that happens, the cost of money, or interest, increases. Or the number of lenders may increase, so the cost of money will decrease, and so on. Interest rates, therefore, are in a constant state of change. Constantly changing market interest rates mean constantly changing bond prices.

Here's how the changes work. Suppose you buy an International Skunk Works, Inc. bond. Suppose the bond you buy matures in ten years, which means the bond is expected to live longer than the skunks. Assume you pay $1000 for the bond. Also assume its coupon rate is 8 percent. This means the Skunk Works will faithfully send you $80 every year regardless of market interest rates, or the price of the bond, or the level of the stock market, and so on.

But suppose exactly one year after you purchase your Skunk bonds, interest rates in the market rise from 8 to 9 percent. New bonds being issued will pay their owners $90 a year. Because your bond only pays $80, your bond is worth less than a new bond. Unfortunately, it is also worth less than the $1000 you paid for it. In fact, the price has probably dropped to $950, a loss of $50. Now, that really stinks. But suppose you hold on, and at the end of the second year market interest rates have declined from 9 all the way down to 7 percent. At 7 percent, new bonds will pay their owners $70 each year. Now your bond is worth more than new bonds because it pays $80 every year. In fact, the price of your bond has probably risen to $1051. At this point, you are happy. You are glad you put your money with a bunch of skunks. And so the fluctuations go. When interest rates go up, your bond goes down. When interest rates go down, your bond goes up.

Some may wonder where the prices of $950 and $1051 come from. To understand this, you must understand yields on bonds. Not just one yield but three different yields.

1. *Coupon yield.* This is the price of the bond at par, or $1000, divided by the coupon rate. In the case of the Skunk bonds, the coupon yield is 8 percent ($80 ÷ $1000 = 8 percent). Par remains $1000, and the coupon rate remains $80 for the life of the bond, regardless of what else is going on. Because these are fixed, the coupon yield will always be 8 percent.

2. *Current yield.* Current yield is the current price of the bond divided by the coupon rate. So, when the market interest rates were 9 percent, and the Skunk bonds sold for $950, the current yield was 8.4 percent ($80 ÷ $950 = 8.4 percent). A yield of 8.4 percent is lower than a market rate of 9 percent. Furthermore, when market rates fell to 7 percent and the Skunk bonds sold for $1051, the current yield was 7.6 percent ($80 ÷ $1051 = 7.6 percent). Please note again that the current yield of 7.6 percent differed from the market rate of interest. Despite its differences (which are explained later), the current yield is important. It is especially important to people who plan to hold the bond for only a relatively short time and then sell it. The price of the bond changes all the time, so the current yield changes all the time. Usually, however, the current yield will not equal the market rate of interest.

3. *Yield to maturity.* Bonds usually are priced so that the yield to maturity is close to the free-market interest rate. Many people don't plan to sell their Skunk bonds. They plan to hold them until maturity. When the bonds mature, the Skunk Works will pay them off at par, or $1000 per bond. Therefore, even if your bond is priced at $950 today, it will be worth $1000 on the day it matures. If the price is going to rise from $950 to $1000, you are going to enjoy $50 of price appreciation. That price appreciation is added to the interest you'll be paid when figuring yield to maturity. For example, the Skunk bonds sold for $950 when market interest rates were 9 percent, and the bond still had nine years until maturity. Each year you will receive $80 interest, plus one-ninth of the $50 price appreciation. One-ninth of the appreciation is $5.56 per year ($50 ÷ 9 = $5.56). When the $5.56 appreciation is added to the $80 interest, the total you receive for the year is $85.56. This total, divided by the price of the bond, equals the market interest rate of 9 percent ($85.56 ÷ 950 = 9 percent).

Actually the true pricing is much more complicated than this. To do it precisely (if there is such a thing in bond pricing) you will need a bond buyer's price book or a special calculator. If neither are readily available to you (which they probably aren't), this approach is a good approximation. And in bond pricing a good approximation may be as close as you'll come.

There is one problem with the $5.56 appreciation you're getting—you don't get it. At least, you don't get it in cash. You only get it on paper. You don't really get the appreciation until the bond matures or you sell it. Then you get all the appreciation at one time. But cash or not, that $5.56 is important. It makes a great deal of difference to many people. Therefore, it must be considered when figuring yield to maturity.

Sometimes the bond is selling for more than $1000. For example, when the Skunk bonds had eight years left to go, and market interest rates were 7 percent, the bonds sold for $1051. At $1051, the bonds will automatically depreciate in price $51 by the time they are paid off. Depreciation is just as important as appreciation when figuring yield to maturity.

Because depreciation and appreciation are important, and because they both depend on price, it is good to know how to figure the price. The following formula will provide you with a reasonable approximation of the yield to maturity.

$$\text{Yield to maturity} \quad = \quad \frac{\text{Coupon rate} + \dfrac{(\text{Par value} - \text{Current price})}{\text{Years to maturity}}}{\text{Current Price}}$$

This formula may look complicated, but it really isn't when you start putting the figures in. The real formula is so complicated it is hard to work without a special calculator.

One thing you'll discover, when you do start putting the figures in this formula, is that bonds do go up and down in price as the yield to maturity changes. And the yield to maturity changes as the market rates of interest change. You will discover, as you put the figures in, that the bond prices go down as the market interest rates go up. And the bond prices go up as the market interest rates go down.

The Skunk bonds will go up and down in price, like any bond. Of course, they will each be worth $1000 when they are finally paid off. But they may be worth many other prices before they are paid off. Most people want to know what their bonds are worth all the time, not just when they mature. And if the price is changing, they want to know why. In most cases, the reason for price changes is going to be rising or falling market interest rates.

Bond Quality

All bonds are created with a par value of $1000 per bond, but that doesn't mean all bonds are created equal. Bonds sold by AT&T (Ma Bell) are much more likely to be paid off than bonds issued by Orville Wnklfzzr's Pub & Dry Cleaning Establishment. So, if you are trying to make a decision which $1000 bond to buy, you would prefer to buy Ma Bell's. You would prefer Ma Bell, unless Orville was willing to pay more interest—a whole lot more interest. In this case, let's say Orville agrees to pay $180 a year, or 18 percent, on every $1000 bond. Let's also assume the phone company is only willing to pay $120, or 12 percent a year. You might feel that additional interest makes the Wnklfzzr bonds attractive to you.

Some may wonder how the average person goes about comparing quality between bonds. The difference is not always as obvious as between AT&T and a flea-bitten pub and dry cleaning store. The differences are based on things such as the value of assets behind the bond, the amount of earnings available to pay the interest, and the stability of the business. Determining bond qualities is work for an expert. Fortunately, two companies, Standard & Poor's and Moody's, rate bonds of most major corporations. They rate AT&T as AAA/Aaa; they do not rate Orville Wnklfzzr. Their ratings are very reliable and readily available. Just ask your broker.

The highest ratings are AAA (Standard and Poor's) and Aaa (Moody's). As a practical matter, a lay investor should not buy bonds with quality ratings below BBB/Baa. Bonds rated lower are speculative.

Bond ratings do change from time to time. Let's say Orville is convinced the nation needs a pub and dry cleaning establishment next to every car wash in the country. So he borrows huge amounts of money to build them. He may get so heavily burdened with debt that his business becomes an even poorer credit risk than it already was. Under these conditions, Wnklfzzr bond quality will go down, and so will the bond price.

Then suppose by some miracle Orville is right. The country does need a pub and dry cleaning establishment next to every car wash. Suppose the money starts cascading in. Suppose he pays off a lot of his debt, and he has cash in the bank. Suppose he looks as if he is getting big enough to buy out AT&T—the whole company. Then Orville Wnklfzzr's bond ratings will go up—and so will the bonds.

Unfortunately, such far-fetched stories are just that—far-fetched. Bond ratings do change. And bond prices do reflect changes. But speculative companies rarely get big enough to buy out AT&T. So if you want good-quality bonds, buy them to start with. (Incidentally, in case you didn't know, Wnklfzzr is pronounced Wnklfzr—the first z is silent.)

Bond Length

Length of a bond has nothing to do with the size of the certificate. Length refers to the time left until the bond matures and is paid off.

Usually, the longer the bond has to go before it's repaid, the higher the interest rate. To illustrate, assume that International Worm Breeding, Inc., wants to borrow money. It needs a second loan for ten years to buy branding irons to cut down on worm rustling.

Finally, it needs a fifty-year loan to build posh new dormitories for the worms. Happy worms make better breeders, you know. Anyway, the worm breeders come to you, and you've decided to invest in their bonds. Will you require the same rate of interest on all the loans? Probably not. Probably you'll want a higher rate of interest on the longer loan. Even though it is with the same borrower, your money will be tied up longer. Furthermore, uncertainty about the future increases with length of time. Who knows?—someone may invent synthetic worms in ten years, or synthetic fish in fifty years. Can you imagine what those developments would do to International Worm Breeding?

Just how much additional interest rate you'll get for a longer loan depends on market conditions. There have been times when so many borrowers needed short-term loans at the same time that short-term rates were above long-term rates. This condition is a financial aberration and is symptomatic of stress in the money markets. Such conditions are usually corrected within twelve to twenty-four months.

Length of the bond versus the yield to maturity can be plotted on a graph. The following is typical:

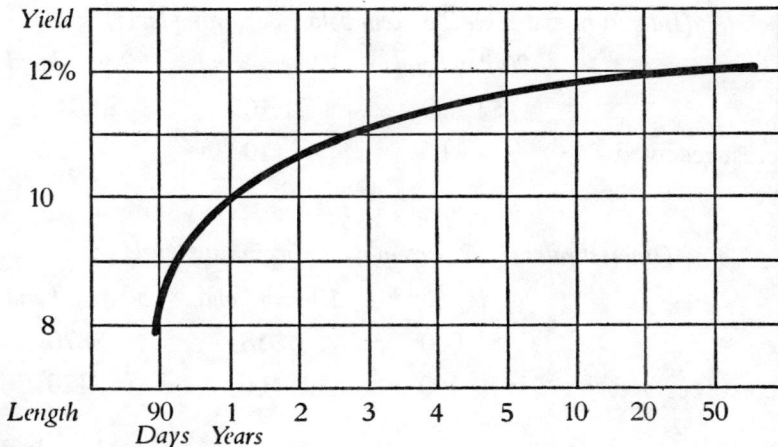

Notice how yield rises with time. If you connected the dots, they would form a curve. This curve is called the *yield curve.*

Undoubtedly some people are wondering why they should be the least bit interested in lengths and curves. Well, it pertains to your investment objectives. Suppose Worm Breeding is paying 8 percent on their ninety-day bonds, 10 percent on their ten-year bonds, and 12 percent on their fifty-year bonds. If you take the ninety-day loan, you'll get your money back in ninety days. Then you'll have to re-invest it. But you may not be able to reinvest again at 8 percent. Interest rates may have dropped to 6 percent by that time. If you keep investing in short ninety-day bonds, you take a chance that the income from your investment will bounce all over the place.

You may not want your income to bounce all over the place. You may want it to remain stable. If you buy Worm Breeding's fifty-year bonds, the interest you receive will remain constant at 12 percent the whole fifty years. But the price of the bond may bounce around. And the longer the bond, the more bouncing. To illustrate all this bouncing, consider the following situation.

First Year
(Beginning interest rates)

	90-day bond	10-year bond	50-year bond
Price	$1,000	$1,000	$1,000
Interest received	80	100	120

Second Year
(Interest rates decline 2 percent below beginning level)

	90-day bond	10-year bond	50-year bond
Price	$1,000	$1,105	$1,166
Interest received	60	100	120

Third Year
(Interest rates rise 2 percent above beginning level)

	90-day bond	10-year bond	50-year bond
Price	$1,000	$918	$876
Interest received	100	100	120

Look at how the interest you receive bounces around with the ninety-day bond. You get $80, then $60, then $100. If you had obligations and needed at least $80 a year, you would have been in trouble.

But the income trouble may not be as troublesome as the price trouble on the longer bonds. See how much the ten-year bond bounced around in price. It bounced from $1000 to $1105, then to $918. But see how much more the fifty-year bond bounced around. It bounced from $1000, to $1166, to $876. The longer the bond, the more volatile the price. That is good when the price is going up. But it's lousy when the price is going down. (Prices in this example are calculated using the formula on page 361. Please remember the formula is only a good approximation of what actual price experience would be.)

There is a way to use length to your advantage. First, decide how long you want to invest your money. If you need it back in six months to remodel your desert retreat, stay short with your investment. But if this is money you can tie up for a while, you can buy long bonds.

Second, if you can buy long bonds, adjust your length depending on what you think is going to happen to interest rates. If you think interest rates are going up, buy short-term bonds. By going short, you'll get less interest income now, but you'll have a chance to reinvest the money at higher rates in the future. Moreover, the risk of price declines on your bonds is reduced. However, if you think interest rates are going down, buy long-term bonds. You will lock in the high interest rates, and your bond price will go up as the interest rates go down.

You can avoid lots of downs, and enjoy higher income, if you pay attention to the length of your bonds. If you don't pay attention to length, your bond investment might wind up being a "can of worms."

◇ 50 ◇
Is a Convertible Bond
for You?

Contrary to some popular misbeliefs, a convertible bond has nothing to do with insurance on a fold-down, soft-top car. Instead, a convertible bond is a regular bond, issued by a regular corporation, that can be converted into regular shares of common stock. Generally, at the option of the bondholder, the bond can be exchanged or converted into a predetermined number of shares of common stock.

Being able to convert a bond into stock has some real advantages. If things are going badly in the stock market, the convertible bond will act like a regular bond. This means it will not decline as much as a stock. However, when things are going well in the stock market, the convertible bond will act like a stock. This means it will go up more than a regular bond.

A convertible bond can accomplish all this because of its hybrid nature. First it's a bond, then it's a stock. To see how it works, imagine you have been worrying for years about an invasion of aardvarks. Naturally, you would be enthusiastic to find a firm that had just invented aardvark repellent. The company believes the repellent works because there have been no confirmed sightings of aardvarks near their repellent plant in Nome, Alaska. You want to invest, of course. In this particular company, you have three investment choices: common stock, bonds, and convertible bonds. The stock sells for $50 a share and pays $2 each year in dividends. The bond has twenty years to maturity, sells for $1000 a bond, and pays $150 in interest each year. The convertible bond also has twenty years to maturity, sells for $1000 a bond, but pays only $120 in interest each year. However, it has a conversion feature. The conversion feature lets you exchange the bond for sixteen shares of stock any time you want. No one wants to convert today because at $50 a share, the sixteen shares of stock are only worth $800.

To see how the convertible bond works, imagine that the International Society for Prevention of Inhumane Treatment of Aardvarks (ISPITA) starts picketing the company. Here's what happens to the securities.

◇ *Stock.* Investors dump the stock. It plummets 40 percent to $30 a share. At $30, the stock has a yield of 6.7 percent ($2.00 dividend ÷ $30 price = 6.7% yield).

◇ *Bond.* Pro-aardvark militants have not affected market interest rates. The bond is still selling at $1000 with a yield to maturity of 15 percent ($150 interest ÷ $1000 price = 15% yield).

◇ *Convertible.* At first the convertible falls with the stock. But because it pays fixed interest, like a bond, the price is soon low enough that it is selling like a bond. It drops to $800, which gives it a yield to maturity of 15 percent ($120 interest ÷ $800 price = 15% yield). The convertible's decline in value is 20 percent, far less than the 40 percent drop for the stock, but more than the straight bond.

Now assume the leader of ISPITA (the rabble-rousers) takes a job with the repellent company. He becomes vice-president of public relations. The stock moves back to $50, the bond still sells for $1000, and the convertible's price once again returns to $1000.

No sooner has this occurred than the U.S. Congress is inundated by aardvarks. A bill is immediately introduced calling for the purchase of two cases of aardvark repellent. Here's what happens.

◇ *Stock.* Speculators rush to buy the stock. The price jumps from $50 to $75. The move represents appreciation of 50 percent. The stock's yield, with a $2 dividend, becomes 2.7 percent.

◇ *Bond.* Free-market interest rates are ignoring aardvarks, and would like to ignore Congress. The bond continues selling for $1000 at a yield to maturity of 15 percent.

◇ *Convertible.* As the stock price goes up, so does the value of the convertible's conversion feature. The convertible can be turned into sixteen shares of stock. With the stock at $75, the bond is worth $1200, up 20 percent. The convertible is not up as much as the stock, but it is up more than the bond. And the convertible may actually be worth more than the $1200. At $1200, still paying $120 a year interest, it has a current yield of 10 percent, substantially more than the 2.7 percent on the stock.

The yield difference between the stock and the convertible is important. Without the difference, there would be no reason to hold the convertible. To illustrate, assume that after twenty-three months of committee hearings, testimony, political logrolling, filibustering, and debate, and with senators standing knee deep in aardvark chips, a repellent bill is finally passed. The financial fortunes of the company improve dramatically, and the company quadruples the dividend on the stock from $2 to $8.

◇ *Stock.* Investors are ecstatic; the stock goes to $200 and yields 4 percent ($8.00 dividend ÷ $200 price = 4% yield).

◇ *Bond.* Dividend increases do not mean anything to the bondholders. The bond still sells for $1000 with a yield to maturity of 15 percent.

◇ *Convertible.* Theoretically, the convertible's price should go to $3200, reflecting the price increase of the stock (16 shares × $200 price). But convertible holders quickly realize they get only $120 per year income if they hold the convertible. However, they can get $128 a year by converting to sixteen shares of stock (16 shares × $8 dividend = $128). So that's what convertible holders will do—they will convert. And if they all convert, the convertible bond issue will disappear.

Only the aardvarks are outlandish in this story. Convertible bonds really do have different characteristics under different conditions. When the stock is depressed, the convertible declines less. It is a better holding than the stock, but not as good as the bond. The convertible doesn't decline more because it is soon selling like a bond. When the stock is going up, the convertible goes up as well. It goes up because of the value in the conversion feature. However, it usually doesn't go up as much as the stock. But it does go up more than the bond. Furthermore, the annual income from the convertible is usually below the bond and above the stock. Then if the dividend income on the stock does rise above the coupon income on the convertible, investors will exercise their conversion privilege.

Convertible bonds may not protect you or your soft-top car from aardvarks. But these bonds can be good financial protection. They are especially useful when you're not very sure what the stock is going to do.

◇ 51 ◇

Tax Advantages
of Municipal Bonds

A municipal bond is a bond like any other bond, except that the interest is exempt from federal income taxes. Because the bond is issued by a municipal authority, the federal government does not tax the interest. Tax-free interest makes municipal bonds something special. There aren't many forms of earnings the federal government *doesn't* tax. They even tax the interest on their own bonds.

You might imagine that any investment the federal government doesn't tax would be very popular, and municipal bonds *are* very popular. They are so popular that their yields are lower than other bonds—much lower. For example, if a taxable bond is yielding 15 percent, it is not uncommon for a municipal bond of similar quality to yield only 8.0 or 9.0 percent. However, even at these lower yields, municipal bonds are better investments than taxable bonds for many taxpayers, such as taxpayers who are in high tax brackets. For example,

Taxpayer in 50 Percent Bracket

	Taxable bond	Municipal bond
Cost of bond	$1,000	$1,000
Yield on bond	15%	9%
Annual interest	$ 150	$ 90
Less federal taxes at 50%	75	0
After-tax earnings	$ 75	$ 90

As far as after-tax earnings are concerned, this particular taxpayer is better off buying the municipal bond. His or her after-tax earnings equal $90 compared to only $75 on the taxable bond. This taxpayer would be better off with the taxable bond, however, if he or she were in the 30 percent bracket:

369

Taxpayer in the 30 Percent Bracket

	Taxable bond	Municipal bond
Cost of bond	$1,000	$1,000
Yield on bond	15%	9%
Annual interest	$ 150	$ 90
Less federal taxes at 30%	45	0
After-tax earnings	$ 105	$ 90

There is a simple formula that allows the investor to quickly determine if his or her tax bracket is high enough to benefit from buying a municipal bond:

$$\text{Tax bracket (\%)} \quad = \quad 1 \quad - \quad \frac{\text{Municipal bond yield}}{\text{Taxable bond yield}}$$

In our example a taxpayer in the 40 percent tax bracket is right on the fence between a municipal and a taxable bond:

$$\text{Tax bracket (\%)} \quad = \quad 1 \quad - \quad \frac{9\%}{15\%} \quad = \quad 40\%$$

Taxpayer in 40 Percent Bracket

	Taxable bond	Municipal bond
Cost	$1,000	$1,000
Yield	15%	9%
Annual interest	$ 150	$ 90
Less federal taxes at 40%	60	0
After-tax earnings	$ 90	$ 90

If the taxpayer's tax bracket is above 40 percent, he or she should buy the municipal bond. If it is below 40 percent, he or she should buy the taxable bond. If it is right at 40 percent, the taxpayer should flip a coin.

Making purchase decisions by flipping coins is never a good idea. Making purchase decisions based entirely on after-tax earnings isn't a good idea, either. Bonds vary substantially in quality. What good is tax-free interest if the bond goes into default and doesn't pay any interest? Determining the quality of municipal bonds is very hard—much harder than determining the quality of corporate bonds.

Determining quality is difficult because it is often hard to identify clearly where the revenues will come from to pay the bonds and how certain they are to continue. Furthermore, the underlying asset may not be worth anything if its original purpose doesn't pan out. For example, suppose you buy sewer bonds issued by the city of Last Gasp, Wyoming. Suppose that just after the sewer project is completed, Fred's Barbershop—the largest employer in Last Gasp— closes down. The community may suffer economically and be unable to make the payments on the sewer. What are you, the bondholder, going to do? Repossess the sewer?

Fortunately, Standard & Poor's and Moody's rate many of the large municipalities. Unfortunately, many municipal bond issues are not rated by these services. If you are a layperson, it is good advice to stick with good-quality rated bonds.

Federal taxes are not your only problem. You have local taxes as well. You should consider the effect of local taxes when considering municipal bonds. Most states do not tax interest on bonds issued by municipalities within their own states. But a few states do. Many states tax interest on municipal bonds from outside their state. No general rules can be given, because of the wide differences between states. Check with your local tax officials to determine the law in your state.

◇ 52 ◇
Series "EE" Bonds

A Series EE bond, or savings bond, is a bond issued by the federal government. The "EE" stands for "earnings"—your earnings. If you have any earnings left over after paying taxes, the government would like to have them. This seems to confirm what some citizens already believe: The government wants everything you make.

The government doesn't really look at it as wanting everything you make—they look at EE bonds as promoting thrift. They want you to be thrifty so the government can finance the huge deficits it runs. Regardless of the logic, EE bonds can be a good, thrifty thing for many people to buy.

Certainly they are different from taxes—there is no law saying you must have them. Furthermore, the government will buy them back at maturity, plus interest. The government doesn't return your taxes with interest. So, to you, EE bonds are a form of savings.

As savings, EE bonds have some unique characteristics:

1. They can be purchased through payroll deduction at many large employers.

2. EE bonds do not pay interest in the normal way. They pay the interest all at one time, when they mature and are cashed in. So instead of getting daily interest, as on a savings account, a $50 EE bond gets paid off at $100 per bond in eight years. That equals an interest rate of 9 percent.

The interest rates you will earn to various dates of redemption are as follows (rate schedule as of May 1, 1981):

Redemption at the end of year	Annual yield	Redemption at the end of year	Annual yield
Year 1	5.92%	Year 5	8.52%
Year 2	6.51%	Year 6	8.69%
Year 3	7.50%	Year 7	8.86%
Year 4	8.24%	Year 8	9.00%

3. EE bonds are purchased and paid off in the following amounts:

Purchase price	Value at maturity	Years to maturity	Compound annual rate of return
$ 25	$ 50	8	9%
37.50	75	8	9
50	100	8	9
100	200	8	9
250	500	8	9
500	1,000	8	9
2,500	5,000	8	9
5,000	10,000	8	9

4. If you do not want to cash your EE bonds in at maturity, you can hold them for ten more years and they will continue to increase in value.

5. If at some point you need to receive cash from your bonds, you may trade your Series EE bonds for Series HH bonds at their accumulated value. Series HH bonds pay interest by check semi-annually.

6. You can cash your EE bonds in at any time. However, you may be penalized for cashing in your bonds early. Instead of getting 5.92 percent compound interest rate, you may receive as little as 4.5 percent.

7. EE bonds are guaranteed by the federal government. Even if they are lost or destroyed, the government will replace them.

8. Usually there are other secure investments readily available to you that pay higher rates of interest. For instance, depending on the money markets you can probably buy an insured savings certificate at a bank that pays more interest.

9. For tax purposes, you can either choose to declare your interest as it is earned or all at one time when the bond is cashed in. This may create some tax advantages for you.

With all these characteristics, the biggest advantage of Series EE bonds is their payroll deduction feature. The government really understands the importance of payroll deductions—notice how your taxes are collected. When your EE bond savings program is set up on payroll deduction, it becomes a form of forced savings. The money is taken out before you can get your check-writing hands on it. Because you never have to handle the money, you don't have to worry about spending it before you get a chance to save it. And for many people that is an important feature.

EE bonds are not generally considered the greatest investment in the world. But they are safe, and secure, and better than nothing. And if the payroll deduction forced savings feature is important to you, then you should seriously consider EE bonds. After all, you should be thrifty, even if the government isn't.

◇ 53 ◇
Why Buy Real Estate?

Real estate may be the oldest form of investment but its popularity is still strong even today. There are several reasons why it is still a very popular form of investment.

1. *Ease of entry.* Owning some form of real estate is generally within reach for a majority of Americans.

2. *Love of ownership.* Most people have a subjective drive to own some real estate: a house, some land, or a building. This love may be the most important factor in the desire for real estate ownership in many cases.

3. *Rising prices.* Most people have witnessed steadily rising real estate values. These increases have made real estate an attractive investment. There is a growing population, but only a fixed amount of land. In this case, the laws of supply and demand dictate rising real estate prices.

Because real estate is easy to buy, and because people love to own it, and because it keeps going up in value, it is no wonder that real estate is still a very popular form of investment today.

Real estate's popularity comes in many different forms. The following table lists the most common types and compares their overall suitability to the ordinary investor. As you study the table, there are four columns to give special attention to:

◇ Column 2: *Suited to ordinary investor.* Because of the risks, or the sophistication, required, or the effort needed, many real estate investments are not appropriate for the ordinary American.

◇ Column 5: *Owner effort required.* Unlike many investments, real estate can require great amounts of physical effort. Many investors underestimate their effort when they buy.

◇ Column 10: *Cash flow before sale.* Many real estate investments not only require a lot of money for the initial purchase, many also require a lot of money while the project is being held. Investors need to be prepared for this cash flow.

◇ Column 10: *Overall investment risk.* Sometimes investors do not realize there is risk associated with real estate. It is possible to lose a lot, perhaps everything, in real estate.

Comparison of Real Estate Characteristics

Col. 1 Types of real estate	Col. 2 Suited to ordinary investor	Col. 3 Source of financing	Col. 4 Where to buy or sell	Col. 5 Owner effort required
Single-family houses	Yes	Thrift institution, bank, mortgage co.	Agent	Substantial
Condominiums	Yes	Thrift institution, bank, mortgage co., developer	Agent or developer	Substantial
1–4 unit rentals	Yes	Thrift institution, bank, mortgage co.	Agent	Heavy
Apartment building	Wealthy	Thrift institution, bank, insurance co., REIT, pensions	Commercial agent	Heavy plus a manager
Commercial shopping centers	Sophisticated, wealthy	Banks, insurance co., REIT, pensions, private investors	Commercial agent	Heavy plus a manager
Commercial office building	Sophisticated, wealthy	Banks, insurance co., REIT, pensions, private investors	Commercial agent	Heavy plus a manager
Industrial building	Sophisticated, wealthy	Banks, insurance co., REIT, pensions private investors	Commercial agent	Heavy plus a manager
Raw land	Yes	Thrift institution, bank	Agent	Low
Land development	Sophisticated	Bank, REIT	Developer	Extreme
Recreational land lots	Yes	Developer	Developer	None
Agricultural	Yes	Bank	Agent	Substantial
Real estate syndications	Wealthy	Syndicator	Syndicator	None

Col. 6	Col. 7 Price appreciation potential		Col. 8 Maximum depreciation rate	Col. 9 Cash flow before sale	Col. 10 Overall investment risk
Inflation	Created value				
Good	Fair		None	Negative	Low
Fair	Poor		None	Negative	Low
Good	Fair to good		175%, 15 yrs	Moderately positive	Low
Fair to good	Fair to good		175%, 15 yrs	Moderately positive	Moderate
Fair	Fair to excellent		175%, 15 yrs*	Moderately positive	Moderate to high
Fair	Fair to excellent		175%, 15 yrs*	Moderately positive	Moderate to high
Fair	Fair to excellent		175%, 15 yrs*	Moderately positive	Moderate to extreme
Poor to fair	Excellent		None	Negative	Low
Poor to fair	Excellent		None	Highly negative	Extreme
Poor	Poor		None	Negative	High
Fair	Fair to good		None	Positive	Moderate
Fair	Fair to good		175%, 15 yrs*	Positive	Moderate to high

*Subject to recapture provisions on all depreciation.

Some of the terms used in the comparison may be unfamiliar. Most will be discussed in the following sections. The types of real estate are familiar to most people, but they are worth elaborating on anyway.

⋄ *Single-family houses.* This category refers to "Home Sweet Home": a dwelling for a single family—your family. In many ways, your home should not be considered an investment. It should be considered a shelter for your family. The love of ownership is a driving force in the purchase of a single-family house.

⋄ *Condominiums.* These are the same as single-family houses except they are attached to other condominiums. Instead of a yard between yourself and the neighbors, there is a wall.

⋄ *1–4 unit rentals.* These are single-family structures, or duplexes, or fourplexes. They are just like regular houses except that your main purpose in owning them is to rent the units and make money.

⋄ *Apartment buildings.* These units are also owned for rental and investment. The distinction between apartments and 1–4 unit rentals is size, required investment, and unit management. All these factors are greater with apartments.

⋄ *Commercial shopping centers.* These buildings house businesses dealing with the retail public. These businesses run from pet stores to department stores, from shoe repairers to jewelers. The cost of shopping center ownership is high, professional management is needed, and usually a large part of the rental income is tied to the success of businesses that operate there.

⋄ *Commercial office buildings.* These buildings contain business offices. Business offices house everyone from corporate executives to dentists, from bureaucratic pencil pushers to inhumane electronic computers. Leases are usually long, and the tenants are usually stable. However, they usually demand a lot from their landlords.

⋄ *Industrial buildings.* Industrial buildings are where things are made, packaged, inspected, stored, and so on. Frequently the buildings are very specialized. If the businesses that operate there fail, the buildings may become practically worthless.

◊ *Raw land.* Raw land is not currently being used for any economic purpose.

◊ *Land development.* In order to convert uneconomical raw land to economical developed land, a land developer must get involved. He or she arranges for permits, proper zoning, adequate financing, construction of buildings, and somebody to buy it all. Development can be a very risky business even for the most sophisticated operator.

◊ *Recreational land lots.* These are lots, or frequently future lots, in a large land development. Typically the land is in a potential resort. Typically the buyer makes payments for years before he or she gets any claim to ownership. Typically the developer uses the payments to complete the development of the lots. Typically things don't go as well as the buyer imagined. And typically the buyer winds up frustrated, disappointed, and angry.

◊ *Agricultural.* These are farms and ranches. The land has economic value for its ability to grow agricultural products.

◊ *Real estate syndications.* In these financial arrangements, a real estate syndicator arranges for investors to give him or her money. He or she invests the money in real estate. The investors receive the financial benefits associated with ownership. The syndicator takes care of the operating headaches associated with ownership. Syndications are marvelous ideas. Unfortunately, far too many are ill conceived and don't work out to be marvelous investments.

There are still many other forms of real estate. And there are ways to make money on all of them. Money can be made through operating profits, increases in value, and tax advantages. But making money isn't the only reason to own real estate. Many people just love it. We can't be sure why real estate was so popular when our ancestors were fighting over which cave to live in. But it is easy to see why it's so popular today.

Real Estate Investing Is Easy—Isn't It?

No! Absolutely not! Many people today think real estate investing is easy—it's not.

It seems that nearly everyone has a cousin who flunked kindergarten and then went on to make a fortune in real estate. And even people without cousins can see neighbors all around who made money on their houses. (See Chapter 56, "Are Houses Great Investments?") All this makes real estate look like a sure thing, but it's not.

As evidence that real estate is not a sure thing, we can look at history—fairly recent history. Between 1973 and 1976, the U.S. real estate market suffered a cataclysmic depression. It is impossible to calculate the total dollars lost in real estate nationwide. Some $5 billion in losses were experienced by the real estate investment industry alone. The depression left major American cities with more than 40 million square feet of unused office space to be worked off, 44,000 vacant condominiums in Florida to be rented, more than 60,000 acres of improved but undeveloped residential land to be built on, and hundreds and hundreds of bankruptcies among developers, contractors, investors, and owners. It took years to work through the problems. Those without staying power didn't make it. The 1973–1976 period was an unhappy time in U.S. real estate history.

This bit of history is remembered here mostly for its therapeutic shock value, not for the purpose of convincing anyone to abandon all ideas of real estate ownership. Real estate can be rewarding. But your rewards, and enjoyment, will be greatest if you bear in mind the following special characteristics of real estate ownership.

1. *Physical work.* Many real estate owners try to operate by themselves the real estate ventures they own. Managing any piece of real estate is hard work. It is physical work, it is emotional work. Be sure you are realistic about the work and that you are well suited to it.

2. *Fixed location.* Real estate cannot be moved. If anything at all goes wrong with the location, you're stuck.

3. *Regional influences.* The fundamentals of real estate are very regionalized. The economic situation of the city, and even of the neighborhood, affects the property. This may be either good or bad, depending on which way the fundamentals are going.

4. *Illiquidity.* Real estate can't usually be sold in a big hurry. A month is usually required, as an absolute minimum, just to close after the buyer says he or she will take it. And it can take

months, even years, to get that buyer. This can create real problems if you need to unload the property in a hurry.

5. *No trading market.* You are never really sure what your property is worth, because there is no trading market for real estate, like a stock exchange. Without such a market, you can't be sure how much the value of your property is going up—or down.

6. *Heavy financial leverage.* Most properties are mortgaged to the rooftops. This is great when things are going well. It is a disaster when things are going badly.

7. *Speculation.* Real estate, like any investment, may be subject to wild speculation. As soon as people start believing there is no way to lose, buying too much of the same thing, and paying too much money, you've got speculation and you've got problems—big problems.

No!—Real estate investing isn't easy. Yes!—It may be very rewarding. It very likely will be rewarding to even investors that flunked kindergarten if they understand it, work hard at it, and use plenty of good old basic common sense.

◇ 54 ◇

The Fundamentals
of Making Money
in Real Estate

One of the most important fundamentals in making money in real estate is to figure out if you really want to make money in real estate.

For many people, making money is just an excuse to be in real estate. Many people are really more in love with the idea of owning real estate than with the idea of making money. The first thing you need to decide is which is which for you. If your real, true, deep-down subjective feeling is that you really want to own some property for the love of it, then quit trying to convince your friends that you're doing it for the money. Having a hobby is OK. If it is a hobby, you can afford to be more lenient with your analysis and look at fundamentals that are important to you. Who knows, you might make some money, too.

For example, there's a family that fell in love with the mountains while on vacation. After a year of stewing about it, they sold their home in Wichita, Kansas, and purchased a small resort high in the Colorado Rockies. The tourist season was short, and anyone with a pencil and the back of an envelope could see the place couldn't support them financially. They knew it, too. But they loved mountains. He got an extra job delivering mail all over the eastern front range. She worked as a nurse, sometimes as far as two winding-road hours away, in Denver. And the whole family worked like pioneers to keep the twelve small cabins clean and rented. A financial success? Twenty-five years later, the land is probably worth something, but they never earned enough to buy a Cadillac or take a world tour. Would they change anything? Not on your life. Was this piece of real estate a good investment for them? For them it was, even though they could have earned more putting their money in a savings account.

Not everyone wants that type of life. Many people are happy being doctors or teachers or carpenters, and so on, and many of these people want to own real estate strictly as an investment. If you are serious about investing in real estate, just for the money, you will analyze the fundamentals very critically before you buy. You won't let your love for the property cloud your objectivity, and you will run the real estate like a business after you own it.

As a business, real estate has many fundamentals in common with all businesses and a few unique ones. The unique ones are of most interest to someone contemplating an investment in real estate. The following sections deal with the unique characteristics of real estate. The following sections deal with the unique characteristics of real estate. They include revenue, expenses, inflation, created value, depreciation, cash on cash, and leverage.

Revenue

Revenue in real estate usually means rental. Because most real estate is an operating business as well as an investment, revenue is very important.

It is fundamental to realize that each piece of real estate is capable of generating its own unique rental stream. Really no two pieces are identical. Therefore, as you analyze a potential real estate property you must examine the market and make a judgment about the revenue it can generate. Here are some of the key considerations:

Type of property. Residential units like apartments typically collect monthly rent. Retail property frequently collects monthly rent based on square footage plus a percentage of the sales. Commercial property may generate revenue based on basic space rental plus amounts for various services supplied by the landlord, e.g., maintenance, security, etc. Hotels collect rent based on daily occupancy. There are numerous other examples.

Location. Rental practices vary from state to state and city to city. Practices may even vary from one part of town to another. For instance, in many communities apartments typically rent subject to a one-year lease. However, in many locations one-month leases are used.

Neighborhood is important as well. In fact, all real estate experts will tell you this aspect of location is the single most important fundamental of real estate. A lovely duplex may collect $1000 a month rent in a good neighborhood. The same duplex may struggle to collect $700 in a slum. A shopping center on the off ramp of a busy freeway will do better than the identical property buried among some warehouses far from any decent roads.

Competition. Competition may hit you from several angels. First, your neighborhood may be overbuilt. Because real estate has large fixed costs, there is a tendency for landlords to drop their rates quickly to attract tenants.

In most communities residential properties suffer competition from small landlords. Owners of one or two rental units tend to price too cheaply. Further, they tend to get to know their tenants personally and then find it difficult to raise rents as much as they could. These small landlords represent a significant portion of most markets.

Rents do rise, of course. But often they rise more slowly than inflation (and always more slowly than the landlord wants). Rent increases are held down by leases, by fear of losing tenants, by fear of rent controls in some markets, and by large numbers of landlords not keeping abreast of the current market conditions.

Competition in real estate is a complex problem. Smart landlords will spend considerable time understanding the competition.

Vacancy. Renters do move around. In some parts of the country turnover in rental units is 150 percent a year. A turnover of 100 percent is not at all uncommon. And all this occurs despite leases. Leases can usually be broken as easily as a frayed thread. Study the local area to make an estimate. How long the unit will stand vacant before it is rented again is also an issue. There are two variables to consider: (1) How long will it take you to clean up the unit for re-rent? (2) How long will it take to get a suitable tenant? Some specialized commercial property can take years to rent, while some big professional organizations fire managers that can't rerent apartments in two days or less.

Lost rental due to vacancies is not the only loss of rent you may experience. Renters, particularly apartment renters, are sometimes slow in paying. In fact, many will get behind a couple of months, if you let them. Once they're that far behind, they often skip out. Professional management organizations are really tough collectors. Local laws permitting, such organizations start eviction proceedings within ten days of a missed payment. And within those ten days, they contact the delinquent renter four times. They rarely accept sob stories in lieu of cash. Most owner-landlords do not have the stomach to be that tough. So the owner-landlords' losses are higher.

Expenses

There are expenses associated with real estate. There are expenses associated with all businesses. Real estate expenses vary from property to property. In general, you can expect the following types of expenses and cash outlays.

⋄ *Principal.* Nearly every piece of real estate has a loan against it. The principal of the loan must be repaid, of course. Principal payments are *not* deductible from income taxes. All other items in this list are deductible.

⋄ *Interest.* This is the cost of borrowing the money. In most mortgages, there is one level payment for the life of the loan. In these cases, the interest paid is heavy during the early years, and the payments to principal are light. It is not unusual for 95 percent of the payments to go to interest in the early years of a mortgage. These heavy interest payments have their pro's and con's. The pro is that interest is deductible from taxes, giving you a big deduction in the early years. The con is that very little equity buildup occurs through payments. You have to count on inflation to give you an equity cushion.

⋄ *Taxes.* Property taxes and special assessments will be levied by the state, the city, and often by several other political subdivisions as well. The better your property, the higher your taxes. Property taxes are also deductible from income taxes.

⋄ *Insurance.* You will need insurance protection against damage and liability. Insurance may even be needed if there are no buildings on the property. You may need liability coverage even on raw land.

⋄ *Maintenance.* These costs will vary from property to property. It is the one cost you have some control over. You can decide to keep things in good shape, or not. But even your flexibility on maintenance is limited in many communities. Most areas have ordinances requiring upkeep. In fact, in many cases you'll have upkeep on raw land, because you'll be required to mow the weeds.

◇ *Miscellaneous.* There are many other expenses you may encounter depending on your property: utilities, advertising, manager's salaries, security, legal fees, and many more.

As with any business, you need to make a careful estimate of expenses and revenues before you buy anything. A careful analysis of expenses is especially important with real estate. Expense analysis is more important with real estate than with almost any other investment because it is a business. And expense analysis may be more important with real estate than with most other businesses because most of the expenses are fixed. They are fixed whether you have any revenue or not.

The revenue may vary a lot. You may lose renters, or renters may be slow in paying. Or you may not sell the property when you want. But despite all the possible revenue problems, the expenses will continue at a constant level. The payments are constant, the taxes are constant, the insurance is constant, the maintenance must continue, and so forth. The bottom line is that in real estate, if something goes wrong with your expected revenue, you can be sure something will go wrong with your expected profits. And with these kinds of things going wrong, you will find other things going, too. In fact, you'll find you can go broke—fast.

Inflation

Real estate values tend to increase over time. Land values rise because there is a fixed amount of land and a growing population. The buildings on the land *go down in value*. In recent years, however, the cost of new construction has risen so fast that the value of even old buildings has increased. Inflation has become all-important to real estate investors. Much of the modern real estate industry is based on the idea of inflation. Constantly rising prices will make even a poor investor look smart—eventually.

Inflation also has a way of attracting unsophisticated investors into the market. What these unsophisticated people should be told is that real estate prices don't always go up—in a straight line, at least. Prices often get ahead of themselves. Then they may go down, or nowhere. These down or nowhere periods can last for years and years and years. If you buy property at the wrong price and the wrong time, and in the wrong place, you may not be able to hold out for years and years and years. It is possible you will lose money, maybe lots of money, perhaps all your money. It is not wise simply to assume that inflation will make your investment look good.

Determining what the rate of inflation will be is not easy, because real estate is a very localized type of investment. True rates of real estate inflation have been about 3 percent for the past forty or fifty years. In the last ten years, they have been more like 8 to 12 percent. The last decade has been a period when inflation in the whole world has been nearly out of control. Many people think real estate inflation has been even greater than general inflation. In fact, the prices of many pieces of property have risen at extremely rapid rates. But if you intend to do a hard-nosed analysis of a piece of real estate, you are well advised to be very cautious in your inflation outlook as it pertains to the sales value of your property. Many real estate deals don't make any sense at all unless a high rate of inflation is assumed. Such deals should be avoided. You can't control inflation. You can't turn it on or off. Because you can't influence inflation, don't make a big decision that depends on it.

Created Value

Frequently value increases in real estate are created. Value is created by adding improvements to the property, or near it. This type of value increase is not really inflation, although many people confuse the two. You might ask, "What is the value of canvas and paints?" Not a great deal when purchased at the store, but possibly enormous after the master artist has finished his or her work. It wasn't inflation that increased the value of the paints.

Artistic work in real estate can take many forms. Great imagination, skill, and perseverance may be required. And after all that, hope for some dumb luck, too.

Sheepherder Sam (a real guy with a fictitious name) was the scroungiest character you ever met in your life. He smelled so bad his sheep kept moving just to stay upwind from him. All he owned in the world was a small house trailer and 2000 acres of barren, desolate Arizona desert. He didn't even buy the land—he inherited it. And he was lucky to still have it, considering the number of poker games it had been in. Sam couldn't think of a thing to do with the land, except raise sheep. Then one day a development company offered him $500 an acre for his land. Sam took it. By dumb luck, he made $1 million.

What about the development company? The company was
headed by a true real estate artist. He knew that a freeway would be
needed going north of the city. So he spent hours studying public
documents about the land out in that direction. Before long, he
could see the conclusion the engineers were obviously going to
come to: A major interchange would have to be right in the middle
of Sheepherder Sam's desert. He also figured out that Sam's land
was desert for only about 150 feet down; then there was water. And
with all that going for it, Sam's desert could become a whole new
suburb. Well, the ending to the story is obvious. Sam made $1 mil-
lion; the developer made $10 million.

There are many ways to create value—buying old homes and re-
furbishing them; adding a feature in an apartment building, then
raising the rent; changing office space to retail space; and so on.
There are lots of ways to improve the value of the land.

Improved value is the way most people make money on their
real estate. The city grows into them, or a shopping center goes up
nearby, or a freeway comes close, or something makes the property worth more. Most people do not use great artistry to bring this
about. Most people are a little lucky, just like Sam. But you can improve your luck by using common sense. You can see which way
the population is moving and try to get in front of it.

Be careful not to get in front of the population too late, however.
A good way to lose money on real estate is buying land near major
new developments well after everyone else already knows about
them.

Willard heard about a new airport from a secretary who worked
for the city council. He knew land values would rise. He also knew
it would take years to work out all the problems, convince the public, sell the bonds, and so on. He was right—it took more than eleven years just to break ground for construction. Not one of the
original city councilors was still in office when the airport was finished.

Willard kept track of progress, and two months before the airport opened he bought land along a major access road. He was im-
pressed to find out the land had appreciated four times in value in
the last ten years—and no developments had even started yet. But
Willard knew developments were starting. The papers had announced several new hotels would be built. He figured his land
would be perfect for a restaurant or something. He figured that
within a year he could unload his land at a huge profit. Willard was

almost right again. His land was perfect for a restaurant. People did contact him about buying it. But in five years he did not receive one offer even equal to what he had paid. To this day, Willard can't figure out where he made his mistake. After all, he had been right about so many things.

Being right about creating land values is something you'll have to do by yourself. There is no way this book, or any book, can tell you how to predict accurately increases in value due to improvements. There are millions of different situations. But although there is no way to generalize about the numbers, some general questions can help sharpen your judgment. If you come up with positive answers to these questions, add something in your analysis for improved value.

⋄ Are there obvious ways to improve the use of the property (for example, by putting a building on a vacant lot, or remodeling an old apartment)?
⋄ Does the area need this type of real estate?
⋄ Is the population growing toward the area?
⋄ Are public amenities adequate (for example, schools, roads, and sewers)?
⋄ Do the political attitudes and laws favor growth or stagnation?
⋄ What are the demographic and income patterns?
⋄ Is there a solid, growing employment base?
⋄ Does the value of your project depend on the success of a major development near by? If so, how long must you wait? Do you have the jump on most people?
⋄ What has been the recent experience of similar property nearby?

In real estate, location is everything. With proper location, you can benefit from the generally improved land values. And with proper location, you can exercise your own artistic real estate skills and create even more value. But location is important. After all, what would Michelangelo's Sistine Chapel painting have been worth on the ceiling of the emperor's dungeon?

Depreciation

Depreciation is a favorite subject for real estate investors. Through the magic of depreciation, many investors can make money while they are experiencing a loss. Many pessimistic people feel they are going to lose money on their investments anyway, so they figure they might as well make money while they're losing it.

Making money while losing it is possible because of depreciation. Depreciation is deductible for tax purposes, which saves cash, but it is not a cash expense. Instead, *depreciation* is a theoretical accounting term. In the case of real estate, it is very theoretical. As assets such as buildings get older, they depreciate. One day the asset is so old and depreciated it must be scrapped. In theory, if money is put aside every year to cover depreciation, there will be enough on hand to replace the old asset with a new one. The government allows you to deduct this theoretical money you are putting aside every year from your taxes. And that's fine with trucks and machinery, but when it comes to buildings, no one ever puts the money aside. People don't put the money aside because they don't need to. Most pieces of real estate "appreciate" in value rather than "depreciate" in value. So when the first investor is tired of owning the building, he or she can sell it, usually for more than he or she paid for it in the first place.

The numbers on depreciation work this way: Suppose a wealthy tight-rope walker earns $100,000 a year risking her neck to give people a thrill. At that income level, she would like to get some tax deductions. So she buys a building. Assume the building makes absolutely no profit—but it does develop $52,500 worth of depreciation. Look at the comparison of her cash in the bank with and without the building (page 391).

This tight-rope walker can balance on more than a high wire. She invested in a building that makes absolutely no cash money. The cash coming in the door from rents is equal to the cash going out the door from operations. So the whole building showed a loss of $52,500 when depreciation was considered. When her loss was offset against her personal income taxes, she wound up paying $19,565 in taxes or $29,435 less than the $49,000 she would have paid without the building. That meant she put $29,435 more in the bank than she would have without the depreciation.

Depreciation is obviously something real estate owners want to know a lot about. The first thing to know is how to calculate it. There are a number of rules governing real estate, and it's impossible to cover them all here. One rule does apply across the board: You cannot depreciate the land—only the building.

Tax Comparison

	Without building	With building
Tight-rope-walking salary	$100,000	$100,000
Expenses for parachutes and ulcer medicine	2,000	2,000
Taxable income before building (A)	$ 98,000	$ 98,000
Add Building Income:		
Rent (cash)	$ 0	$100,000
Expenses (cash)	$ 0	100,000
Building cash profit	$ 0	$ 0
Depreciation expense (non-cash)	0	52,500
Taxable income (loss) on building (B)	$ 0	$ (52,500)
Net taxable income (line A − B)	$ 98,000	$ 45,500
Tax rate	50%	43%
Taxes	$ 49,000	$ 19,565

The 1981 Economic Recovery Act made substantial changes in depreciation rules. Here we will discuss only those relating to real estate.

First, the basis for depreciation is known as "straight line" depreciation. The value of the property is divided by the years of usable life. The usable life of a building is generally defined by the regulations. Thirty-five and forty-five years are most common.

To see how this works assume the tightrope walker's building cost $450,000 and has a useful life of forty-five years for depreciation purposes. Her straight line depreciation will be $10,000 a year.

Building cost	$450,000
Useful life	÷ 45 years
Annual depreciation	$ 10,000

Second, new tax law allows the use of accelerated depreciation. The accelerated depreciation rules increase the deductible depreciation in two ways: (a) by assuming a fifteen-year life rather than a forty-five year life, and (b) by multiplying the straight line depreciation by 175 percent. Now the tightrope walker's depreciation jumps from $10,000 to $52,500.

Building cost	$450,000
Useful life	÷ 15 years
Straight line depreciation	$30,000
Acceleration factor	× 175%
First-year depreciation	$ 52,500

The depreciation will decline every year, because as depreciation is deducted from taxes it is also subtracted from the depreciable cost of the building. So, in the second year the depreciation is $49,688.

Building cost	$450,000
Previous depreciation	− 52,500
Remaining depreciable value	$397,500
Remaining useful life	÷ 14 years
Straight line depreciation	$ 28,393
Acceleration factor	× 175%
Second-year depreciation	$ 49,688

The tightrope walker is allowed to use the 175 percent acceleration factor until the amount of her annual depreciation declines below fifteen-year straight line depreciation or $30,000. At that point she may use straight line until the building is fully depreciated.

Third, no salvage value assumption is required when calculating real estate depreciation.

Fourth, the building will probably be subject to recapture if accelerated depreciation is used. Recapture means much or all of the depreciation that was taken will be subject to ordinary income taxes when the property is sold.

For real estate there are different recapture rules for residential and all other real property. For residential property any gain on the sale of the property is subject to recapture to the extent the accelerated depreciation exceeds fifteen-year straight line depreciation.

For example, assume the tightrope walker's building is an apartment house and she sells it after two years for $550,000, or $100,000 more than she paid. Her taxes would look like this:

Selling price	$550,000
Purchase price	450,000
Gain	$100,000

Two years accelerated depreciation	$102,188
Two years straight line depreciation	60,000
Excess depreciation taken	$ 42,188

Gain on building	$100,000
Less excess depreciation subject to recapture and ordinary taxes	42,188
Gain subject to long-term capital gains tax	$57,812

For nonresidential real property *all* the accelerated depreciation is subject to recapture.

For example, assume the tightrope walker's building is a warehouse and she sells it in two years for $550,000. Now her taxes look like this:

Sale price	$550,000
Purchase price	450,000
Gain	$100,000
Less two-year accelerated depreciation subject to recapture and ordinary income taxes	102,188
Excess gain	($ 2,188)

Since there is no excess gain over depreciation, none of the gain will qualify for long-term capital gains taxes.

Recapture takes a lot of the fun out of accelerated depreciation. It means that real estate owners have to think thrice before adopting a depreciation schedule. Quick tax write-offs are good, but so are long-term capital gains. How long you plan to own the building is the key.

If you are thinking about real estate, a thorough understanding of depreciation is an absolute must before you put down any money. You will want to know how much the depreciation can help your cash flow. Making money while losing is something you ought to know about, especially if you are pessimistic about investment losses.

Cash on Cash

"Cash on cash" is a fancy concept used by real estate insiders to refer to projects that earn money. Many real estate projects do earn money, even before the tax consequences are considered. Incredible as it sounds to the uninitiated, many real estate projects are conceived and operated on the idea of a positive cash flow only after depreciation and personal income taxes are considered. That is, the projects are expected to lose money. Consider the following examples of rental properties.

	Positive operating cash	Negative operating cash
A. Income from rents	$ 50,000	$ 50,000
B. Cash expenses		
Interest	$ 30,000	$ 32,000
Property taxes	8,400	10,000
Utilities	6,000	6,500
Operating expenses	600	700
Total cash expenses	$ 45,000	$ 49,200
C. Cash from income and expenses— positive (negative) (A − B)	$ 5,000	$ 800
D. Less repayment of principal	2,000	2,300
E. Cash flow from operations— positive (negative) (C − D)	$ 3,000	$ (1,500)
F. Noncash depreciation	$ 14,000	$ 18,800
G. Profit (or loss) for tax purposes (C − F)*	$ (9,000)	$(18,000)
H. Tax shield for investor in 50% tax bracket (G × 50%)	$ 4,500	$ 9,000
I. Total cash flow (E + H)	$ 7,500	$ 7,500

*Principal repayment is *not* involved in the calculation of Line G. Repayment of principal is a negative cash item, but is not deductible for tax purposes.

Here are two projects both able to receive $50,000 in rents. The positive building operates somewhat more efficiently than the negative building. It is also financed at a lower rate of interest. For these reasons the operating profits (Line C) are substantially higher for the positive building than for the negative building. After the principal is paid, the positive building is still positive; it has positive cash on cash. The negative building does have its advantages. It has a very heavy depreciation schedule. Depreciation provides a tax shield. When the depreciation is considered for an investor in a 50 percent tax bracket, both buildings wind up having the same cash flow.

In theory, real estate projects such as the negative building are attractive. In theory, they allow you to make money while losing it (see the section on *depreciation*). But actual real world experience frequently proves the theory wrong. What seems to make the theory wrong is not the after-tax cash flow, but the economic viability. Real estate projects, after all, are businesses. And any business that cannot generate sufficient cash revenues to pay cash expenses is probably not viable over the long run.

Why do people invest in real estate projects that do not have positive cash on cash? Oftentimes the potential investor is in love with the idea of the real estate itself. An investor in love with a project may be mentally prepared to find any reason to move ahead with the project. A positive cash flow after taxes may seem like a good reason to invest, even if some of the numbers don't make good sense. The idea of using real estate only as a tax shelter is often enough to get the real estate lover to move in.

A more fundamental reason why projects may lose money is because they are new. New projects cost more to build than the old ones did. Rents, however, are set near existing market levels. The existing market will be determined by the older buildings already in place. Furthermore, a new building will take time to fill with tenants. And, if it is a commercial building, it will take time for customers to find the tenants. All this means that a new building is likely to experience operating losses for awhile.

The question is whether the investor can wait a while. If the investor's project is a negative project, one designed to "make money while losing it," he or she will find additional cash must be poured in all the time just to keep it going. As this outpouring takes place, tax refund time is likely to seem farther and farther away. Then because the project is probably not economically viable to begin with, surprises in estimates seem to come along. More often than not, the surprises will be bad. Often the investor then finds that losses are bigger than expected. Soon the hot, impassioned love affair begins to cool like some fleeting infatuation. Unfortunately, by the time the investor figures all this out, he or she may already be married—without any painless way for annulment. What, then, should a wise suitor do? Marry for money, not for love. Be sure your intended building has plenty of cash on cash.

Leverage

Leverage is when a little does a lot. It's like when you need to turn over a heavy rock, and you can't. So you use a strong board for leverage, and then you can. It is like when you want to get your boss to give you a raise, and you can't. So you get the union's help, and then you can. And it is like when you want to buy some property with a little money, and you can't. So you go get a loan, and then you can. Leverage is important in real estate transactions.

Leverage is easier to use in real estate than you might imagine. Good pieces of real estate are considered prime loans by banks and other lending institutions. Frequently they will lend you 80 percent and up to 100 percent on the value of a good piece of real estate. They'll lend these large amounts because of inflation. If you get in a tough spot and can't repay, they can repossess the property. Frequently it will have gone up in value since they made the loan, and they can sell and make a profit on the repossession.

Naturally, you wouldn't ask for a loan you didn't think you could repay. In fact, you may wonder why you want to borrow money and use leverage at all.

Assume you want to be a big real estate tycoon. So you break every piggy bank in the house, cash in your Series EE bonds, and hold a garage sale, all of which nets you $20,000. With $20,000 burning a hole in your pocket, you go looking for something to buy. What you find for $20,000 you don't want to buy. But let's say you find a nice duplex for $100,000. You'll soon discover that with your $20,000 as down payment, the bank will lend you $80,000 to buy the duplex, and you're in business, using leverage.

The advantage of leverage doesn't stop with the purchase. Let's assume your duplex investment throws off $4000 in cash every year after everything is paid for. Actually $4000 on a $100,000 investment is only 4 percent and that's not very good. But $4000 is 20 percent on your $20,000 investment, and that's terrific. Leverage helps again.

Leverage helps a third time, when you decide to sell. Let's say you own the duplex for ten years and that its value goes up only 4 percent per year. After ten years, you can sell it for $148,000. An increase of $48,000 on a $100,000 duplex in ten years is only 48 percent, which is not nearly as good as the money would have done in a savings account. But an increase of $48,000 on your $20,000 investment is 140 percent in ten years. No savings account can match that.

Using other people's money to leverage your own is an important part of most real estate transactions, and it is easy to do. It is easy because the banks are usually eager to make the loan. They frequently make the loan more against the value of the property than against your obvious ability to repay. In fact, loans are so easy to get that there is a terrible temptation to overuse leverage. It works so well that people easily forget leverage works both ways.

An example of overusing leverage is a young college student with barely a penny to his name. While in the process of renting a duplex to live in, Jack discovered the local banks would lend 100 percent of the value of a duplex if the owner agreed to live in one side and rent the other. Jack thought it made much more sense to buy rather than to rent, under those conditions.

His conditions went smoothly. And a few months later, at semester break, Jack began asking himself, "What would happen to the loan if I moved?" He read the contract—the answer was, nothing! So he moved. He moved to another duplex that he financed 100 percent because he was living in half of it. It didn't take long before he wanted to move again. After four moves in one year, Jack's wife told her budding real estate baron "no more moving!"

This was only a mild setback for our creative genius. He soon found banks would make him the 100 percent loan if he simply said he *"intended to move into the duplex."* In a couple of years, he had ten duplexes he was "intending" to move into, with a value of three-quarters of a million dollars, and he had never put up a single dime. Talk about leverage!

At the rate he was going, Jack figured he would own the whole town before he graduated. Then trouble developed. A recession caused a major plant in the area to close down. Suddenly he was having a tough time keeping his duplexes rented. The rent checks weren't coming in as fast as the loan repayments needed to be going

out. He figured the thing to do was regroup fast. Sell a few duplexes. He was sure they were worth more than he paid for them.

He was wrong. The market was soft. Because he'd never put a
dime in them, there was no cushion. If he sold, he wound up needing cold cash to pay off the loans. He couldn't afford to keep them,
and he couldn't afford to sell them. So at twenty-two he declared
bankruptcy and walked away from them. The banks got hurt, and
they deserved it. Their bad lending practices tempted him into his
troubles to start with. But Jack got hurt much worse, and he also
deserved it.

Of course, in today's market it is unusual to find any lending institutions willing to lend 100 percent of the market value. Also,
lenders today take far greater pains to see to it that someone who
signs a sworn statement that he or she intends to live in a property
actually moves in. Nevertheless, overleverage through the use of
second mortgages or contracts for deed is still possible, with the
same bad results.

You probably deserve to use leverage in your real estate investments, and it is a good idea. But it is risky, it is bad business, and it
may be downright immoral to overuse leverage. As a rule of
thumb, you are overusing leverage if you don't put 15 percent
equity or more into your commercial real estate investments. You
can easily find any number of authors and real estate moguls who
will emphatically, even angrily, disagree with the opinion just expressed. Usually that's because they are overusing leverage to an
almost sinful level themselves. You'll have to make your own
choice. But in the long run the rocks will roll over you, your bosses
will fire you, and your real estate investments will bankrupt you if
you don't put some effort and equity behind your leverage.

In most cases real estate held for investment is also a business. It
is a business with many unique fundamentals. A thorough understanding of the fundamentals is necessary to enjoy either a successful investment or a successful business. Fundamentals are even more
important if you want them both to be successful.

◇ 55 ◇
Analyzing a
Real Estate Investment

If you are seriously considering making an investment in real estate you will want to analyze the project carefully. To do a good job of analysis you will need a thorough understanding of how the fundamentals of making money in real estate (Chapter 54) apply to your project. You will need to pull all the fundamentals together and work out the numbers. It will take some effort. But it is effort you should give. Real estate investments tend to be very big and making a mistake can be costly.

The first step is to estimate your cash flow. The following Cash Flow Projection may be helpful.

Cash Flow Projection

Revenues		
Gross rent	$XXX	
Less vacancy time	XXX	
Net revenues		$XXX
Tax deductible cash expenses		
Manager's fee	$XXX	
Regular maintenance	XXX	
Rerent maintenance	XXX	
Rental expense	XXX	
Utilities	XXX	
Property taxes	XXX	
Special assessments	XXX	
Insurance	XXX	
Interest payments (no principal)	XXX	
Miscellaneous	XXX	
Total tax deductible cash expenses	XXX	
Profit (loss) before non–cash expenses		$XXX

Tax deductible non-cash expenses
  Depreciation   XXX
  Total profit (loss) $XXX

Taxes
  Taxable profit (loss) $XXX $XXX
  Tax rate (%)   .XX
  Tax liability (shield)   XXX
  Net profit (loss) $XXX

Cash flow
  Net profit (if loss, use
  "tax shield" figure here) $XXX
  Less principal payment on mortgage   XXX
  Net cash flow   SXXX

Your cash flows will change every year. Rents will rise, expenses will change, depreciation may decline if you use accelerated methods, interest deductions will decline and principal repayments will increase. Therefore, to do a good job of analysis you must project your cash flows for several years—five at minimum; ten years is better.

At the end of that period of analysis there is one large additional factor to be concerned with—the value of your real estate. For the analysis you are doing you should assume you will sell the property in five or ten years (whether you plan to sell or not). When assuming the sale of the property consider the following:

Future sales price $XXX
Less: selling expenses $XXX
    mortgage repayment   XXX
    tax consequences*   XXX
Total   XXX
Net cash flow from sale $XXX

*Note: Don't forget depreciation recapture if you used accelerated depreciation methods.

The reason for developing all these cash flows is to be certain your property returns at least as much cash to you as it required to buy and hold it, and then some. After all, you want this to be a profitable investment.

But a dollar today is worth more than a dollar tomorrow. Sophisticated real estate people take this problem into account by "discounting" the dollars they'll get in the future. You must discount the future cash flows in order to do a decent evaluation. The discount rate should be the interest rate you could earn on some other investment with about the same amount of work and risk. Usually there aren't any really good comparisons, so you wind up estimating a discount rate. For instance, 12 percent is a common discount rate used in the industry today. In some ways this seems low when you consider you can get 12 percent for no work and minimum risk in many non–real estate investments. Real estate requires lots of work and plenty of risks. So you should earn more interest on real estate. In this case, however, assume you think 12 percent is enough.

The following table gives rates of 6, 8, 10, 12, 14, and 16 percent for ten years. The logic of the table says that at a 12 percent discount rate you would just as soon have $0.567 today as $1.00 five years from today. (Sounds reasonable when you think about inflation.) Put another way, the table says that if you invest $0.567 today at 12 percent, it will equal $1.00 in five years.

Discount Rates

Year	6%	8%	10%	12%	14%	16%
1	.943	.926	.909	.893	.877	.862
2	.890	.857	.826	.797	.770	.743
3	.840	.794	.751	.712	.675	.641
4	.792	.735	.683	.636	.592	.552
5	.747	.686	.621	.567	.519	.476
6	.705	.630	.565	.507	.456	.410
7	.665	.584	.513	.452	.399	.354
8	.627	.540	.467	.404	.351	.305
9	.592	.500	.424	.361	.308	.263
10	.558	.463	.386	.322	.270	.227

Here's how you use discounting in your analysis. Assume you are considering an investment of $40,000 in real estate. You believe you can earn 12 percent in alternative investments, so you will use a 12 percent discount. You estimate your cash flows for five years and assume the project is sold at the end.

Year	Estimated cash flow ×	12% discount factor =	Discounted cash flow
1	$ 473 ×	.893 =	$ 422
2	527 ×	.797 =	420
3	577 ×	.712 =	411
4	621 ×	.636 =	395
5	657 ×	.567 =	373
5	70,000 ×	.567 =	39,690
Totals	$72,855		$41,711

You invest $40,000 today. Over the next five years you receive $72,855 in cash flow, which sounds like a lot, and it is. But you don't get the cash until sometime in the future so you need to discount it. The discounted value of that cash is $41,711, which is still good. This means the project is earning just a little more than the 12 percent you wanted, so you would make the investment. If the discounted flow added to less than $40,000, you would pass it by.

After all the fundamentals of revenues, expenses, inflation, created value, depreciation, cash on cash and leverage are thoroughly analyzed, you'll have a good idea whether the investment is worthwhile or not. You are also likely to think that doing all the analysis to get that idea is a lot of work, and it is. But it is necessary work. Real estate investments are generally big investments. And big investments should be taken very seriously. For serious investors, fundamental analysis is a must.

◇ 56 ◇
Are Houses Great Investments?

No, houses generally are not great investments. Houses are great places to live. Houses are great for a feeling of ownership. Houses are great for a sense of belonging. And houses can be the least expensive form of shelter. But houses are normally not great investments.

To assert that houses are not usually great investments might be considered downright un-American. Everyone knows how much houses have gone up in value. Everyone knows you can deduct your interest and property taxes from your income tax. Everyone knows many people who have sold their homes and made a bundle. And everyone, except the unpatriotic, knows that houses are great investments.

Unfortunately, not everyone knows the true cost of house ownership. Or at least not everyone thinks about the true cost of house ownership. All things considered, most people will agree houses are often poor investments—but great places to live. The following is a real case. The situation is typical, even above average. It involves a nice four-bedroom, 2½-bath home, in an excellent suburb, close to schools, churches, and shopping. The house was well built and well maintained. It sold new for $48,000. It sold again only eight years later for $101,000—an increase in value of 110 percent.

Original cost	$ 48,000
Equity investment	9,600
Mortgage	$ 38,400
Selling price	$101,000
Less sales commission	− 7,708
Net selling price	$ 93,292
Mortgage repayment	$ 35,730
Accumulated equity in home	$ 57,562

On the surface, this looks like a great investment. The original equity investment was $9600. That built to more than $57,000 in just eight years. But even though it looks like a great investment, it wasn't. In judging an investment only as an investment, *all* costs of owning, keeping, operating, and maintaining that investment must be considered.

		Actual cash spent due to ownership (8 years)
Original equity investment		$ 9,600
Closing costs		1,250
Mortgage payments ($38,400 mortgage, 10%, for 30 years)		
To principal		2,270
To interest	$30,318	
Less income tax deductions	− 7,579	22,739
Insurance payments		3,200
Property taxes	$11,000	
Less income tax deductions	− 2,750	8,250
Maintenance and repairs		5,280
Improvements: air conditioning, humidifier, soft water, patio, drapes, storm windows, extra insulation, carpets, wallpaper, shelves, minor remodeling		10,700
Sales commission		7,708
Miscellaneous costs of selling		450
Subtotal		$71,447
Utilities		19,200
Total actual cash spent		$90,647

Now the true total cost of this investment can be compared with its selling price.

	Actual cash received
Selling price	$101,000
Less mortgage repayment	− 35,730
Actual cash received	$ 65,270
Minus actual cash spent	− 90,647
Net gain (or loss)	$(− 25,377)

An actual net cash loss of $25,377 on an investment is *not* "great." In fact, losing that much money on an investment is downright lousy. People often think they are making a lot of money because the house goes up in price and they accumulate a sizable equity. But the big equity comes from "forced savings." In a sense, the mortgage, the maintenance, the improvements, the everything else that an owner spends on a house is a form of forced savings. Some of those savings are returned to you in the form of equity when you sell the house. But these forced savings are not very efficient savings. If this homeowner had forced him- or herself to put this money in a savings account paying only 5.25 percent he or she would have accumulated $117,990 in eight years. But by being forced to save the money in a house, he or she only accumulated $65,270.

What makes the house a poor investment is the fact that not all the forced savings are returned. Some of them are lost. What's lost is the cost of living in the house. So houses shouldn't be judged as investments at all. They should be judged as places to live, to relax, to enjoy, to love, to grow, and to be together. Houses are places for homes. And as places for homes they are terrific. One reason they are terrific places to live is that they can be inexpensive. For example, if the family in this house had rented something comparable to live in, which would have been hard to do, the family members would have spent a lot more money. Eight years of comparable apartment living would have cost them about $72,000, including utilities. Compare this with the cost of $25,377 to live in the house. The total cost of living in a house can be much cheaper than living anywhere else. Remember, however, that much of the expense reduction in house living is not realized until after the house is sold, when you aren't living there anymore.

Who cares whether houses are good investments or just nice places to live? Not enough people, unfortunately. Many families rationalize themselves into buying houses that are far too expensive, on the idea that it will be a great investment. Then they become "house poor." Burdensome chunks of their income get tied up in payments, maintenance, utilities, and so on. The nicer the house, the bigger the forced savings payments. The financial burdens can create pressure on the inhabitants of the house. The result often is that the house does not become a place to live, to relax, to enjoy, to love, to grow, and to be together. Rather, it becomes a place to fight, to quarrel, to fret, to argue, and to worry. When this happens, the house is not a home; it may be a prison.

Price Trends in Housing
(New, single family homes)

Ted's case is a perfect example of a house becoming a prison. Ted was one of those guys who really did have a rich uncle who really did leave him some money. Ted had mixed emotions when his uncle died. He was glad to be getting some money, but he was sorry it was going to take so long to come. He felt bad about his uncle too, but he never mentioned it. Some people keep their grief bottled up inside.

Most of Ted's grief seemed to center around the eight years it took to satisfy all the terms of his uncle's trust so Ted could receive his money. But the delay gave Ted, and his wife Janet, lots of time to think about what to do with the money. They wanted to invest it in something that would build value for them over the years. They talked to several financial advisors, who suggested several possibilities. But Ted and Janet thought up the idea of a house all on their own.

A house seemed like an excellent idea to them: a beautiful place to live, and appreciation of their investment. What they didn't appreciate, however, was the cost of maintaining a big house. They purchased a beautiful home for $201,000. They invested all the $122,000 inheritance and carried a $79,000 mortgage. The mortgage payment was $812.60, which was OK. But taxes and insurance brought the monthly tab to $1020.93 a month, which was a real shock to their $2050 monthly salary. The house was twice the size of their previous house. However, every utility bill was more than doubled, somehow. Their old furniture, which had looked fine in the old house, looked wretched in the new one. The large lot required large amounts of fertilizer, weed killer, and water. Everywhere they turned things cost more—lots more.

The house is probably appreciating in value, just as they hoped. And eventually Ted and Janet will accumulate sizable equity. In the meantime, they are saddled with enormous forced savings and they are broke. They have never been so broke. You might say they are "house broke." But no matter what you say, it all means they are very unhappy.

Homeowners should not be unhappy. House ownership is a great idea when the house is a home. It's absolutely American to live in a house you can afford and call a home, isn't it? Many more houses would be homes if the families buying them were willing to look at them as places to live and not as investments.

Should You Sell Your House to Get the Equity Out of It?

No! Selling your house is a very inefficient way to get the equity out of it. If your primary objective is to convert the illiquid equity in your home to liquid cash, you are better off to refinance. This is true whether you want the equity for spending or for investment. It may make sense, however, to sell your house if your objective is to get a nicer house, or a bigger house, or a better house. The equity in your old house may help you get the new house you want. But sell your home to get the equity only if you really want to move; don't sell it just to turn your equity into cash.

Converting house equity into cash may be an unusual thought for many people. Many people feel that converting house equity to cash is like spending their life savings, and in some ways it is. But many other people seem to want to spend that equity. Many of these homeowners can't stand to see that equity just sitting around doing nothing. They feel it is their patriotic duty to somehow turn the equity into cash and spend it. By spending, they can do their fair share to keep the economy going. One way to get cash for the house equity is to sell the house—and then, of course, go buy a new house.

The Condies thought this way. In 1973, they purchased a nice house for $32,700. In 1980, they realized their house was worth $64,500. They figured their equity was right around $39,600. That seemed like a lot of money to the Condies. They could think of many things to do with the money, if they could just get their hands on it. Several of their friends were getting their hands on their equity by selling their old houses and buying new ones. The Condies found a new house they liked that cost $72,000. They could buy it for $14,400 down. They would then have a bigger mortgage but the transaction would leave $25,200 free cash in their hands. This free cash could be used for new furniture, a new car, a trip, even some savings.

Furniture, cars, trips, and savings all sounded good to the Condies. They really didn't care that much about the new house. They liked the old one just fine. And the new one was actually a little bit smaller. But they forged ahead anyway.

After they had forged ahead to the point of no return, they realized they weren't going to get the full $25,200 they had been thinking about. Then a "friend" pointed some things out to them. For example, they did not have to sell their home to get at the equity. They could have refinanced the old house. The lending institution that had the mortgage on their old house would have been tickled to give them a new mortgage, a bigger mortgage, on the old house. The lender did it for somebody every day. All the Condies had to do was ask.

The Condies didn't ask. But if they had asked, they would have been much better off financially. Here's the line-by-line comparison.

The Condies became absolutely ill when they saw these figures. Sure, they had a newer home, and it was a bit nicer. But, they maintain to this day, they really didn't care that much about the new house. Furthermore, they hated to leave their old neighborhood. They really just wanted the equity out of the home to do a few things. Well, they got $18,559 free cash to do a few things. But they could have done a few more things by refinancing. They could have gotten $26,343 extra cash by refinancing. Worse yet, their new monthly payments are $220.47 more than they would have been if they had refinanced. That extra $220.47 will cut down on the few things they can do in the future. The Condies are definitely not enjoying their new house and the extra cash as they thought they would.

Many people really want or need a new house. Maybe they need more room, or maybe they like the new floor plan, or maybe they just like having a brand new house. That's OK. But if they talk themselves into moving on the idea that they can make better use of their equity, then they've probably made a big financial mistake.

	Selling and Buying	Refinancing
Sales price of old house	$64,500.00	$ 0.00
Cash received from refinancing old house at 80% of market value	0.00	51,600.00
Real estate commission to sell	− 4,515.00	0.00
Cost of moving including movers, trucks, pad rental, utility hook-ups, three nights in motel, and miscellaneous (not including wear and tear on furniture and nerves, lost time, disruption of family life, and trauma in finding new friends for children)	− 1,215.00	0.00
Payoff on old loan	− 24,900.00	− 24,900.00
Prepayment penalty at 1% of outstanding (waived for refinancing)	− 249.00	0.00
Closing costs, loan origination fees, title search, appraisal, mortgage origination tax, title guarantee, etc. (Certain fees lowered or waived on refinancing of existing smaller mortgage)	− 662.00	− 357.00
Down payment on new house	− 14,400.00	0.00
Extra cash left over	$18,559.00	$26,343.00

Mortgage Details

	Selling and Buying	Refinancing
New mortgage	$57,660.00	$51,600.00
New interest rate (The interest on the old mortgage had been 7¾%; the lender would have been happy to refinance the loan, and at a rate below the current market.)	12%	10%
New mortgage payment (monthly)	593.10	452.83
Insurance payment (monthly)	30.00	26.88
Taxes (monthly) (The new house was appraised at its sales value. The old house was still being appraised near its original sales value.)	150.00	72.92
Total monthly payments	$ 773.10	$ 552.63

◇ 57 ◇
How Can You Finance a Home?

In Chapter 56, "Are Houses Great Investments?," I showed that houses aren't good investments at all, but they are cost-effective places to live. It may seem strange, therefore, to devote a chapter in the middle of the investment section of this book to explaining the most sophisticated new ways of financing this noninvestment.

There are two reasons for placing this chapter here. First, despite what I said in Chapter 56, I know most people will go right on believing their homes are investments. Second, the techniques for financing homes apply to all forms of real estate—not just homes. In the 1980s, you will not last long as a real estate investor if you do not become acquainted with these various forms of financing.

There are many creative ways to finance a home—conventional mortgage, second mortgage, contract for deed, variable rate mortgage, shared appreciation mortgage, municipal rate mortgage, government-subsidized mortgage, and so on.

Only a few years ago, nearly all homes were financed using straight conventional mortgages. However, the soaring interest and inflation rates of the 1970s made alternatives to the conventional mortgage increasingly necessary. Today there are many creative ways of financing a home. Most of these new financing vehicles are somewhat regional in scope. Local law, custom, or competitive environment may make some forms of financing unavailable where you live.

A Bit of History

Before the Great Depression of the 1930s, homes and farms were typically financed with notes or mortgages at a local bank. The entire amount of these notes came due every six or twelve months. The banker and the owner had an unwritten understanding that on the due dates the owner would go to the bank and pay the interest and a portion of the loan principal. Then a new six- or twelve-month note would be written for the unpaid balance. These mortgages worked fairly well for years—despite the fact they inspired some of the best melodramas of all time.

In the 1930s, unfortunately, the melodramas became all too real. Instead of booing and hissing makebelieve villains, millions of Americans found themselves with real "villains." Not that the banks were such villains—they were caught up in it, too. As the economy plunged into depression, owners became financially strapped. When their mortgages came due, they hoped their friendly bankers would accept less than the usual payment. But their friendly bankers were having troubles of their own. The banks needed money badly to satisfy persistent withdrawals. Instead of being willing to accept less than the usual payment, bankers wanted more than usual. Often, the banks demanded the full amounts.

Owners couldn't come up with the full amounts, so the banks foreclosed. Soon the banks held more real estate than they wanted or could sell. Real estate prices collapsed, and—without cash—so did the banks.

Out of this chaos was born today's conventional mortgage. The conventional mortgage has served as one of the soundest financial instruments ever conceived. It has survived depression, wars, space races, and changes in government. It will be interesting to see if it can survive inflation.

Conventional Mortgages

Conventional mortgages are the most common type of home financing in America. A conventional mortgage is a loan, secured against the value of the real estate. Typically, the mortgage will be written for 75 or 80 percent of the value of the house. Conventional mortgages usually have a life of twenty-five to thirty years. Equal monthly payments are made over the life of the mortgage. The major issuers of conventional mortgages are thrift institutions, banks, and insurance companies.

Consider the following example: A home is sold for $80,000. The lender requires a 20 percent down payment and is willing to write a mortgage for 80 percent. The mortgage carries a 12 percent interest rate and has a thirty-year life. Monthly payments for principal and interest will be $658.31.

Sales price of home	$80,000.00
Down payment at 20%	16,000.00
Mortgage at 80%	$64,000.00
Interest rate	12%
Months to pay (30 years)	360
Monthly payments	$ 658.31

This conventional mortgage is an excellent form of financing for the borrower. In many ways, ordinary home buyers can borrow on terms far superior to those granted major corporations. First, the borrower can borrow large amounts of money. Borrowing two or three times a homeowner's annual income is possible. In this example, the loan is for $64,000. This loan might be made to a family with a total income of $30,000 or maybe less. Furthermore, the loan might be equal to 70 or 75 percent of all the family's assets. Major corporations would have great difficulty borrowing two or three times their revenues and 75 percent of their assets.

Second, the loan is very long—twenty-five or thirty years. Many corporations find it difficult to sell thirty-year bonds in today's environment. Length is an advantage, because it reduces the monthly payments.

The following table shows the required monthly payment of this mortgage, assuming different lengths.

Years	*Monthly payments*
10	$918.21
15	768.10
20	704.70
25	674.06
30	658.31
40	645.44
50	641.64
100	640.00

Incidentally, thirty-year loans are about as long as you'll find. A major reason is that beyond thirty years the monthly payment doesn't decline much.

Third, monthly payments are convenient. Loans that require huge lump sums can catch the borrower unprepared and embarrassed.

Fourth, the interest rates are very favorable. Usually, the interest rate on a new mortgage is very competitive with rates available to America's most creditworthy corporations and even the government. When mortgage rates reach 15 percent, homeowners may wonder if they are favorable. But 15 percent or more is what many good companies must pay to borrow money during such times.

The interest will raise the total price of the home a great deal. In our example, interest payments raise the total cost by $172,991.60, as follows:

Original mortgage (principal)	$ 64,000.00
Interest rate	12%
Monthly payments	$ 658.31
Number of monthly payments (30 years)	× 360
Total payments	$236,991.60
Less original mortgage (principal)	− 64,000.00
Total interest paid	$172.991.60

Another interesting thing about mortgage interest is that interest is about all you pay in the early years. For instance, in the first year only about $19.35 of each monthly payment goes to reduce the principal of the mortgage—while $638.96 goes to the payment of interest. In this example, it will take about twenty-four years of payments before more will be going to principal than interest. It's the price you pay for financing a home—fortunately, interest is tax deductible.

Fifth, the borrower has substantial protection against foreclosure. Usually the protection exceeds that available to major corporate borrowers. For instance, a corporate borrower would probably have to agree to a lengthy list of conditions. These might include dividend restrictions, minimum income, equity, and limits on future borrowings, to name a few. In fact, there is often a clause saying the lender can demand full payment anytime he or she "feels unsecured." And to police all this, the corporation must file frequent, audited financial statements.

By contrast, all the homeowner must do is fill out some basic financial information one time, and then meet the monthly payments. The lender isn't constantly snooping around checking on the borrower's financial condition. How many mortgage lenders would have a right to "feel unsecured" if the homeowner lost his or her job? People do lose their jobs all the time, yet their homes are not repossessed. Even if the homeowner does miss some payments, foreclosure is difficult. Usually many months are required before the lender can legally put the owner out. In the meantime, there are frequent chances to get caught up again.

The conventional mortgage is so favorable to the borrower that untold millions of Americans would be unable to own homes if they were forced to borrow on terms comparable to those required of major corporations.

Second Mortgages

Despite all the good qualities of conventional mortgages, they present problems to some borrowers and to some lenders. One problem for many borrowers is the down payment. In our example, the new owner was required to make a down payment of $16,000.

Sales price	$80,000
Mortgage	64,000
Required down payment	$16,000

But $16,000 is a lot of money—especially for young couples. Sometimes they can borrow a big chunk of the down payment by using a second mortgage. The second-mortgage market is not well established. A primary source of second mortgages is well-to-do relatives. If you don't have rich relatives, check with a local mortgage banker to see if they can lead you to a source.

When second mortgages are made, they usually carry higher interest rates and shorter payment periods than the first mortgages. This can result in very heavy monthly payments. Following our example, assume the new owner can only put $4000 down. He or she is able to obtain a $12,000 second mortgage. Assume that the second mortgage carries a 15 percent interest rate and a ten-year life.

Sales price	$80,000.00
First mortgage (12% for 30 years)	64,000.00
Balance	$16,000.00
Second mortgage (15% for 10 years)	12,000.00
Down payment	$ 4,000.00
Monthly payment, first mortgage	$ 658.31
Monthly payment, second mortgage	193.60
Total monthly payments	$ 851.91

A second mortgage might appeal to people in a better position to make large monthly payments than large down payments. And if it really appeals to them, third, fourth and further mortgages are also sometimes available.

Mortgage Insurance

Mortgage insurance is more appealing to many people who need low-down-payment financing. Lending institutions can accept lower down payments and bigger mortgages if the mortgage is insured against default.

The government offers mortgage insurance through its well-known FHA (Federal Housing Administration) program. If you apply for a mortgage insured by one of the FHA government programs, the lending institution can lend you 90, or 95, or even 97 percent of the home's value. That means that your down payment can be as low as 3 percent, which would be $2400 in our example ($80,000 × 3% = $2,400). The lender can take this risk because if you fail to pay the lender can collect from the government. The government will then foreclose on your house.

Unfortunately, not everyone likes or can use FHA. Lenders especially don't like to use them. In a word, the government is very bureaucratic. It has all kinds of rules, inspections, and forms, which lead to delays, hassles, and extra expense. Generally speaking, lending institutions and real estate agents will steer customers to other alternatives if possible.

One possible alternative is insurance provided by a private mortgage insurance company. These private corporations have succeeded in cutting out most of the red tape the government requires. This means their approvals are much faster and more certain.

With private mortgage insurance, borrowers can get mortgages for 90 or 95 percent of the value of the home. Of course, the borrower must pay a premium. Often the premium is added to the interest rate. The premium typically runs 0.25 percent for a 90 percent mortgage and 0.50 percent for a 95 percent mortgage. Sometimes the premium is a single payment made at the time of closing. The single payment can run 2 percent of the home price. Assume in our example a 0.25 percent premium will be added to the conventional mortgage rate of 12 percent, giving a total rate of 12.25 percent. The following illustrates the effect of private mortgage insurance on our example.

	Uninsured mortgage	*Insured mortgage*
Sales price	$80,000.00	$80,000.00
Down payment percentage	20%	10%
Down payment	16,000.00	8,000.00
Mortgage required	$64,000.00	$72,000.00
Interest rate	12.0%	12.25%
Monthly payment (30 years)	$ 658.31	$ 754.44

The down payment required to get into the home falls from $16,000 to $8,000. But the monthly payment increases from $658.31 to $754.44, due to a larger mortgage and a higher interest rate. Many borrowers have good jobs and can make the payments, but they may not have the cash for down payment. Mortgage insurance can make the difference.

The Veterans Administration (VA) offers qualified vets a "guaranteed" loan program similar to the FHA program. It usually has the same interest rate, but offers no down payment. Check with your lender.

Contracts for Deed for Sale

Another vehicle for reducing both down payments and monthly payments is the contract for deed. Some states have a similar instrument known as a *contract for sale*. These contracts have grown tremendously in popularity in the past several years.

Contracts for deed are used in a number of situations. Their uses and terms can vary with each deal, depending on what the parties can negotiate. In general, they are subject to state usury laws but that's about all.

Perhaps their most typical use is a situation where a home is being resold. The existing mortgage is assumable by the new buyer and has a low rate of interest. However, substantial equity has built up in the home. The seller is willing to take a small amount of cash and a contract for deed for the equity.

The contract for deed is different from a second mortgage. There are some legal differences, but usually the big difference is in the repayment schedule. A second mortgage is paid off in equal monthly payments, but the contract for deed may have small

monthly payments, with a lump sum payment due in the future—
say, five years.

Go back to the example of our $80,000 house. This time, assume
there is a mortgage on the house that was originally written for
$45,000 at 8 percent. The monthly payment is $330.19. The mortgage is assumable. Naturally, the new buyer would love to keep the
8 percent mortgage. To do so, the buyer must come up with
$40,000 cash—and can't.

Sale price	$80,000
Less existing mortgage	40,000
Required equity	$40,000

The seller, however, can wait for the money. So they negotiate a
$30,000 contract for deed with an interest rate of 10 percent, which
is well below the market. The buyer will pay only interest for five
years. But at the end of the fifth year, the whole $30,000 is payable
in one lump sum.

Here's the arithmetic:

	Amounts	Monthly payments
Sales price	$80,000	
Remaining principal of existing mortgage ($45,000 original, 8%, 30 years)	$40,000	$330.19
Contract for deed (5-year note, 10%)	30,000	250.00[a]
Down payment	10,000	
Totals	$80,000	$580.19

[a]Payment of interest only for 5 years.

Here's what the seller is thinking: (1) he (or she) wants to sell; (2)
he doesn't need the cash right now; (3) to make the sale, he'll accept
a low interest rate; (4) he won't cut the selling price of the house as
much as he might otherwise; and (5) if the buyer defaults, he can repossess and resell the house—probably at a profit.

Here's what the buyer is thinking: (1) he (or she) wants to buy
the house; (2) he would like to assume the old mortgage with the

favorable interest rate; (3) he can't come up with the cash for the down payment; (4) he can't meet the monthly payments for a new mortgage at higher rates, or new mortgages simply are not available; and (5) in five years, either his financial circumstances, and/or the financial markets will have improved greatly, allowing him to pay off or refinance the contract for deed.

Contracts for deed are frequently carried by the seller or by someone else who has an interest in seeing the sale closed. All things considered, they are not usually great investments. But curiously enough, a secondary market for these contracts has developed. This allows the seller to get most of the equity out if he or she in fact does need it. Real estate agents know where these secondary markets are.

Many homes have been sold on contracts for deed that might otherwise still be on the market. But buyers and sellers should be aware of some potentially serious problems. First, there is no assurance that home prices will continue rising as fast as they have been. In fact, the odds are prices will cool off some in the 1980s. This could mean less equity cushion than everyone is counting on.

Second, there is no assurance that financial markets will allow refinancing in the future.

Third, be especially cautious if you are at the end of a series of contracts for deed. That is, A buys from B, who buys from C, who buys from D, and so on. Everyone accepts a contract from his or her buyer. Everyone counts on the final balloon payment at the end to meet his or her own balloon payment. If someone's balloon pops, it could set off a chain reaction that pops your balloon.

These are just words to the wise—not advice to avoid contracts for deed. But you might go back and reread the section called "A Bit of History" near the beginning of this chapter. See if you see any similarities in the widespread use of contracts for deed and the situation homeowners were facing during the Great Depression.

Wraparound Mortgages

Occasionally there are circumstances where a property has a modest existing low-interest-rate mortgage that is assumable. The new buyer does not have sufficient equity to buy the home and assume the existing mortgage. These circumstances are right for a wraparound mortgage.

Go back to the example of our $80,000 with an original 8 percent, $45,000, mortgage. Payments are $330.19 a month. In this case, a lender may be willing to write a new mortgage for 80 percent of current value.

Sales price	$80,000
Loan ratio	80%
New mortgage	$64,000
Required equity	$16,000

But also assume the new lender assumes the existing mortgage. In effect, the lender has not tied up $64,000 in the loan. He or she has only tied up $24,000. He or she has also assumed an obligation to repay the old mortgage.

Equity from buyer	$16,000
Cash from lender	$24,000
Assumption of existing mortgage	$40,000
Sales price	$80,000

Under these circumstances, the lender can reduce the interest rate on the new mortgage to the new buyer and still come out all right.

Assume that new mortgages are going for 14 percent today. The lender needs at least that *on the cash tied up,* and would like more. In this case, he or she has $24,000 tied up—not $64,000. (To simplify the math, assume the new and old mortgage have identical maturity dates. Each runs for twenty years to maturity.)

The lender writes the new mortgage at 10.67 percent, which is well below the market of 14 percent. Then he or she gets a payment each month of $646.22. From this the lender makes the old mortgage payment of $330.19. This leaves a net of $316.03. This equals 15 percent, not 14 percent, on the $24,000 the lender has out.

The wraparound is good for the seller. He or she sold the property without having to fool with a contract for deed.

The wraparound is good for the borrower. He or she bought the property with a modest down payment and a single mortgage carrying a below–market interest rate.

The wraparound is good for the lender. He or she made a loan at 1 percent above the going market.

And it's good for the agent. He or she made a sale. That is why good agents are alert to these possibilities. The agent is the first place to ask about a wraparound. It is the agent's livelihood to know how to do them.

Variable-Rate Mortgages

In recent years, not all the problem of getting mortgages has been related to the inability of borrowers to qualify or to produce down payments. A great deal of the problem has been caused by the inability of financial institutions to write mortgages and make money.

Take the savings and loan institutions, for example. The original idea was that depositors would open savings accounts on which these institutions paid 5.25 percent interest. The savings and loan institutions would then lend the money out in the form of mortgages (often to the same people) at 7.25 percent. The savings and loan people made a profit on the difference in rate.

Then interest rates rose, and people could make more than 5.25 percent in other forms of savings. So people pulled money out of their savings accounts. That put the savings and loan institutions in a real liquidity crunch.

So the savings and loan officers asked the regulators for the right to pay more interest. The regulators gave them savings certificates. Then billions flowed into the savings certificates, some paying up to 14 percent. Unfortunately, most of the money came out of the old 5.25 percent passbook savings account. This meant that the savings and loan institutions were paying more for their deposits. But that old 7.25 percent mortgage loan was still paying only 7.25 percent. Profitability collapsed. So the savings and loan officers asked the regulators for mortgages whose rates change with market interest rates, and the regulators have given them variable-rate mortgages also known as *adjustable* and *floating-rate mortgages*. The use of variable-rate mortgages is spreading around the country.

Here's how variable-rate mortgages work. The mortgage will probably be written at a rate below the current conventional rate, depending on the market. But the rate can be adjusted. In many cases the adjustments may be as much as 1 percent. This change in rate is reflected in the monthly payment the homeowner makes. Usually the adjustment is tied to something like the Government Treasury Bill (T-Bill) rate. If the T-Bill rate rises, the savings and loan institution can raise the mortgage rate. If the T-Bill rate falls, the mortgage rate declines. As you would guess, there have been more increases than declines. (Incidentally, avoid rates that are tied to the lender's cost of money. For technical reasons the rate will be less volatile than other indexes, but it is more likely to rise than to fall.)

The effect on our example is as follows:

Sales price	$80,000.00
Mortgage (30 years, 12% variable up to 1% each 6 months)	$64,000.00
Initial monthly payments	$ 658.31

Situation 1. Interest rates rise by 1% end of first 6 months.

Mortgage rate 12% + 1%		13%
Monthly payment	$	707.96

Situation 2. Interest rates rise by 1% end of second 6 months.

Mortgage rate 12% + 1% + 1%		14%
Monthly payment	$	758.31

Situation 3. Interest rates rise by 1% end of third 6 months.

Mortgage rate 12% + 1% + % + 1%		15%
Monthly payment	$	809.24

This homeowner has seen the monthly payment rise by $150.93 in eighteen months. That would be a shock to many family budgets. Of course, it can swing the other way—and it probably will, someday.

In some cases, the payment can remain the same even while the interest rate adjusts. This can be accomplished either by adjusting the number of payments or by accruing the interest and adding it to the principal.

The first case is unlikely to be popular. If interest rates are rising, it is difficult to lengthen payments enough to make a difference.

In our example, if interest rates rose only from 12.00 to 12.34 percent, payments would stretch from 30 years to 100 years in order to maintain a flat payment of $658.31. Consequently, in order to write variable mortgages that work under flat payment assumptions, the initial length would need to be short—20 years or less. That, of course, would mean rather high payments right from the start.

The second case is more workable. Here interest differences are accrued and added to or subtracted from the principal. In the example where interest rates rose from 12 to 15 percent, the monthly payment rose from $658.31 to $809.24. If the payment remained level at $658.31, there would be unpaid accumulated interest of approximately $1800 by the end of the thirtieth month. This means that, instead of the principal declining somewhat, the homeowner would actually owe more. He or she may find the principal owing after 2.5 years to be $65,200, when the original mortgage was only $64,000.

There are two hopes in this situation. The first is that interest rates will go down. With enough declines, the homeowner may even wind up paying less than $64,000.

The second hope is that the home will appreciate. This was an $80,000 home. If it is sold in thirty months for $100,000, then the increase in principal from $64,000 to $65,200 is not too bad. It can easily be paid, and the homeowner still has a sizable equity.

Borrowers do not like variable-rate mortgages, but they will accept them. They will accept them because they prefer them to the alternative, which is probably no mortgage at all. Someday variable-rate mortgages may be the only mortgages available.

Shared-Appreciation Mortgages

Another way to make lenders more willing to write mortgages is to give them part of the appreciation of the home. In addition to the cash flow and liquidity problems many mortgage lenders have had in the past, they have also had poor investments. They would write a mortgage with a fixed rate of interest for a long period of time. Inflation meant the interest rate was soon low, and the mortgage was being paid back with dollars that weren't worth as much as they used to be. Homeowners got just the reverse. They were paying back with inflation-cheapened dollars, and they were enjoying the appreciation in their homes as well.

To make the mortgage more attractive to lenders so they will keep lending, many homeowners are now willing to share the appreciation they hope to get in their houses. Here's how it works. The lender makes the mortgage at a rate below the current market rate. Then when the home is resold, the lender gets part of the equity and the homeowner keeps the rest. Assume that the lender in our example is willing to write a shared-appreciation mortgage. The rate is 10 instead of 12 percent. This reduces the monthly payment from $658.31 to $561.64. But the lender is entitled to receive one-third of the future appreciation in the home. The lender doesn't get this until the home is resold.

Original sales price	$ 80,000.00
Shared-appreciation mortgage (10%, 30 year,	
+ ⅓ of future appreciation)	$ 64,000.00
Monthly payment	$ 561.64
Future sales price (5 years at	
10% annual appreciation)	$128,840.00
Less original sales price	− 80,000.00
Appreciation	$ 48,840.00
⅓ share to lender	$ 16,280.00
⅔ share to homeowner	$ 32,560.00

This extra payment when the home is sold makes the mortgage more palatable to the lender. It raises the return and gives the institution a modest hedge against inflation. In many cases today, shared-appreciation mortgages are written "40/40." The lender cuts the interest rate by 40 percent and later takes 40 percent of the equity.

Shared-appreciation mortgages are not yet available in many parts of the country, and even where they are available, they are not common. But their usage is growing. Today there are no real standards pertaining to rates and percentages of sharing. The preceding example should not be used as a guideline. Where such mortgages are used, borrowers are not very excited about sharing their appreciation. In the end, however, the borrowers seem willing to share a piece of the future in order to get the money today.

Municipal Rate Mortgages

Many cities have gone into the mortgage-lending business. Here's how it works. The city raises money by selling municipal bonds. The interest paid on a municipal bond is not taxable to the investor. This means cities sell bonds at very favorable interest rates—say, 10 percent. The city then lends the money to homeowners for mortgages. Because the city's interest rate is very favorable, the interest rates on the mortgages they make can be favorable—say, 11 percent. The lending rate is a little higher than the borrowing rate to cover costs. Where can you beat a mortgage rate like that?

Of course, there are a few requirements. The obvious one is that you must build a new home within the boundaries of that city. Sometimes the cities require you to build a certain type of house, in a certain section of the city, with local union labor, and so on. And—very important—in many cases, these loans are available only to moderate-income families.

To the city, it is a good deal. They attract new growth to their city; their bonds are paid off with the mortgage payments, and they get additional revenues from property taxes on the new homes. To the buyer, it's an inexpensive way to finance a new home—if you can live with the requirements. However the system does seem to violate the federal government's idea of bureaucratic fair play. There are indications that government will try to prohibit such usage of municipal funds in the future.

Government-Subsidized Mortgages

From time to time, the federal government gets concerned about the ability of families to afford homes. Over the years, there have been a host of programs to help. One example was the FHA 235 program of the 1970s. Under this program, a qualifying family (certain maximum income, certain percentage of minorities, certain previous credit history, and so on) could buy a qualifying house (certain price limitations, certain building restrictions, certain FHA guarantees, and so on) with a government-subsidized mortgage. The government would agree to pay perhaps one-third of the interest, calculated by a complex equation.

Here's the effect of the government paying one-third of the interest. In our example, a $64,000 thirty-year, 12 percent mortgage has $658.31 monthly payment. In the first year, interest on the mortgage is about $638.96; only $19.35 goes to principal. The government pays one-third of $638.96, or $212.99. This reduces the first-year payment to $445.32 ($658.31 − $212.99 = $445.32). This obviously is very helpful to a financially struggling borrower.

The government subsidy doesn't stay at this level, however. Every year it decreases. That is because every year more of the payment goes to principal and less goes to interest. The homeowner will see payments gradually increase until in the last year he or she is paying nearly the full amount of $658.31. This is consistent with the hope that the homeowner's salary will increase over the years.

Government programs are fairly inactive at this time. But who knows what they will be doing next year?

The range of ways to finance homes has expanded dramatically in recent years. It has expanded in response to some of the most stressful financial times in U.S. history. If the financial markets continue to be chaotic, we can expect this list of creative ways to finance homes to grow. You can keep track of what's available by talking to real estate agents—it is their livelihood to know. But before you commit to a new-fangled form of home financing, be sure you understand all the implications. Here are a few questions to ask yourself:

1. Is there a deferred payment schedule? Is there a large balloon payment at some point?

2. What happens if the home does not appreciate in value as fast as you estimate?

3. What happens if your income doesn't increase as much as you hope?

4. Who could foreclose on you, and under what circumstances?

5. What requirements and restrictions do you assume?

6. Does your successful completion of your obligation depend on someone else successfully completing an obligation?

7. Where are the weak links?

The conventional mortgage is an excellent form of financing, particularly for the borrower. It is a well-tested form of financing. Some of the new forms may someday prove to be better—that's progress. But at this time we must wait and see.

◇ 58 ◇
Gambling with Commodities

Just a few years ago, commodities futures were something that very few people considered. They were left to the supersophisticated and wealthy individuals. But with news of fortunes made (lost fortunes rarely make the headlines), more and more people have become interested in commodity futures.

"What are they? How do I get into the market? Where is the profit made?" I am asked such questions fairly regularly, and sometimes they dismay me. When the questions come from a wealthy individual with hundreds of thousands or even millions in assets, I feel comfortable. If this person gambles in futures and loses, he or she probably can sustain the loss. But more and more frequently I get questions about commodities from people such as schoolteachers, blue-collar workers, or others whose assets are closer to $25,000. If these people gamble and lose, they could be wiped out. In the commodities futures market, what most people who invest don't realize is that you can lose *more* than your investment. Your entire estate may be at risk!

Although on the surface commodities futures seem similar to other investments such as stocks, bonds or even real estate, they are not. They are a breed apart. They involve heavy speculation and marginal investing. The term *margin* as used in the stock market is somewhat different in meaning from the term *margin* as used in commodities.

But perhaps the best way to understand both the risks and the rewards of the futures market is to jump right in and gain some understanding of the operation of the market itself.

Futures contracts are just what they say they are. They are a contract or an agreement to buy or sell something in the future. But why would there be a need for such an agreement?

Futures contracts originated many years ago as a means of ironing out the cycles that seem to occur in commodities. They were a means for both buyers and sellers to avoid extreme fluctuations in price. For example, all growers of wheat typically harvest their grain at about the same time. This pattern has certain repercussions for the growers. Some years have bountiful rainfall, few pests, and bumper crops. This should make the farmers happy. But if all the farmers have bumper crops, there is an oversupply of wheat. When the farmers bring grain to market, they will be competing with other farmers to sell it. The price will drop.

However, the buyers of wheat (those who purchase for large grain-processing concerns such as bread and cereal manufacturers) have slightly different concerns. They are thrilled when the farmers have a year of bumper crops because the prices are low. But they are concerned when there is a bad year. In a bad year, little rain, or an attack of locusts, or any number of other calamities might reduce the size of the crop. In such circumstances, the wheat buyers are competing with each other for a short supply. The price rises.

Buyers wish to be protected against high prices, growers against low ones. Is there any way to do this?

What we're really dealing with here is risk. Both the farmer and the buyer want to eliminate at least some of the risk inherent in their business. The way they found to cut down on risk was to give the risk to someone else. They called in the speculator.

The term *speculator* as I'm using it here is different from the way I used it in earlier chapters. Earlier, I meant someone who was taking too much financial and/or emotional risk for the gain that person was likely to make. In futures, the speculator assumes the risk for the grower and buyer in exchange for a profit.

But how can such a system work? How can the grower or the buyer transfer the risk to a third party?

The risk is transferred by means of the futures contract. Although in practice it is very sophisticated, in theory it is actually quite simple. Let's take the case of the grower first. The grower is concerned that in the case of bumper crops, the price might fall. How can he or she avoid this risk?

Here's how. He (or she) calls in the speculator and makes him an offer something like this. He tells the speculator, "I want to be assured of getting at least $3 a bushel when I bring my wheat to market in September, six months from now. To be assured of it, I am willing to sell my crop right now, in April, at $3 a bushel to you. I will guarantee delivery at that price six months from now.

The speculator considers this interesting offer. He can buy the farmer's wheat six months in the future for $3 a bushel. Is there any money to be made in this?

There certainly is. If it turns out that instead of a bumper crop there is a big crop failure and the price soars to, say, $4 a bushel, the speculator can buy this farmer's wheat in September for the guaranteed rate of $3 a bushel and turn right around and sell it to eager buyers at $4. He makes $1 profit per bushel! If he agrees to buy 100,000 bushels, that's a very handy $100,000 in profit.

But things could go the other way. What if there is a bumper crop? What if the price of wheat plummets so that by September it's down to $2 a bushel? Our speculator would be forced to buy the farmer's wheat at $3 and turn right around and sell it to disinterested buyers for $2. He'd lose $1 a bushel or $100,000.

The speculator tends to make a lot of money or lose a lot of money. So what does he do? He checks the long-term weather forecast. He checks past crop history. He investigates to see how many acres are planted, and so on. We'll say he concludes prices are going up, so he signs the futures contract with the farmer.

Now let's consider the buyer of wheat. Remember, he's concerned about a short crop and high prices. Our buyer also would like to be assured that he can buy at prices no higher than $3 a bushel. So he calls in a different speculator.

Our buyer tells Speculator 2, "I want to be assured of paying no more than $3 a bushel. So I will sign a contract today guaranteeing to buy 100,000 bushels of wheat at $3 six months in the future." Is there money to be made here?

Speculator 2 considers. If the price of wheat should drop to $2 by September when the contract comes due, he can quickly buy all the wheat he needs for the $2 price and turn around, forcing this buyer to pay him $3 a bushel for it, according to the signed futures contract. He stands to make $100,000 profit.

But what if the price moves up to $4? Then Speculator 2 would be forced to buy the wheat at the higher price and sell it to the buyer according to the contract for $3—a dollar loss or $100,000 on the whole contract.

Speculator 2 also looks at weather, crop history and so on. He concludes that a bumper crop is coming. So he takes on the futures contract.

This is how the futures market works in simplified fashion. Please notice several very important items in our example:

1. By using the futures contract, both the buyer and grower were able to eliminate much of the risk of fluctuating prices.

2. The two speculators, in hoping for big profits, assumed all the risk that the buyer and grower eliminated.

3. Speculator 2 signed a contract agreeing to sell 100,000 bushels of wheat to our buyer six months in the future, even though he didn't own any wheat at all at the time. This last point is often the most confusing to newcomers to the market. It is called "selling short." It means selling a commodity that you don't own. In our example, the speculator was able to do this because he felt confident that come September he could always buy wheat from a grower and fulfill his contract.

4. The grower, the speculators, and the buyer all felt confident that the others would live up to their ends of the bargain.

Their guarantee was the deposit or "margin" as used in commodity futures. Even though contracts are signed, how can the grower really be assured that the speculator will actually come up with the $100,000 in cash come September should the price fall from the agreed-on $3 per bushel to $2? How can the buyer be assured that the other speculator will come up with the $100,000 he agreed on come September, should the price rise from the agreed-upon $3 to $4 per bushel? How can the speculator be assured that if the price goes to $4, the farmer will actually deliver the wheat? (Won't he be tempted to try to break the contract and sell for more?) How can the other speculator be assured that if the price falls to $2 the buyer will actually follow through with the purchase? (Won't he be tempted to try to break the contract and buy elsewhere for less?)

To guarantee performance by all parties, a deposit or margin is established. It is the difference between the price agreed on in the contract and the actual future price of the commodity today.

Again, this concept is not difficult, but it may take a few moments to consider. In our example, the grower has agreed to sell for $3 a bushel in September. If it's lower in September, he wins. If it's higher, he loses. Now let's say that in May the price of wheat rises to $3.10 a bushel. That's a difference of ten cents a bushel. Of course, by September the price may very well drop below $3. But in the short term, our grower has guessed wrong. He's lost. Our speculator now tells our grower, "If you want me to honor your contract at $3 in September, you have to immediately come up with that ten cents a bushel you guessed wrong."

Ten cents a bushel times 100,000 bushels is $10,000. In order to keep his contract, the farmer must now put up $10,000 in cash. This is his margin.

Let's say that by June the price of wheat again rises to $3.20 a bushel. It's risen another ten cents. Again the speculator says, "If you want me to honor your contract at $3 in September, I want you to put up another ten cents a bushel to me now." (Our speculator is really feeling pretty good about now, because his gamble is paying off. The farmer has agreed to sell at $3, and the market is already $3.20. If it stays the same way until September, the speculator has $20,000 on his gamble. This money, of course, is exactly the amount the farmer must put up.)

In July, the price goes up another ten cents to $3.30 and the farmer puts up another $10,000. In August, it's up to $3.40, and once again our farmer dips into his bank account for another $10,000. Our farmer has put up $40,000 in all. And our speculator has won $40,000 in his gamble, thus far.

But in September the farmer's gamble pays off. A bumper crop is harvested, and the price of wheat drops to $2.10. The contract calls for the speculator to buy the wheat at $3.00 even though the market price is only $2.10. The farmer has saved himself a loss of $90,000. However, remember that the price was up to $3.40 a bushel in August. When it drops to $2.10, that's a drop of $1.30 per bushel. For 100,000 bushels, that comes to $130,000. Our farmer not only saves himself a loss of $90,000 on the sale of the wheat, but also gets back the $40,000 margin he had to give the speculator.

Saved on loss from wheat	$ 90,000
Return of money invested	40,000
	$130,000

But what of our poor speculator? Now we're going to make this example a bit more true to life. We'll say that our speculator didn't deal with the farmer directly. Instead, he went to a commodities brokerage house. (There are hundreds of these across the country.) The commodities broker was just a middleman to facilitate the contract between grower and speculator.

The broker told the speculator, "I can get you a contract with a farmer for $3 per bushel. However, to guarantee that you will pay off if the price should drop, you are going to have to put some money up front. It will be divided into two parts. The first part will be a deposit that I will use in case the price drops. This is just in case the price fluctuates down a few cents. For example, the price of wheat rarely stays at exactly $3.00. It could go down to $2.99 or $2.98 before rebounding back to $3.01 or $3.02. I will use this deposit you give me to guarantee the contract in case the price drops a few cents. A drop of only one cent on 100,000 bushels is a loss for you of $1000. A drop of two cents is a loss of $2000. Therefore, I will require that you give me a deposit of $2000 against such a loss. In addition, there's always a chance that the price could drop even further, very rapidly. Therefore, to guarantee that I will have time to call you on the phone and have you deposit more money should the price fall more than two cents, I want a maintenance *margin*. The maintenance *margin* will be $1500, or equivalent to the price of $.015 movement in the price of wheat."

Our speculator understands, therefore, that he must come up with a total of a $2000 deposit and a $1500 margin, or $3500, to get a contract with our farmer. But he is sure the price for wheat is going to go up, not down, so he agrees.

Please notice that the $3500 the speculator puts up is the total amount of his *initial* investment (plus the broker's fee, which usually runs less than $100 for the contract).

It is at this point that many newcomers to the futures game make a big mistake. They think that this $3500 investment is like the amount paid for stock or the down payment on a home. They think that this amount is all that they have at risk.

Nothing could be further from the truth. Let's see just what our speculator truly does have at risk.

Our speculator agreed to buy 100,000 bushels at $3.00 a bushel. Of course, he figured the price would go higher and he could sell for a profit. But let's say a catastrophe occurred. Let's say that there was a nuclear accident, and all of the farmer's wheat was contaminated with radiation! Suddenly, no one would buy it at any price— no one except the speculator who according to written contract had agreed to buy it, come flood, famine, pestilence, or nuclear accident, for $3 a bushel. In that case, our speculator would have to come up with $3 times 100,000 bushels, or $300,000. Our speculator was at risk for $300,000! This, even though his initial investment was only $3500.

Newcomers to commodities investing never seem to realize this risk potential. They are at risk for the entire amount of the contract. But let's see how it worked for our particular speculator.

By August, you'll recall, the price had risen to $3.40 a bushel. Because the contract price was for $3.00, our speculator had made $.40 a bushel profit, or $40,000. (Remember, this was the money our farmer had to deposit into his margin account to maintain the contract.) Our speculator was feeling great. He had $40,000 in his account, which he was able to withdraw down to the $3500 limit set by the brokerage firm. He had made $40,000 already on his contract.

Then came September, with the surprise news of the bumper crop. Prices plummeted. One day it was $3.40, the next it was $3.30, the next $3.20, and on down. Every day our speculator had to go to the bank and make a withdrawal to maintain his contract.

After he had lost $30,000 of his profit, he went back to his broker and said, "Stop this contract! I want out. I'm getting killed. Is there any way out?"

"Certainly," said the broker. "You have a contract to buy at $3.10. But there are other speculators who have contracts to sell at $3.00. (You recall our other speculator who agreed to sell at that price to the buyer of wheat?) "You can do the same as they did. You can agree to sell at the September future price of wheat, which at the moment is $3.10. If you have a contract to buy at $3.00 and a contract to sell at $3.10, both contracts will cancel each other out. You'll be out of the market, pocketing the difference, which in this case happens to be ten cents a bushel, or $10,000."

"Great!" said the speculator. "I'll take my $10,000 and run."

"No sooner said than done," said the broker, and he put in a call to his brokerage house's agent right on the floor of the commodity exchange. He told this floor agent to sell one contract of September wheat at $3.10.

But the floor agent replied that the price had already fallen to $2.95. And it was going down so fast that it was at limit and the market closed.

The broker looked up at the speculator apologetically. He said, "I'm sorry. You're too late. The commodities market has limit rises and falls. What that means is that if the price goes up or down too fast, to protect everyone from being hurt we close the market. In the case of wheat in this market, the maximum price the commodity can fall in one day is $.15 per bushel. It has already done that. We can't execute any new buy or sell orders until the market opens tomorrow.

"Oh, and by the way," the broker continued, "The September price is now $2.95. Your margin was at $3.10. You owe us the difference, or $.15 a bushel. That comes to $15,000."

The speculator went home flabbergasted, but withdrew the money from savings and gave it to the broker. He had now lost all the $40,000 in profit plus an additional $5000 of his own money, plus still had his original deposit and margin invested.

Because of the sudden news of a bumper crop, the price continued to fall. It was down the limit each day, and no one could buy or sell new contracts. Finally, after over a week it ended up at $2.10. By this time our speculator owed his broker the difference between the $3.00 contract price and the actual price of $2.10, or $.90 a bushel. For 100,000 bushels, that came to exactly $90,000. For an initial investment of $3500, our speculator had lost $90,000! Quite an investment.

Just how realistic is this example? In some ways, it is very realistic, particularly in explaining the loss potential. When a commodities brokerage house accepts a client, it insists on seeing a financial statement. It wants to be sure the speculator has sufficient assets to cover a loss such as this.

In addition, in order to establish a contract, the speculator has to pledge his or her assets in case of loss. If the speculator doesn't willingly come up with the money, the brokerage house can take legal action to obtain it.

How often is the market up or down the limit?

Not very often. For each commodity handled (and there are dozens and dozens), limit moves don't normally occur more than once or twice per year. But they do occur, and when they do a speculator can get caught—and burned.

The reader must remember that when you enter the commodities market, you are not the grower or the buyer. You are the speculator. You are taking the grower's or the buyer's risk in order to make a profit. You are gambling with enormous sums of money. You may win big. But you could also lose big.

Our example is also unrealistic in many ways. For one thing, I've been talking as if there actually was delivery of a commodity, wheat in this case. There almost *never* is. Of all the contracts handled on the Chicago Board of Trade, studies indicate that less than 2 percent ever go to delivery! In all other cases, the buy contracts are offset by sell contracts, and vice versa.

The purpose of the commodities futures market is *not* to buy a commodity. It is to reassign the risk. That is the simple reason that delivery is so rarely done. (There are reasons why delivery is sometimes taken, such as when it is difficult to actually obtain the commodity on the spot market. The term *spot market* means the cash price.) Also, another major reason for exchanges working as they do is to provide liquidity. The majority of buyers and sellers are speculators. If only growers and processors were in the markets, they would probably be too illiquid to operate successfully.

Also unrealistic is the idea that growers or suppliers would dig into their pockets for $40,000, as did our wheat grower when the price went against him. The minute he saw the price of wheat rising above $3.00 to, say, $3.03, he offset his contract and got out of the market. As long as the September price was rising above his $3.00 mark, why should he bother with a contract? He'd be making money in the spot market.

Of course, the minute the price started to drop, he'd try to get back in, to execute a sell contract. Certainly by the time the price broke $3, he'd be in the market trying to protect himself again. However, if he was out and the market was down the limit, he'd be unable to get in. He'd be taking the loss in the actual reduction of price for his wheat. If he was out of the market and the price was down the limit from $3.00 to $2.10, he would have lost $90,000 in actual cash on the sale of his crop.

In actual practice, speculators are in and out of the market not only on a daily or hourly basis, but on a minute-by-minute basis. And the market price moves up and down like a roller-coaster, sweeping speculators, growers, and buyers along with it.

Chances for Making a Profit

My description of the commodities futures market has been brief—far too brief actually to give a true working understanding of how it operates. Anyone who is seriously thinking of investing in this market should spend some time, hopefully several months, reading the literature available on it as well as contacting the various exchanges, which have their own literature. Also, play the commodities market first on a piece of paper, with play money. See how well you would have done before you spend a penny. If you find that you would have lost money, maybe that's a good indication you should stay out.

◇ 59 ◇
Strategies for Winning
in the Futures Market

Although studies have indicated that 85 percent of the speculators lose *all* of the money they invest (some much more) in commodities futures, there is always that 15 percent that makes money. How do they succeed?

Here are three reasons why people do make it big in commodities.

Day Trading

"Day trading" simply means opening a contract and closing out in the same day. Here, the speculator is trying to take advantage of the price movement that occurs during a single day.

For example, the price of T-Bills (a commodity sold on most exchanges) may move up or down significantly in one day. Frequently the market will open high, drop way down, and then close about where it was when it closed the preceding day. Or it could move in the other direction—dropping at the opening, moving higher, and then closing lower. A day trader tries to take advantage of these movements.

In almost all cases, the only successful day traders are those who are right there on the floor of the commodities exchange. These are members of brokerage exchanges and a few individuals. They can watch price movements as they occur. Some experts have argued that such floor trading actually *causes* such daily fluctuations. Because the day traders are right on the spot, they can take advantage of them. People who are right on the floor get caught up with the excitement of price moves and are able to react instantly. Floor traders typically make great amounts of money by day trading.

But speculators who are hundreds or even thousands of miles away, in a broker's office, usually *lose* on day trading. The long-distance speculator has little opportunity to get the feel of the market. He or she doesn't know what's actually going on in the minds of the floor traders. (One clue that floor traders sometimes use is to glance around and see how many buy or sell orders other floor traders are holding. By judging the volume moment to moment, they can actually predict the market's course for the next few minutes.

Sitting far away, the speculator only sees the market on a television screen, after the fact. This is the first element of delay.

Then, once the speculator sees what the market has done, he or she spends time deciding how to act. This is the second delay. Finally, there is the time spent in communicating the order to the broker and in the broker calling the floor trader via phone lines once the decision to act has been taken. This lag can take a half or a full hour. During that time, the market could easily have reversed itself.

Day trading is perhaps the most risky method of all in commodity futures.

Trending

There is a way for a distant speculator to make money in commodities futures: by trending the market.

Trending the market means spending a great deal of time and effort in judging both "fundamental" and "technical" analysis. It means trying to find long-term trends and taking advantage of them.

Fundamental analysis means learning what factors influence the market up or down. If we're interested in soybeans, for example, we can learn about weather conditions, acres of beans planted, new farming techniques being employed, pest control measures, and so forth.

Technical analysis examines the past history and patterns of the market. It considers such factors as how the market tends to perform in a given month each year, how many times the market has risen (or fallen) from the present price range in the past, and so on. Fundamentalists look at market factors; technicians look at charts and graphs. A speculator who wants to trend the market will probably spend months and months examining market factors, charts, and graphs before making a move.

A speculator who is trending should understand that the best he or she can hope for is to be right 40 percent of the time. That means being wrong 60 percent of the time. Therefore, the trending speculator will have a reserve of money available. For example, playing with $50,000 is not uncommon. With this money the speculator will gamble, perhaps $5000 at a time, hoping to hit a trend. The speculator will keep playing the market, buying long (offering to purchase a commodity) or selling short (offering to sell a commodity), hoping that he or she will be able to buy into a long-term upward or downward price trend.

If the trender is successful in getting into a long-term price movement, he or she will stick with the market, usually for a long ride up or down—making money all the way. Good trenders usually try to bail out before the market peaks or hits bottom. The philosophy is that it's better to make a little by getting out too soon than lose a lot by staying in too long.

Emotions

The final key to success in the market has nothing to do with the actual market at all. Rather, it has to do with the speculator's emotions.

Emotions in commodity futures are strong, stronger than most beginners ever dreamed of. It is one thing to calmly tell your broker to buy September plywood. It is quite another to sleep well that night, knowing that you are committed to close to $100,000 in a highly volatile investment.

New investors are frequently riddled with emotions they don't know how to handle. First, there is fear—fear that they have made a bad move and bought or sold at the wrong time, fear that they really don't know what they're doing and shouldn't be in this field, fear that they will lose far more than they can afford.

At the other extreme is greed—greed that says they have a chance to win a fortune, if only they don't blow it; greed that says they should not only stick it out, but invest more money; greed that blinds them to the reality of the market.

The great problem with fear is that it drives the speculator to sell a good contract too soon and a bad one too late. The great problem with greed is that it tends to make the speculator want the market to behave as he or she demands. The market, however, is slave to no one. It is totally free and operates according to its own whims.

I hope that I've made my own position on the market clear. I'm not against speculating in commodities if you have the assets to do so, and if you understand that speculating is far more like gambling in Las Vegas or Atlantic City than most brokerage houses care to admit.

My own feeling is that only about 2 percent of the population really should be into commodities futures. If you happen to be among that 2 percent, then I suggest you first write to the commodities exchanges. They are almost all more than willing to send free brochures describing their activities. Next contact several brokers. Commodity brokerage houses are usually part of stock brokerage firms. All large ones are bonded and backed up by some insurance.

The following is a list of commodities typically traded on exchanges. It includes food stuffs, metals, money, and lumber. All have different underlying fundamentals, and they all have plenty of risk and lots of volatile price action.

Commodities Typically Traded on Exchanges

Copper	Coffee	British pound
Gold	Cotton	Canadian dollar
Heating oil	Orange juice	Japanese yen
Platinum	Potatoes	Swiss franc
Silver	Sugar	West German mark
	Corn	GNMA
Lumber	Oats	Treasury bonds
Plywood	Soybeans	Treasury bills
	Soybean meal	
	Soybean oil	
	Wheat	
	Barley	
	Rye	
	Flaxseed	
	Rapeseed	
	Cattle (feeder)	
	Cattle	
	Hogs	
	Pork bellies	
	Cocoa	

◇ 60 ◇
Investing Dollars in
Gold and Silver

Gold and silver are very legitimate assets. In fact, they have been a major form of money for thousands of years. In the last four or five years, they have performed both very well (prior to February 1980) and then again not quite so well. The person who is going to buy them as an investment, however, should scrutinize their risk potential very carefully.

To begin, let's do away with some of the mystique surrounding gold and silver. They have not, as some promoters claim, always done well or always gone up in the "long term." For extended periods of history, the price of gold and silver has been steady. For many years, gold was about $22 an ounce. For nearly thirty years after World War II, it remained at $35 an ounce. (From 1933 until 1975, U.S. citizens were prohibited from owning investment gold.)

Over the long haul, silver has not had a much better track record. During the 1800s, with massive silver discoveries in the Comstock Lode, silver was so plentiful that its price plummeted. It was only through heavy lobbying that silver interests succeeded in getting the U.S. government to back some of its paper currency with silver and thereby absorb the surplus.

After 1964, when the United States stopped issuing most silver coins and redeemed its outstanding silver certificates, the price remained low. The United States had a stockpile of over 2000 million ounces, and it proceeded to sell this stockpile to the highest bidder, keeping the price around $2 per ounce.

In modern times, the price of those precious metals has gone up only since the early 1970s, when the U.S. government stopped redeeming in paper currency from foreign countries with gold and stopped selling from its silver stockpiles (under 140 million ounces as of this writing).

From a low of about $40 an ounce in 1973, the price of gold soared to almost $900 on the open market in early 1980, only to fall back to half that level 18 months later. Silver sold for about $5 an ounce at the beginning of 1979 and then soared to about $50 an ounce at the beginning of 1980. A little over a year later, it plummeted almost all the way back down.

This big rise in price during 1979 and early 1980, I believe, gave the American public a real consciousness of gold and silver. Before that, these were exotic investments, something only foreigners or supersophisticated investors dabbled in. After the big price booms, everyone got into the act. Long lines of people formed outside gold and silver dealers as the average American waited either to sell his or her family silverware or to buy some precious metal.

Even the big price drop after early 1980 didn't daunt the American public. Although very few people actually bought the precious metals, everyone watched them closely. Most seemed to be determined to catch the next big price rise and take advantage of it. People had seen fortunes made, and weren't going to miss out next time.

I have no quarrel with this idea. But as we wait for gold and silver to jump in price once more, it would be well worth our time to understand why they tend to move as they do.

Gold

Gold is a proxy for a hedge against international tension and international inflation.

That may be a mouthful to say, but it does help capture the reason for gold's price moves. Let's break it down. First let's look at international tension more closely.

INTERNATIONAL TENSION

Historically, gold has been the currency of last resort. During both World War I and II, families in occupied parts of Europe were able to buy food, clothing, and shelter with gold when their regular paper currencies would buy nothing. It has often been said that every French family has some gold coins hidden in the doorposts of their homes against a future war emergency.

Even today, this feeling pervades most of the world. In the Middle East, where tensions are high, wealthy individuals tend to trade their dollars or other currencies for gold. In the event of a crisis, they want money that is not only spendable but also transportable—something wealthy people can take with them if they must flee the country. For example, when the Ayatollah Khomeni took over Iran wealthy Arabs stockpiled gold.

Sometimes people purchase gold just because there is tension. When the Soviet Union invaded Afghanistan, the volume of gold demand increased enormously. When there was trouble in Poland, again purchasers far outnumbered sellers. The same was true for nearly a year and a half when the Iranians held fifty-two Americans hostage. Whenever international tensions rise, people around the world trade their regular money in for gold.

The effect of all this trading is to send the price of gold up. As more and more people demand gold, the price is forced up. That is why we can almost measure the change in the price of gold by world tensions. When there is a major crisis somewhere in the world, the price of gold is likely to be rising.

But when we enter a calm period with little or no crisis, people tend to dispose of their gold.

So it's simple—buy on tension, and sell on calm. Or is it simple? Why didn't gold rise during the war between Iran and Syria, or during the war of nerves Russia waged against Poland in 1980–1981? Because the Syrians and Iranians had their oil shut off and had to sell gold to sustain their economies. And Russia was running heavy expenses, with troops in Afghanistan and on the Polish border. They had to sell gold to meet expenses.

Gold cannot be rented out to bring in income as real estate can. It pays no dividends as do stocks. It yields no interest as do bonds or T-Bills. It simply sits there. It does, in fact, cost money to hold if one considers the cost of insurance and safety deposit boxes. Therefore, when gold is not going up in price, it is a highly disadvantageous investment.

Consequently, we can expect the speculators to buy and sell very quickly. Perhaps more quickly than you can figure out whether the current situation is a good world tension—or a bad world tension.

INTERNATIONAL INFLATION

If gold only responded to international tension, then perhaps we could eventually learn to plot its course and, if we were careful, invest for profit. Gold, however, also responds to international inflation. This aspect of gold is somewhat more difficult to understand, although its effects are obvious.

Inflation is evidenced by an increase in prices. However, things have not become more valuable: Rather, the currency we use to purchase them has become less valuable.

When investors see that inflation is occurring and their currency is becoming less valuable, they tend to look for hedges—places they can put their money where it won't depreciate. One such hedge has traditionally been gold investments.

Therefore gold is a kind of international currency. Around the world, when inflation rises in France, people trade francs for gold. In Germany, they trade Deutschmarks for gold. In Italy, they trade lira for gold, and so forth. The idea is that gold will retain its buying power, while the regular currency of these countries will not.

This pattern can be most clearly seen in terms of oil. Oil has often been described as *black gold,* for good reason. The relationship between gold and oil is strong.

As we all know, oil is the backbone of our modern civilization. Yet during the past decade it soared in price. From a few dollars per barrel, it rose to over $40 a barrel.

Many people attribute this price rise entirely to an increase in value of oil. But that would not be correct. During this same time period, our U.S. dollar depreciated in value by nearly 50 percent due to inflation. In terms of 1972 dollars, therefore, we might say that oil only rose in value to $20 a barrel. The rest of the increase was due to our own inflated currency.

So during the last ten-year period it took more and more dollars to buy the same barrel of oil. In fact, it took nearly ten times as many nominal dollars to buy a barrel of oil in early 1981 as it took to buy a barrel in early 1971.

Now let's look at gold. One ounce of gold back in early 1971 was valued at about $40. One ounce of gold would buy, therefore, about 10 barrels of oil back then. But early in 1981, gold was valued at about $500 an ounce. With oil at $40 a barrel, that same ounce of gold would buy 12.5 barrels! Gold had retained (actually increased) its buying power, while the dollar had lost 90 percent of its buying power—at least in terms of oil. It's easy to see why investors have turned to gold.

People in Germany, France, England, Italy, Switzerland, and virtually every other country in the world regularly trade their own currency for gold in order to avoid the effects of inflation.

The critical factor to understand is that these people buy gold (and thereby send the price up) *when there is the threat of inflation.*

When there is little or no threat of inflation, however, people are content to stick with their countries' currencies. The future price of gold, therefore, depends to a great extent on what inflation will do. If we continue to have high inflation, we can expect gold prices to remain high. However, if inflation drops, we can also expect the price of gold to drop.

I have no crystal ball regarding worldwide inflation. But in Chapter 2 I noted there are significant reasons that the inflation rate in the United States may tend to drop. Declining U.S. inflation should help cool worldwide inflation.

One important factor to watch, I believe, is the worldwide price for oil. As I write this, after nearly a decade of oil shortages, we are having a period of oil surplus. Middle Eastern, African, South American, and other oil producers simply can't find enough buyers, and the price of oil is falling. Right alongside, the price of gold is also falling.

Of course, I don't anticipate this oil glut will last too long, but while it does the price for both oil and gold may be depressed.

OTHER FACTORS

Although international tension and international inflation strongly influence the price of gold, they are not the only influences. (Actually, if they were, it still would be fairly easy to predict the future price of gold and speculate on that.) There are many other factors involved, not the least of which is the withholding of gold supplies and the strength of demand for jewelry gold.

WITHHOLDING GOLD

The Union of South Africa is the largest producer of gold in the world, currently providing about half the free world's annual supply. Yet during the past few years, whenever the price of gold dipped below what South Africa considered to be a minimum level (in the past about $500), that country withheld gold from the market.

The effect of this withholding was to buffer any drops in the price. By keeping the supply down whenever the price drops it is possible, in theory, to establish a floor for the price of gold. South Africa apparently succeeded in doing this for more than a year after the price initially plummeted in early 1980. Whether it will be able to continue maintaining this floor, of course, remains to be seen.

JEWELRY DEMAND

Even though we've spoken of the demand for gold by investors as if it were the only use for this precious metal, it is not. In fact, more than half of all gold produced each year is used by the jewelry trade. This gold goes into rings, bracelets, earrings, watches and so on. This may come as a shock to many investors, but is, in fact, the case.

An interesting thing happens to the jewelry demand for gold when the price rises. The demand declines almost proportionately.

This phenomenon was first observed in the period between 1974 and 1976 when gold took its first major price jump in this century. At that time, gold rose from about $40 an ounce to just under $200 an ounce largely in anticipation of the new American market. For the first time in over four decades, Americans would be legally allowed to own gold. Many speculators hoped that we would flock to the yellow metal, driving the price up.

As the price rose—driven up by speculation—the demand for jewelry gold fell. The higher price for gold resulted in higher prices for jewelry and buyers backed off. They didn't make purchases. By the time gold peaked, at about $200 an ounce, jewelry demand had dropped to only about 25 percent of its former levels!

Because jewelry demand at that time amounted to nearly 75 percent of total gold demand, the price of gold was not able to sustain high prices without it. It began to fall, and within a year had dropped back down to just over $100 an ounce—a drop in price of 50 percent.

But as the price dropped, people began buying jewelry again, and the jewelry demand revived. Eventually, after a few years, so did the price of gold.

Almost an identical phenomenon occurred in the period from August 1979 to early 1980. The price of gold rose from about $220 an ounce to almost $880. And jewelry demand fell almost to zero. After early 1980, the price, no longer sustainable without the jewelry demand, also fell.

The supply and demand picture for gold also gives another insight to what causes its price to fluctuate. There are, of course, more factors—including simple speculation in the market and auctions of gold by governments such as the United States and government-like agencies such as the International Monetary Fund. So it is extremely difficult for an individual investor to get accurate information and to pin-point all of the factors so that an informed judgment can be made.

Silver

Many would-be investors regard silver as a poor man's gold. Silver frequently costs only about 1/20th to 1/30th the price of the yellow metal.

But silver has a mind of its own. Although it does tend to be swept upward or downward when gold is fluctuating strongly, it does not at all operate according to the same factors as gold.

To begin, silver has never been an international proxy for a hedge against inflation and tension, as gold has. People don't tend to run to silver in times of trouble or to buy it as protection against inflation nearly as much as they buy gold. Part of the reason is the U.S. government.

As mentioned earlier, the U.S. government for years was dumping silver from its stockpile. This has artificially kept the price of silver low. Investors, therefore, never got into the habit of using silver as a hedge. (Some speculators, however, saw that this inexperience with silver could prove to be a boon if they could control the market. Investors unfamiliar with silver might jump right in and buy if they thought it was indeed poor man's gold and acted accordingly, as we'll see shortly.)

SPECULATION IN THE SILVER MARKET

The second big difference between gold and silver has to do with how the market for each is established. Let's compare: The market for gold is established when buyers and sellers of the actual, physical metal get together and work out an acceptable price. The two most famous "price fixings" occur in the Rothschild's bank in London and among three of the biggest banks in Zurich, Switzerland. The morning and afternoon price fixes are announced world-wide and establish the price of gold. (A secondary price for gold is established on the commodities market, where gold futures are bought and sold. As noted earlier, commodities futures is highly speculative. The biggest futures market is in the Commodities Exchange of New York (COMEX), and its daily prices are also widely quoted.)

The important point to understand, however, is that with gold the ultimate price is primarily determined by the fixings where the actual, physical metal is bought and sold.

For silver, however, there are no such "price fixings." Rather, the physical silver is bought somewhat secretively by the major users. The price they pay is tied in some cases directly to the price of silver in futures contracts, usually at either the Chicago Board of

Trade or the Chicago Mercantile Exchange. Therefore, the price of silver in the United States is determined primarily by the commodities futures market.

But as we've noted, this market is highly speculative. So a few investors can decide to buy heavily and thereby influence the price without regard to actual supply and demand conditions or without regard to investors as a whole.

This is, in fact, what happened during the big price increase in early 1980. Several speculators in the Chicago markets gained control of vast quantities of silver on futures contracts. Then, instead of canceling out their contracts with offsetting contracts (as explained in the chapter on commodities), they demanded actual, physical delivery!

Of course, they had to have enormous amounts of money—billions of dollars—to do this, but they accomplished the feat.

Sellers, who were for the most part speculators, suddenly found they couldn't cancel out their contracts. They were forced to actually buy physical silver to deliver to these buyer speculators. (In practice, the exchanges themselves handle the purchase and transfer of physical silver.)

The many "long" (purchase) contracts, combined with sellers dashing around to find actual silver to sell, forced the price up to $50. The price rose almost entirely through speculation. Investors and users had little to do with it.

Some of these speculators have claimed that they could have sustained the price at $50 if the exchanges had not changed their rules and required larger margins—up to 50 percent of the contract value, in some cases. In any event, people sold their old silverware, silver jewelry, silver trays and dishes, and so forth at high prices. Great quantities of the metal flooded the market, and price went down as fast if not faster than it had gone up.

Therefore, the opportunity for a few speculators to corner the market and influence prices is very strong in silver, unlike gold. And the price of silver at any given time may well be an artificial price caused by this speculation.

SUPPLY AND DEMAND

The demand for silver comes primarily from a single source—the photographic industry. Silver is used to create the images we see on film. It has been estimated that between 70 and 90 percent of the silver used worldwide is used by the photo industry.

The demand for silver from the photo industry tends to remain constant, regardless of price. (This differs considerably with gold demand from jewelry users.) During the time that silver jumped up nearly ten times its value to $50 an ounce, the photo demand dropped only about 25 percent. Demand remained fairly constant.

The supply of silver, however, varies greatly. Supply of silver comes from many sources, including new mining and old scrap. Old scrap includes the silverware and old jewelry that was traded in by the average person during the big price jump.

Whenever the price of silver rises, it seems to pour into the market. In India alone, an estimated 3 billion ounces of silver is held in the form of jewelry. In India, unlike most of the world, people buy silver as proxy hedges instead of gold. It is kept in India largely through laws prohibiting its export. But during times of high prices, it escapes through the black market and is sold. The threat of legalizing the sale of silver from India is like an axe hovering over the price of the precious metal.

Another axe with a sharp blade is the remaining 139.5 million ounces of silver in the U.S. strategic stockpile. The Reagan Administration has announced that it no longer considers the metal to have any strategic value. It wants to sell the entire stockpile. Because the 139.5 million ounces are almost an entire year's supply of silver, such a sale could have a disastrous effect on the market.

Investing in gold and silver is not the "sure thing" that some promoters claim it is. Gold and silver do not always go up in price, in either the short or the long run. Trends predicting what the price of these precious metals will be are not easily discovered. And the person who is less than an expert in the field stands a good chance of getting burned. That's why I would rank the investing in both these precious metals as high risk.

I'm reminded of a friend of mine who bought some physical silver back in 1979, when the price was only $10 an ounce. In a few months, it jumped to $25.

She was astonished by her success and wanted to buy more. She quickly discovered that by combining commodity futures with silver she could control vast quantities of the metal with only a small deposit and margin.

She bought several contracts when the price was $25 an ounce. Within a month, it had shot up to $50. Because each contract was for a 4000-ounce bar, a jump in price of $1 meant a $4000 profit for her. She held three contracts, so each time silver went up $1 an ounce she made $12,000 profit. But it went up $25 an ounce. Her profit was twenty-five times $12,000, or $300,000!

She had made $300,000 on an investment of less than $15,000. She did so well, in fact, that she said she was never going to sell her silver. She was going to wait until it reached $1 million.

Unfortunately, before it went up again, it went down—down the limit. The market was closed, and she could not bail out until it reached the $24 mark. She lost the $300,000 she had made, plus her original deposit of $15,000.

I suppose it's easy to say, "Easy come, easy go." But, she felt rather bad about it. She had believed that silver was a sure thing. It was not, as she gloomily found out.

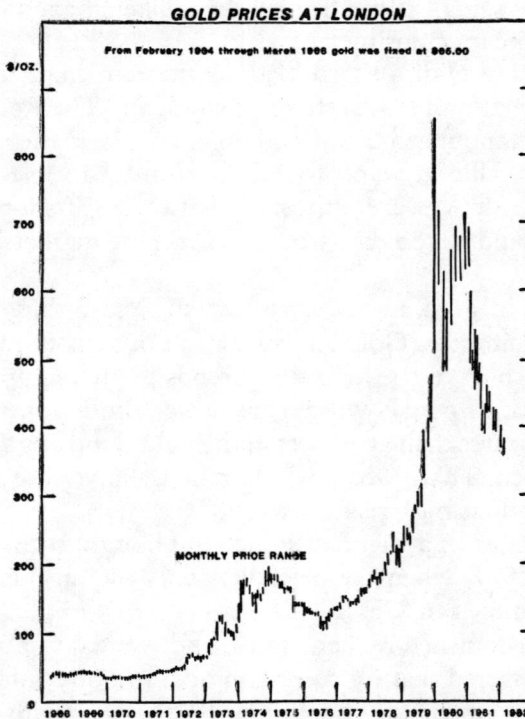

GOLD PRICES AT LONDON

From February 1904 through March 1908 gold was fixed at $85.00

$/OZ.

900

800

700

600

500

400

300

MONTHLY PRICE RANGE

200

100

0

1966 1969 1970 1971 1972 1973 1974 1975 1976 1977 1978 1979 1980 1981 1982

◇ 61 ◇
How to Profit in Gold and Silver

For those who feel they have sufficient assets to be able to take a plunge in gold and silver and withstand the possibility of loss, the question arises, "What do I invest in?" In other words, what form should the gold and silver take? A 4000-ounce silver bar such as used for the futures commodity market would cost $40,000 if the price of silver were $10 an ounce. What do you buy if you have considerably less to invest?

Gold

There are many options open for the person buying gold. However, the investor must always consider resale when buying. It's important to buy a form of gold that is resalable. If that is the criterion, then perhaps the best form of gold to purchase is a South African krugerrand. The krugerrand is recognized the world around as a standard of gold and is quickly accepted in every bullion store.

The krugerrand contains exactly 1 ounce of pure gold, so its price is easy to calculate. It's the price of gold at the moment, plus a small premium—usually about 5 percent. (The premium goes to the dealer and wholesaler, for marketing the coin.)

If the price of gold is $500, a krugerrand might be expected to sell for about $525 ($500 per oz + 5% premium, or $25 = $525).

If for some reason a South African krugerrand is not preferred, then the next choice would probably be a Canadian maple leaf. This coin, like the krugerrand, also contains exactly 1 ounce of pure gold, and its price is calculated similarly. However, the maple leaf is .999 fine, while the krugerrand is only .916 fine, and the maple leaf has about a 6 percent premium. (Don't let the fineness fool you. There's still exactly one ounce of gold in each coin.) The maple leaf is not as well known as the krugerrand, but selling it should present no problems.

After these two coins, there are many others well recognized and some not. The biggest problem with the rest is that they usually do not contain exactly 1 ounce; hence the calculation of their value is somewhat difficult. They include the British sovereign, the Austrian 100 corona, the Mexican 50 peso, and many, many others.

One point that newcomers may not realize is that the premium on the coin goes up as the weight goes down. A krugerrand may have only a 5 percent premium, but a half-krugerrand containing 0.5 ounce may have a 7 to 8 percent premium, and a quarter-krugerrand containing 0.25 ounce may have a 10 percent premium. The same holds true for other smaller gold coins.

Silver

Outside of commodity silver bars, most people who purchase silver buy it in the form of silver coins. Prior to 1964, the United States issued silver coins in the denominations of dime, quarter, and half-dollar (and, earlier, the dollar). These for convenience are sold in bags of $1000 face value. Each bag contains about 714 ounces of pure silver. Their value is determined by multiplying 714 times the price of silver. If silver is $10 per ounce, the bag should be worth about $7140. Bags, however, also have premiums, which can either raise or lower the price.

For both gold and silver, there are also numerous ingots (bars) available. Silver ingots are produced by Englehard Industries and Johnson Mathey. Gold ingots are produced by a wide variety of sources including Credit Suisse and other major world banks.

A special word of caution when buying ingots: The guarantee of purity when buying gold coins is the fact that the coins are manufactured by government mints where quality standards are rigidly maintained. However, no government supervision may be involved in buying ingots. Therefore, some of the ingots could contain less gold or silver (or the precious metal in less fine a quality) than is stamped on them. This, in fact, has happened in the case of a few of the less well-known firms. Sticking with a well-known firm should avoid this problem.

Counterfeiting

Gold and silver coins and ingots are readily available from a wide variety of sources, including banks, bullion dealers, coin dealers, and currency traders. In most cases, the coins sold are authentic. However, recently fake coins, primarily krugerrands, have turned up in California, Texas, and Massachusetts.

These fake coins, containing only a few dollars' worth of real gold, were generally sold by less established dealers or through the mail. Frequently they were sold by individuals who offered to discount them. In one case, three schemers in Boston were offering to sell krugerrands for $300 when the market price of gold was $500. A buyer presumably could buy the coin, walk to the nearest dealer or bank and sell it for a $200 profit.

Needless to say, the greed of the buyers resulted in the sale. The principle to be learned, however, is to be careful of any type of precious metal that is discounted. In terms of world currency, gold and silver are as transferable as dollars or Swiss francs. No one discounts dollars, and no one discounts gold.

Similarly, staying with established dealers helps to ensure that the gold coin purchased is authentic. Most reputable dealers will instantly refund the purchase price or exchange any fake coin they inadvertently sell for an authentic one.

◇ 62 ◇
Investing in Diamonds

Over the past few years, some Americans searching for just the right investment have selected diamonds. As with gold, silver, and rarities, the desire to escape the ravages of inflation is usually the motive behind the search for the right investment. What is unusual is the selection of diamonds as the investment medium. Traditionally diamonds have been a store of wealth. But they have not been an inflationary hedge until fairly recently.

The history of diamonds as assets is long and studded with brilliant examples of how the precious stones helped their owners. Napoleon is rumored to have paid for his final war by the sale of French national diamonds. The czars of Russia kept much of their wealth in the form of diamond jewelry and diamond "eggs." The royal crown of Hungary, St. Michael's crown, has many uncut diamonds set in it as a symbol of wealth.

No one seriously challenges the fact that diamonds are both an expression and a storehouse of wealth. But only within the past decade have diamonds come to be widely considered as a true inflationary hedge. The reason is their phenomenal price growth.

Although it is impossible to chart accurately the diamond market (diamonds are unlike silver or gold or stocks in that each is unique), generally diamonds have grown in value enormously. They had a steep price rise during the early 1970s and then, about the same time that coins and other rarities were taking off, shot up in value (between 1978 and 1980). Since that time, they have actually lost some of their value.

Investors watching the diamond price appreciation have jumped on board. Those that got in early have made money, a great deal of money. Those who came on board later are now wondering just how wise their decision was.

It may sound as if diamonds were just another form of rarity, similar to coins or paintings. Certainly their price behavior during the 1970s was similar. However, diamonds have one aspect that makes them totally unlike any other investment in the world, with the possible exception of physical oil. Diamonds are bought and sold in what is basically a *controlled* market.

A controlled market is simply one in which either the supply or the demand of a commodity is controlled by some force. In the case of diamonds, the force is the supply. The DeBeers corporation controls about 80 percent of all the rough diamonds in the world. ("Rough" diamonds are the stones as they come out of the ground, before they have been cut and polished.) It is DeBeers' control of the supply that makes the diamond investment so unlike any other investment.

To understand how DeBeers control influences diamond values, we have to go back a while in time. I have heard diamond promoters say that diamonds have had a long history, dating back thousands of years of continual price appreciation. Some will even go so far as to say that diamonds never decline in value. They may plateau for a while, but decline—never!

Nothing could be further from the truth. In the nineteenth century, when diamond mining in both Brazil and South Africa was heavy, the price of diamonds rose and fell depending on the supply and the inventory. New diamond strikes depressed prices as increased numbers of the precious stones came onto the market. The drying up of the Brazilian mines led to higher prices.

Even early in this century, the prices of diamonds fluctuated up and down depending on the supplies coming from the giant Kimberly and other mines in South Africa. But generally speaking, it was true that prices were edging upward, overall. Then came the Great Depression.

The largest group of buyers for diamonds has always been and continues to be the jewelry trade. Diamond use in jewelry accounts for perhaps 60 to 70 percent of all quality diamond usage. (By far the greatest demand for diamonds overall, albeit for low-quality diamonds, comes from industrial usage in drill and saw blades.)

When the Great Depression of the 1930s hit, jewelry purchases virtually came to a halt. With people literally starving and out of work, very few had the wealth to purchase jewelry diamonds. Many who owned diamonds wanted to sell them to get money to live on. But there were no buyers. During the early 1930s, many of the diamond mines in South Africa had to close down because they couldn't make enough money even to pay their overhead.

It was at this time that Sir Ernest Oppenheimer, who was chairman of the board of Anglo-American, the parent company of DeBeers, fashioned a plan for saving the diamond industry. This plan was so ingenious and worked so well that it alone was responsible for the world-wide acceptance of diamonds as a modern hedge against inflation. And the plan may account for diamonds' remarkable price appreciation.

The plan was simple enough. Because DeBeers controlled most of the world's rough diamonds, it would choose and establish a price at its "sights" (meetings held about a dozen times yearly, where DeBeers sells rough stones to brokers). The price would reflect where the diamond market "should be."

It was a bold plan, to fix the price of diamonds much the same way that OPEC fixes the price of oil. But Oppenheimer executed the plan with such grace and finesse that it makes OPEC's efforts look clumsy by comparison.

During periods when there was prosperity and diamonds sales were high, DeBeers would *slowly* raise the price, forcing it to remain low and thereby generating even more sales to the jewelry trade. (Low prices during prosperity encouraged people to buy diamonds.)

During periods of recession or economic difficulties, DeBeers would reduce the volume of diamonds offered at its sights and increase the quality, thereby forcing prices to remain steady, or even to increase slightly.

During periods of great economic difficulty when there was a real threat to the market, DeBeers, using money it had set aside from earlier, more prosperous times, would actually buy diamonds back and thereby maintain price levels!

It was an incredible financial ploy and one that has worked steadily since the Depression. Diamonds slowly moved upward in price—until the mid 1970s.

Then investors, looking for inflation hedges and totally unaware of what the DeBeers Corporation was doing, saw diamonds. They bought and bought. Suddenly the price stopped moving upward slowly. It *shot* up.

This did not correspond with the DeBeers plan for slow, steady price movements. A sharp increase could force prices so high that jewelry sales of diamonds could falter (in much the same way as gold sales faltered when the price of gold rose too high).

At first DeBeers threw more rough diamonds onto the market, thereby undercutting demand with increased supply, and steadying the price. Then it imposed surcharges on the price, implying that it could take those surcharges off at any time, thereby dropping the price.

For several years, it worked. But with the inflation-produced panic of 1979 and 1980, average people from across the globe and in particular the United States suddenly threw their wealth at any hard asset they could find. By then, diamonds were becoming increasingly popular as investments. The price shot up, more than doubling for many grades of the precious stones. (This is the same phenomenon we saw with rarities and collectibles.)

In the aftermath of the panic buying, the market became soft. Many investors realized they had bought too high and paid too much. Today they are trying to sell and get their money out. The result is an overall drop in the price of the precious stones as the market recoups.

However, the diamond market remains distinctly different from the market for other rarities and collectibles. While in paintings, coins, and so forth a soft market is quickly reflected in lower prices or sharply decreased volume, in diamonds DeBeers acts to take up the slack. The giant company, according to reports, has begun to reduce volume and even to offer to purchase diamonds back, all to sustain the price.

Will DeBeers be successful? Will diamonds continue their upward march in price?

Both these questions might well be answered with a guarded "yes." If past history is any judge, the march upward in diamond prices will eventually continue, although probably at a much slower pace than in the past. As to when, that's very difficult to say, but probably before 1985.

But this hopeful outlook for diamonds does not necessarily mean that they are a panacea, an investment that can't lose. There are problems with investing in diamonds.

Discount

The biggest problem is the discount. When an investor buys diamonds, he or she can only buy them from a dealer who charges at least 30 percent in commission. Therefore, the investor is buying the precious stones at 30 percent above market prices. For example, if I buy 1 ounce of gold tomorrow and then sell it the day after, if I buy wisely in the form of a krugerrand, I could lose no more than 2 to 5 percent of my purchase through discounting (assuming that the price of gold hasn't changed). If I buy a diamond tomorrow and try to sell it the day after, chances are I will be forced to sell for about 30 percent less than I paid.

Buying at a disadvantage can make sense if the market is moving upward quickly. However, if it is stagnating, such buying means tying up a great deal of money in a no-return investment for what could very well be two or three years. It may very well take that long for the market to rise to the point where the investor can just get his or her money back, let alone make a profit.

My point is that the money spent investing in a diamond during a stagnant period could better be spent instead on some other item, such as stocks, bonds, or real estate, that will give both a return and an immediate appreciation.

The key to making money in diamonds, therefore, is to buy at precisely the right moment. Buy just before the market makes a move upward, and then sell a few months later, and you may do quite well. Buy when a stagnant period is approaching and it may be years before you can get your money out.

How does one know at what point in the cycle the diamond market is? Again, as for collectibles, you either have to be your own expert or find a real expert whom you can trust.

Where to Buy Diamonds

If you decide to go into diamond investing, a few words should be said about the working of the market itself.

Unless you are in the diamond trade, your chances of being able to buy an investment-quality diamond at anything less than a retail price are nonexistent. It is basically a closed market. It is closed by two factors. The first is that diamonds are graded according to weight, cut, clarity, and color, and only a diamond expert with years of experience can determine the true quality of a diamond. Unless you're an expert, you have no chance of knowing the true quality of what you might be buying, if you try to buy wholesale.

Secondly, the wholesale diamond clubs and exchanges do not welcome casual buyers of single stones. They operate as most other wholesale markets do—wholesalers sell to retailers. The investing public is generally not invited.

Knowing that you are going to have to buy retail, how do you choose from whom you are going to purchase? Your options include jewelry stores, large diamond investment corporations, and salespeople who sell diamonds in seminar-like meetings.

My own observation is that the sales seminar meetings are probably the worst choice. The sellers tend to be inexperienced in the field and often do not themselves know the true value of the merchandise they are handling. You wouldn't give your savings to an amateur banker. Don't give them to an amateur diamond salesperson, either.

Jewelers, however, generally do know the quality of what they sell. But they tend to charge the highest markups. Typically, a jeweler has what is referred to as a "keystone" or turnaround price for anything he or she handles. This is the amount of markup he or she must charge in order to make overhead. It is often between 100 and 300 percent. Buying from a jeweler can mean paying such a high price that the investment potential of the diamond is virtually lost.

That leaves diamond investment companies. Many of these have sprung up over the past four or five years. Some are quite legitimate and offer authentic diamonds with reasonable discounts. Some, however, are very fraudulent operations and are only out to cheat the buyer.

In judging the growth of the diamond investment company, there are certain guidelines to watch for, such as the following.

1. How long has the company been in business? Length of time indicates honest business operations.

2. Will the company guarantee the diamond in writing? If the company is willing to buy the diamond back should it prove not to be as sold, this is an indication of good intention. This is the minimum guarantee any investor should expect.

3. Does the company have a true liquidation program? Selling diamonds can be tricky. Every city has diamond dealers willing to buy diamonds. But are these dealers going to pay reasonable prices? Quite often the easiest way of disposing of a diamond at sale time is to go back to the person you bought it from. If the company who sold you the diamond has a long record of buying back diamonds from its clients, that is another good indication of honesty.

4. Does the company try to educate you, the investor, or try to high-pressure you into making a purchase? If the company tries high pressure, that indicates it's out for the quick sale and isn't interested in the long term. If the company spends time educating the client, that indicates the company is looking for long-term business—another good sign.

5. Finally, do you get a written certificate of authenticity? Diamonds today come with pedigrees. These are certificates stating both the quality of the diamond and, in some cases, an estimate of value. For the investor who knows nothing about appraising a diamond, these certificates are the lifeblood of the investment.

But there is virtually no regulation of certificates in the United States. You or I or anyone else could issue one without any experience in the field at all. Therefore, it is not just a matter of getting a certificate. It is a matter of getting a certificate from the right authentication laboratory.

There are at least a dozen major authenticating laboratories across the country and around the world whose reputations are excellent. I'll just mention three. In the United States, the largest and most well known is the Gemological Institute of America's (GIA) lab in California. GIA certificates are well recognized and are usually reliable.

Also in California, perhaps the second largest lab is that of a private diamond company, International Diamond Corporation. This company's labs handle tens of thousands of diamonds annually and are highly regarded in the industry.

In Europe, the European Gemological Laboratory (EGL), a sort of counterpart of the American GIA, is also well recognized.

If you invest in diamonds, you should be wary. Besides timing, you must watch out for the schemers who want to take your money. Diamond investing is a new field and, as in all new fields, there tend to be many crooks. It will probably be a few more years before the diamond field gets sufficiently organized to police itself.

People who have invested in diamonds in the past have made money, a great deal of money. I suspect that those who invest in the future may also do fairly well. But diamonds are not a panacea either. They are simply one more investment avenue whose risks and rewards must be weighed against all other potential avenues of investment.

◇ 63 ◇
Choosing Rarities
and Collectibles

A painting that sold for $500 ten years ago may be worth $20,000 today. A stamp that brought $1500 at auction in 1973 may be sold today for more than $7000. A rare old coin that fetched only $300 in the early 1970s is today going for over $12,000. And on and on goes the list, including everything from antique furniture to carousel horses. We seem to be living in an age of collectibles, and the people who seem to be making the most money are those who invest in such items.

At least that's the way that it "seems." With the high prices recorded for rarities of all types over the past decade, it would "seem" that only a fool wouldn't jump into the field with both feet. However, actually the contrary is true. Only a fool *would* jump in, without first taking the time to consider the risks as well as the rewards.

I'm not saying that profits haven't been made or aren't continuing to be made in rarities, antiques, and collectibles. They have been, and they are. I am asking, however, whether you or I could easily participate in those profits.

The Last Ten Years for Collectibles

Rarities and collectibles have been around for a long, long time. Baron Rothschild began his banking fortune more than a century ago with rare coins he had collected. Italian counts and noblemen in Renaissance Italy collected works of master artists. Even in ancient Rome the creations of the artists were recognized and appreciated by people of great wealth and station. Isn't it odd, therefore, that only in the last ten years has the average investor suddenly become interested in this field? What has changed in the last ten years?

Two things are different. The first is the average person's awareness of inflation. The second is awareness of the price appreciation of rarities and collectibles. The average investor has put these two awarenesses together and come to the conclusion that there's money to be made, lots of it, in rarities.

But is there money to be made for *everyone* today? Consider how the field of rarities and collectibles operates. Let's take rare coins, which have seen phenomenal growth over the past decade.

In the past, only a very small group of individuals called *numismatists* collected rare coins. These were true collectors, those who sought out the rare coins from circulation or retrieved them from the mint before they reached the hands of merchants. They bought these coins usually in order to obtain a collection. A collection might consist of one coin issued by the United States from every date and mint. Or it might be a "topical" collection consisting only of coins that contained eagles on the reverse. (In coin collecting, the front of the coin is the "obverse," the back is the "reverse.") Or it might be all the cents the United States had produced. (The United States *never* produced a "penny." Only Great Britain has produced pennies.)

In any event, the primary goal of these numismatists was hobby enjoyment. Just as a fisherman might spend a great deal of money on rods, reels, and equipment, so these collectors spent a great deal of money on their coins. Even today if you talk with a true collector, he or she rarely mentions selling their collection. The joy, for them, is in the collecting and the saving of the pieces. Selling often comes about only on the death of the collector.

Over the years, it happened that the only old coins that remained in existence in *top quality* were those saved by collectors. The others were worn out, lost, destroyed, or returned to the mint, where they were melted down. New collectors coming into the hobby found that in order to create their collections, they had to buy old coins from collectors who already had them. The older collectors were frequently willing to sell duplicate pieces that they might own.

However, because of the demand from new collectors and the scarcity of true collector coins, the prices began to rise. It now cost new collectors more to buy old coins than it cost the original collectors.

This price rise, however, was not as steep as most people believe. Between 1900 and 1950, the price of American coins from the period of 1800 to 1850 may only have doubled in value. An investor would have done better to have put money into stocks for the same time period.

But the true collectors didn't care that much about appreciation. They were, after all, into the hobby for the joy of it, not for the profit.

Between 1950 and 1960, the price of coins doubled again and twice between 1960 and 1970. Of course, we're talking now about a not too considerable sum of money. An 1849 "capped-bust" quarter cost $5 early in this century, and was only up to about $80 by the beginning of the last decade.

But then inflation became a significant concern in the United States, and the average person became aware of it. That same average person began looking for areas to put money that would act as a hedge against inflation, areas in which the money would appreciate in buying power faster than inflation was taking buying power away. One area that seemed a good bet was coins. (Rare paintings, stamps, antique furniture, and so on were, of course, equally appealing.)

Investors began looking at rare coins, began buying them. After all, hadn't they doubled in value many times?

So now we have something new in the field of numismatics. As never before, we have great numbers of people buying coins not for their beauty or as a hobby, but strictly for their price performance.

This produced a significant and dramatic change in the field. It produced *volume*. Before the 1972, there were relatively few coin collectors. Although figures such as 8 or 12 million have been bandied about by various publications, a check of auction records for the period, including bids as well as purchases, indicates that there were probably fewer than 100,000 hard-core collectors—perhaps as few as 20,000. Of course, millions had saved "pennies" as children and occasionally would express an interest in the field. But very few true collectors spent time and money on their hobby.

Suddenly, into this small group came a great infusion of investors. These investors didn't care for the beauty of a coin nor if they completed a collection. They cared only for the potential price appreciation. They bought indiscriminately, both top-quality coins as well as some rather poor specimens.

The result was an instant rise in the price of coins. Beginning about 1975, coins began to rise swiftly in value—all types of rare coins.

This price appreciation only convinced more investors to come into the field. But these new investors noticed that the top-quality material seemed to be appreciating faster than the lower-quality material—so they bought only the best.

The result was that the price of top-quality coins (uncirculated material in the MS-60 to MS-65 category) doubled in value between 1970 and 1975 and then doubled again by 1978. It doubled once again in value between 1978 and 1979 and, incredibly, once again in the six-month period between November 1979 and April 1980! Needless to say, those who had purchased rare coins as investments were feeling quite good.

But what about people who were just thinking of going into the field? Times were not quite so good for them. Prices for coins were already very high. The 1849 quarter mentioned earlier had by now risen in value to about $700 in uncirculated condition. That's a lot of money for one quarter.

In addition, the opportunity for future price appreciation was double. What really happened was a kind of collective panic on the part of investors. During 1979 and 1980, inflation in this country was into double digits, perhaps for the first time since right after World War I. Investors projected this inflation into the future, and talk was rampant of inflation topping 20 percent by 1981 and 50 percent by 1985. Investors were ready to buy anything that might protect them from this inflationary threat. Rarities, including coins, seemed a good bet.

By late 1980 and through 1981, however, cooler heads prevailed. Inflation remained high, but was not accelerating. Those who had bought coins in panic now took a closer look at what they had, and they didn't like what they saw. They had bought coins at what might be real prices of years in the future. If they were to try and sell their coins, they couldn't find buyers at the prices they paid, not even at sizable discounts. The field had been overbought. Volume of sales decreased dramatically as owners of high-priced coins waited for the market to catch up with what they had paid.

What about today? Is this a good time to go into coin investing? I think not. I suspect the field is very overbought for all coins in top grades. (I also suspect, however, that coins in lower grades may still be underpriced today because they were overlooked in the panic buying.)

The point to be made here is that although it was possible to make money, considerable money in coins during the last decade, it is not clear that the same rewards will be available in the near future. It could very well be the case that the coin field could stagnate for several years. And as with gold, coins do not produce income. If they are not appreciating, they are a drag on the investor.

The same holds true for virtually every other area of rarities and collectibles from paintings to bottles. This brings up three other points regarding investing in collectibles.

Sometimes You Need To Be an Expert

I was recently talking with an expert in western paintings, another field that has seen phenomenal price appreciation. He told me that certain paintings were still going up in price. Most, of course, were overpriced. But a few were still climbing.

As an example, he cited the case of a relatively obscure western painter, Charlie Dye. Charlie Dye painted westerns in somewhat the style of the great Charlie Russell. But for some reason few people had heard of Dye, while nearly everyone had heard of Russell.

Then Dye's paintings began to click. They were selling in the range of $5000 apiece in 1975 (depending on size).

Charlie Dye passed away a few years ago, and with him went the potential to produce more paintings. Today, few people have heard of the Dye paintings. Yet it would be hard to buy even a small one for less than $40,000, and others command far greater prices.

The point is that an expert in the field knows what to look for. An expert in western art recognized the significance of the Dye paintings early on and, I'm sure, bought several. The expert is the one who made the profit.

Getting back to coins, I'm sure the case is similar. The hobbyist who has devoted many, many years to learning the field may have his or her eye on several coins that only he or she realizes are truly rare. Buying these coins even today may result in substantial profits in the future when their quality and rarity become generally recognized.

But what of the nonexpert investors? What of the individual who doesn't know western paintings or coins or stamps or furniture or antiques? What are the chances that this person will make a wise purchase, one that will mature and return a healthy profit?

I'm not saying that a novice investor will always buy badly. But the odds are against novices. I believe that in order to succeed in the rarities and collectibles field, one must spend time learning—a great deal of time. Then, and only then, will it be possible to make intelligent investments.

One time-shortening method that has been widely publicized is that of hiring an expert. Go into any coin shop and the owner will tell you that he or she is an expert and can tell you exactly which coins to buy. Or check with bigger dealers, who frequently hold investment seminars for people who want to put in a certain amount of money each month. The dealers will recommend the best buys in coins. And then there are even the syndicates organized to buy top-flight material. Just invest the price of one share (anywhere from $1000 to $100,000) and be a part owner of some of the world's rarest coins.

Are these good investments? It really depends on the expert and the advice he or she gives. Would you trust the advice of your stock broker or your commodities broker? Have you made money that way? If you would and you have, then perhaps you would do well by trusting the advice of dealers.

My own feeling, however, is that you must become your own expert in the field of rarities and collectibles in order to succeed.

You Need to Understand How the Market Works

Most rarities and collectibles work in markets that are very unusual to the layperson. Paintings, for instance. The current value of paintings is pretty well established by the numerous art dealer auctions held throughout the world. By studying the trade, you can keep abreast of prices at the auctions—or can you?

Today many paintings are purchased by the wealthy with the ultimate idea of turning the painting into a profitable tax shelter. Here's how Mrs. Iva Gotrocks buys a Grand Master for $100,000. Mrs. Gotrocks doesn't know much about Renaissance surrealism, but she is assured the painting is a bargain by her advisor—her tax advisor. She drags the painting home and hangs it in the broom closet. Five years later, she generously donates the painting to a local art museum. Then she deducts the current market value from her taxes. The amount she deducts is $500,000, which in her 50 percent tax bracket, saves $250,000 in taxes. She gets a wing of the museum named after her, everyone in town loves her, and she actually had a positive cash flow of $150,000 ($250,000 tax shelter minus the $100,000 original purchase price).

But where did she (and her advisor) get the $500,000 value? Well—from an auction. Similar paintings by the same painter are selling for $500,000. So this should be a defensible price to the Internal Revenue Service. However, the IRS is starting to question it. First, all auctions (not just art auctions) use price limits of some sort. If the bids do not exceed the limits, the item doesn't sell. Therefore, it is possible to keep a sale from being recorded at an embarrassingly low price. Secondly, art dealers know that it's terribly important that prices keep moving up. Third, the IRS has started to wonder if the limits are occasionally rigged. In fact, they wonder if a lot of art doesn't change hands among the dealers just to keep prices moving up. If prices should drop, there are a lot of Mrs. Gotrocks who may decide they don't need any more tax shelters hanging in the broom closet, and that would mean a lot less business for art dealers.

If a market really does work this way, you would want to understand it before you bought.

You Should Avoid Instant Rarities (Unless You Like Them)

Finally, one last danger with collectibles and rarities has to do with the instant product. These are easily recognized in most cases (but not always). They are a product of the quick turnover and demand for items in this field of the last decade.

An instant rarity is exactly what it implies. It is a painting or a coin or a piece of furniture that has been manufactured to be a rarity. In the field of painting, this is frequently called a *lithograph* or a *serigraph*. In the field of coins, it is called an *art medal*. And so on.

But haven't signed lithos and art medals appreciated dramatically in price?

A few have. Those created by well-loved masters who produced only a few have done almost as well as some of the better paintings. But in general, in most fields the mass-produced "rarities" have not fared particularly well, except during panic buying. When the investor thinks he or she only has a few moments to dump dollars and get into some sort of inflation hedge, even instant rarities seem appealing.

But in normal times, the market for these items is flat. True collectors and expert investors wouldn't touch these. And the novice investor, if he or she isn't pushed by panic, will usually opt for the genuine article.

Buying instant rarities and collectibles can be a one-way ride for the unsuspecting investor. After the purchase is made it's extremely difficult to resell, even for the original purchase price, let alone a profit. So if you buy an instant rarity it's important to buy it because you like it, not because you think you can make money.

◇ 64 ◇
The Bottom Line

The bottom line is "Only you can count on helping you when it comes to financial freedom."

Most of us only have a stream of spendable income available to us during our lifetimes. Usually the income comes from paychecks we receive during our working years. Despite how the income comes, it must support our consumption for our entire lives.

During our lives, all of us consume a stream of the world's economic resources. We consume food, water, lumber, steel, oil, wool, human services, and so on. Most of the resources we will consume must be paid for out of the income we earn during our working years. The more income we earn, the more resources we can consume. A rich person can buy two suits of clothes; someone less wealthy only gets one. The goods and services of the world go in greatest quantity to those who can afford them.

Basic needs for resources, however, have nothing to do with income. Each person needs roughly the same amount of food and other resources to stay alive.

Our personal stream of income is a function of four things:

1. *God-given talents and abilities.* We all have some kind of talent. Whether we can turn our talent into income or not is another matter.

2. *Environmental circumstances.* Some people are born in poverty and never get out. Some people are born rich and never want to get out. Most of us are somewhere in between.

3. *Luck.* Some people just happen to be in the right place to get the right job or win the quiz show. Others just happen to be in the wrong place and get fired, or beaten, or robbed.

4. *Initiative, hard work, and management.* Regardless of our talents and abilities, our environment, or our luck, we can always improve our situations through initiative, hard work, and good management.

These factors influence the amount of wealth a person may enjoy during his or her lifetime. People can do little about the first three. But people are not helpless—they can do something about the fourth. Probably the most important variable in earning money is an individual's own initiative, hard work, and good management. It is amazing how initiative and hard work can improve talents, turn bad luck into good, and change circumstances for the better. And the fortunate thing is anyone can work hard, use or exercise good management—our society encourages it and rewards it.

To begin good management can help us in matching our streams of income to our streams of consumption. The following bar charts illustrate the point. The first chart represents the basic resources absolutely needed to maintain life. The chart in the middle represents actual consumption by a typical American. The chart on the right represents the consumption desired by the typical American.

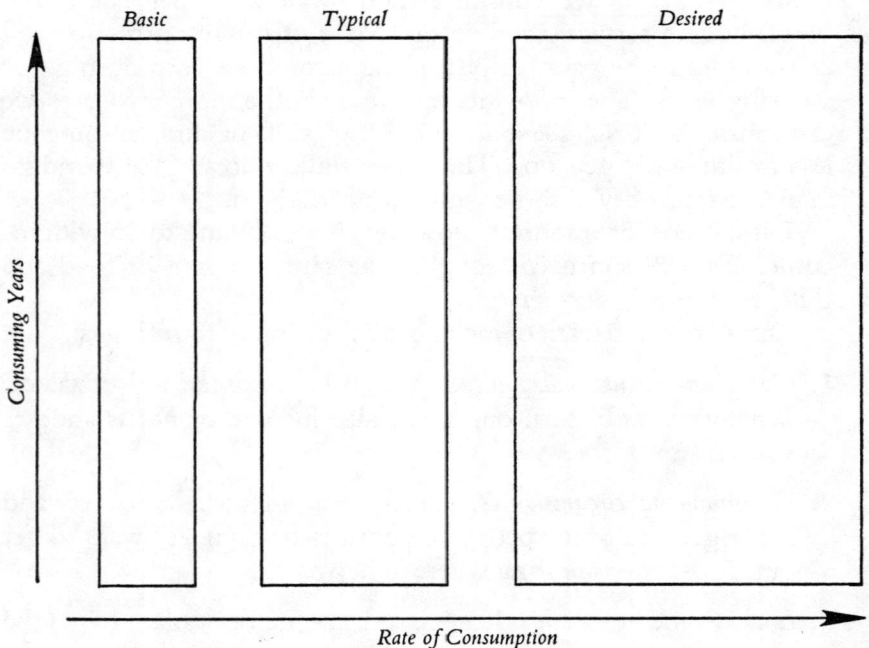

When the stream of income is laid over the stream of consumption, the charts can illustrate potential problems. For example, there is the case where a person is trying to live a typical life with a less than typical income (left). Worse yet is the person trying to consume everything he or she desires on a typical income (right).

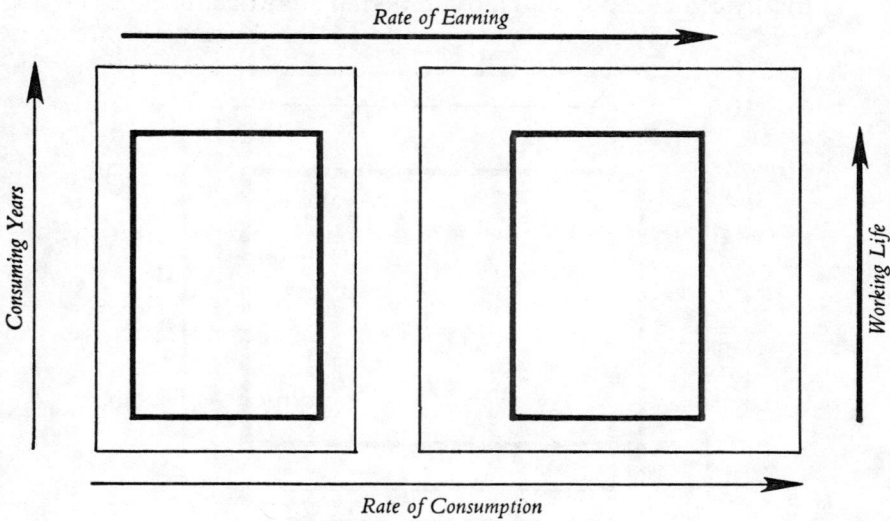

People with charts like these have financial trouble all their lives. Other people do better. They successfully match their *current* spending with their *current* earnings and enjoy a degree of comfort most of their lives. But sometimes they forget they won't be working all their lives. They forget they must accumulate something in the way of investments or pension for the years when they won't be working. Their charts look something like the following one.

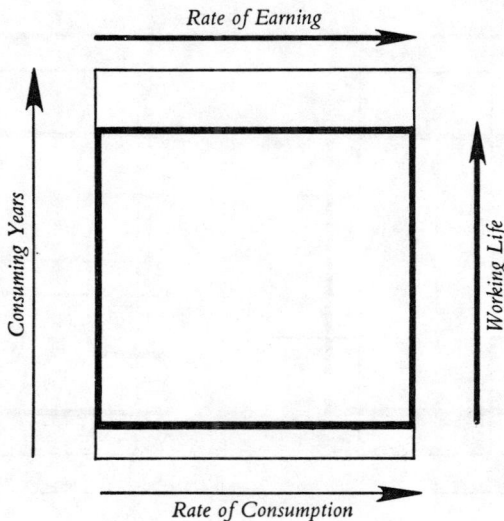

People with charts like this manage to live comfortably most of their lives, but they tend to have miserable retirements.

Ideally our charts would look something like this.

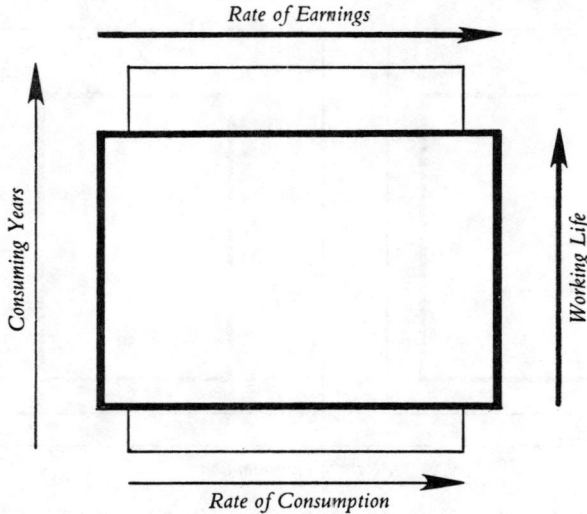

Here we have a fortunate person who has managed to live not only *within* his or her income but *below* it for a number of years. With the excess money, this individual has made investments, and these investments, as they pay off, have allowed this person to increase consumption.

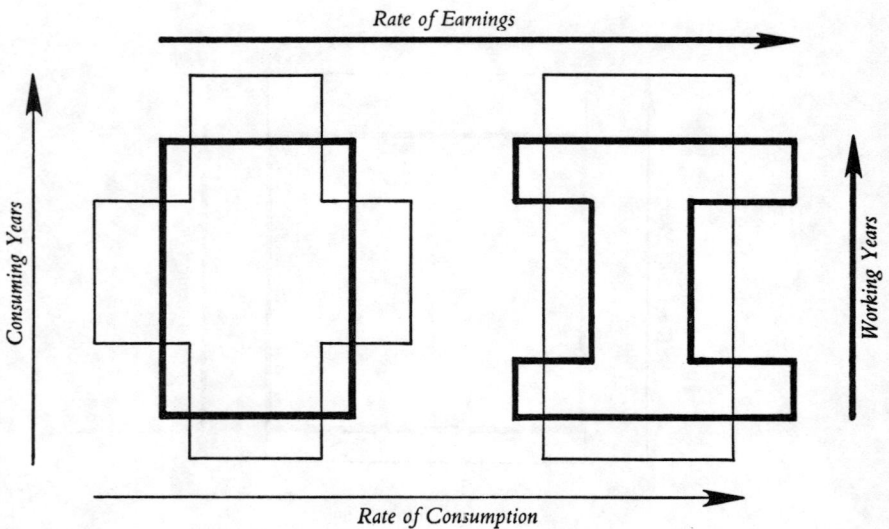

It should be noted that in our last chart we did not indicate the age when retirement could occur. For the person who works hard, manages money wisely, and makes sound investments, the retirement age need not be in the sixties, as is commonly the case today. It could be in the fifties, the forties, or even earlier. An early retirement is a form of financial freedom.

With more and better investments producing ever greater income, our individual not only can consume more of what he or she wants, but at retirement, when work stops, there will be plenty of money left for living a comfortable life.

That is the bottom line of this book—achieving financial freedom. This is what the last individual has done. Both during working years and during retirement, there is no serious threat to his or her financial security—that is what financial freedom is all about.

◇ 65 ◇
Financial Freedom

According to *Webster's Third International Dictionary,* freedom is "a quality or state of not being coerced, or constrained by fate, necessity or circumstances in one's choices or actions." Are you free financially? Or do you find your choices and actions constrained by fate, necessity, or circumstances?

I can tell you from numerous financial counseling sessions, most Americans do not feel financially free. Despite the highest living standard in the world, despite the highest personal income in history, and despite all outward appearances to the contrary, millions and millions of Americans are not free.

And millions more are trapped today than were trapped even five or ten years ago. The financial upheaval has buried them. Many many more will be financially trapped next year and the year after that if they do not make immediate financial adjustments.

Their spending is constrained by high prices. They are coerced by heavy debt and extraordinary interest rates. In general, people may feel more anxiety about finances today than at any time in history.

But it is possible to be financially free. Freedom comes from understanding the environment (and financially the environment is all new). Freedom comes from understanding yourself. (We are often our own worst enemies.) Most of all freedom comes from wise personal management. Freedom comes from successfully avoiding financially destructive traps. And, finally, freedom comes from wisely investing your money today so that it gives you more freedom tomorrow.

I know you can be financially free. It is my sincere desire and hope that this book has helped you find your financial freedom. If it has, I feel greatly rewarded for having shared these principles with you.

472

INDEX

473